WINGS OVER SUEZ

WINGS OVER SUEZ

Brian Cull
with David Nicolle and Shlomo Aloni

GRUB STREET · LONDON

Published by
Grub Street
4 Rainham Close
London SW11 6SS

First published in 1996
Copyright © Grub Street 1996
Text copyright © Brian Cull, David Nicolle and Shlomo Aloni 1996

This amended paperback edition first published 2006

British Library Cataloguing in Publication Data
Cull, Brian
  Wings over Suez: the only authoritative account of air
  operations during the Sinai and Suez wars of 1956
  1. Sinai Campaign, 1956 2. Sinai Campaign, 1956 – Aerial operations
  3. Middle East – History – 20th century
  I. Title II. Nicolle, David, 1944- III. Aloni, Shlomo
  956'.044

ISBN-10: 1 904943 55 1

Edited by John Davies

Typeset by Pearl Graphics, Hemel Hempstead

Printed and bound in India by Replika

Brian Cull is the author of the following Grub Street titles:

Air War for Yugoslavia, Greece and Crete, 1940-41 with Christopher Shores
    and Nicola Malizia
Malta: The Hurricane Years, 1940-41 with Christopher Shores and Nicola Malizia
Malta: The Spitfire Year, 1942 with Christopher Shores and Nicola Malizia
Bloody Shambles, Volume 1 with Christopher Shores and Yasuho Izawa
Bloody Shambles, Volume 2 with Christopher Shores and Yasuho Izawa
Spitfires Over Israel with Shlomo Aloni and David Nicolle
Twelve Days in May with Bruce Lander and Heinrich Weiss
Hurricanes Over Tobruk with Don Minterne
Hurricanes Over Malta with Frederick Galea
Hurricanes Over Singapore with Paul Sortehaug
Buffaloes Over Singapore with Paul Sortehaug and Mark Haselden
Spitfires Over Malta with Frederick Galea

CONTENTS

ACKNOWLEDGEMENTS

First and foremost, the authors wish to thank their respective ladies, without whose understanding and co-operation we would all be much the poorer. Brian Cull thanks Val, who does increasingly more work with each book: editing, proofreading and indexing. Without her constant help and encouragement the production line would rapidly grind to a halt. David Nicolle similarly thanks Colette; while Shlomo Aloni dedicates his contribution to Tal Aloni and also wishes to express his deep gratitude to his wife Nili for her enthusiastic support over the years, as well as thanking their respective families.

Brian Cull, on behalf of the authors, wishes to acknowledge the major contributions made by the many former members of the Royal Air Force and Fleet Air Arm, without whose generous offerings this account of the Suez operation would be but a poor imitation: in particular, our thanks are extended to Rear Admiral Ray Rawbone CB AFC and Air Chief Marshal Sir David Harcourt-Smith GBE KCB DFC, not only for their personal recollections but since each kindly contributed a Foreword.

We are also grateful to the following gentlemen for their respective contributions: Vice-Admiral Sir Edward Anson KCB (895 Sqn), Captain Bruce Clark (899 Sqn), Cdr Bill Cowling (830 Sqn), Lt Charlie Dwarika (809 Sqn), Lt Cdr Brian Ellis (HMS *Albion*), Captain Roy Eveleigh DSC (802 Sqn), Lt Cdr John Hackett JP (809 Sqn), Lt Cdr Bill Henley DSC (893 Sqn), Lt Cdr Graham Hoddinott (810 Sqn), Lt Cdr Peter Lamb DSC AFC (810 Sqn), Captain Keith Leppard (897 Sqn), Captain Paddy McKeown (802 Sqn), Cdr John Morris-Jones MBE (895 Sqn), Captain Ben Neave (893), Lt Cdr Dick Needham (890 Sqn), Lt Cdr Ron Shilcock (809 Sqn), Lt Cdr Jan Stuart (849 Sqn), Lt Cdr Jim Summerlee (SAR HMS *Eagle*), Cdr Maurice Tibby (800 Sqn), Lt Bob Wigg (809 Sqn), Lt Cdr John Willcox (893 Sqn), Captain Jack Worth (800 Sqn); and to Mrs Nancy Bailey, widow of Capt Pete Bailey (SAR HMS *Eagle*); we also thank Mrs Drucie Mills, widow of Cdr Donald Mills OBE, for permission to use extracts from *It Is Upon The Navy*; and to Linda Haywood, from whom copies of that book are available at 17 Pennine Close, Hereford. Thanks are also due to: Air Vice-Marshal George Black CB OBE AFC (802 Sqn), Sqn Ldr Joe Blyth DFC AFC (8 Sqn), Wg Cdr Michael Bradley AFC (208 Sqn), Flt Lt Chris Bushe (208 Sqn), Bob Byrne (249 Sqn), Grp Capt Peter Ellis DFC (6 Sqn), Captain Tony Gronert (249 Sqn), Sqn Ldr Dick Hadlow (8 Sqn), Wg Cdr Harry Harrison (6 Sqn), Wg Cdr Bernie Hunter MBE (58/13 Sqn), Flg Off Bryn Jones (8 Sqn), Sqn Ldr Tom Lecky-Thompson (249 Sqn), Sqn Ldr Jock Maitland DFC (US) (249 Sqn), Flt Lt Denis Moyes (249 Sqn), Wg Cdr Geoff Quick, Grp Capt Charlie Slade (249 Sqn), Sqn Ldr Tam Syme DFC (249 Sqn),

Flg Off Nick von Berg (8 Sqn), Sqn Ldr Dave Williams MBE (249 Sqn), Wg Cdr Allen Woods AFC (148 Sqn); and Mrs Emmie Bickel, mother of the late David Bickel (RAF Habbaniya), Brian Courtney, son of the late Grp Capt R.N.H. Courtney DFC, Mrs Christine Yates, widow of Flt Lt Ted Yates (88 Sqn).

Air Commodore Henry Probert MBE kindly gave permission for extracts from the RAF Historical Society's: *Suez 1956 – Air Aspects* to be used within the narrative. Our thanks also go out to Mr Graham Mottram, Director of the FAA Museum, Yeovilton, to Mr Dave Richardson (Research Officer) and Mrs M. Gittos (Keeper of the Records), who gave generously of their time and made available for study records relating to Fleet Air Arm activities during Suez; Lt Cdr Michael Lawrence and staff of the FAAOA; the staff of AHB3 Ministry of Defence; Mrs P. Williams of RAFPMC; the staff of the Public Record Office; the staff of Bury St Edmunds Public Library in obtaining hard-to-find books for reference purposes; the staff of the Newspaper Library, Colindale; Général Silvestre de Sacy and M. Georges Rech, and their staff, of the Armée de l'Air Service Historique. Jocelyn Leclercq, Albert Grandolini and Pierre Hervieux – our French contributors – provided material, photographs and translations which have richly enhanced the narrative.

David Nicolle wishes to thank his Lebanese friend Ass'aad Dib for the translations of Ali Muhammad Labri's history of the Egyptian Air Force. He also acknowledges the assistance he received from several former REAF officers including the late Air Vice-Marshal Abd al-Moneim Mikaati, Air Commodore Ibrahim Gazerine, and Air Vice-Marshal Sa'ad al-Din Sherif. He also thanks the staff of the Royal Geographical Society for their splendid help with his queries regarding maps of Egypt for the period in question. Shlomo Aloni acknowledges the help he has received from former IDF/AF officers: Maj Ezra Aharon, Col Ya'acov Agasi, Brig Gen Menahem Bar, Lt Col Israel Ben-Shachar, Lt Col Elyashiv Brosh, Maj Aryeh Dagan, Maj Aryeh Fredlis, Maj David Gatmon, Maj Avraham Greenbaum, Maj Hugo Marom, Lt Col Chaim Niv, Maj Eldad Paz, Maj Ze'ev Sharon, Maj Ze'ev Tavor, Maj Aryeh Tse'elon, Col Adam Tsivoni, Col Yoash Tsiddon, Col Itshak Yavneh, and Lt Col Uri Yarom. Also Dalya Ash, widow of the late Maj (R) Shimon Ash; and Micha Kaufman and Bat-Sheva Naftali of the IDF Archive.

We congratulate Chris Thomas for another superb dust-jacket illustration, and thank Seymour Feldman DFC of Albuquerque (former IDF/AF test pilot) for his contribution; our thanks to Dr Ing. Gianni Cattaneo of Aer Macchi for information on Macchi MC205Vs and Vampires supplied to the REAF/EAF; to John Havers for information and advice on Middle East civil aviation matters; to Flt Lt Andy Thomas for the generous loan of many of the excellent photographs used within; to Ray Sturtivant, the acknowledged FAA aircraft expert, for his kind assistance; to researcher/writer Michael Schoeman of South Africa for his contribution and encouragement; to Frederick Galea and Fred Coleman of the Malta War Museum Association for photographic assistance; to Bruce Lander for practical assistance; to Richard Barfield for information. And, as ever, Brian Cull acknowledges on a personal level Mr Jack Lee's inspirational influence.

The authors jointly thank Mr John Davies of Grub Street for his continuing support in publishing this series of important historical studies of air conflict in the Middle East. In this context, an account of the 1967 Six-Day War is contemplated.

Brian Cull, David Nicolle and Shlomo Aloni

FOREWORD

by

Rear Admiral A.R. Rawbone CB AFC

(Commanding Officer 897 Squadron HMS *Eagle*, 1956)

At sea in HMS *Eagle* in 1956, I was one of those privileged to take part in the Suez conflict and to witness at first hand an important milestone in our military history. Meant to unseat an ambitious dictator and re-establish stability in the Middle East, the campaign was overshadowed by a marked change in public reaction to political domination by force of arms. In some ways it was a last gasp for gunboat diplomacy.

Provoked by the nationalisation of the Suez Canal and aware of the destruction of pre-conceived aims in the region, the British and French governments drew a veil of secrecy over this sensitive area, shielding diplomatic intrigue and political intent. In consequence, for those who sensed future naval action, the build-up to the subsequent operation appeared to lack political direction and urgency. Without clear military objectives the situation was little short of an enigma. Officers and men were left to speculate and use their initiative to prepare for confrontation. Many aircrew and sailors were inexperienced and had never seen action. Individual ships practised essential war drills but there was little opportunity to exercise Fleet operations and inter-service co-operation. Liaison with our French allies was inevitably minimal.

Nevertheless, once committed to battle the response was spirited, positive and decisive. Nasser's Air Force was formidable but his decision to ground his pilots, to save them for the long-term battle against Israel, was an unexpected bonus which allowed almost complete freedom to our air forces and uninterrupted operation of the Carrier Task Force within easy range of most targets in Egypt. Naval aircraft inflicted a heavy toll on Egyptian ground forces and were largely responsible for the complete decimation of its Air Force in the first three days. The airdrop by British and French paratroops, and the landing of the Royal Marines, provided a firm base and springboard for the occupation of the whole Canal. Unfortunately, it was not to be!

Throughout all these operations we were very conscious of the increasing international pressure against a military solution. The reported movement of Soviet aircraft in support of Egypt and the antagonistic political stance taken by America, Russia and the United Nations were factors ever present in our minds and difficult to ignore. At sea, Admiral Power had to make it clear to the American Fleet Commander that he would not tolerate any interference with the execution of Anglo-French carrier operations, and the conflict has a special fascination as the first major action in which British forces were deployed against a background of serious public disquiet at home. Overall, this was unsettling to those in action and Ships' Companies were dismayed but not entirely surprised when United Nations pressure stalled an overwhelming military success some 48 hours before the Canal Zone could be occupied.

In many ways the action was unreal. For those who served in the Second World War or Korea, the almost passive resistance experienced in some areas was unexpected and, to anyone with a conscience, it was weird and disconcerting. There were also interjections of a lighter vein such as the sudden arrival of a civil funeral party in the middle of a furious battle across a cemetery. A respectful lull was observed by both sides before battle recommenced. Perhaps only in Egypt!

With hindsight, the British and French action at Suez has generally been regarded as a political failure. Those less kind have regarded it as a disaster. A lack of political foresight and will handed diplomatic success to President Nasser. The Arab nations and America emerged as the main beneficiaries. Unfortunately, political failure tended to wash over the military action as well, almost as though our political masters wished to bury the whole matter in the mists of time. In fact, all services felt proud of their conduct and success. The Carrier Task Force in particular felt that it had entirely met the operational requirement and had been mainly responsible for an overwhelming victory at minimum cost. Unfortunately, the military was not given a clear set of directives early enough. If there was a weakness it was clearly in the preparation and work-up to the campaign. Fortunately it did not matter, but it may have had a more critical bearing had the Egyptian Air Force decided to fight. One can only conclude that in 1956 politicians had much to learn. In spite of that, the military did all that was expected of it – and did it decisively.

Brian Cull and his co-authors mix meticulous research and tactical narrative with personal recollections from many who took part and vividly bring to life the atmosphere in which the conflict was fought. They also link together the successes, failures and problems faced by all arms of the services, many of which would have remained unknown to most except for this dedicated analysis. They skilfully unravel the power politics and diplomatic machinations which eventually led to an embarrassing withdrawal from Egypt without achieving the aim. The consequences were bound to be controversial.

Wings over Suez is an impressive, very well researched and well written account of this most intriguing conflict.

Ray Rawbone

FOREWORD

by

Air Chief Marshal Sir David Harcourt-Smith GBE KCB DFC

(Flight Commander 8 Squadron Cyprus, 1956)

I was very pleased when Brian Cull contacted me and told me of his plans to write a book on air operations during the Suez campaign. I have felt for a long time that this small piece of military history needed greater exposure. I suspect that the reason so little is said or written about the Suez affair is, in a large measure, because it is the source of considerable embarrassment and not something of which we are particularly proud.

Although *Wings over Suez* does not attempt any deep analysis of this short war, it does not disguise the view that 'Suez' was a political disaster, particularly for Anthony Eden, as well as a military shambles, with indecision and dithering being the order of the day. It also tested the special relationship with the United States to near breaking point and it did much to further discredit the British in the eyes of the Arab world. It was a sad epilogue to a once great Empire.

From a military viewpoint, I have always felt that it was a rather crude example of a large hammer to crack a rather small nut. Most of the Staff Planners involved in the operation had been in the Second World War and it was apparent that all too often they were still mentally fighting a large-scale operation in Europe. What was required was flexibility and audacity and a degree of risk-taking to bring the military operation to a swift and decisive conclusion.

On a personal level, *Wings over Suez* will rekindle memories for those who took part in the fighting. Apart from the squadron commanders, most of the aircrew found themselves in a new and potentially dangerous situation. In the event, the opposition was slight; nevertheless, the six days of combat did make us more professional in our flying and with a greater awareness of our own capabilities and shortcomings.

Wings over Suez is a well researched, factual account of the air operations but with sufficient personal recollections from many of the aircrew who took part to bring the text to life.

WINGS OVER SUEZ

REVISION TO ORIGINAL EDITION

Page 58: The photograph caption is incorrect. The three IDF/AF instructors are standing at the rear, not seated as suggested.

Page 83 and Page 91 onwards…: By the end of 1955, 80 MiG-15bis fighters had been delivered, plus six MiG-15UTI trainers. They arrived in the bare metal finish seen on Czechoslovakian Air Force machines but their stencilled instructions were in English. Such a sudden and abundant supply of sophisticated jet fighters necessitated plenty of support personnel, and the first Czechoslovakian technical experts reached Egypt in mid-October 1955. The following May another group arrived under the command of Major General Reinlem. This group included three pilots (Kapt Ludovit Solar, Lt Egon Skala and Lt Jiri Plzak), two technical experts plus an interpreter. They were based at Kabrit and Abu Suweir in the recently liberated Canal Zone. The last British armed forces actually left Abu Suweir in April 1956. Other Czech personnel went to the EAF College at Bilbeis.

The flying instructors in the Russian advisory mission included some of the most experienced men in the Soviet Air Forces, some pilots having participated in World War II or in the more recent Korean War. They faced a huge task because the EAF had so few trained jet pilots and as a result the Soviet advisors flew operational as well as training sorties. None flew combat missions in the Suez conflict, though some were caught up in the fighting while ferrying EAF aircraft out of the country.

Although the EAF was confident that its new jets could face the Israeli Air Force on equal terms, the MiGs themselves were held back by significant limitations. The MiG-15bis was an underpowered and rather crude first-generation jet; however, it was strong and stable. While the Mystère II was superior at low and medium altitude, the MiG-15's lower wing loading made it better at high altitude. Unlike the MiG-15, the Mystère IV was supersonic in a shallow dive and it could out-turn a MiG, though the latter had superior climb. The MiGs did not have power controls and strong 'g' forces tired their pilots quickly. Above all, the Mystère's armament was much more effective; the MiG's heavy cannon fired 400 rounds a minute while the Mystère's, admittedly smaller cannon, fired three times faster.

According to Soviet sources, the MiG's biggest shortcoming was its very limited endurance, which often meant it had to carry external fuel tanks. The EAF found these to be in very short supply during the Suez War and after only two or three combats – during which the wing tanks were dropped – the MiG squadrons ran out of replacements. Furthermore, the pilots often had difficulty detaching their tanks, which proved particularly dangerous in combat situations. If only one separated, the aircraft easily went into a spin, especially if the pilot was using violent manoeuvres as an emergency method of detaching reluctant tanks. Even if the pilot recovered, spinning with a single drop-tank often severely deformed the wing.

Initially the high landing speeds of the MiGs also caused problems for EAF pilots. Having been accustomed to more forgiving British types, several Egyptian pilots overshot the runways. Nor was pilot confidence helped by the early and primitive ejector seats in the MiGs. Some of those pilots who had ejected suffered broken arms. On the other hand, the MiG-17 – the first of which entered EAF service a few days before the outbreak of the Suez War – was regarded as a perfection of the ideas first seen in the MiG-15. Both Egyptian and Syrian MiGs were still being assembled and tested at

Dekheila when the Suez War broke out, whereupon all available aircraft were rushed to their operational squadrons along with their pilots.

Syrian connection

During 1956 several Syrian Air Force pilots with jet experience on Meteors arrived in Egypt for conversion to the MiG-15. Their new aircraft were similarly shipped to Egypt because Syria reportedly lacked airfields capable of operating high-performance jets. These Syrian MiGs were assembled by a new group of Czech advisors commanded by Major Josef Medun. They included two pilots (Kapt Josef Saksun and Lt Pavl Hladila) with five technicians, plus two doctors, two interpreters and a cook. The Syrian aircraft consisted of 20 S-103s (MiG-15bis) and four CS-102s (MiG-15UTI), which arrived crated during April 1956. However, their mission was marred by tragedy when one Czechoslovakian pilot lost his life on 16 August. A recently assembled CS-102 (c/n 1612792) was declared ready to be test-flown by Kapt Saksun. At 1120, he took off, climbed to 650 feet and made a circuit of the airfield. He then climbed to 13,000 feet and completed several manoeuvres without any problems. The aircraft was above the brilliant white salt-encrusted surface of Lake Maryut, which lay to the south of the airfield. The completion of Saksun's final manoeuvre left his aircraft in a steep dive towards this salt lake and as the MiG came down to 5,000 feet, Lt Hladila tried to contact Saksun by radio but got no response. A short while later it was all over – the MiG had smashed into the salt lake at high speed. A subsequent accident commission suggested that the pilot had become disorientated by the lake's brilliant white salt crust, noting that over the years some Egyptian pilots had been lost in similar accidents. It was also thought possible that Kapt Saksun suffered thermal shock as the temperature in his aircraft's cockpit probably reached 45°C. By the outbreak of the Suez War, the Syrians had completed their initial conversion training and had moved with their MiG-15s to Abu Suweir.

Page 111: The two Il-28 jet bomber squadrons were commanded by Sqn Ldr Mustafa Hilmi (8 Squadron) and Sqn Ldr Fawzi Desouqi (9 Squadron). Pilots had been drawn from Meteor squadrons and transport units respectively.

Page 123: An Egyptian account of the resulting large-scale dogfight was recorded by Soviet Colonel A. Bozhenko, one of the Warsaw Pact advisors in Egypt:

> "Four Egyptian fighters were attacked [or more likely threatened] by four [three] Mystères as they took off. These Mystères were then in turn attacked by two Egyptian fighters from the standing patrol. This Egyptian pair was now attacked by the four other Mystères. The situation was now as follows: six Egyptian pilots, four of whom were very inexperienced, fought eight [six] enemy planes. Veteran fighter pilot Capt [Sqn Ldr Mahmud] Sidki was on the airfield at this time. He was now ordered to take off and join the combat. He bravely attacked a Mystère but the enemy saw his aircraft and avoided Sidki's fire. Both aircraft turned away and climbed. During one turn, Sidki intercepted the enemy and fired a burst but the Mystère pilot again avoided being hit; he was clearly an experienced [sic] enemy. However, Sidki intercepted the Mystère as the enemy manoeuvred and a sharp burst of fire smashed into the Mystère's wing. The Egyptian pilot did not see where the enemy fighter fell because he was himself now attacked by another Mystère. Sidki pulled to one side, executed a combat turn, climbed and counter-attacked but the enemy pilot broke away."

The Mystère, flown by Segen (Lt) Yosef Zuk landed at Hatzor with a damaged wing.

Page 125: Sqn Ldr Mustafa Hilmi and his crew of an 8 Squadron Il-28 was lost during an operational sortie against Israel, possibly crashing into the Mediterranean. Kamal

Zaki was promoted to command. Only one other night raid by an Il-28 was flown during the war, by Flt Lt Hamid Abd al-Ghafar, who was later killed in an accident.

Pages 129/130: The Egyptian Vampire pilot of 40 Squadron who baled out and was captured was Plt Off Ahmad Farghali; the survivor of this disastrous sortie was Plt Off Gabr Ali Gabr.

Page 131: Israeli Mustang pilot Seren (Capt) Uri Schlessinger of 116 Squadron was reported shot down by AA (as recorded) although Egyptian Vampire pilot Plt Off Zuhayr of the Flying Training Unit claimed a Mustang during the fighting.

Page 132: The Egyptian pilot who ditched in Lake al-Bardawil was Plt Off Abd el-Rahman Muharram. He was one of the youngest pilots in his squadron, having only graduated in 1955, and was a close friend of Fuad Kamal to whom he related his story:

> "Abd al-Rahman Muharram escaped from the Israelis after being hit in the wing by going down to extremely low altitude, flying at zero feet and making sharp manoeuvres. Before ditching in Lake Bardawil there were no enemy aircraft close to him and the story that an Israeli flew alongside and could see the MiG pilot's face is nonsense."

After safely ditching in the lake he was able to escape back across the Suez Canal.

Page 133: The Egyptian account of this combat was recorded by Colonel Bozhenko:

> "Four [MiG] fighters, commanded by Sqn Ldr Abd el-Aziz Khalifa [real name Nazih], flew to Sinai. After making an attack on an Israeli column in central Sinai, the Egyptian pilots saw a pair of Ouragans approaching. Khalifa decided to divide into pairs and enter a dogfight. He gave his orders and within a moment, the aircraft reformed. Khalifa and Flg Off Kefi formed the first pair, while Flt Lt Badr and Flg Off Zein formed the second. The Khalifa/Kefi pair took on the enemy leader, while the Badr/Zein pair took on the Israeli wingman. Both Ouragans dropped their auxiliary tanks and started to manoeuvre. Khalifa intercepted the enemy on his next manoeuvre and opened fire from a range of 150 metres. He hit the Ouragan's wing and the Israeli fighter fell. Badr and Zein then attacked the second Ouragan, which exploded in the air a few seconds later."

Despite these claims, one Ouragan force-landed at Halutza and the other landed safely at Hatzor.

Page 134: The Egyptian MiG pilot shot down by Mystère pilot Seren [Lt] Ya'acov Nevo was Plt Off Fuad Kamal (not Plt Off Iwais as suggested), who nonetheless survived ejection from his blazing aircraft.

Page 152: Sqn Ldr Kamal Zaki witnessed the attack on Luxor by the F-84Fs:

> "The French aimed at the pilots first, hitting one pilot in the leg, before attacking the planes. We took the wounded man to hospital. After the planes were destroyed the rest of the squadron personnel left the base and I remained at Luxor on my own, in command of nothing at all."

One Il-28 survived unscathed and was flown to safety at Jeddah in Saudi Arabia by Sqn Ldr Sidki. There he remained for 40 days, his wife giving birth to a son while he was away.

Page 155: The photograph allegedly depicts part of the wing of Plt Off Fuad Kamal's MiG shot down on 31 October. The Israeli pilot on the left is Amos Lapidot and on the right is Ran Ronen.

Page 160: One of the RAF's three B-29 Washingtons (from 192 Squadron), equipped to carry out electronic surveillance, had also arrived in Cyprus; its main achievement was to discover that the Egyptians shut down their air defence radars at midday each day, which proved to be a great help when the attack was launched. Shackletons from Malta were also engaged in maritime reconnaissance sorties in the area, one of these being intercepted by four MiGs led by Sqn Ldr Shalabi al-Hinnawi over the Mediterranean, north of Port Said: "At three o'clock that afternoon a British aircraft was detected over Port Said. Four of our aircraft were scrambled and intercepted. We got behind, and in range. We thought it was a Halifax. There was no fire so I asked our Ground Control 'Should I open fire?' I was at about 600m range. The answer was 'Don't fire, because the English have not yet declared war.'" A lucky escape for the RAF crew.

Page 161: While Cyprus-based British aircraft continued to investigate all intruders at this time, the EAF was similarly engaged in Egyptian air space, two Meteor F.8s flown by Sqn Ldr Mustafa Hilmi and Flt Lt Allaa Barakat of 5 Squadron, intercepting a civilian aircraft that had strayed over a military zone. It proved to be that of the US Ambassador, the pilot of which was obliged to land at Fayid.

Page 193: Sqn Ldr Ware's 148 Squadron Valiant was intercepted by Sqn Ldr Salah el-Din Hussein in a Meteor NF13, who claimed to have scored hits. Cairo Radio later exaggerated this as a kill.

Page 201: Shortly following the first of the morning's raids against Kabrit, pilots were instructed to fly any airworthy aircraft to Almaza, as Flt Lt Talaat Louca recalled:

"I went to the Ops Centre at our air base. It was early in the morning, at about 6 o'clock. We were ordered to get into the nearest trench because the British would attack the base at around 9 o'clock. At five minutes to nine all the Canal Zone bases were attacked and strafed. Our aircraft had already been dispersed but were still open to the sky. They were ready for operations and some were already bombed up. During a pause between the first and second raids our Operations Officer told us to try to get some aircraft to safety at Almaza. My Vampire was ready to go and the external starting battery was already plugged in but I needed a mechanic to help me by unplugging it. There wasn't a mechanic available so I decided to try to pull it out by taxiing and swinging to the left. This worked OK and I took off. I had two bombs on board and dropped them from 100m into the desert. Perhaps the blast damaged the aircraft because I couldn't retract the undercarriage, but I flew towards Almaza anyway. Then I heard on the R/T that Almaza was also under attack, but I kept my eyes open and landed safely. I stayed at Almaza for a while but my Vampire was destroyed on the ground in another air raid."

Page 273: Regarding the death of Lt deV Antoin Lancrenon of 14 Flotille, Russian advisor Colonel Bozhenko wrote:

"The Egyptian MiG pilots showed us the wreckage of the crashed French Corsair on the airfield, shot down by anti-aircraft fire. What we saw could hardly be called wreckage. Instead numerous tiny fragments were scattered over a square kilometre area. The only trace of the pilot was his left hand, which was found 200m away from the point of impact. But this at least enabled the Egyptians to learn the French pilot's name, which was on his finger-ring."

Page 274: It transpired that Lt Dennis McCarthy's Wyvern had not been shot down by AA fire, but had fallen victim to an Egyptian MiG flown by a Soviet advisor/fighter pilot Kapt Sergei Anatolievich Sincov (a Korean War ace with three kills) who, it was believed, was ferrying one of two MiG-17s to probably Syria to avoid destruction. The Wyvern was sighted just north of Port Said when attacked – obviously unknown to

McCarthy – before the MiGs continued their journey.

Page 317: The pilot of the MiG-17 that strafed British positions at Gamil airfield was Flg Off Nabil Kamil who was on a solo mission from Almaza. The Soviet advisor Colonel Bozhenko, recorded Kamil's account of his sortie:

> "Nabil was on his own near Port Said. He strafed British-French troops but eight enemy fighters appeared right away. They spotted the Egyptian pilot and attacked his aircraft. Nabil picked up speed, executed some sharp manoeuvres, fired his guns and broke through the enemy formation, then executed a combat turn and got away at low altitude."

This event was, not surprisingly, remembered with pride in the EAF. Additional details were provided by Flt Lt Alaa Barakat, who recalled that two MiGs were involved rather than just the one flown by Kamil: "Two MiGs [from Almaza] flew missions over British-held Gamil airfield near Port Said. One returned undamaged, but the other came back with 32 holes in it. This latter was flown by Nabil Kamil. Then President Nasser ordered no more flying because it was pointless and would lead to losses for no gain." Plt Off Fuad Kamal added: "I think the mission was just to show that the Egyptian Air Force still existed, nothing else."

Although the physical damage inflicted was small, the psychological and political impact was huge. These final EAF sorties were primarily political. It was clear that the UN would very soon impose a ceasefire, as both the USA and the USSR were demanding that the British and French stop their aggression. So the seemingly desperate and suicidal missions by Nabil Kamil and his colleague had a very clear purpose. They were part of the Egyptian Government's announcement to the world in general, and to the Arab World in particular, that Egypt had not been defeated. A more immediate result of these missions was that the British established regular patrols by Sea Hawks. One reported seeing a swept-wing fighter later in the morning. They believed it to have been an Israeli Mystère, but it is more likely to have been an EAF MiG. RAF Hunters were also sent to seek out and destroy the MiGs. One such fighter sweep by Hunters at 33,000 feet over the Delta and as far south as Cairo saw a solitary MiG but they were unable to intercept it as it was flying at high speed in the opposite direction.

Pages 335-338: Syrian Meteor F.8s had been scrambled on several occasions, but had rarely seen the enemy and certainly not brought one down. One of their pilots was Lt Hafiz al-Asad who, when the war began, was moved from his original posting at al-Mezze to Nairab, just out-side Aleppo. Shortly after 0880 hours on 6 November, the final day of the shooting war, the Syrian frontier post at Abu Kamal, on the River Euphrates, telephoned to say that a British Canberra had been sighted flying in from the direction of Iraq. This Canberra was operating at extreme range from Cyprus on a mission to photograph airfields in Iraq and Lebanon as well as Syria. Lt al-Asad was sent in pursuit and not only found the British reconnaissance aircraft, but was able to open fire from a distance before the Canberra escaped towards Cyprus. The crew that al-Asad pursued had found their targets covered with cloud and on their return they also reported being "chased by Meteors in unidentified markings".

Air HQ in Cyprus insisted that a second Canberra immediately be sent to get the required photographs of Syrian airfields and the oil pipeline. By this time, Syrian Meteor pilots were practically living in their cockpits, and the problem they faced when trying to intercept the British and French reconnaissance overflights were formidable. Sqn Ldr Tahir Zaki, an Egyptian air attaché in Damascus and former CO of Egypt's No.20 (Meteor) Squadron, was working with Major Moukabri, and explained:

"The Syrians had no radar, so I gave the SAF commander a plan to shoot down these Canberras using just telephones for communication. Above all we needed a direct telephone link between Latakia and the main airfield at Damascus."

The appearance of the Canberra was duly reported by telephone, this time entering Syrian airspace over Latakia. Six Syrian pilots had been sitting in readiness in their aircraft since 1000 hours, two apparently in Nairab and four in al-Mezze. Tahir Zaki continued:

"Since these were two targets [the Syrian ground observers were mistaken in this, unless a French RF-84 was also flying a reconnaissance mission], the Syrians had to send up more than one aircraft. One of the interceptor pilots was Hafiz al-Asad. But the actual shooting down was by al-Garudy and al-Assasa, the CO of the Meteor squadron."

There is some confusion in the Syrian and Egyptian accounts at this point, since it is not clear whether al-Garudy and al-Assasa formed a pair, or were each leading a pair of Meteors. The latter was probably the case since the Syrians thought they shot down two Canberras while the Canberra crew believed that they had been attacked by two different pairs of Meteors.

"When the Canberra passed over Latakia they telephoned us in Damascus and we told the pilots to start their engines and to take off. The Canberra was over Aleppo by then. There was usually low cloud over Damascus at that time of the morning during that time of year, so we told the pilots to stay hidden in these clouds. When they got the message that the Canberra had passed over Homs they were to climb out of the clouds and prepare to attack. The result was a successful interception."

Major Moukabri, the SAF ground controller, recalled that the two Meteor pilots (or pairs of pilots) could not see the Canberra until they were advised to look down. They then made a stern attack.

About 40 minutes before sunset, on the same afternoon that Hunter's Canberra was shot down, Hafiz al-Asad was again scrambled in pursuit of another intruder. It may have been an American U-2, since the CIA was also looking for the 100 or so MiGs that were supposed to have arrived in Syria. Al-Asad tested his brakes before taking off and found them faulty, but took off anyway. He failed to find the intruder and now, with darkness falling and his radio unserviceable, he had to land back on an airfield which had no night-flying aids. He could hardly see the runway and the wind direction had changed during his flight. As a result al-Asad landed downwind and overshot. His faulty brakes could not cope. The Meteor smashed through a small orchard and headed for a stone wall. Al-Asad opened the cockpit hood while steering with the rudder, was bounced over the wall by a water conduit and just missed the tents of a Palestinian refugee camp. The aircraft smashed down again, tearing off its undercarriage. The engines seized up and the Meteor finally came to rest on its belly. Al-Asad leapt out and dived into a ditch, fully expecting the burning aircraft to blow up. Then he heard people from the refugee camp running about amongst the trees, apparently looking for his body because the aircraft's cockpit was empty. "No doubt," he recalled, "they expected to find a corpse hanging from a branch ..."

Lt al-Asad was subsequently reprimanded and given a suspended gaol sentence for taking off with defective brakes and thus endangering the aircraft. Many of his colleagues, however, blamed the base commander for sending him on a mission so close to nightfall from an airfield lacking night-landing facilities.

Chapter One

AFTER THE WAR WAS OVER

"We do not seek to be masters of Egypt. We are there only as servants and guardians of the commerce of the world."

British Prime Minister Winston Churchill to the US Congress

The Arab-Israeli war in Palestine, which led to the establishment of the State of Israel, ended in January 1949[*] but Israel's struggle to survive amid the hostile environment of the Middle East had not. It was not until 27 April 1951 that Britain finally fully recognised Israel, although both the US and USSR had done so within days of the cessation of hostilities.

Records show that during 1949 a total of 239,576 Jews arrived in Israel, with a further 447,172 arriving over the next four years, by which time half the population comprised Oriental Jews. Israel's Prime Minister, David Ben-Gurion, wrote:

"They come from Iraq, from Kurdistan, from North Africa. They come from countries where their blood was unavenged, where it was permissible to mistreat them, torture them, beat them. They have grown used to being helpless victims. Here we have to show them that the Jewish people has a state and an army that will no longer permit them to be abused."

In reality, of course, the murderous anti-Semitism characteristic of so much European history had never been seen in the Arab and Islamic world. There, toleration had been the norm and persecution very rare. Nevertheless, both Jews and Christians had remained second-class citizens until modern times; in practice, if not necessarily in law. Nevertheless, and in spite of facing an economic depression and the immigration of hundreds of thousands of Jews from all over the world, Israel had no option but to keep its armed forces strong. Furthermore, dispossessed Palestinian Arabs, individually and in groups, frequently crossed the ceasefire lines into Israeli-held territory. Some crossings were merely attempts to harvest recently lost fields or orchards, though they still led to clashes with Israeli forces. On other occasions they were revenge attacks aimed at newly arrived settlers, though as yet there was no co-ordinated Palestinian resistance movement. For Israel all such incursions posed a threat, but maintaining a large operational army required modern equipment.

---

[*] See *Spitfires over Israel* by Brian Cull and Shlomo Aloni with David Nicolle, published by Grub Street in 1993.

The war which put Israel on the map had been a disaster for the Arabs, most obviously for the indigenous Arab population of the area formerly known as Palestine. Hundreds of thousands had been forced to flee as refugees. The entire Galilee had fallen to the Israelis and only the West Bank, East Jerusalem and the Gaza Strip remained of the territory originally allocated to the Arabs by the United Nations' Partition Plan of 1947. Even there the Arabs lost their independence, for the proposed Arab State never came into existence. Adel Sabit, a cousin of Egypt's King Farouk and a prominent member of the Arab League, wrote later:

> "The 1948 War with Israel was possibly one of the worst-managed wars in modern history. It was an extraordinary production, conceived, prepared for and put into effect by an international team of kings, presidents, prime ministers and politicians, all obeying different loyalties and several secretly ready to betray one of the others for opportunist reasons. In all of this Farouk was to become the innocent victim, and his country, Egypt, was to pay the highest price in men, money and other costs of war. Egypt lost several thousands killed and wounded, together with its prestige, and the King eventually lost his throne."

How innocent King Farouk had been remains a matter of opinion, but he certainly became a victim. The disastrous war also led to serious problems for most of the other Arab governments involved. The Syrian government was soon to be toppled in a military coup. King Abdullah of Jordan (incorporating both Transjordan and the annexed West Bank) was assassinated by an outraged Palestinian. King Farouk was overthrown by Colonel Nasser's Free Officers' Movement in 1952 and, a few years later, the Iraqi monarchy also toppled, though in a much bloodier manner.

Much of the Egyptian officer corps, particularly that of the Army, felt humiliated by the defeat in Palestine. Many officers also believed that they had been badly let down by their own government. The armed forces had been thrown into a war ill-trained and ill-equipped as part of an ill-conceived political gamble. Defeat by such a small settler state as Israel seemed almost incomprehensible to many, particularly the Egyptians, who saw their country as the natural leader of the Arab world. A large part of the Egyptian officer corps felt that King Farouk no longer deserved their loyalty and as a result disaffected groups such as the Free Officers' Movement grew stronger. Britain's unwillingness to help the Royal Egyptian Air Force modernise also led to bitterness within Egyptian circles. At the same time anti-colonialist and anti-imperialist ideas made many in the Egyptian officer corps see their country's future in terms of the Third World rather than as part of a Mediterranean dominated by Europe. However, the Palace clique which controlled Egypt made little effort to answer criticism, instead resorting to bribery, corruption and occasional oppression in an attempt to stifle dissent.

Following the end of the Second World War in 1945, Britain had in principle agreed to withdraw from Egypt by September 1949, although she only – and even then rather reluctantly – moved her forces into the narrow strip of land bordering the Suez Canal. Despite the surrender of her mandates, Britain was still the dominant power in the Middle East and retained the vast military base in the Canal Zone, together with the impressive airbase at Habbaniya in Iraq.

Under the pretext of ensuring the use of the Canal as an international waterway, Britain endeavoured to maintain her influence amongst the emerging oil-producing nations of the Middle East. In the Canal Zone were a number of vast but rundown former RAF airfields dating from the Second World War. These airfields – Ismailia (on the northern shore of Lake Timsah), Abu Sueir (ten miles west of Ismailia), Deversoir (at the northern end of the Great Bitter Lake, on the western bank of the central section of the Canal), Fayid (in the desert, two miles from the Bitter Lakes), Fanara (a flying boat base six miles south of Fayid), Kasfareet (eight miles south of Fayid), Kabrit (at the southern-most point of the Great Bitter Lake), and Shallufa (five miles north of Suez) – were also vital as staging posts for RAF aircraft flying to the Far East, while the British Chiefs-of-Staff felt that the threat posed by the Soviet Union to the 'friendly' nations bordering the eastern Mediterranean warranted a continued British presence in the area. The RAF's air echelon (205 Group, RAF Middle East Air Force) of the British military force occupying the Canal Zone during the 1949-50 period comprised:

324 (Fighter) Wing

6 Squadron, Deversoir	Tempest F6/Vampire FB5	Vampires
213 Squadron, Deversoir	Tempest F6/Vampire FB5	arrived late
249 Squadron, Deversoir	Tempest F6/Vampire FB5	1949
13 Squadron, Fayid	Mosquito PR34	
39 Squadron, Fayid	Mosquito NF36	
208 Squadron, Kabrit	Spitfire FR18	

Transport Wing

Kabrit (70, 78, 114, 204 and 216 Squadrons)	Valetta C1
683 Squadron, Fayid	Lancaster PR1

The Lancaster PR1s of 683 Squadron were equipped with cameras for vertical photography and were employed on colonial development duties in East, Central and South Africa. Units of the Squadron operated in very remote areas, on survey work in conjunction with a Radar Air Survey Liaison Section, while detachments of Lincoln heavy bombers and Mosquito light bombers from Bomber Command in the United Kingdom were sent to Shallufa for a month at a time, operating under the codename *Sunray*, to accustom crews to the terrain and climate under which they might have to operate should relations with the Eastern bloc countries continue to deteriorate.

Although the immediate post-Arab-Israeli War period was one of relative peace, Britain considered it necessary to retain a strong military presence in the area despite its commitment to NATO in Europe and its bases in the Far East. The RAF was stretched to fulfil its role as peacekeeper in a world then threatened by communist infiltration, particularly in Malaya and Korea, where fighting flared up in 1950. Nevertheless, upgrading of RAFMEAF's operational aircraft was underway and Vampire FB5 jets, in particular, were soon to be seen and heard in ever increasing numbers.

For the RAF in the Middle East, 1949 had started badly with the loss of four Spitfire FR18s of 208 Squadron and a Tempest F6 of 213 Squadron, all shot down on 7 January by Israeli fighters and ground fire.* The next RAF fatalities occurred on 25 January with the crash of an Iraq Communications Flight Proctor, HM406, which ran out of fuel and ditched in the Euphrates with the loss of the pilot and his passenger, the commander of RAF Iraq Levies. 249 Squadron, having recently arrived at Deversoir from RAF Habbaniya (Iraq), was still equipped with Tempest F6s and was awaiting conversion to the Vampire FB5. A Mosquito PR34 (RG261) of 107 MU exploded in the air near Kasfareet on 5 July, killing both crew members. Another serious accident occurred on 14 July when two Spitfire FR18s of 208 Squadron collided during mock combat, with the loss of both pilots; TP292 crashed in the Great Bitter Lake and TP450 near Abu Sultan. The final fatal incident of 1949 in which the RAF was involved occurred on 28 November, when a Valetta (VW160 of 204 Squadron) swung on take-off from Deversoir and hit a building, killing an occupant.

RAF Middle East Air Force suffered a further 18 fatalities due to flying accidents in 1950, the majority of which occurred in two tragic incidents. 213 Squadron suffered the loss of one of its new Vampire jets when VZ188 crashed head-on into Lincoln SX957 of 148 Squadron while participating in a fighter affiliation exercise on 11 May. All 11 airmen in the two aircraft were killed and the wrecks fell about ten miles from Deversoir. The second serious accident occurred just before Christmas when a visiting Transport Command Hastings (TG574 of 99 Squadron) lost a propeller, which caused it to crash near Habbaniya; all five members of the crew were killed. 249 Squadron lost two pilots during the year, one whilst flying Tempest F6 NX252 near Deversoir on 10 February, and the other in Vampire FB5 VV622 on 8 December at Abu Sultan. Meanwhile, the Royal Egyptian Air Force was having problems of its own.

* See *Spitfires over Israel*.

4

Chapter Two

EGYPT'S MILITARY EXPANSION 1949–52

"Soon there will be only six kings left: the King of England, the King of Egypt, and the four kings on the playing cards."

King Farouk of Egypt (shortly before his own downfall)

The REAF had taken a severe knock during the 1948/49 War; its morale was low and the heavy fighting of the final two weeks of the war had considerably reduced its front-line strength. When the Israelis eventually withdrew from Sinai, as part of the ceasefire agreement, a token unit of REAF fighters and transports was sent to their former main base at al-Arish to observe. Other squadrons were concentrated at Helwan, Almaza, Dekheila and at al-Ballah, which had been leased from the British in the Canal Zone.

Further deliveries of Italian aircraft gradually enlarged the REAF fighter force. To follow up the first much-delayed batch of 24 Macchi MC205Vs (s/n 1201–1224), of which only a handful remained serviceable, Egypt ordered a second batch of 18 (s/n 1225–1242) in February 1949 (see Appendix I). Dr Ing Gianni Cattaneo of Aer Macchi revealed:

"A second contract for the supply of a further 18 C205Vs was signed on 23 February 1949 by Ibrahim Sa'ad Messiry Bey for the Egyptian Ministry of Defence, and General [Eraldo] Ilari for Aer Macchi. The contractual amount was 270,000 [Egyptian] pounds and the deliveries were effected progressively with seven aircraft in July 1949, two aircraft in August, five aircraft in September and four aircraft in November. The assistance of the Aer Macchi team continued till the end of the year, with [Commandante Guido] Carestiato [Aer Macchi Chief Test Pilot] attending in September to the test and acceptance operations. The aircraft were intensively used in the build-up of the REAF, with frequent incidents due to the inexperience of the pilots, the shortcomings of the previous training and the unreliability of the engines. The DB605, built under licence in wartime in Italy by Fiat, suffered due to the scarcity of proper material and processes, and the operational record was disappointing. A third batch, anticipated several times, did not materialise. A new operational era was dawning also in REAF planning, with Meteors and Vampires on the horizon. Aer Macchi, confident in this further batch, had already put aside 20 aircraft that were subsequently reconditioned and supplied to the Italian Air Force; they served well in the training role at the Advanced School at Lecce until the early 1950s."

British fears that Egypt might turn to Italy as its major aircraft supplier proved unfounded; some of these aircraft were later resold to Italy to serve as advanced trainers. Italy also overhauled some of the REAF's war-weary C-47 Dakotas at a time when Britain and America refused to touch Egyptian military aircraft, the arms embargo still being in force.

General al-Sharawy, an Army officer, was in command of the REAF but Air Force officers hoped to have one of their own take control in the near future. Meanwhile, professional relations between the REAF and RAF forces based in the Canal Zone remained good despite the increasing tension between their governments. Egyptian use of the RAF's al-Ballah airfield in the Canal Zone encouraged this close collaboration, while the RAF organised operational training courses for the pilots of 1 and 5 Squadrons REAF immediately following the end of the Palestine war. At first Wg Cdr H.M. Tawfiq, the REAF Station Commander, had only wanted ground attack training but under British prompting the Egyptians eventually went through a whole course in air fighting tactics and formations, navigation and weapons training, using both Spitfire LF9s and Fiat G55s. At this point the British government preferred military co-operation with Egypt rather than Iraq or Syria, as the REAF had shown itself better able to make full use of its equipment in the recent war. The REAF had already enquired about the possibility of British advisers returning to Egypt, though only in a civilian capacity because of the Egyptian government's concern about the impact uninformed advisers might have on their increasingly volatile public opinion. In private, however, senior and junior officers admitted the REAF's need for guidance. As Air Commodore G.W. Hayes, the British Air Attaché in Cairo noted:

> "All the training that was arranged was done on the Service to Service 'old boy' basis, as the Egyptians did not seem prepared to publicise the fact that the Royal Air Force was assisting the Royal Egyptian Air Force."

Hayes' report added:

> "It was very soon apparent that there was good material, but that in the ranks of Flight Lieutenant and above, and more particularly in the more senior ranks, there was a reluctance to fly on exercises other than those which entailed simple local flying in good weather. One of the main drawbacks was lack of leadership."

One of the RAF's foremost fighter pilots, Sqn Ldr (Acting Wg Cdr) John Baldwin DSO DFC, headed a small team of instructors seconded to the REAF to help train and organise; Baldwin's subsequent report was not very complimentary, although he acknowledged the potential therein:

> "Since the authority to draw up plans and commence joint training for the Egyptian Air Force using RAF facilities was given in February [1949], considerable progress in this direction has been made, and pilots of 5 Fighter [Squadron] and one Flight of 1 Fighter Reconnaissance Squadron REAF have been given a brief operational training course. The training programme has now been completed and the REAF propose to bring in a second lot of pilots for another training programme. During the course of training it has

been possible to assess very clearly the standards of training and potential abilities of the Egyptian fighter/ground attack pilots. Their standards of training were in every subject well below our own. Details are as follows:

(a) Air Fighting Tactics and Formations: The tactics and formations used were of pre-Battle of Britain pattern. The standard of Squadron Drill was of a very low order.

(b) Navigation: The triangle of velocities was a completely unknown quantity to the pilots.

(c) Weapon Training: Most of the pilots had never shot at a ground target and had the results assessed. Consequently, when they first tried hardly one of them could hit the target.

(d) Morale and Discipline: Morale was fairly high among the pilots, particularly the more junior. Some of the senior Flight Lieutenants could not be trusted to take to the air at all. Morale was lower among the ground crew, but was quite fair. Discipline was moderate though it tends to be more show than effective.

The very considerable improvement made by the Egyptian pilots during the course was only gained by certain of the RAF instructors giving up almost all their spare time for seven days a week during the course.

Conclusions: There would seem to be no basic reason why the REAF should not reach a similar standard of those in our own squadrons provided they get sufficient training of the right type. They are severely handicapped by poor VHF R/T technically and at present by poor R/T discipline. On their present showing a complete OCU course lasting some three to four months and with each pilot flying some 70–90 hours is necessary to bring them to an acceptable standard. After that a regular yearly training programme similar to our own would be essential if they are to maintain the standard."

After winter rains flooded the small al-Ballah airfield, the entire training programme moved to the base at Helwan while the REAF pressed for the use of a less waterlogged Canal Zone airfield. On this, however, the British refused to budge.

King Farouk tried to boost his popularity by proclaiming the need for a Pan-Arab Air Force with 2,000 to 3,000 aircraft to support a Pan-Arab Army of a million men, this to be built around a model training division supervised by ex-Wehrmacht (German Army) officers. The British were aware of this proposal. Few ideas could have been more calculated to alienate British and American public opinion and to increase Western sympathy for Israel. On a more realistic level, the REAF embarked on a publicity programme to boost morale and improve the Air Force's standing with the Egyptian public. A collection of historical aircraft was assembled at Almaza from various airfields and every major REAF type was said to have been represented.*

---

* The collection apparently included a Moth trainer, an Avro 626, an 'Egyptian' Audax, a Hawker Hart, a Gladiator, a Lysander, a Hurricane and a Spitfire; most were destroyed during the Anglo-French attack of November 1956.

The REAF's confidence was heightened by the delivery of several aircraft that had been held up by the United Nations arms embargo, while new orders were hurriedly sent to Britain. Egypt, despite her ambiguous relationship with Britain, still preferred British weaponry. In the summer of 1949 the Egyptian government proposed an expansion plan calling for three to six fighter squadrons, two light bomber-squadrons, one medium bomber squadron and two transport squadrons. Britain, however, urged Egypt to concentrate on a defensive role by building up its fighter units. After a great deal of haggling an Egyptian 'shopping list' was finally agreed, to include nine Lancaster B1 and nine Halifax A9 four-engined bombers to replace the unsatisfactory Stirlings; three Meteor F4s and one T7 trainer to supplement the two F4s ordered earlier; a further seven F4s were ordered later in the year. These fighters were essentially the same as those serving with the RAF, though with provision for desert survival equipment in the rear fuselage. Egypt also ordered 20 Vampire FB52 jet fighter-bombers, the first of an agreed but never attained total of 66 such aircraft; Fury FB11s and Spitfire F22s were soon added to the list.

The first of a small number of Halifax C8 transports had earlier arrived in Egypt, having been purchased for meteorological work, air–sea rescue and bomber-training. They lacked tail turrets as the rear gunner's position had been covered over, although subsequent Egyptian Halifax A9s had tail turrets, but no guns. Once again the REAF's experienced scrap-scroungers set to work. Guns were even taken from British or American Second World War scrapped machines and fitted to a few of these bomber-transports, while Prince Abbas Halim (a cousin of the King and former member of the German Air Force who had reportedly flown actively during the First World War), though not recognised by the REAF as its official agent, set out to order gun turrets on his own initiative, much to the confusion of all concerned. Ultimately, the REAF's Halifaxes and Lancasters ended up with twin Browning .5 inch guns in all three turrets, which British RAF observers regarded as highly unorthodox. The REAF was plagued by its inexperience in operating heavy aircraft, and this time the RAF did not help as such 'offensive' bombers were regarded as politically more sensitive than 'defensive' fighters. Which left the Egyptians to learn by experience – always a hazardous approach.

One Halifax was soon lost in an accident at Almaza. As the heavy transport roared down the runway, with Wg Cdr Abd al-Latif al-Bughdadi at the controls, a curtain of flames burst from one wing. It seemed an age before the blazing aircraft rolled to a halt. Flames were licking horribly close to the fuselage as the rear door swung open and everyone on board bundled out – 40 mechanics on their way to England for a Vampire maintenance course. Miraculously, no one was hurt except for a few bruises and some dented dignity, but the aircraft was a write-off. Someone had apparently overfilled the tanks, fuel had spilled into the wings and there it ignited when the engines heated up, a lucky escape by any account.

As the Cold War confrontation with the Soviet Union developed, Britain felt little confidence in Egypt's ability to defend the Canal against a Soviet threat. At first this merely led to combined air-defence exercises, but even these were potentially sensitive in Egypt and were done with the minimum of publicity. In October 1949 the joint RAF/REAF *Exercise Gestic* tested the air defences of the Canal Zone but an accompanying joint British and Egyptian public air display was cancelled. In contrast a big parade and flypast over Cairo in

November, which included the first appearance by REAF jets, commemorated the centenary of the death of Muhammad Ali, founder of modern Egypt, and was accompanied by an outburst of Egyptian nationalism.

During 1949 technical discussions had also worked out an air defence arrangement for the Canal Zone. This called for joint British and Egyptian maintenance of air bases which could, if needed, accommodate 20 RAF and allied squadrons. Britain suggested a co-operative Anglo-Egyptian defence system, but the Egyptian government, while agreeing to the maintenance of the air bases, insisted that the five RAF squadrons then based in the Canal Zone be withdrawn to other countries in the region. If war threatened then the treaty would permit these RAF units to return. The Egyptians also wanted the British to equip five REAF jet fighter squadrons and train these to defend the Canal. British support for this concept rapidly evaporated, however, when an Egyptian general election voted the more nationalistic Wafd Party into power in Cairo late in 1949. The British Air Attaché, Air Commodore Hayes, commented:

> "Unless considerable improvement is made in all directions, it is my opinion that it may be safe to assume that the Royal Egyptian Air Force could not be assessed as a valuable asset to forces concerned with the defence of the Suez Canal and the Delta area as in relation to the defence of a Middle East base in a war against a major power, unless the leadership of the Egyptian Air Force was vested in British officers."

All these political manoeuvrings caused the supply of new British aircraft to the REAF to be both intermittent and unpredictable. Meanwhile King Farouk's own Royal Flight was growing into what sometimes seemed to be a private air force. A Macchi MB308 light aircraft (SU-AGG) had arrived before the end of the Palestine war as a gift following the conclusion of the Italian Macchi MC205V order, though this did not officially form part of the REAF's Royal Flight. Two Westland-Sikorsky S-51B Dragonfly helicopters had been sold to the REAF by Britain in September 1949 and continued to be the subject of a tussle between the REAF and its Royal Flight. One of the REAF's C-46 Commandos was also sent to Italy where it was fitted out with a bathroom and bedroom so that the King could fly non-stop, and in some style, to and from London. The King's favourites, however, remained his two Grumman Mallard amphibians. By the time the 1952 Revolution erupted, the Royal Flight consisted of no less than 13 aircraft. There was even a special REAF unit known as the Farouk Squadron with Vultee BT-13 Valiants, which were used for anti-malarial DDT spraying over the towns and lakes of Egypt.

Egypt received its first jets on 27 October 1949, when a Meteor F4 (s/n 1401) and a Meteor T7 (s/n 1400) two-seat trainer landed at Cairo, flown from the UK by British ferry pilots (the trainer piloted by Sqn Ldr W.A. Waterton AFC, a Gloster test pilot, who remained in Egypt for nearly a month to help train Egyptian pilots), although political pressure led to the associated training programme being cancelled three weeks later. The British Air Attaché (Air Commodore Hayes) wrote:

> "The first appearance in public of the jet aircraft aroused considerable interest. The demonstration of these jet aircraft was regarded as a matter of great importance and the Egyptians undoubtedly felt proud to have been

One of the two Grumman Mallards of the REAF's Royal Flight, s/n 08. These amphibians were King Farouk's favourite aircraft. (*Authors' collection*)

able to fly jet aircraft over this particular parade . . . the hundreds of thousands of spectators stood open-mouthed when the Meteors flew over at high speed and shouted in Arabic, exclaiming that the sight was wonderful and miraculous."

The Meteors were followed in December by a single Vampire FB5 and two Vampire FB52s. By the start of 1950 the REAF's strength had increased considerably to 281 aircraft, 89 of which were operational types. Front-line fighter units still flew Fiats or Macchis as the Meteors were not yet operational, while the remaining Spitfire LF9s had been transferred to the advanced training role. The REAF also bought eight Sea Otter amphibians from the British civil register for target-towing duties.

REAF's first Meteor T7, s/n 1400, which arrived in October 1949. (*Authors' collection*)

The REAF's inventory was large but remarkably varied at this time and, according to Air Commodore Hayes' annual report, included the following types of aircraft:

Unit and Location	Aircraft	Unit	Reserve	Comments
1 Squadron, Helwan	Macchi C205V	12	6	Awaiting arrival of Fury FB11s
2 Squadron, Helwan	Macchi C205V	12	6	
3 Squadron, Almaza	C-47 Dakota	12	2	
4 Squadron, Dekheila	Anson	5	0	General Reconnaissance
	Dove	3	0	Squadron, attached to
	Beechcraft	2	0	the Navigation School,
	Sea Otter	7	1	Dekheila
5 Squadron, Helwan	Fiat G55	12	6	
6 Squadron	Fiat G55	12	6	One Flight, al-Ballah One Flight, al-Arish
7 Squadron, Almaza	C-46 Commando	12	6	
8 Squadron, Almaza	Stirling IV	6	1	About to move to Cairo West on arrival
	Halifax C8	3	0	of Halifax A9s from UK
10 Squadron, Heliopolis	Dove	3	0	
	Bonanza	3	0	Communication Squadron
	Anson	2	0	
	Norseman	1	0	
Flying Training School, Almaza	Sokol	24	18	The ten Magisters in
	Magister	10	10	reserve were to be
	Chipmunk	4	0	scrapped when further
	Harvard	10	8	Chipmunks received
	Spitfire LF9	18	10	

The FTS moved to Bilbeis approximately March 1950.

Royal Flight, Almaza	C-47 Dakota	2	0	
	C-46 Commando	1	0	
	Beechcraft	2	0	
	Mallard	1	0	One further Mallard
	Catalina	1	0	yet to arrive

Additionally, two Sikorsky S-51B helicopters were on order for the Royal Flight: G-ALMD in REAF colours was shipped to Almaza on 16 December 1949, and was followed by G-ALKC on 12 February 1950.

Farouk Squadron	Vultee BT	6	2	Used for DDT spraying

Miscellaneous Aircraft (continued)			
	Serviceable	U/s	
Lodestar	1	1	
B-17	0	1	salvaged from abandoned wrecks
P-47	1	1	salvaged from abandoned wrecks
Avenger	0	1	salvaged from abandoned wrecks
Lysander	1	0	
Stinson AT-19	1	0	
Beechcraft	3	0	modified and equipped for bombing training
Meteor F4	0	1	awaiting further deliveries from UK
Meteor T7	1	0	awaiting further deliveries from UK
Vampire FB5	1	0	
Vampire FB52	2	0	awaiting further deliveries from UK
Halifax A9	3	0	awaiting arrival of six more from UK
Lancaster B1	0	0	awaiting arrival of nine from UK

The nine Halifax A9s imminently due from Britain had previously served with the RAF in former Palestine, from where they had been flown to England, refurbished by Aviation Traders Ltd, and were to be ferried to Egypt bearing civil registrations (see Appendix II). A second Meteor F4 (s/n 1402) arrived for the REAF on 16 January 1950, followed by three more (s/n 1403–1405) by the end of February; the final seven, plus two more T7s, arrived in ones and twos during March, April and May, the last on 22 May, the British government sometimes embargoing deliveries then releasing them.* This made a mockery of the REAF's training and expansion schedules. It also undermined Britain's reputation for reliability and encouraged a feeling in the REAF that Egypt should look elsewhere for military supplies. This growing dissatisfaction would not however, lead to a major shift in policy until after the Revolution of 1952.

Though Egypt was getting some jet fighters, older generation piston-engined fighters were also purchased, including 19 reconditioned ex-RAF Spitfire F22s and a T9 two-seat trainer which were delivered during 1950–51; the trainer arrived on 13 April 1950, bearing the civil registration G-ALJM, and became s/n 684. The first two F22s, PK435 (wearing delivery registration G15-88) and PK484 (G15-89), arrived on 14 June 1950; the last – PK524 (G15-102) – arrived on 8 February 1951 (see Appendix II).

The Vampire was generally agreed to be a delight to fly and would earn a special place in the affections of REAF pilots. The first Vampire to reach Egypt was a standard FB5 (s/n 1500) although all subsequent Vampires were FB52s, plus a dozen T55 trainers. Shipments only came to an end with the Suez crisis of 1956, by which time four Egyptian fighter-bomber squadrons operated these aircraft. In October 1949 Egypt had placed an order for a dozen Vampire NF10 two-seater night fighters, but this order was held up and then dropped when another embargo came into effect. Not only were night fighters virtually banned

* The final seven Meteor F4s (ex-RAF VZ420-426) were allocated the serial numbers 1406–1412; the REAF eventually acquired 12 Meteor F4s and three T7s. An even bigger order for Meteors had been sent to Glosters in October and November 1949, but it was never completed.

from Egypt for many years, the REAF was not even permitted proper night flying facilities. Pilots and navigators had to be trained on antiquated Ansons, which themselves had little – apart from slow flying speed and rugged construction – to help them in the darkened skies of Egypt. Eventually Britain did deliver a dozen Meteor NF13s to fill this yawning gap in Egypt's defences.

Unconfirmed intelligence reports suggested that an unidentified jet fighter had exploded in Israeli airspace in April 1950. The British speculated that this unidentified aircraft was an Egyptian Vampire since the Israelis did not at this time possess any jet aircraft, therefore the finger was pointed at Egypt although the Egyptians denied losing such an aircraft. To add to the intrigue and mystery, REAF intelligence reported that eight crated S92 jet fighters (Czech-built Messerschmitt Me262A-1As) had been delivered secretly to Israel, although this was not correct.

In May 1950 the embargo on arms sales to Egypt ended despite the failure of Middle East peace talks. This followed a Tripartite Declaration issued by Britain, France and the United States of America, in which they guaranteed the existing Arab-Israeli armistice lines against future violation. Events were now proceeding on two quite separate levels. The British government negotiated, imposed and then lifted arms embargos while trying to force Egypt to act in accordance with Britain's wishes. On quite another level the REAF and the RAF carried on in a spirit of mutual respect and even friendliness, despite the political problems. In some ways they still reflected the old imperial relationship, with a patronising but supportive attitude on the part of the British and a respectful reticence on the part of the Egyptians. At the same time the Egyptians were growing both in confidence and their resentment at British interference.

The period from 1949 to 1952 saw efforts to develop Egyptian airborne forces and an Air Force College. In the summer of 1949 work started on a Parachute Training School, a dozen Airspeed Horsa transport gliders were purchased and 3,000 British-made Irving Type X (paratroop) parachutes were ordered, with a view to creating an airborne force in the Egyptian Army, but this was abandoned early the following year. In 1950 an Air Force College was established at Bilbeis, modelled on the famous RAF College at Cranwell, to where 16 newly arrived Miles Magister trainers were sent, these having been purchased from the British civil register. The REAF also bought a number of Czechoslovakian Mraz M-1D Sokol trainers in an effort to circumvent another threatened British arms embargo.

The Egyptian Army was also attempting to upgrade its anti-aircraft capability, wishing to acquire three types of radar stations, but difficulties with the British arms embargo meant that Britain's reliability as a source for equipment was under strain in the Army as it was in the Air Force. Britain had provisionally agreed to supply Marconi AMES 13, 14 and 21 radars back in October 1948. Two sets of AMES 21 radars were ordered in May 1949 but Egypt was still trying to obtain these three years later. Only one radar station of uncertain value had been set up at al-Arish by the end of 1951 and by 1952 Egypt was looking elsewhere, even for light anti-aircraft guns, one such order being placed in Switzerland.

King Farouk, though happy to wear the uniform of a REAF Air Marshal when occasion arose, developed a deep mistrust of his Air Force's political leanings. A REAF officer was never put in command of the REAF, that post being consistently occupied by an Army general. In fact, Air Vice-Marshal Abd

King Farouk and his entourage of ADCs and senior officers watching a flying display at Bilbeis in 1950. The Air Force officer immediately beyond the King's left shoulder is believed to be Hassan Aqif, his senior personal pilot. (*EAF*)

al-Moneim Mikaati, the Deputy Commander, found himself fighting day to day to uphold the interests of the Air Force and its officers. Small and perhaps insignificant changes were, however, permitted in the hope of maintaining morale and strengthening the corporate identity of the REAF. Earlier, new serial numbers had been introduced as a symbolic break with the past. Then someone had taken a fancy to the wing-tip stripes worn by some visiting RAF aircraft; thereupon all fighter units had adopted three black wing-tip stripes. Every opportunity was seized to publicise the REAF.

Recruiting and training more aircrew was now a priority for the REAF. Many men who would make names for themselves fighting the Israelis in the 1960s and 1970s joined the Air Force at this time. According to then confidential British reports, current REAF personnel included excellent material with high morale and good general discipline, though the REAF still suffered from poor leadership, low operational standards and bad R/T discipline among the pilots.

Egypt had been investigating the possibility of a senior retired RAF officer advising the REAF on its future plans. Thus, Air Marshal Sir William Dickson GCB KBE DSO AFC, who was soon to retire as Commander-in-Chief of the RAF Middle East Forces, was asked by the Egyptian Minister of War whether he would like this job despite his age. This fascinating proposal came to nothing, but four days later Air Marshal Dickson visited the REAF Officers' Mess at Heliopolis and handed over a silver model of an eagle in flight to Air Vice-Marshal Mikaati. This was destined to be the prize in an Egyptian inter-squadron air gunnery and bombing competition. In reply Mikaati announced, somewhat fatefully perhaps, that 'there will never be a breakdown in the true friendship between the two air forces'. However, the existence of British forces and air bases in the Suez Canal Zone was now becoming increasingly unacceptable to an Egyptian government which was eager to establish its position as leader of the Arab countries. Egypt therefore focussed its attention on removing this final British military presence. The British, for their part, were still professing their willingness to leave, as they had been doing since the Battle of Tel al-Kebir in 1882, but as yet seemed peculiarly unable to go. To Western countries, however, the Suez Canal remained a vital strategic waterway.

There were some in the British Foreign Office who were aware that constantly interrupting supplies to the Royal Egyptian Air Force was undermining Britain's influence with that Service; but the degree to which the Egyptian armed forces were growing impatient, both with their own government and with Britain, does not seem to have been appreciated. How far such frustration contributed to the success of Colonel Nasser's Revolution of 1952 remains unknown, but may have been considerable. The British aviation press showed no sign that it sensed trouble; nor did British aircraft manufacturing companies. Instead, these concentrated on making as much publicity as they could out of their delivery flights to Egypt. In fact selling military aircraft to the REAF appeared to be regarded as an extended air race, with Hawker and de Havilland machines trying to knock a few minutes off the latest London-to-Cairo record flight-time. A dozen Fury FB11s arrived during early 1950 and one of these, s/n 703, made an attempt on the London–Cairo speed record during its ferry flight in February, in the capable hands of Hawker's Assistant Chief Test Pilot, Sqn Ldr Neville Duke DSO DFC AFC. The Fury reached Almaza 6 hours, 32 minutes and 10 seconds after leaving Blackbushe, at an average speed of 360 mph, including a stop over at Luqa (Malta), a record until eclipsed two months later (on 24 April)

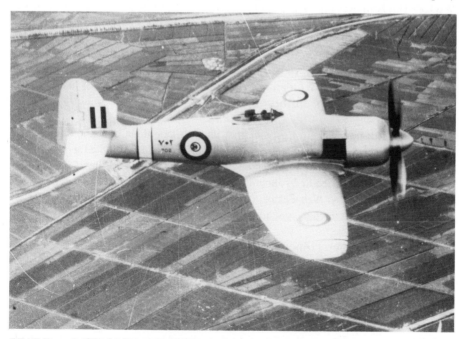

REAF Fury s/n 702 of 1 Squadron REAF over the Nile Delta. Usually based at al-Arish close to the Israeli frontier, Furies were replaced by Vampires in 1955. (*EAF*)

by the new Comet jet airliner. On the same date, a REAF Vampire FB52 (s/n 1513) arrived at Almaza on a ferry flight from Hatfield, setting a new time of 7 hours and 20 minutes for a single-engined jet, an unofficial record which lasted several years.

Meanwhile, professional liaison between REAF and RAF carried on as usual despite the Canal Zone issue. An interception exercise on 12 January 1951 between Vampire FB5s of the RAF's 213 Squadron from Deversoir and REAF Furies from al-Ballah ended with a mid-air collision, when VV562 flown by Flt Lt G. Sharrett clipped a Fury when about 20 miles east of Ismailia. Luckily both pilots were able to bale out without injury. As a result of this accident no further interceptions were carried out at unit level. The loss of the 213 Squadron Vampire was the first of RAFMEAF's eight serious air accidents to occur during 1951, which included two fatal Vampire crashes (VX989 of 249 Squadron on 7 September and VZ338 of 32 Squadron on 22 October) and four Mosquitos (in which one crew member was killed), but the most serious accident involved a Valetta (VW156) of 78 Squadron. During a supply dropping demonstration near Fayid on 2 May, a parachute caught on the tailplane and the aircraft fell out of control, killing all eight crew on board.

At the end of April 1951, Acting Wg Cdr R.N.H. Courtney DFC arrived at Ismailia to take over from Wg Cdr John Baldwin as Head of the RAF Training and Liaison Mission. His first duty was to set up a training airfield at al-Ballah, where the REAF's Meteor and Vampire trainers were to be based. He was also responsible for advising the REAF of all matters concerned with the organisation, operation, equipment and management of al-Ballah and other Egyptian airfields. In addition, as Head of the Mission, he was responsible for control of costings, billings and repayments for all services given to the Egyptians by the Mission. Two RAF Proctors were placed under his command at Ismailia and Wg Cdr Baldwin accompanied him on a familiarisation flight in one of these on 29 April. Wg Cdr Courtney took up an REAF Meteor F4 (s/n 1405) for the first time on 18 May and flew Meteor 1409 the following day. On 22 May he led a formation of five F4s flown by Flg Offs Shalabi al-Hinnawi and Zaky, Plt Offs Bahig and Mansour, flying 1408 on this occasion. Two further flights followed in Meteor 1406 before he handed over flying training to members of his Mission. Of this period, Wg Cdr Courtney recalled:

> "I was accompanying an Egyptian pilot on a training flight over the desert when it became apparent that we were going off course. I asked the Egyptian pilot where we were, and he admitted he didn't really know. When I asked him what he intended to do about it, the Egyptian pilot suggested that Allah might intervene on their behalf. I felt that a conventional course of action would be more effective, and advised him of the required heading."

Mrs Courtney and her 11-month-old son joined Wg Cdr Courtney at Ismailia, where they lived off base in a flat. Mrs Courtney remembered that when one training course ended, some of the officers and pilots from the REAF took her and her husband out for a meal. This also included a trip to the Pyramids and the Cairo Museum, followed by the presentation of a silver dish from the grateful students.

An illustration of the well-defined Arab sense of humour concerned an RAF Dakota which had developed an engine fire when flying over Egypt at about

Wg Cdr R.N.H. Courtney was Head of the RAF Training and Liaison Mission in 1951, and was issued with an official ID card in Arabic. (*Brian Courtney*)

this time; the British pilot reported:

> "It was during the period of Ramadan and Biram, when everything stops for several days, and devout Moslems spend their time alternately fasting and feasting. After a rather trying time, I managed to put down safely in a cloud of smoke, but received no attention from the aerodrome fire tender. My rather pointed remarks at the crash crew's complete passivity while I had been in the circuit was received with a courteous, 'Sir, it is Ramadan. But we prayed for you.'"

Egyptian and British forces held full-scale joint manoeuvres in June 1951 to test the Suez Canal's defences against a hypothetical invader coming from the north. The manoeuvres were given the rather inappropriate name of *Exercise Contentment*, and RAF aircraft based in Cyprus played the part of aggressors in what could be seen as a remarkable preview of the Suez War of 1956. The REAF's 1 Squadron flew its Furies alongside 'defending' RAF squadrons based in the Canal Zone, while Meteor F4s of the newly formed 20 Squadron REAF defended the western flank from their bases near Cairo. The British reported that the Egyptians played their part admirably in *Exercise Contentment*, but once again political tensions soon overshadowed professional co-operation. Later in the year, during November, an REAF Meteor T7 flown by Sqn Ldr Omar Bakir, the Commanding Officer of 20 Squadron REAF who was regarded as the REAF's best fighter pilot, hit a hangar during a display; both Bakir and his passenger were killed.

The RAF's 205 Group retained a sizeable force in the Canal Zone during the period 1951–52, the main units based at Deversoir (where 324 Fighter Wing was disbanded), Kabrit and Fayid:

6 Squadron, Deversoir	Vampire FB5	(to Habbaniya 10/51)
32 Squadron, Deversoir	Vampire FB5	(to Shallufa 2/52)
213 Squadron, Deversoir	Vampire FB5	
249 Squadron, Deversoir	Vampire FB5	
13 Squadron, Fayid	Mosquito PR34/ Meteor PR10	(to Kabrit 2/51)
39 Squadron, Fayid	Mosquito NF36/ Meteor NF13	(to Kabrit 2/51)
208 Squadron, Kabrit	Spitfire FR18/ Meteor FR9	(to Abu Sueir 9/51)
219 Squadron, Fayid	Mosquito NF36	(re-formed 3/51)
70 Squadron, Kabrit	Valetta C1	(to Fayid 2/51)
78 Squadron, Kabrit	Valetta C1	(to Fayid 2/51)
114 Squadron, Kabrit	Valetta C1	(to Fayid 2/51)
204 Squadron, Kabrit	Valetta C1	(to Fayid 2/51)
216 Squadron, Kabrit	Valetta C1	(to Fayid 2/51)
683 Squadron, Fayid	Lancaster PR1	(to Khormaksar 1/52)
651 Squadron, Ismailia	Auster AOP6	

205 Group lost 13 aircraft during 1951 as a result of accidents, in which ten personnel were killed. The worst incident concerned a Valetta of 78 Squadron (VW156) which crashed near Fayid with the loss of eight lives when a parachute caught in the tailplane during a supply dropping demonstration. The other two fatalities occurred when a Mosquito PR34 of 13 Squadron crashed near Kabrit (one killed) on 17 July, followed by a Vampire FB5 (VZ338 of 32 Squadron) which crashed near Shallufa on 22 October.

A dispute in mid-June 1951 between Britain and Persia, when the Anglo-Iranian Oil Company's refinery at Abadan was seized and promptly nationalised, gave cause for grave concern for the safety of British nationals. As a result, 27 Hastings aircraft of RAF Transport Command were flown to Fayid, ready to airlift troops to safeguard and help carry out a mass evacuation of the threatened civilians, should the need arise. To provide air cover for the transports, two of the Canal Zone's fighter units, 6 and 249 Squadrons, flew to Shaibah in Iraq, where they were joined by Brigand-equipped 8 Squadron from Aden. In the event, the crisis evaporated into an uneasy peace and 8 and 249 Squadrons returned to their respective bases in October, while 6 Squadron moved to Habbaniya in Iraq, but not before 249 Squadron lost an aircraft and pilot while operating from Shaibah.

Political unrest was never far away from the surface in the Middle East, as witnessed on 16 July 1951 when Riyad il-Sulh, the former Prime Minister of Lebanon, was shot dead in Amman (Jordan); four days later, King Abdullah of Jordan was assassinated in the Old City of Jerusalem as he entered the Aqsa Mosque to attend noonday prayers. The elderly monarch was shot in the back of the head and died instantly in view of horrified onlookers, including his grandson, 16-year-old Prince Hussein, who was also hit by a bullet fired by the assassin. Miraculously the bullet ricocheted off a medal on the young prince's uniform and he was not hurt, though the assassin was immediately shot dead by the King's bodyguard. A state of emergency was proclaimed throughout Jordan and a curfew was imposed in the Old City, its western boundary forming part of the frontier with Israel. The dead King's younger son, the Emir Naif, was pronounced Regent, since his elder son, the Emir Talal (Prince Hussein's father), was in Beirut undergoing treatment for a nervous breakdown. Nonetheless, he was soon to return to take his rightful place, albeit briefly. The King's death was mourned by many, including the British government.

In October 1951 the Egyptian Prime Minister announced that his country was abrogating the Anglo-Egyptian Treaty of 1936. Four days later Britain, France, the USA and Turkey offered Egypt a partnership in their new Middle East Defence Organisation, but as Egypt was still trying to get foreign troops out of the country this ill-timed proposal was rejected. The country had no wish to see the British presence in the Canal Zone replaced by four non-Arab armies. The fact that one of these armies would be Turkish did nothing to help. Egyptians, like most other Arabs, still considered the four centuries of Ottoman Turkish occupation that had so recently ended as a long period of cultural oppression. Almost at once trouble flared up in the Canal Zone, where several British soldiers and a number of Egyptian policemen were killed as the cycle of terror intensified. The AOC 205 Group, Air Vice-Marshal V.E. Groom CB CBE DFC, was reported as saying:

> "When the emergency first started brewing, the RAF and the Army discussed what should be done to ensure the safety of personnel and families and the smooth running of the RAF machine as a whole. Orders were sent out to all stations to go about their normal business but to safeguard personnel. The RAF was sensitive to the vulnerability of aircraft on the ground and a comprehensive system of guard duties [has] been devised to protect them.
>
> Some burdens [have] been placed on the shoulders of the airmen and airwomen, but all [are] taking things in good part. Much of the best Egyptian labour remained with the RAF and defections [are] far less than the Egyptian government had hoped. Some 400 families [are] now accommodated in two RAF stations in the Southern Zone, but because of the responsibility laid upon the RAF, a proportion must return to England as soon as possible.
>
> With regard to the Royal Egyptian Air Force, [we will] take no deliberate action against them, and relations between the RAF and REAF had always been most cordial. [My] men have been instructed to take no action which might be construed as hostile towards the Egyptians, unless they attempt to stop the British from carrying out normal work and duties."

It says something for the commonsense of the REAF that the crew of an RAF aircraft which made an emergency landing at an Egyptian airfield, at the very height of these troubles, could later thank their Egyptian counterparts for courteous treatment in the very highest tradition of international conduct. This did not unfortunately cut much ice with the politicians of either side and, in the last month of the troubled year, Egypt ordered all REAF officers then training in Britain to return home. As a result of the troubles, the RAF Training Mission was abandoned, as related by Wg Cdr Courtney's son, Brian:

> "There was considerable unrest, and at one point the local population at Ismailia rioted. Mum was alone with me [then barely a year old] in the flat, and fires were being started, and the crowd outside were banging on the

door. Fortunately for us, our Egyptian servant very courageously went out alone to talk to the crowd. Despite being hurt by a thrown stone, he managed to persuade the crowd to move on. All the RAF personnel were on the base during this incident, and could see the smoke from the fires. However, they were not allowed to leave the base until the crowds had dispersed, so this was a very worrying time for them as well."*

The wave of violence reached its peak in the new year, starting on 25 January 1952 with a British Army attack against the barracks at Ismailia which housed Egyptian military police, whom the British believed were turning a blind eye to the many acts of terrorism, being carried out. The one-sided battle, during which tanks went into action, lasted several hours before the garrison surrendered shortly before midday; almost 900 policemen threw down their arms, following the deaths of 41 of their comrades with a further 73 wounded. Three British soldiers had been killed and 13 wounded in the action. When news of this latest humiliation reached Egyptian hard-liners in the various militant organisations, leaders of these groups planned an immediate response.

Early next morning (Saturday 26 January), hordes of young men described as 'students' crowded into the streets of Cairo, chanting 'We want arms! Let us fight for the Canal!' They were soon joined by workers and policemen and then, just before midday, the first major act of revenge occurred when the Badia Cabaret, a favourite haunt for Europeans, was torched, followed by the Rivoli Cinema, the Metro Cinema, the British Turf Club – where nine British civilians were murdered together with the Canadian Trade Commissioner – and other places frequented by foreigners. Groppi's famous Tea Rooms went up in flames, as did the Jewish-owned Circurel's departmental store, followed by the British-owned Robert Hughes store, Ford's showroom – full of new motor cars – Weinstein's (a German stationers), the TWA office, Barclays Bank, and the Ritz Café; one of the last to be bombed and torched was the grand Shepheards Hotel. Many Europeans, mainly British, died horrible deaths in the bloody frenzy. It was not until 1700 hours that the Egyptian military put in an appearance, then 150 soldiers attempted to restore some form of order amongst the tens of thousands on the streets. But the troops refused to open fire on their countrymen, although looting was rife and fires continued to break out. Late that evening came the announcement over the radio of a curfew and martial law. Black Saturday fizzled out, but by then 17 civilians and 50 Egyptian police officers had perished in the riots while in excess of four million pounds' worth of damage had been caused to British-owned property in the city.

At local level retaliation by British troops was severe, including the burning down of at least one Egyptian village, thought to be harbouring some of the ring leaders of the riots, while Britain's response was to send more troops and aircraft to the Canal Zone, a squadron of Lincoln bombers (eight aircraft of 148 Squadron flying to Shallufa from the UK) and two Vampire squadrons arriving at Deversoir in January 1952, 6 Squadron from Habbaniya and 73 Squadron from Malta. Contingency plans were even drawn up for an attack on the REAF

---

* Wg Cdr Courtney had flown fighter operations during the Second World War. Following the departure of the RAF Training Mission from Egypt in late 1951, he was given command of 32 Squadron at Shallufa in the Canal Zone, flying Vampire FB5s, having reverted to the rank of Squadron Leader.

to cover a British ground advance against Cairo. Meanwhile REAF aircraft flew fully armed with other armed aircraft held on standby.

Although the majority of REAF officers took a neutralist position as far as the worsening Cold War between the West and Soviet bloc was concerned, feelings naturally ran higher on Egypt's relationship with Britain. While personal contacts between the REAF and RAF remained friendly, the Egyptians clearly wanted the British out of their country. They also hoped that their own Air Force would grow much stronger. Yet this did not look likely in the foreseeable future. The British government still used various pretexts to delay delivery of an extraordinary list of equipment that Egypt wanted to purchase. By May 1952 this list included no fewer than 161 aircraft, enormous numbers of spare engines, static Link Trainers, parachutes, tyres, maintenance equipment and assorted other items. The list of aircraft ordered by Egypt but currently held up by the British authorities included 20 Balliol trainers, at least 34 Chipmunk trainers, eight Sea Furies, six Lancasters, three Meteor T7s, 24 Meteor F8s, six Spitfire T9 trainers, 20 Spitfire F18s, 22 Vampire FB52s (plus 18 more to be assembled in Egypt), 16 Vampire night fighters, and two Westland-Sikorsky S-51B helicopters. The Egyptian Army and Navy were suffering similar problems. Not surprisingly, frustration and resentment against Britain, even against the West as a whole, grew steadily worse throughout Egypt's armed forces.

On paper the REAF's strength now looked quite formidable, but in reality Egypt lacked sufficient trained pilots to make use of its front-line strength. The British-trained Fury and Meteor squadrons were regarded as the best, 20 Squadron REAF with its Meteor F4s being the élite, while the locally trained Vampire pilots were not yet up to the same standard. Most conversion training was done in the squadrons themselves. There was neither a Fighter Control nor an Early Warning system, except for a barely serviceable radar unit near the Israeli frontier at al-Arish. Pilots averaged only 10 to 20 flying hours per month. The bomber squadrons had no live bombing nor air firing experience and were in no sense really operational. Since the REAF had no proper maintenance facilities, operational aircraft were either grounded indefinitely or continued flying when they were due for major overhauls. Leadership was, in the opinion

Egyptian Meteor F4, s/n 1411 (*Authors' collection*)

of Air Commodore Hayes, the British Air Attaché, very weak at the top. Air Vice-Marshal Mikaati was regarded as very knowledgeable but not very strong, allowing himself to be overruled by Grp Capt Ibrahim Gazerine, acting as the Minister of War's mouthpiece. Conditions on REAF airfields were less crowded since many units had been dispersed away from Almaza. The Egyptians were also upgrading three landing grounds in Sinai by laying concrete runways. In general, however, British observers considered that the REAF's operational standards were declining rather than improving.

The REAF's Order of Battle as at January 1952 was assessed by the British Air Attaché to be:

Unit and Location	Aircraft	serviceable	u/s	
1 Squadron, al-Arish	Fury FB11	9	3	
2 Squadron, Helwan	Spitfire F22	10	9	
3 Squadron, Almaza	C-47 Dakota	10	2	
4 Squadron, Dekheila	C-47 Dakota	1	0	
	Beechcraft	4	2	
	Sea Otter	0	5	
5/6 Squadron, Bilbeis	Fiat G55	4	15	
	Macchi MC205V	4	8	
7 Squadron, Helwan	C-46 Commando	10	6	
8 Squadron, Cairo West	Halifax A9	4	4	Conversion unit for Lancasters
9 Squadron, Almaza	Lancaster B1	5	4	
10 Squadron, Heliopolis	Bonanza	3	0	
	Dove	5	0	
	Anson	2	1	
20 Squadron, Almaza	Meteor F4	9	1	
	Meteor T7	1	0	
30 Squadron, Almaza	Vampire FB52	20	5	
Farouk Squadron, Heliopolis	Vultee Valiant	5	1	
Royal Flight, Almaza	C-47 Dakota	2	0	
	C-46 Commando	1	0	
	Beechcraft	2	0	
	Mallard	2	0	
	S-51B helicopter	2	0	
	Morane 502*	2	0	
Air College, Bilbeis	Chipmunk	9	10	
	Mraz Sokol	10	20	
	Magister	2	8	
	Harvard	12	12	

* Licence-built Fieseler Fi156 Storch

During mid-1951 the REAF had sold ten of its ageing Macchi MC205Vs, all in poor condition, to the Syrian Air Force.

It was not until after the 1948–49 War that the Egyptian government had sponsored private sector defence manufacturing. The Egyptian aviation industry originated as early as the 1920s and 1930s with the development of several domestically designed aircraft. These included an unusual aircraft, the Aerogypt (with an aerofoil-shaped fuselage), powered by three Douglas Sprite engines. Although several prototypes were built, it was never produced in quantity. Initially, Egypt had been willing to work with any group or country to obtain technology and expertise before the authorities encouraged the development of an indigenous arms and aircraft industry beginning in 1949. In that year agreements had been reached between Egypt, the British Bristol Aircraft Company, and America's Pratt and Whitney engine company, for the overhaul of civil and military aircraft and engines.

With assistance from several West German companies, a factory for the production of the German-designed Bucker Bu 181D Bestman trainer had been established at Heliopolis in 1950. The first Egyptian-built aircraft entered service with the EAF in January 1952. Eventually more than 300 of these aircraft were built at the Egyptian Aircraft Construction Factory, located in Heliopolis. Known as the Gomhouriya (Republic) this type remained one of the EAF's primary trainers well into the 1990s. Plans for the production of a jet fighter in Egypt had been announced as early as July 1950 by Defence Minister al-Ferik Muhammad Heidar, following which British firms set up a factory at Helwan to build the Vampire jet fighter, but increasing Anglo-Egyptian friction over the continuing British presence in the Canal Zone slowed progress on this project and, during the height of the crisis in 1951, Egypt dismissed the British personnel who were working at the Helwan factory.

Meanwhile, some Egyptian officers concentrated solely on their professional

The REAF's Royal Flight included two Westland-Sikorsky S-51 Dragonfly helicopters. One, s/n F10, is seen dropping sweets to children to celebrate the birth of the Egyptian Crown Prince. (*Authors' collection*)

duties, but others took a closer interest in politics. This would eventually lead to a division within the Egyptian Army, Air Force and Navy between political and professional officers (a division which would lead to disaster in the Six Day War of 1967). However, there was no evidence that the politically motivated Egyptian officers were neglecting their military duties. King Farouk, ever eager to court popularity by trying to push the British out of Egypt, failed to recognise the serious discontent among his officer corps. Even some senior men who had a stake in the status quo had begun to grow very restless with the political situation.

Unknown to the King, and to most of these senior officers, a number of middle-ranking Egyptian officers were planning a revolt. Colonel Nasser's Free Officers' Movement had been born many years earlier in the stern fortress of Mankabad overlooking the Nile in Upper Egypt. Many Army and Air Force officers had joined its ranks, though the Navy seems to have remained almost entirely loyal to King Farouk until the end. A crackdown by the King's security police in 1949 had necessitated a reorganisation of the Free Officers' Movement and a secret central executive committee of ten was set up. Six members, including Nasser, came from the Egyptian Army, and four from the REAF: Wg Cdr Gamal al-Din Mustafa Salim, whose Army brother was also on the committee, Wg Cdr al-Bughdadi, Sqn Ldr Hassan Ibrahim and Sqn Ldr Abd al-Moneim Abd al-Raouf (who had tried to fly General Aziz al-Masri out of Egypt during the Second World War). The membership of this committee changed little over the following three years and was to form the basis of the later Council of the Revolution. Other REAF officers played a leading role in the Movement and they included Wg Cdr 'Ali Sabri, Chief of Air Force Intelligence, who had particularly good connections with the American Air Attaché in Cairo. This would be a factor of some importance when the Revolution came in July 1952.

The Free Officers' Movement made the final decision at the end of June 1952 to overthrow King Farouk. Only one REAF officer was present at this fateful meeting, newly promoted Wg Cdr Ibrahim. The other REAF members were with their squadrons. Zero hour was to have been midnight, 21 July, but preparations took longer than expected and the uprising was delayed for 24 hours. The plan called for Wg Cdr al-Bughdadi to seize control of Almaza, the REAF's main base. Then he and Wg Cdr Ibrahim would brief pilots stationed there on the coup. None doubted that the REAF would support their revolution. Meanwhile Wg Cdr Salim was to fly his brother, Colonel Salah Salim, and two other Army officers, Colonel Abd al-Hakim Amr and Colonel Anwar al-Sadat, to Sinai. There Wg Cdr Salim was to take control of the al-Arish airbase and win over the squadrons based in that area.

There were many reasons for the military coup which overthrew King Farouk. Not only had the Egyptian Armed Forces been humiliated by their recent defeat in the Palestine War but they, and the country at large, felt that the monarchy was still too subservient to the British who occupied the Canal Zone. The country's ruling class was regarded as feudal, oppressive and corrupt. Some of these criticisms were certainly valid and the 1952 coup did usher in a completely different era for Egypt. Nevertheless, the Revolution did not solve all the country's problems and in some respects added new ones.

The coup eventually took place in the early hours of 23 July. It went exactly according to plan and was almost bloodless, although one of the Royal Flight Dragonfly helicopters was reported shot down when Grp Capt Aqaba attempted to escape the country.* Two men died when the Cairo Military Headquarters building at Kubri al-Kubba was stormed by revolutionary forces, and a further two men were wounded in a skirmish at Almaza Air Force barracks. Notwithstanding, most REAF officers and men enthusiastically welcomed the revolution and from dawn onwards Egyptian Meteors, Vampires, Lancasters and Halifaxes flew above Cairo, Alexandria and the main Nile Delta towns in a show of support. The daring of the fighter pilots as they swooped and wheeled, almost at rooftop level, made watchers proud of their Air Force, encouraged support for the coup and discouraged potential resistance. General Mohammed Neguib, one of the revolutionary movement's leaders, considered that such a show of force would be a powerful psychological weapon and the aggressive low-level flying of the fighters clearly discouraged any resistance. The coup leaders in Cairo were kept informed of developments in Alexandria:

> "We are in constant communication with our men at both palaces . . . Meteor and Vampire jets are flying back and forth over the two palaces. Above them are flights of four-engine bombers carrying demolition bombs. We have a flight of Hawker Furies alerted for interception in case the King tries to slip away by air . . . Shots have been fired . . . [later] The Royal Guard has surrendered . . . Farouk has finally agreed to abdicate . . ."

Early on the morning of the coup, Air Commodore Hassan Aqif, the King's chief pilot, had arrived at Almaza to prepare the Royal C-47 (s/n 113) for a scheduled flight. The base was already in revolutionary hands and Aqif was refused admission. However, he remained loyal to his King to the end and travelled overland to Farouk's palace outside Alexandria. There he guarded the King as the latter tried to raise support in the Egyptian Navy, having seen an Egyptian naval vessel train its guns on a REAF bomber that had overflown the Palace. Since most naval vessels were at Alexandria, Farouk decided to make a dash for the Ras al-Tin Palace which overlooked the harbour. The royal Mercedes was summoned and while the King drove, Aqif sat in the front passenger seat with a sub-machine-gun across his knees. Behind sat the King's infant son, Prince Ahmad Fuad, and his British nurse. As the King, who had the reputation of being something of a demon driver, sped along the Corniche road, a jeep-load of soldiers, who had been instructed to keep an eye on him, tried to follow. Although their Army jeep could not keep up with the Mercedes, Farouk's hopes were soon dashed. His Navy was bottled up in Alexandria Harbour beneath fortress guns and the watchful eye of the REAF circling overhead. When at last Farouk agreed to abdicate, Aqif had to follow him into exile, being one of the eight men from the royal entourage that the new revolutionary leaders insisted had to go.

Over the next two days REAF transport squadrons were kept busy ferrying various members of the Free Officers' Central Committee – known as the Council of Ten – from place to place during the complicated negotiations which succeeded in cementing the coup. As such, they probably did a great deal to

---

* There remains some doubt concerning the authenticity of this incident. If the shooting down of the helicopter did occur, it would seem that it was only damaged, since it was reported to be still on the strength of the EAF at the end of 1955. There is also doubt regarding the identity of the pilot.

avoid unnecessary bloodshed. Once the Free Officers group had firm control, they debated what they should do with the King. Wg Cdr Salim argued in favour of putting him on trial, but most of the coup leaders accepted Colonel Nasser's advice that Farouk be sent into exile while his infant son, Ahmad Fuad, be proclaimed the new King of Egypt. General Neguib and Colonel al-Sadat flew from Cairo to Alexandria in a Dove of 10 Squadron REAF on 25 July to arrange King Farouk's departure from Egypt and, in fact, it was General Neguib and Wg Cdr Salim who bade Farouk, resplendent in white dress uniform of an Admiral in the Egyptian Navy, farewell when he sailed with his wife, Queen Narriman, and their four children, from Alexandria in the royal yacht *Mahroussa.** The King's cousin, Adel Sabit, speculated later:

> "If Farouk had, that first morning of the *coup d'état*, taken his car and driven straight to the Alexandria Garrison HQ at Mustafa Pasha Barracks, he would have been able to assume command of a substantial military force which considerably outnumbered the Cairo rebels. In addition, the Egyptian Navy remained loyal. But he preferred to remain inactive and let events overtake him. Some years later I expressed my astonishment at his passive inaction . . . and received this curious answer: 'There would have been bloodshed and people would have died . . .' Clearly, the same inertia and lack of decision that caused the Army to lose the 1948 War was as prevalent as ever."

REAF reconnaissance aircraft commenced regular flights over the Canal Zone, striving to observe the British air and ground forces stationed there. The coup leaders were clearly worried about possible British intervention but this never occurred. The new AOC of 205 Group, Air Vice-Marshal D.H.F. Barnett CBE, a New Zealander, had been instructed not to interfere and although all RAF aircraft were brought to a state of readiness, they were grounded temporarily during this period of unrest. Barnett had only recently taken up his new post, having been promoted to fill the vacancy left by the accidental death of the previous AOC, Air Vice-Marshal David Atcherley CB CBE DSO DFC (having succeeded Air Vice-Marshal Groom), when the 13 Squadron Meteor PR10 (WB161) he was flying disappeared over the eastern Mediterranean on 7 June while en route to Cyprus from Fayid.†

Although the RAF retained a low profile, Wg Cdr 'Ali Sabri was nevertheless kept busy making contact with the most important foreign embassies in Cairo. As Chief of Air Force Intelligence, Sabri was acquainted with Lt Colonel David L. Evans, Assistant Air Attaché at the US Embassy. The Free Officers were well aware of the importance of American reaction to their coup and Sabri was given the important task of reassuring the American ambassador that Egypt's new rulers were not anti-Western, and he also made sure that the British Embassy knew that the Free Officers' Movement had drawn up plans for guerilla resistance should Britain interfere.

---

* This vessel subsequently returned to Egypt and still sails as the Egyptian presidential yacht, while at the same time being one of Egypt's oldest and most historic vessels afloat.
† Air Vice-Marshal Atcherley, a celebrated Second World War fighter pilot whose twin brother was also an RAF staff officer, was one of five fatalities suffered by RAFMEAF in 1952, when a total of 17 aircraft were lost in accidents; two of these were Vampires (WG892 and WL576 of 6 Squadron) which collided on 30 April, killing one pilot; the same unit lost WL567 and its pilot on 9 September, and a Mosquito NF36 (RK988 of 219 Squadron) had crashed earlier, on 12 February, with the loss of both crew members.

To those not immediately involved in the coup, the dramatic events had come somewhat as something of a surprise, though not entirely so. Air Vice-Marshal Mikaati was the most senior REAF officer although Army General al-Sharawy retained overall command of the Air Force. Mikaati had been waiting for a staff car to take him to Military Headquarters when the conspirators struck. When it failed to arrive, he telephoned HQ and only then learned of the Revolution, which also explained the unusual amount of air activity that morning. But it did not clarify his own uncertain position. Some of his fellow senior officers had already been arrested. No one came for Mikaati, so he put on his best uniform and went to see General Neguib and the other coup leaders. Was he to be arrested or was he to continue to work? Neither, was Neguib's reply, since Mikaati was known to have a very low opinion of King Farouk and his palace clique, and his efforts in defence of the interests of the Air Force were appreciated by all in the REAF. There would be no question of arrest, yet similarly the revolutionaries could hardly allow Mikaati to continue working. He was a member of the old guard, identified too strongly with the *ancien régime*. He would have to stand down and make way for a younger man.

Air Commodore Hassan Mahmud was in a London hospital having his appendix removed when news of the coup reached him. His next surprise was a telephone call to his hospital room, in which Egypt's new Prime Minister asked him to take charge of the Air Force. After serving as a Group Captain during the Palestine War, Hassan Mahmud had been the Egyptian Air Attaché in London for several years. His British contacts were wide-ranging and friendly, and this was expected to be a great help in his new job. However, the Egyptian government's hopes of a new and improved relationship with Britain were unfounded. The British, it seemed, were no more sympathetic to the new Egypt than they had been to the old. As soon as Air Commodore Mahmud arrived back in Cairo he agreed to take command of the Air Force, but only on condition that no officer should be promoted ahead of his peers merely for being on the right side of the recent coup. Nasser and the other Free Officers agreed. Other REAF officers of the old guard had been more closely associated with King Farouk's palace clique and were not treated so leniently.

Of the other notables involved in the coup, Wg Cdr Salim later became Egypt's Minister of Communications and Deputy Prime Minister before leaving the government in June 1956. Wg Cdr al-Bughdadi became Minister of Rural and Municipal Affairs before taking over as Minister of War. Wg Cdr Ibrahim became Minister of National Production; he also left the government in June 1956. These enthusiastic and technically trained Air Force officers brought a new outlook to the stagnant Egyptian political process. But other Air Force officers found it harder to accept Egypt's new direction. Wg Cdr al-Raouf, though an early member of the Free Officers' Movement, had also been closely associated with the Moslem Brotherhood, an Islamic fundamentalist revolutionary organisation which strongly disapproved of the Free Officers programme of socialist-inspired economic and political reforms.

There were also many others in the Egyptian Air Force who felt unfairly treated by the new government. Despite earlier assurances, many senior officers were forced to retire so that junior men, more loyal to the new regime, could be rewarded with a promotion. Such men were often innocent victims of a perhaps inevitable purge, yet their sacrifice sometimes left bitterness in families that had provided Egypt with loyal officers over many generations. A series of

Egypt's Revolutionary Command Council, 19 June 1953. Seated from left to right: Wg Cdr al-Bughdadi, Lt Col Nasser, President Neguib, Maj-Gen al-Hakim Amr, Major Salim, Lt Col Anwar al-Sadat. Standing from the right: Lt Col Hussein al-Shafi, Maj Khalid Moheiddin, Wg Cdr Gamal Salim, Maj Kemaleddin Hussein, Sqn Ldr Hassan Ibrahim, Lt Col Zakaria Moheiddin. (*Authors' collection*)

investigations and prosecutions, known as the Defective Arms Trials, also started soon after the Revolution. These attempted to uncover supposed profiteering by various military officers and government officials during the 1948/49 War. The Air Force's unsatisfactory Stirling bombers featured prominently and among those accused was Prince Abbas Halim, who had been closely involved in various unofficial procurement programmes for the REAF. The Prince was eventually cleared of all charges, along with 13 others accused, but these events also contributed their share of bitterness. It was not so easy to avoid political show trials involving leaders of the corrupt old regime and parties, and Wg Cdr al-Bughdadi found himself saddled with the unpleasant task of chairing these ventures into doubtful regions of distorted justice.

THE SYRIAN AIR FORCE

After the 1948/49 War, a new Syrian military regime came to power in a coup later claimed to have been engineered by the American Central Intelligence Agency (CIA). This military government worked hard to build up an effective air force, a task made more difficult by the continuing conflict with Israel, as well as confusion and political intrigue within Syria during the early 1950s.

Not much is known about the Syrian Air Force during this period, although 30 Fiat G55s and G59s were sold by Italy to Syria in 1950 and the first batch apparently consisted of Daimler-Benz DB605-powered G55 fighters. All subsequent deliveries comprised Rolls-Royce Merlin-engined G59A-2 fighters and G59B-2 two-seat conversion trainers. Syria also took delivery of an unknown number of Fiat G46 primary trainers to supplement ageing Harvards supplied by France in the late 1940s, on which pilots did their initial training at

28

an airfield east of Aleppo. The SAF also received ten ex-REAF Macchi MC205Vs and ten reconditioned Spitfire F22s from Britain, including ex-RAF PK658 which became s/n 504.

Al-Mezze was home to Syria's handful of Fiat G55s and G59s where they formed the SAF's only real front-line strength, backed up by the Spitfire F22s, until the arrival of a dozen ex-RAF Meteor F8s (WK814–817, WK824–827, WK862–865, which became S101–S112) from Britain in September 1952 which, together with two T7 trainers (ex-WL471 and WL472), had been held up by the British arms embargo of October 1951. Two further T7s (s/n S91 and S92) were retained in England and were used to train Syrian pilots who went to England specifically for that purpose. Other aircraft acquired during this period included Chipmunk trainers, French-built versions of the Junkers Ju52/3m transport, C-47 Dakotas, Beechcraft D-18s and Fairchild F-24s, and 18 Macchi-built Vampire FB52s purchased from Italy.

THE LEBANESE AIR FORCE

The Lebanese Air Force was founded in 1949 when a few Prentice trainers were received from Britain. Although there were a number of small airfields built for the Armée de l'Air during the French mandate, there was only one base – at Khalde near Beirut – suitable for operating large jet aircraft. Although it was hoping to acquire jet fighters, the LAF possessed only communications and transport aircraft at this stage, including four refurbished converted Savoia-Marchetti SM79P tri-motors (s/n L112-L115), and a Macchi MB308 donated by Aer Macchi to the Commander-in-Chief of the Lebanese Armed Forces.

Decorative Harvard of the Lebanese Air Force, with its s/n L130 in both Western and Arabic script. (*John Havers*)

THE ROYAL IRAQI AIR FORCE

Britain had supplied the RIrAF with 30 Fury FB11s (s/n 231–260) between 1948 and 1950, together with two two-seat T20s (s/n 261 and 263), a few Auster AOP6s and T7s and several Bristol 31M Freighters. During the final stages of the Palestine War the Iraqis detached four of the Furies to al-Arish in support of the REAF, where one was damaged beyond repair in an accident. Although the remaining three flew defensive patrols, no Israeli aircraft were encountered and they were withdrawn when al-Arish was abandoned by the REAF in December 1948. Of the first dozen Furies delivered, only three were operational by January 1949: four had been written off in accidents and five were unserviceable but repairable; two of these crashed later during the year, and a further two during the early months of 1950, including s/n 242 at Habbaniya in January, while Lt Colonel Mahmoud Ayoub was killed landing another at Mosul in March of that year.

With the fighting over, the RIrAF ordered further Furies from Britain, 25 FB11s (s/n 302–326), ten of which were diverted from Fleet Air Arm stock; these were WJ293, WJ298, WM483–WM486, WN480–WN483, and three T20 trainers (s/n 327–328), which arrived between 1951 and 1953, the year in which Chipmunk trainers were acquired, the latter eventually delivered to the RIrAF Flying College at Raschid.* Under King Feisal III, who was also Commander-in-Chief of the Armed Forces, the control of the Air Force, still an integral part of the Iraq Army, was the responsibility of Maj-General Rafiq Arif as Chief of General Staff. Brigadier Kadhim Abadi, as Air Officer Commanding, had direct day-to-day control of all Air Force matters.

The Anglo-Iraqi Treaty of 1936 allowed Britain to maintain a presence at Habbaniya, the largest airbase in the Middle East, although the Tempest F6-equipped 249 Squadron was the sole occupant until joined by a detachment of Vampire FB5s of 6 Squadron from Deversoir; the remainder of the Squadron followed in June 1951 by which time 249 Squadron, equipped with Vampire FB5s, had moved to Deversoir. The following year (1952) saw the arrival of another Vampire FB5-equipped unit, 185 Squadron from Cyprus, although disbandment for this unit was but a few months away. Lancaster PR1s of 683 Squadron from the Canal Zone also arrived at Habbaniya on temporary attachment for mapping duties over the Persian Gulf.

THE JORDANIAN ARAB LEGION AIR FORCE

Jordan's Arab Legion, partially officered and completely armed by the British, possessed only a few communications and transport aircraft, a miscellany of Tiger Moths, Dragon Rapides, Proctor Vs (including TJ-AAJ, AAK, AAL, and AAM) and Auster AOPs, the Jordanian budget too small to support more than a token air arm. It was commanded by a seconded RAF officer, Wg Cdr Jock Dalgleish. Under the terms of the 1948 Anglo-Jordan Treaty, the RAF was permitted use of the airfields at Mafraq and Amman, which it shared with the Jordanian air arm. More than 40 small airstrips were scattered throughout the kingdom.

In May 1950, an advance party of 324 Wing from the Canal Zone arrived at Mafraq, followed next day by a detachment of Vampire FB5s of 6 Squadron from Deversoir to carry out trials to establish the effect of jet aircraft operating from a compressed sand runway. Although far from ideal, this type of runway was shown to be suitable for occasional periods of operations and, having completed the trials, the Squadron returned to the Canal Zone.

---

* In February 1960, four Fury FB11s, two of which were s/n 234 and 259, were given to Sherifian Royal Aviation, which later became the Moroccan Air Force; however, only two of these gained full Moroccan Air Force markings. In 1972, 24 surviving Furies were purchased by two American civilians from open storage in Iraq and shipped to the USA. These were: s/n 237, 241, 243, 249–250, 252–255, 302–305, 308, 310, 312, 314–316, 318, 324–327, the latter a T20.

Proctor Vs at Luton circa 1948 prior to delivery to Jordan. (*Peter Arnold collection*)

A skirmish between Israeli forces and the Arab Legion on the road to Aqaba, at the beginning of December 1950, resulted in the death of a Jordanian soldier. Though within Jordanian territory, this road ran within a few yards of the ill-marked border; a situation which caused trepidation in the British camp, since RAF vehicles frequently used this road to transport supplies from Aqaba to Amman and Mafraq. Protection of the British convoys was the responsibility of the RAF Regiment, which was, as a result of further Israeli threats, reinforced to provide greater protection for both airfields and convoys.

The Royal Jordanian Air Force came into existence in late 1952, following the succession of Crown Prince Hussein to the throne, who replaced his ailing father in August of that year. Egypt, endeavouring to gain favour, promptly supplied a gift of three Gomhouriya primary trainers for its use.

Chapter Three

ISRAEL AND THE ARMS RACE 1949–1953

"The Israelis will destroy themselves if they go on spending 60 per cent of their budget on armaments. We are not going to make that mistake."

Colonel Nasser to British Labour MP Richard Crossman

The arms embargo imposed on Israel and the Arab states during the 1948 War was lifted after the armistice was signed in 1949. Nevertheless, the main traditional arms suppliers remained reluctant to sell in this volatile part of the world. Britain, for example, maintained the unofficial arms embargo it had imposed even before the first Arab-Israeli War broke out in 1948. As yet the oil wealth of a few Arab states had virtually no influence on their ability to procure arms. Meanwhile, all sides did what they could to circumvent the embargos. This often meant purchasing weaponry from unlikely or at least non-traditional sources. Here again the Israelis' wide network of Zionist and other sympathisers stood them in good stead.

By the end of the 1948/49 War, Israel's Chel Ha'Avir (the Air Force) could boast with some justification that it was the best air arm in the Middle East. From the embryonic Sherut Avir (Air Service) of November 1947, with its handful of obsolete light aircraft and a few dozen enlisted men, it had developed into a force which had taken on and defeated the Royal Egyptian Air Force, the Syrian Air Force and the Royal Iraqi Air Force, and had even challenged the Royal Air Force in the skies above the desert sands of Sinai. By January 1949, when the fighting officially ended, Chel Ha'Avir had expanded to a complex organisation with in excess of 6,000 enlisted men and women, of whom 150 were pilots, albeit mainly foreign volunteers. It was only natural, once the war was over, that highest priority was given to the training of Israeli pilots to take the place of the volunteers, many of whom had started to return to their native shores.

When the air arm was founded in 1947 it classified its own inexperienced pilots as air cadets; they had been given occasional training, but worked as mechanics in their spare time. As operational activity increased, the training of these cadets locally became impossible and a training facility abroad was sought. The first step in that direction was the establishment of a flying school at Bakersfield, California, during early 1948, under the aegis of the daughter of a rich cattleman who was also the owner of Bakersfield Air Park, just outside Los Angeles. From this private airfield operated a large fleet of Stearman PT-17 biplanes for agricultural use, which were made available to train a group of young Israelis.

The group comprised eleven men and two women, all of whom had sacrificed comfortable lives as students at American universities to answer their country's call. The course had officially opened on 1 March 1948 and required the students to log in excess of 200 flying hours in a period of less than four months: the primary stage comprised 70 hours on Fairchild PT-16s and PT-19s, followed by 70 hours on the basic Vultee BT-13, and finally 70 hours on the twin-engined Cessna AT-17. By 7 June 1948 the first five cadets had graduated, followed just over a week later by the remaining eight, all of whom were flown or shipped to Israel during the month, where they were posted to the various light aircraft units. Three members of the course lost their lives during the 1948/9 war, with a fourth taken prisoner; another sustained injuries and a sixth was killed in an aircraft accident shortly after the end of hostilities.

At roughly the same time as the Bakersfield graduates reached Israel, another group of young Israelis commenced flight training at the Czechoslovak Air Force Air Academy at Hradec Kralove. The story of this group dates back to March 1948 when two young Haganah representatives in Italy, Mordechai Fein (changed later to Moti Hod) and Avraham Yoffe, received a special stipend of 75,000 Italian lire to commence a civil flying course in Rome. The flying school chosen was Alicca and since costs were considered reasonable, it was decided to send a further group of cadets, all of whom held private flying licences, for advanced training. Thus, on 13 May 1948, eleven would-be fighter pilots boarded a Dakota for Rome. However, none possessed entrance visas for Italy and they found themselves conveyed to Prague, there to reside until formalities had been sorted out. Within a few weeks seven of the group arrived in Rome and commenced training, using Lombardi FL-3s and FL-5s, but soon developments in Czechoslovakia culminated in all but one of the students moving to that country where they entered the Czech Air Academy to complete their training.

At Hradec Kralove the students flew initially the Avia C2B-1 basic trainer, which was the Czech version of the German-designed Arado AR96B, a type roughly equivalent to the American Harvard or British Miles Master. The major obstacle was the language barrier since few of the Czech instructors spoke English. To overcome that difficulty, three foreign volunteers were sent to aid the Czech instructors, among whom were Harold Green and George Lichter, both Americans. By September 1948 the basic stage had been completed, with the students each having accumulated 90–100 hours on the Avia C2B-1; the group then commenced its advanced training at Ceske Budejovice on the Avia CS199, the two-seat version of the Avia S199 fighter, which had been developed from the German Messerschmitt Bf109G. It was not generally liked by the pilots since it had a tendency to pull to starboard on take-off. However, when relations between Israel and Czechoslovakia turned sour in late 1948 the training course was cut short, although by then five of the students had advanced to flying the Spitfire LF9, a type the Czechs were about to sell to Chel Ha'Avir.

The fledgling fighter pilots returned to Israel in November/December, two flying Spitfires as part of the *Velveta 2* ferry operation.* Of the group of twelve, the four most promising were posted to the fighter unit – 101 Squadron commanded by Syd Cohen (a former SAAF fighter pilot) – for further instruction, the others joining light aircraft units until the Flying School was opened. Those

---

* See *Spitfires over Israel*.

who joined 101 Squadron – Moti Hod, Dani Shapira, Israel Ben-Shachar and Yeshayahu Gazit – were given an improvised but thorough operational conversion course on the Harvard before progressing to the unit's Spitfires. Among the instructors were Rudy Augarten, Jack Doyle and Caesar Dangott, North American veterans of the recent war. The reward for the hard work came on 14 March 1949 when Prime Minister Ben-Gurion, together with the IDF Chief-of-Staff Ya'acov Dori, and the commander of Chel Ha'Avir Aharon Remez, attended the formal graduation ceremony at Shmuel Field (later renamed Hatzor, but formerly RAF Qastina), when the four pilots received their coveted 'wings'. Ben-Shachar described his training with 101 Squadron:

"When we arrived at 101 they laughed at us, they were all World War II aces. First of all they gave us blue hats instead of the red hats (which fighter pilots had); we were clowns, and in the evening we were not allowed to enter the bar. We thought that we were to participate in a great war. They took two Harvards (s/n 08 and 12) and Rudy Augarten and Dani Dangott instructed us and, during the fighting, we did a Harvard course. We flew about 40 hours and at last we received our wings . . . it was an enlightening experience to serve in a fighter squadron in wartime. We were there when they shot down the British Mosquito. We flew with all the 101 pilots – [Arnie] Ruch, [Denny] Wilson, [John] McElroy, and all those guys. What we learnt from them accompanied us through the years. They were wild guys but in the air (they had) aerial discipline. We learnt the USAF discipline from Augarten and the USN discipline from Dangott, two different approaches and we had to learn a lot from both."

The initial success of the flying course in Czechoslovakia resulted in the organisation of a small group of Czech Jewish youth, who elected to join Chel Ha'Avir upon completion of their training syllabus. These included Hugo Maizel (who changed his name to Marom on arrival in Israel), Josef Plazec (who became Yossef 'Joe' Alon), Joel Costa and Monic Melnitzki (the latter changed later to Moshe Tadmor). As with the earlier course, their training in Czechoslovakia was abruptly halted in December 1948 and they departed by train for Romania, and hence by ship to Israel, arriving in February 1949. As with the majority of the first group, they were posted to the light aircraft squadrons for further experience.

Yet a third group, including Nachom Biran and Menahem Bar, had been despatched to Czechoslovakia during the previous summer, but they had only managed to finish the primary stage of their training before being sent back to Israel, where they were given a short flying course within the liaison squadrons and eventually received their 'wings' on 9 May 1949. There was a fourth concurrent flying course in progress at Rome, seven cadets graduating successfully having carried out their basic flight training on the indigenous Lombardi FL-3, before advancing to the Ambrosini S-7 and the British Proctor. However, by late 1948 Chel Ha'Avir's own Flying School was established and in excess of 600 candidates for a flying course, drawn from all Israeli Defence Force (IDF) units, were gathered for initial tests, though only 77 passed the elementary stage. But since there were no instructors available at the time, students had to content themselves with basic theoretical studies at a camp near Jaffa, where many trained as bombardiers for service aboard Chel Ha'Avir's C-46 converted bombers during the final phase of the War of Independence.

By early 1949 a number of Piper Cubs and Stearman PT-17 Kaydets were available for use as trainers, at which point the students were sent to St Jean, an abandoned former RAF airfield near Acre, some 20 miles north of Haifa. But, with the end of the Arab-Israeli war, Chel Ha'Avir was about to be reorganised. New winds were blowing. Cuts in the armed forces were demanded. The move was not unexpected, since economic depression followed the ceasefire. Many of the foreign volunteers, sensing the imminent change, now returned to their homelands, including Syd Cohen, commander of 101 Squadron, who went back to South Africa to continue his medical studies, while Jack Doyle and Denny Wilson returned to their native Canada. The cuts inflicted upon Chel Ha'Avir included the closure of some of its bases, while some of its units were disbanded and others amalgamated. Hatzor airfield (formerly Shmuel Field) was handed over to the Army and 101 Squadron, which had been based there and was commanded by Rosh-Tayeset* Ezer Weizman, and moved to Ramat David on 30 May 1949. Many of the foreign volunteers had already left the Squadron and, in most cases, the country: George Lichter returned to the United States in February to his textile business; Rudy Augarten also returned to the United States to resume studies at Harvard; while Lou Lenart and Slick Goodlin (two American volunteer pilots) signed on with a private charter service to ferry Jewish refugees from Iraq to Israel.

Soon after 101 Squadron's move to Ramat David, three more of the American volunteers – Red Finkel, Mitchell Flint and Caesar Dangott – departed Israel. By then half a dozen Israeli pilots had joined the Squadron, although a handful of volunteers remained, notably American Buck Feldman, Joe Cohen (ex-Indian Air Force) and Bill Kaiser, a South African. They remained to help train the Israeli pilots to operational standards. During the summer of 1949 George Lichter returned to Israel, although his offer of help was not taken up by Weizman.

The two resident units at Ramat David, 103 Squadron with its C-47s and 69 Squadron with B-17s, moved to Tel Nof (formerly RAF Aqir), while the two units based at Tel Nof, 106 Squadron (which handed its C-46s over to 103 Squadron) and 35 Squadron, were disbanded. The latter unit's Harvards were passed on to the newly created Flying School, which was activated at Kfar Sirkin (formerly RAF Petah Tivqa), some ten miles east of Tel Aviv. The Flying School was named in memory of Modi Alon, the legendary commander of 101 Squadron who fell in the War of Independence. Also at Tel Nof were the three liaison/observation units, 1/Tel Aviv Squadron, 2/Negev Squadron and 3/Galilee Squadron, now amalgamated to form 100 Squadron, although one Flight was to remain based at Beersheba in the Negev for observation duties in that area. The Technical School was formed at Haifa airport, using a deserted high school building, while Air Headquarters was relocated in Jaffa from Tel Aviv. Thus, Chel Ha'Avir's Order of Battle as at 1 June 1949, following the defence cuts, was:

---

* Chel Ha'Avir adopted the RAF system of rank:

Pakad-Avir	= Pilot Officer	Rosh-Tayeset	= Squadron Leader
Pakad-Tais	= Flying Officer	Rosh-Kanaf	= Wing Commander
Pakad-Teufa	= Flight Lieutenant	Rosh-Lahak	= Group Captain

Ramat David	101 Squadron	19 Spitfires, 3 Mustangs
	Station Flt	1 Auster, 1 Piper Cub
Haifa	2 TTB	2 Harvards
Sirkin	Flying School	8 Harvards, 4 Kaydets
	114 Squadron	6 Consuls, 3 Ansons, 2 Harvards, 1 Norseman
Tel Nof	22 Wing	6 Spitfires, 5 Piper Cubs, 5 Rapides, 2 B-17s, 2 C-46s, 2 Harvards, 2 Norseman, and one each: BT-13, Beaufighter, C-47, C-54, Hudson, Lodestar, Bonanza, S-199, Kaydet (all u/s except one Norseman and the Kaydet)
	69 Squadron	1 B-17
	100 Squadron	10 Piper Cubs, 2 Bonanzas, 1 Rapide
	103 Squadron	5 C-46s, 4 C-47s, 2 Hudsons, 1 Mosquito PR16

Stearman PT-17 Kaydet (s/n 06) in the early 1950s light colour scheme. Later these trainers were camouflaged. (*IAF Magazine collection*)

The Order of Battle did not include many aircraft, especially Spitfires, which were yet to be assembled. A further 27 unassembled Spitfires and two Mustangs had arrived in Israel and a further dozen Mustangs, procured in the United States, were awaiting shipment to Israel. The main problem facing Chel Ha'Avir was a lack of pilots; 101 Squadron had 25 pilots, of whom seven were experienced foreign volunteers, but of the 18 Israelis the majority were not experienced and eight were, in fact, on operational conversion training. On 69 Squadron there were only two Israeli pilots capable of flying the B-17 bombers, the other seven being foreigners; and of the 37 transport pilots, only a dozen

Spitfire s/n 24 was an ex-Czechoslovak example which served with both 105 and 107 Squadrons. (*IAF Magazine collection*)

were Israelis, while only eight of the 22 navigators were Israeli. With many of the foreign volunteers returning home, the problem of the lack of trained aircrews was deadly serious.

During this period of cut backs it seems that the commander of Chel Ha'Avir, Aluf-Avir Remez, failed to face the reality of the situation, instead concentrating on the future rather than the present, which led to his resignation. Just prior to this dramatic anti-climax to what had been a meteoric career, Remez had presented Prime Minister Ben-Gurion with his ambitious plan for the Air Force, in which he envisaged no fewer than seven wings comprising 292 aircraft in 15 squadrons and in excess of 6,000 personnel:

Wing 1: for day and night air defence with three squadrons comprising (a) 27 Spitfires, (b) 16 Mosquitos or P-38s (c) eight Spitfires and Mosquitos, the latter an Operational Conversion Unit;

Wing 2: for tactical operations with two squadrons of (a) 22 Spitfires and (b) 22 jet fighters of an unspecified type;

Wing 3: for tactical and strategic bombing with two squadrons comprising (a) 24 C-47s and (b) 16 B-17 and B-25s;

Wing 4: for transport and coastal patrol with two squadrons comprising (a) 16 C-46s, C-47s and C-54s, and (b) 12 PBY-5A Catalinas, Hudsons and Venturas;

Wing 5: for liaison and observation with two squadrons comprising (a) 20 Dragon Rapides, Norseman and Ansons, and (b) 30 Piper Cubs and Auster AOPs;

Wing 6: for training with four squadrons comprising (a) 30 Stearman PT-17 Kaydets (b) 30 AT-6 Harvards (c) 12 Spitfires (d) 12 Ansons.

The purpose of Wing 7 was not indicated but it was probably a non-flying unit. Of the total of 292 aircraft specified, 87 were to be for reserve.

Israel Ben-Shachar inspects the damage caused to his Spitfire by the propeller of another after a mid-air collision in 1949. (*Israel Ben-Shachar*)

The only positive step taken at this time was the formation of a second fighter unit, 105 Squadron, based alongside 101 Squadron at Ramat David and equipped entirely with Spitfires. The new squadron was to serve as an OTU for the graduates of 1 Flying Course and by the time the second flying course graduated (in December 1950) it became an independent unit under the command of Rosh-Tayeset Bar. The new unit's aircraft were adorned with yellow and black diagonal tail markings and yellow spinners, whereas 101 Squadron's Spitfires displayed red and white tails and red spinners.

During this period Chel Ha'Avir had to fight hard for recognition and credibility, since its officer personnel had gained a certain reputation for indiscipline. This attitude was highlighted when an air cadet, who had been dismissed from the flying course, stole a Piper Cub on 11 June 1949 and flew it to Turkey; he was duly arrested and sent back to Israel, but the harm inflicted on the image of Chel Ha'Avir was difficult to eradicate.

Once the United Nations arms embargo was lifted on 11 August 1949, after the ceasefire agreements were signed at Rhodes, both Israelis and Arabs frantically trawled the arms markets. Israeli intelligence reports of the period were hysterical concerning the aircraft procurement campaign in Egypt. As early as March and April 1949 it was reported that three de Havilland Vampire jet fighters were seen in REAF colours at an Egyptian base; they were, in fact, RAF Vampire F3s – probably aircraft of 73 Squadron from Cyprus on a visit; this unit had received its first Vampires the previous October, the first jet fighters in the Middle East. Another report indicated that Egypt had placed orders with Britain for 110 Vampire and Meteor jet fighters, dozens of late mark Spitfires and Sea Furies and up to two dozen Halifax and Lancaster heavy bombers. The Syrians were reported to have ordered a dozen Fiat G55 fighters from Italy and two dozen Meteors from Britain. Although the numbers were exaggerated, the aircraft types mentioned in these reports were reasonably accurate. Israeli procurement agents had their own feelers out, but little was forthcoming at this time.

Chel Ha'Avir was keen to have all forms of conventional modern warfare available for use by its pilots and in mid-1949 began to experiment with napalm bombs. The chief maintenance pilot, Buck Feldman, had been approached to demonstrate the weapon, as he recalled:

"I had been summoned to the IAF base at Ekron where I was briefed as to what was to be carried out during the test flight. Military observers were to check the flame spread over a designated target area near Nabi Rubin, located south of Tel Aviv in an isolated area of desert terrain. The date was 28 September 1949, a beautiful autumn day. After taking off [in Spitfire s/n 2016/21], I flew to the designated site and carried out a dummy run and observed the handling characteristics of the aircraft. The second run-in on the target was to be the actual drop. The starboard bomb released satisfactorily; however, immediately, I experienced a severe yaw to port accompanied by a strong port wing drop. The port bomb had turned 90° and was jammed on its carrier, covering the port wheel well completely. After several violent manoeuvres, I had realised that it was impossible to jettison the bomb. My radiator coolant temperature was rapidly approaching the red line. I finally made the decision to abandon the aircraft and, after climbing up to about 7,000 feet, carried out the prescribed procedure for a Spitfire bale out. Whilst flying inverted, one of my legs was momentarily caught in the cockpit. This caused a delay in clearing the aircraft, causing me to hit the vertical fin. I landed OK; however, strong, gusty surface winds caused me to be dragged a couple of hundred yards. I eventually managed to release myself from the parachute harness and a few hours later was picked up by military personnel, none the worse from this experience. The aircraft had been completely demolished. During this escapade some silly clot suggested that I carry out a belly landing back at Ekron."

This was the first successful bale-out in the short history of Chel Ha'Avir. The principal duty of 105 Squadron, like that of its sister unit, was the air defence of Israel. Since no radar chain was in service and the early warning system was primitive, Israel's airspace was frequently intruded, either deliberately or by mistake, and the eager young fighter pilots set themselves the target to put an end to any intrusion that lacked authorisation. Although peace agreements had been signed with her Arab neighbours, the IDF kept a constant vigil along Israel's borders, and from time to time called upon Chel Ha'Avir to help investigate violations.

Spitfire IXE 2016/21 had a short but colourful career in Israel. It participated in combat with RAF Tempests in 1949 but during the same year was lost when test pilot Buck Feldman was obliged to bale out during a bombing test. (*Aaron Finkel*)

One of the first opportunities for Chel Ha'Avir to flex its muscles came on the morning of 17 May 1950 when four Spitfires of 105 Squadron, which were due to give an air support demonstration for the officers of the North Command, were waiting at Ramat David for the order to take-off. At this point Rosh-Tayeset Grisha Bar On (formerly Braun), observed a large four-engined flying boat flying westwards at an altitude of about 2,000 feet, and promptly scrambled accompanied by Pakad-Teufa Yoffe. Jettisoning the 50kg bombs slung under the wings of the Spitfires for purposes of the demonstration, Bar On and Yoffe closed rapidly on the intruder, an RAF Sunderland, some 15 miles offshore. The flying boat's captain, Flt Lt Ted Yates, allegedly ignored the Israeli Spitfires initially and changed his heading from west to south, flying parallel to the Israeli coast towards Egypt. At this, Bar On lost his patience and fired a couple of bursts across the bows of the Sunderland following which Yates wisely decided to alight immediately in spite of the grey sea and high waves. Mrs Catherine Yates, widow of the pilot, remembered:

"Teddy did mention that, at the time the Israeli fighters intercepted, they lowered their wheels and fired across the bows of the flying boat, indicating that they must land."

On witnessing the incident, Rosh-Kanaf Weizman, newly promoted and now Head of Air Department within Air HQ at Jaffa, drove to the harbour, from where he set out in a motor boat to rendezvous with the British aircraft, DP199/C of 88 Squadron, which had been on its way from Hong Kong, via Bahrain, to the United Kingdom. Due to a navigational error, the flyingboat had crossed into Israeli airspace near Lake Tiberius while heading for Egypt. It was reported that the astonished crew were not aware that Israel was no longer under British control (it should be noted that Britain had yet to fully recognise the State of Israel). Weizman ordered the two officers among the crew of eight – Yates and his navigator, Flt Lt Roy Axten – to come ashore and they were taken to Tel Aviv, there to meet Rosh-Tayeset Bar On and Rosh-Kanaf Paul Kaidar, OC Ramat David, with whom they enjoyed a couple of beers before being allowed to depart.

A second opportunity for Israel's air arm to enforce the law came the following month, on 13 June 1950, when two of 101 Squadron's Spitfires intercepted a Jordanian Arab Airways Dragon Rapide, which had been reported on several occasions overflying the Negev on flights from Jordan to Egypt and vice versa. Several attempts to intercept the intruder failed before Rosh-Tayesets Bar and Meir Roof sighted the red-painted aircraft while on a routine training mission. Roof made the initial sighting and took the lead. Although the Rapide's American pilot, Captain C.C. Cloud, attempted to evade the Spitfires, the Israelis did not open fire but signalled the pilot to follow them by the use of hand gestures and lowering their undercarriages and flaps.* The American pilot understood and responded by landing the Rapide at Beersheba, where it emerged that the aircraft carried four civilian passengers – three Jordanians and a Pakistani businessman – in addition to a cargo of oranges. The pilot and

---

* In September 1948 an Israeli Messerschmitt had similarly intercepted an Arab Airways Rapide (TJ-AAQ), which was shot down when it failed to respond to gestures to land – see *Spitfires over Israel*.

passengers were soon released by the Israeli authorities while the oranges were sent to 101 Squadron, but the Dragon Rapide – TJ-AAB – was confiscated and pressed into service with 100 Squadron at Tel Nof. On 18 December 1950, in the hands of Meir Hoffshi, a Bakersfield graduate, the aircraft crashed into the Mediterranean south of Ashkelon, off the coast of the Egyptian administered Gaza Strip. It is not clear if the Dragon Rapide crashed as a result of a technical malfunction or hostile action, but Hoffshi and his seven passengers were killed, their bodies recovered from the sea by the Egyptians and returned to Israel.

A third opportunity for Chel Ha'Avir to flex its muscles came soon afterwards when, on 24 July, an unidentified aircraft was reported in Israeli airspace near the Lebanon border. 101 Squadron's deputy commander, Pakad-Teufa Moshe Peled, was scrambled from Mahanaim and intercepted a Lebanese DC-3 (possibly LR-AAM) of Compagnie Générale des Transports, which refused to be ushered to an Israeli airfield and therefore found itself under attack by Peled before it could reach the border. Three passengers were killed during the attack and, although damaged, the DC-3 was able to reach Beirut and land safely.

Inevitably, as with all air forces, flying accidents occurred as pilots continuously strived to hone their skills. The experienced Joe Cohen crashed to his death in a Spitfire on 21 June 1950 while victory rolling over Ramat David to celebrate his promotion to Pakad-Teufa. The aircraft (s/n 2022/29) hit a hangar and exploded on the runway. However, the IDF/AF's chief maintenance pilot, Buck Feldman, escaped injury when a Mustang he was testing crashed on take-off:

> "I had accomplished a number of test flights of short duration on this P-51, serial number 2313. However, on 23 February 1951, shortly after I had retracted my undercarriage after take-off, I lost power and had to force-land in a field just off the end of the runway at Ekron. A minimum amount of damage was done, and in a few weeks the machine was again test flown. Upon investigation it was discovered that a bolt in the throttle linkage to the carburettor had sheared."

There occurred a potentially fatal incident when Chel Ha'Avir Dakotas were dropping paratroops, in an exhibition before cadets at a training camp. As one cadet jumped, his parachute snagged the aircraft's tailwheel and it was only the quick actions of a NCO in charge that prevented a tragedy. As soon as he realised what had happened he sent a message to the pilot, Pakad-Teufa Oded Abarbanel, instructing him to cut the engines and head out to sea while he tried to haul in the parachute lines, which he eventually succeeded in doing, thereby saving the paratrooper from almost certain death. All three were decorated for their coolness, resourcefulness and daring during the dramatic episode.

Following the resignation of Aharon Remez as commander of Chel Ha'Avir, 38-year-old Aluf (Maj-General) Shlomo Shamir was appointed in his place. Although he had held a private pilot's licence since 1940, Shamir had served in the Army – with the British Army during the Second World War and as commander of the Israeli 7th Brigade during the War of Independence – before being appointed commander of the Israeli Navy in 1949. His appointment to command Chel Ha'Avir met with a certain amount of resentment from its officers, since they wished one of their own to be elevated to this position. One of his first actions was to change the ranks within Chel Ha'Avir, which up to

Mustang 2313 following a forced-landing at Ekron due to engine failure while being test flown by Buck Feldman. It was soon repaired and back in service. (*Buck Feldman*)

his arrival were similar to those of the RAF, to the general ranks used throughout the Israeli Defence Force. Thus:

Pakad-Avir	became Segen-Mishne	= Pilot Officer/2/Lt
Pakad-Tais	became Segen	= Flying Officer/1/Lt
Pakad-Teufa	became Seren	= Flight Lieutenant/Capt
Rosh-Tayeset	became Rav-Seren	= Squadron Leader/Major
Rosh-Kanaf	became Sgan-Aluf	= Wing Commander/Lt Col
Rosh-Lahak	became Aluf-Mishne	= Group Captain/Colonel

Aluf Shamir also decided to transfer Air Headquarters from its cosy location at Jaffa to the tented camp at the former RAF airfield at Ramleh, east of Tel Aviv, in an attempt to stem the bureaucracy then in prevalence; this shock move came in the midst of one of the most severe winters in Israel's recent history, when snow even engulfed the capital. Also transferred to Ramleh at this time was 100 Squadron from Tel Nof, the liaison unit required to provide Air HQ with the services of its Piper Cubs.

Although Israel's relations with Britain were frosty, Britain's military training establishments welcomed overseas students of most nationalities at all levels. One of the first Israeli pilots sent to Britain was Israel Ben-Shachar who was at the time the CO of the Basic Squadron at FTS, with some 1,500 hours as a Harvard instructor under his belt. He recalled:

"In the autumn of 1950 I was on vacation when I got a phone call to report immediately to GHQ . . . they told me go to England. I was on the first group to go and there was no one I could ask how to behave. I hardly knew English but I learnt enough from the Americans on 101 Squadron to manage. As I had previous experience as an instructor and I handled well the Harvard, I felt pretty much at home. The Flight Instructors Course was at the CFS at Little Rissington near Oxford. Of the 49 men who attended the course with me, I was the only foreigner, although on the other courses (there were four courses running in parallel) were pilots from Egypt, Iraq, Lebanon, Pakistan, France and Denmark, but on my course I was the only foreigner.

My instructor was an ex-WWII bomber pilot, Johnny Green, and right from the start he made a deal with me: 'You will teach me aerobatics and I will teach you instruments.' I loved aerobatics. I learnt a lot from the British. I learnt the value of an educated pilot. Every briefing, every exercise, every debriefing were all thorough, based on theory. For example, prior to stalling or spinning the student understood why the aircraft stalled, why the aircraft spun. The course was very serious, most thorough. It was the first time that I really had ground school as it should be, four months, half a day each day. An Iraqi major volunteered to teach me Standard Beam approach. He was the chief instructor of the RIrAF. I also got friendly with an Egyptian, Hezi Yosuf was his name, and there was also another Egyptian, Mohamed Ramadan. The highlight was when it turned out that the Flying Examining Wing's instructors flew with me at the recommendation of my instructor, since at the end of every course there was an aerobatics contest and I won first prize [the prestigious Clarkson Trophy, awarded to the finest all-round pilot on the course].

I was probably the first IAF pilot to fly a jet. The syllabus of my course included five flying hours on the Meteor, but while I was there they had several crashes and they grounded the Meteors. One day they told me that they did a modification. Without a ground school, I had not seen the aircraft, I had never sat in its cockpit. The instructor took me to the front seat. I had never before flown a twin-engined aircraft. I climbed into the aircraft and by the time I woke up and understood what was going on, we were already at 10,000 feet."

The next Israeli to attend the course was Seren Itshak Yavneh who graduated in December 1950. He, too, won the Clarkson Trophy. In February 1951, Sgan-Aluf Weizman was sent to England to attend the RAF's Command and Staff College at Andover.

Even though the War of Independence had officially ended in January 1949, all along Israel's ill-defined borders local skirmishes were almost a daily occurrence. During one of these, on the morning of 5 April 1951, an Israeli patrol was attacked by Syrian forces at Hammat Gadder, the point at which the Israeli-Syrian and Israeli-Jordanian borders meet; seven Israeli policemen were killed in the incident. The decision was taken at top level to retaliate immediately with an air attack by Chel Ha'Avir. The attack was carried out late that afternoon by four bomb-armed Spitfires from 105 Squadron led by Rav-Seren Bar, followed by Rav-Seren Roof with four rocket-armed Mustangs of 101 Squadron, while a Harvard flown by Seren Binyamin Peled with Sgan-Aluf Kaidar as an observer to co-ordinate the attack accompanied the strike. The Spitfires attacked first from out of the sun, their target the local police station at Hammat Gadder, but it was unlikely that the relatively light bombs inflicted any significant damage. The quartet of Mustangs followed with a rocket attack on a bunker and a cluster of tents; two rockets were believed to have struck the bunker and it was reported that a fire broke out in the tented area, while Syrian small-arms fire was experienced in return. However, none of the aircraft was hit. The damage caused during the air attack was light, but the response it provoked in the world press was so intense that it was decided by the Israeli government, for political reasons, not to repeat such an attack. Notwithstanding this, within a month Chel Ha'Avir was again in action.

The main bone of contention along the Israeli-Syrian ceasefire line was the UN-designated demilitarised zone. This basically lay on what had been the Palestinian side of the international border. The Israelis now considered that they had a right to cultivate the area. The Syrians believed that no armed citizens were permitted to enter the zone, but as Israeli cultivators felt the need for armed protection so close to the ceasefire line, the scope for violent misunderstanding and escalation was obvious. Such a situation was made even more tense by the Israeli unwillingness to permit Syrian fishermen from the eastern shore of the Galilee to set sail, which they had always done despite the fact that the waters, legally speaking, all lay within Israel.

At the beginning of May 1951, elements of the Syrian Army commenced an attack on the Tel Motila strongpoint north of Lake Kineret. The Israeli Golani Brigade was responsible for the defence of that area and its 13th Regiment became involved in the battle that lasted for several days. Although Seren Yoash Tsiddon was acting as an air support liaison officer to the Golani Brigade, he was fearful of calling upon Chel Ha'Avir, particularly as Prime Minister Ben-Gurion was at the time on a formal visit to the United States. By 6 May, with about 40 Israeli fatalities to date and the current battle going against the IDF, Tsiddon was urged to call for air support. As he tried desperately to contact Air Headquarters, he heard on the R/T that a flight of Spitfires from 105 Squadron had taken off from Ramat David on a training flight. He contacted the leader, Sgan-Aluf Augarten (recently returned from his studies in the United States) for help. However, Augarten insisted on receiving permission from Air HQ before he would intervene. Tsiddon asked him to nevertheless make a low pass over the area until permission was granted but, in the meantime, Air HQ radioed Augarten to go ahead provided he and his companions did not open fire on the ground forces. The first low pass was followed by others until the Syrians started to retreat eastwards. During one pass Seren Costa was unable to resist firing two short bursts at the fleeing soldiers. The Syrians returned fire and all four Spitfires suffered light damage. However, the day was fortuitously saved by the timely intervention of the Spitfires and peace was restored in the area, albeit temporarily. These events were, not surprisingly, interpreted differently on the Syrian side of the frontier. In Damascus what was known as the 'Battle of Chamalinah' was seen as a brave and successful resistance by the Syrian Army to Israeli aggression.

By the summer of 1951, Aluf Shamir's health had deteriorated to such an extent that he could no longer command Chel Ha'Avir, so he was succeeded by Aluf Chaim Laskov, another former IDF Army officer. Morale was low and discipline was poor in the Air Force Laskov inherited. Poor administration led to logistics problems: fuel stocks were low and allowed for only two weeks of intensive flying; rocket and incendiary bomb stocks were dangerously low and spare parts were scarce. He informed a shocked Prime Minister that Chel Ha'Avir could probably fight only for two consecutive days if an all-out conflict flared up, such was the dire position of the Air Force. He pointed an accusing finger at Air HQ, whose staff numbered 1,253 men and women, about 25 per cent of the total strength of Chel Ha'Avir at the time; Air HQ was accused of swallowing budgets and breeding bureaucracy. With Ben-Gurion's approval, Laskov immediately initiated a programme of pruning surplus personnel from Air HQ and thereby diverting funds to where they were most needed: aircraft, aircrew, armaments and supplies.

At last, on 11 June 1951, Chel Ha'Avir received the first of its long-awaited replacement aircraft, albeit Second World War vintage twin-engined Mosquito two-seat fighter-bombers from France. Three of the ex-Armée de l'Air refurbished machines arrived on this date (flown by ex-RAF pilots), followed by others until a dozen had arrived by 7 August. Following the agreement with the French government for the purchase of these aircraft, John Harvey, a British ex-RAF fighter pilot who had ferried aircraft to Israel during the War of Independence, had been sent to Châteaudun to test fly each overhauled Mosquito, which were then flown to Israel by ferry pilots employed by a British company, Britavia. During one test flight Harvey's Mosquito (s/n 2156) crashed and he was killed; his remains were buried with full military honours in Châteaudun cemetery. Another pilot was sent to Châteaudun to continue the test flights: this was Seren Marom who had graduated from the Flying School less than two years earlier.

In accordance with Chel Ha'Avir's numbering sequence of the period, the Mosquitos were numbered 2103 onwards (Chel Ha'Avir's first Mosquito, a PR16, had been ferried to Israel from England by Harvey during the War of Independence; on arrival it had been allocated s/n 2101). However, for the purposes of ferrying, the letters IAF, for Israeli Air Force, were added before the number. On one of the ferry flights, via Cyprus, a British air traffic controller mistook the letters to mean Iraqi Air Force and after two Mosquitos had departed from Cyprus for Israel, he transmitted to Iraq to expect a delivery for the Iraqi Air Force. The transmission was also received in Israel where it was feared that the Mosquitos had been hijacked. Once the misunderstanding had been established, the IAF acronym was replaced by IDF/AF – Israel Defence Force/Air Force. Thus Chel Ha'Avir became the IDF/AF.

By the end of the year, 36 Mosquitos had crossed the Mediterranean out of a total of 68 purchased from France: 42 FB6 fighter-bombers, 19 NF30 night fighter variants minus their radar equipment, four photo-reconnaissance PR16s minus cameras and three T3 trainers, although six of these were nothing more than scrap and were bought for spares. The deal included all available spare parts and 20mm cannons, but no radio sets. While negotiations had been going on with the French, other aircraft procurement agents had discussed with Canadian authorities the possibility of purchasing aircraft. The Canadians agreed to sell a further six Mosquitos to Israel. The first aircraft was subsequently procured and overhauled by de Havilland of Canada, following which Ray Kurtz, the original commander of 69 Squadron during the War of Independence, was asked to ferry it to Israel. He agreed and flew the machine to Goose Bay where he spent three weeks due to bad weather, by which time his navigator left to get married. However, another volunteer was soon forthcoming, Cy Lerner, also a former member of 69 Squadron. On 17 May 1951 they departed from Goose Bay in the Mosquito, and were never seen again: it was assumed that the aircraft developed a malfunction and crashed into the Atlantic, taking Kurtz and Lerner to their deaths.

The Mosquito deal gave the IDF/AF the possibility of establishing two fighter-bomber squadrons, a single night fighter squadron and a reconnaissance flight.

All urgently required: the night fighters to counter the threat posed by the REAF's Stirling and Halifax heavy bombers already in service, with the possible additional threat from further Halifax and Lancaster heavy bombers should the intelligence reports of their procurement be accurate; while the fighter-bomber and reconnaissance aspects would add new dimensions to the IDF/AF's capability. There remained a major problem however, since the IDF/AF did not possess sufficient pilots to fly the new acquisitions and, as a consequence, the Mosquitos were parked at Tel Nof, from where they were flown occasionally to keep the systems working. The RAF was again approached and agreed to help solve the lack of qualified pilots by accepting initially just one Israeli for a conversion course at RAF Swinderby in Yorkshire. The pilot selected was Seren Abe Nathan, an Indian Jew who had served with the RAF in the Far East during the Second World War. Although he came close to being ejected from the course due to his anti-British political views, he eventually graduated and was soon followed by six more pilots. Seren Dani Shapira was in charge of this party which comprised Segen Dov Erlich, Segen Israel Lahav and Segen Avraham Portigali, plus Segen-Mishne David Orly and Segen-Mishne Moshe Ashel, all of whom arrived in Britain in December 1951. There were a number of incidents during the course, including a confrontation with an RAF instructor who had been a friend of the pilot of the RAF Mosquito shot down by an Israeli Mustang in November 1948.*

Despite the occasional hostility from their British instructors, the group graduated in March 1952 and returned to Israel, where they helped organise the IDF/AF's first Mosquito unit – 109 Squadron – at Hatzor, with Seren Shapira in command. The first Mosquito T3, s/n 2119, was written off in July during a take-off accident while in the hands of Shapira. As more pilots arrived from the Flying School, they converted to the Mosquito and later a second unit (110 Squadron) was formed under Seren Hugo Marom, although serviceability rates were low and the accident level high. In the event, a night fighter squadron was not formed and the NF30s never saw operational service with the IDF/AF. Some of the Mosquitos were, however, equipped with American APS-4 radar which was particularly useful in detecting ships. During this period the IDF/AF had not engaged in any operational activity except for the commencement of a series of long-range reconnaissance flights by the Mosquito PR16s, which had been fitted with underwing auxiliary fuel tanks to improve endurance and range. The first such flight was carried out by Seren Shlomo Lahat, who photographed Alexandria and Cairo.

The low serviceability rates of the period and the relatively high attrition of the weary Mustangs and Spitfires in service with the IDF/AF resulted in the procurement of additional fighters of both types. The Mustang was generally preferred due to its longer range and the heavier loads it could carry, but the Spitfire was also considered valuable especially since it introduced the graduates of the Flying School to the art of air fighting at the OTU.

Following the procurement of some 30 Mustangs in the United States, 101 Squadron converted to that type and it was Laskov's ambition to form a second Mustang unit that led to the procurement of 25 Mustangs from Sweden. The Swedish Mustangs were flown to Israel between December 1952 and July 1953 by Svenska Flygvapn pilots, who were granted special permission to ferry

* See *Spitfires over Israel.*

One of the three PBY Catalinas operated by the IDF/AF between 1951 and 1956. (*IAF Magazine collection*)

aircraft to Israel in their own time. All aircraft arrived safely. Meanwhile protracted negotiations had been under way with Italy for the purchase of 30 refurbished Spitfire IXs, an agreement eventually being reached and all aircraft had arrived in Israel by early 1953. During this period, three PBY Catalina flying boats joined the C-47s of 103 Squadron, and two Hiller 360 helicopters were purchased to serve with 100 Squadron at Ramleh, while two of the B-17s of 69 Squadron were fitted with nose radar for maritime patrol. A number of obsolete aircraft were discharged, the C-46 Commandos being taken over by El Al and the Dragon Rapides by Arkia, Israel's internal commuter airline. Others were transferred to the Technical School at Haifa to serve as instructional airframes. The outcome was that the IDF/AF rationalised its fleet considerably and by mid-1953, before Laskov departed, it had five active air bases and eight operational squadrons:

69 Squadron, Tel Nof	B-17s
100 Squadron, Ramleh	various light aircraft
	Hiller 360s
101 Squadron, Ramat David	Mustangs
103 Squadron, Tel Nof	C-47 Dakotas
	Catalinas
105 Squadron/OTU, Ramat David	Spitfires
107 Squadron, Ramat David	Spitfires
109 Squadron, Hatzor	Mosquitos
110 Squadron, Hatzor	Mosquitos

There were also a number of Airspeed Consul crew trainers with the Training School, these having been procured earlier from the British civil register (see Appendix III).

Two Mosquitos and their crews were lost during August 1953; one, s/n 2113 crewed by Segen-Uriel Ashel and Segen-Mishne Oded Shatil, crashed into the Mediterranean during a training exercise. Next day, while searching for the missing aircraft, a second Mosquito, 2112 crewed by Segens Eliezer Raizner and Yehuda Katz, failed to return. The training of new pilots was a continuous

Pilots of 105 Squadron OTU in 1953 with the unit's CO, Israel Ben-Shachar, in centre front. On the wing, left to right: Rafael Rot, Mordechai Ohad, Helman; standing: Akiva Presman, Azriel Ronen, Aryeh Fredlis, CO, Gad Gotman, Naftali Altman, Yeshayahu Bareket. (*Israel Ben-Shachar*)

process, often fraught with danger for instructor and pupil alike, which sometimes ended in tragedy. One such incident occurred in October 1953, when two Spitfires from the OTU at Ramat David collided shortly after taking off from the base. Segen-Mishe Yitzhak Yalon was killed, although the other aircraft, flown by veteran instructor Ran Sharon, belly-landed in a ploughed field.

The IDF/AF was desperate to acquire jet fighters to update its inventory. The

05 was the only IDF/AF Mustang armed with four 20mm cannon. It was written off in a forced landing at Wadi Hayon in June 1953. The pilot was Seren Adam Tsivoni. (*Adam Tsivoni*)

quest for jets was not a new issue. As early as June 1949, Remez had demanded the procurement of a single squadron of 22 jet fighters, at an estimated cost of $4½ million including spares. However, it was not the question of cost or lack of agreement but purely a question of availability. Only three nations had jet fighters for sale in the late 1940s/early 1950s – the United States, Britain and the Soviet Union – but none would agree to sell to Israel; the US turned down a request for F-84 Thunderjets while the USSR had no desire at that time to become involved in the Middle East arms race. Thus Israel had no choice but to approach Britain, but the Foreign Office was Arab-orientated with close links with most Arab nations, especially Egypt and Jordan, and was still much in presence in the Middle East with large forces in Cyprus, Jordan, the Canal Zone of Egypt and in the Persian Gulf. For the British, Israel meant nothing but trouble and they gambled on the Arab card, in which they saw promise of secured oil supplies and political support. Nevertheless, Britain was asked to supply a squadron of Supermarine Attacker jet fighters and initially talks were fruitful – even supply dates were agreed upon (August 1951 to March 1952). Regarding the suitability of the Attacker for the IDF/AF, an official report claimed:

"From a defence point of view the Attacker would be a valuable acquisition to the IAF as we could probably intercept any aircraft that the Arabs possess, provided early radar warning is supplied. The rate of climb, though not up to the standard of the Meteor F8, is formidable, and the Attacker placed in the hands of capable pilots could prove to be an effective weapon of defence.

From the attack point of view, without any long-range tank, all targets within 150 to 200 miles radius from our operational bases in Israel could probably be reached and attacked with safety. As the aircraft is made to carry a single overload tank under the fuselage, it is probable that rockets and/or bombs could be carried for long-range strikes. This means that any important target in Lebanon, Syria, Transjordan and in parts of Egypt (the upper part of the Nile Valley including the Cairo area) could be attacked with a fair margin of safety from the fuel factor point of view. Thus, considering that the aircraft compares well with all the jet and prop-driven aircraft possessed by the Arabs, it would be a great asset to the IAF and would add greatly to our offensive and defensive strength, not to mention the gained prestige that its acquisition will give to the name of Israel in the Middle East."

But all was to no avail, since the British government then changed its mind and decided against the sale. The next stop for the IDF/AF's search for jets was France, where the aircraft industry was recovering from the effects of the Second World War by building for the Armée de l'Air, under licence, foreign models, including the Mistral, the licence-built Vampire. Among the many types under development was the SO-6000 Triton, a two-seat jet trainer which the Israeli delegation's test pilots, Bill Kaiser and Moti Hod, were permitted to fly. Each flew the aircraft for three hours. The last paragraph of their subsequent report read:

"The plane requires a terrific amount of braking power. Can only do one landing on a flight then must refuel. Can go round again, but only if pilot decides to do it well before landing. Pilot must come in from long way off, put plane down and keep it straight. Landing speed of machine is excessive that it can prove dangerous. Would not volunteer to teach on this machine."

Nevertheless, Hod was suitably impressed but the French made it quite clear that the aircraft was not available; in fact, only three prototypes were ever built. However, a more suitable aircraft was the Dassault MD450 Ouragan (Hurricane), a single-seat, straight wing fighter powered by a single Rolls-Royce Nene engine; although it was slightly inferior to the American F-84G Thunderjet it was comparable in performance to the British Meteor F8. Although the French were willing to sell, Britain and the United States pressed for them to pull out of the deal and the sale was put on hold.

Although the French could not sell the Ouragan to Israel because of American and British pressure, and the Italians could not sell the licence-built Vampire without British permission, it was inevitable that the stalemate would soon have to be broken, particularly as Egypt had already acquired jet fighters. Britain finally relented and accepted an order for Meteor F8 jet fighters, since Egypt had already taken delivery of Meteors and Vampires. Negotiations with Glosters commenced in November 1952, and two pilots, Rav-Seren Bar and Seren Peled, plus a technical delegation, were sent to England to explore the Meteor and its Rolls-Royce Derwent engines. Although the Meteor was already obsolete it was an excellent introductory jet fighter, mainly because of its stable flight characteristics. It was also the only jet fighter available. A contract was duly signed for 11 F8s and four two-seat T7 trainers, at a unit cost of £36,250 for the fighter version and £34,250 for the trainer. The first two Meteor T7s (s/n 2162 and 2163) arrived at Ramat David on 17 June 1953, flown by British ferry pilots. They

Clipped wing Spitfire IXE s/n 64 was unique among the ex-Italian Spitfires. (*IAF Magazine collection*)

were accepted with formal ceremony by Prime Minister Ben-Gurion, and named *Soufa* (Storm) and *Sa'ar* (Tempest). Two months later the first Meteor F8s arrived and the IDF/AF's first jet unit, 117 Squadron, was formed under Rav-Seren Bar.

Less than two years after taking command of the IDF/AF, Aluf Laskov asked to be retired; he was basically a ground forces officer and felt that he lacked proper understanding of the IDF/AF's requirements and, similarly, lacked affinity with the men who flew the aircraft. He evidently took badly the death of one of his young pilots, Seren Costa, whom he witnessed killed when visiting Ramat David shortly after he had taken command; Costa's 105 Squadron Spitfire had caught fire and the pilot fell to his death when his parachute snagged on the aircraft's tail as he baled out. Laskov's successor was 32-year-old Aluf-Mishne Dan Tolkowsky, who had served as a fighter pilot with the RAF during the Second World War and had recently completed his studies at Oxford University. Although he had not served the IDF/AF as an operational pilot, he had flown as member of a B-17 crew during the War of Independence. Thus, the IDF/AF entered a new era – the jet age – with a new commander.

Chapter Four

ISRAEL FLEXES ITS MUSCLES 1954–55

"As a sovereign state we decide our path by ourselves. Israel's survival depends on two factors – her strength and her right."

Israeli Prime Minister David Ben-Gurion

There were now changes in the Israeli leadership, with former Minister of Foreign Affairs Moshe Sharet succeeding Ben-Gurion as Prime Minister, while Pinchas Lavon was appointed Minister of Defence. Ben-Gurion abandoned all his political obligations to retire to the distant kibbutz Sde Boker in the Negev. For the IDF/AF, his retirement was a major blow, since he was a staunch supporter of a strong air force.

The installation of the new Israeli government led to a secret dialogue with the Egyptian leadership, aimed at laying the foundations for proper peace negotiations. However, opinions were still divided in both camps. Each side had its hawks and its doves and neither government felt able to show any sign of weakness and an action by one side was inevitably followed by a reaction on the other side. As a result, a cycle of increasing tension built up in which both countries felt that they were the victims and that the other was the aggressor. The latest round of talks was conducted, on the Israeli side, by Moshe Orbach and led to a tentative agreement whereby Egypt would make peace with Israel in return for Israeli technical aid. However, the talks came to an abrupt end in the wake of the so-called 'Lavon Affair', named after Pinchas Lavon, the new Israeli Minister of Defence. The 'Lavon Affair' was an apparently unauthorised campaign of terrorist attacks by the Israeli secret service against British and other Western interests in Egypt, blamed on extreme Egyptian nationalists, and intended to sabotage any improvement in relations between Egypt and the West.

The exposure by British and Egyptian security services of the 'Lavon Affair' was followed by the fall of Sharet's government, which brought Ben-Gurion back from his brief retirement to once again lead his country out of a crisis. Fuelled by this scandal, the Egyptian government tried to impose a blockade on Israeli shipping using the Strait of Tiran at the southern end of the Gulf of Aqaba. The Egyptians tried to justify the blockade on the grounds that these were Egyptian territorial waters, that Egypt and Israel were still technically at war, and that Israel was stalling on the question of the return of 750,000 Arab refugees to their homes in what had been Palestine. In March 1954, Israel's appeal to the UN that Egypt be obliged not only to open the Strait of Tiran, but to allow Israeli merchant ships to use the Suez Canal, was vetoed by the Soviet Union. While Israel continued to try to use the Gulf of Aqaba and the Strait of Tiran, despite the not entirely effective Egyptian ban, military aircraft of both sides continued to attempt reconnaissance flights over the other side's territory. In this the Israelis were more effective.

Partly as a result of the talks with the Egyptians, the new Israeli government introduced a series of severe budget cuts, many of which affected the IDF/AF and several units were disbanded and establishments closed down; 107 Squadron was stood down while 69 Squadron handed over its three B-17s to neighbouring 103 Squadron, and was similarly disbanded. The Flying School at Kfar Sirkin was closed down and the base handed over to the Army. The training of new pilots was divided between the Technical School at Haifa and Tel Nof air base, although later all trainees received their induction and flying training at Tel Nof.

With the arrival in Israel of the Meteor jets, the two main aims of Rav-Seren Bar, commander of the IDF/AF's first jet unit, 117 Squadron, was to convert as many pilots as possible to the new aircraft; the first five to attend the course established by Bar and his flight commander, Seren Peled, were: Rav-Seren Hod, who was the deputy commander of Ramat David; Seren Aharon Yoeli, an instructor from the Flying School; Seren Alon, who had learned to fly on one of the Czech courses in 1948; Seren Ya'acov Nevo, also from the Flying School; and Rav-Seren Shapira, who had been flying Mosquitos. The last two Meteor F8s from the initial batch ordered had arrived at Ramat David on 21 January 1954, by which time the first fighter squadron had become operational.

Two pilots, Seren Gideon Lebanon and Segen David Ratner, lost their lives within two weeks of each other in March and April 1954; the former, a QFI, in a Fokker S11 trainer of the Flying School, the latter over the Gulf of Aqaba in either a Spitfire or a Mustang. Additionally, one of the two newly acquired Hiller 360 helicopters was damaged in a low-flying accident. Another incident during this period concerned the temporary 'disappearance' of an Israeli Dakota

The first IDF/AF jet pilots (left to right): Ya'acov Nevo, Moti Hod, Benny Peled, Joe Alon, Dani Shapira, Aharon Yoeli, Menahem Bar and Avraham Yoffe. (*IAF Magazine collection*)

whilst flying at night from northern Israel to Tel Nof. When the aircraft failed to arrive at its destination, another was sent aloft and intercepted a distress signal to the effect that the overdue aircraft had run out of fuel and was about to land. Its whereabouts were unknown until its unexpected arrival at Tel Nof the following morning; it emerged that the Dakota had strayed off course and the inexperienced crew found themselves over the Mediterranean. When land was eventually sighted they realised they were over the Canal Zone where, with almost empty fuel tanks, a landing was made at RAF Ismailia. There, the friendly station commander agreed to supply fuel and sent the Dakota on its way, presumably without informing the Egyptian authorities.

Since the previous summer, Piper Cubs of 100 Squadron had been participating in *Operation Matate* (Broom) which was aimed against Bedouin smugglers who freely crossed the deserted border between the Negev and Sinai in the Nitzana area, west of Beersheba. The Cubs used by 100 Squadron had received many local modifications: some were able to carry supply packs of up to 40kg slung under the wings, while others were fitted with a .3-inch machinegun under the port wing, fired electrically by the pilot, and one had a four-wheel landing gear installed to enhance its ability to land on rough terrain. The Cubs were used to sweep the area of operations, where they searched for and attacked any smugglers discovered. They were also used to transport military commanders to observe the area, were on standby for the evacuation of casualties, and were sometimes used as communication relays. They were also used in one spectacular operation in early June 1954.

The Israeli Navy had been instructed to survey the sea route from Eilat south to the Tiran Straits, between Sinai and Saudi Arabia and, for that purpose, an old wooden vessel, the *Bar Giora*, was despatched from Eilat with seven Israeli sailors on board. The sailors were disguised as fishermen to hide their real identity and thus avoid contact with the Egyptians and Saudis. The *Bar Giora* departed Eilat on the evening of 31 May, but encountered a storm which, coupled with mechanical failure, led to the abandonment of the vessel off the small Saudi town of al-Maqnah in the Gulf of Aqaba at noon the following day. A message detailing their plight was received at Eilat, following which a Mosquito was sent to make contact; meanwhile, a Saudi police patrol launch arrived on the scene, together with many civilians from a nearby village. Although help was offered, the Israelis rejected this and awaited developments. Since the Israeli Navy was unable to react fast enough, the only means available to evacuate the men were the Piper Cubs of 100 Squadron at Ramleh.

That evening, six Cubs flew to Beersheba, where they refuelled and joined forces with another Cub, all seven aircraft departing for Eilat at 2300, but bad weather forced them to return. Airborne again at 0455, they landed at Eilat to refuel before heading out to sea. Only one Cub was equipped with radio and it also carried some spares, including a wheel and a propeller, in case one of the aircraft was damaged on landing in Saudi Arabia. Three Cubs led the other two pairs and were accompanied by a Mosquito, which also acted as a communication relay. At about 0830 the stranded sailors were located and, with astonished Saudis looking on, the first three Cubs landed and evacuated one sailor per aircraft, followed by the next pair, then the final pair. As soon as the last sailor had been safely evacuated, four rocket-armed Mustangs from 101 Squadron, led by Sgan-Aluf Weizman (commander of Ramat David), wrecked the abandoned *Bar Giora* and thereby destroyed all evidence of the Israeli 'invasion' of Saudi Arabia. Later the same day a Mosquito flown by Segen Zoric Lev was sent to photograph the remains of the *Bar Giora*, using a hand-held camera operated by the navigator. Having secured the photographs Lev, against orders, flew some 75km south to the southern tip of the Sinai Peninsula and photographed Sharm al-Sheikh. On the return flight one of the Mosquito's engines began to overheat and had to be shut down, but it was nevertheless able to reach Hatzor safely on one engine.

The high number of accidents attributed to the indiscipline of young pilots grew steadily and to such an extent that orders were issued to punish severely those caught violating flight safety regulations. The first pilot to be convicted was the very same Segen Lev who, while flying a routine exercise to the Yehuda Desert west of the Dead Sea, took the Mosquito down to almost ground level along the Sodom road, forcing car drivers to swerve in panic. But inevitably one driver held firm – and the Mosquito clipped the car's roof as Lev attempted to climb at the last moment. On returning to Hatzor, where only minor damage was found to the tips of the propeller blades, Lev admitted his indiscretion to the base commander, following which he and his navigator were incarcerated in the military jail for 35 days. Worse was to follow, however, since the Chief of Staff, Rav-Aluf Dayan, decided to make an example of Lev and, having served his sentence, dismissed him from the Service.*

Over the Tel Aviv waterfront on 3 June 1954 there occurred a collision between a Meteor and a Mustang of 101 Squadron during a simulated dogfight; the Mustang pilot, Seren Avraham Yodfat, was killed, but the crippled Meteor was able to reach base and land safely. Another pilot, Segen Ahud Dolinski, was lost in a night flying accident three weeks later. During the year the IDF/AF had relaxed somewhat its strict regulations and had given its approval for aerobatic flying to be introduced, but tragedy struck on 8 August at an air display organised at Ramat David for 200 visiting youths soon to join the Israeli Defence Forces. Three Mustangs led by Segen Omri Ariav were performing a series of manoeuvres for the benefit of the young audience when two collided and crashed in fields at nearby Kfar Yehoshoa, taking Ariav and Segen-Mishne Itschak Zelinger to their deaths. Two more pilots were lost in accidents during September 1954: Segen-Mishne Johnny Kurar was killed when his Meteor crashed in the Negev, followed four days later by the death of Segen-Mishne Adam Schirer in another crash.

The heavy attrition meant that the IDF/AF still relied heavily on piston-engined fighters and, because of the political inability to procure more jets, more piston-engined aircraft had to be purchased to replace losses and to create a reasonable reserve in case of emergency. Thus, the first of 14 Mosquito TR33s arrived from the UK in October, having been refurbished by Eagle Aviation. A further 30 Mustangs were bought from Italy but only about 20 went into service with the IDF/AF, the remainder being used for spares. An unexpected surprise was the approval by the British government for the sale of seven Meteor FR9s† then being operated in the UK by Flight Refuelling Ltd for experiments

---

* After a year spent working on his parents' farm and repeated requests to be allowed to rejoin the IDF/AF, Lev was reinstated; he went on to fly Mystères during the Sinai War before becoming a squadron commander, and commanded Ramat David in the early 1970s. During the 1973 Yom Kippur War he was shot down and killed while flying a Douglas A-4 Skyhawk.

† The Meteors were WB123, WB140, WL259, WX963, WX967, WX975 and WX980.

with in-flight refuelling. Once refurbished, they were flown to Israel and arrived between January and May 1955.

In response to the tension building on the Israel-Sinai border, a detachment of Meteors from 117 Squadron at Ramat David had been sent to Hatzor, some 30km from the border. The move soon paid dividends when, one morning in July 1954, a pair of Meteors were ordered to scramble in an attempt to intercept an incursion by Egyptian aircraft, although only the leader, Seren Yoeli, took off since the other Meteor suffered a mechanical failure. Yoeli pressed on alone but the Egyptian Fury had already recrossed the border and was on its way back to al-Arish, the pilot probably having been warned by Egyptian ground control. Ignoring orders not to cross the border, Yoeli raced at low level towards al-Arish and arrived over the airfield just as the Fury was about to touch down, 'so I came down after it and buzzed it so low that it ran off the runway and flipped over', related the elated Israeli pilot. However, on his return to Hatzor he was ordered to report to Aluf-Mishne Weizman, who fined him 25 Israeli pounds, a not inconsiderable sum, for crossing into Egyptian airspace.

From Hatzor, in July, the newly formed 115 Flight equipped with Mosquito PR16s began regular long-range reconnaissance flights, using specially lightened aircraft fitted with underwing fuel tanks when necessary, which increased endurance to five hours and an operational radius of almost 1,000km. Prior to the formation of the special Flight, Mosquitos had ranged far and wide, including sorties over the Sinai Peninsula, the Egyptian mainland, Syria and Jordan. The localised flights were concentrated over the Yehuda and Shromron areas of the West Bank (under Jordanian control) and the Sinai Peninsula, while more risky long-range flights were undertaken to Siwa Oasis, in the Western Desert of Egypt (where Israeli agents were imprisoned), Mersa Matruh naval base and Luxor air base in the Nile Valley. Also visited by the Mosquitos were Iraq's H-3 air base which guarded the oil pipeline, and Syria's main air base at al-Mezze just outside Damascus. Throughout this period of reconnaissance in hostile skies not a single Mosquito was lost. Occasionally the intruders were tracked, but although attracting anti-aircraft fire none was intercepted by the EAF. At least one of these sorties was undertaken by Sgan-Aluf Leslie Easterman, commander of Hatzor air base, who had been awarded the DFC by the RAF during the Second World War, when he had flown Lancaster bombers.

Tensions inevitably increased and on 28 September 1954 there was another incident, when radio contact was lost with a small Israeli vessel, the *Bat Galim*, flying the national flag and carrying wood, leather and meat from Ethiopia. A B-17 of 103 Squadron was despatched to search for the missing vessel in the Strait of Tiran. To allow his crew, which included an Israeli naval officer, to identify the many ships sighted, Rav-Seren Michael Keren (formerly Mischa Kenner) maintained the big aircraft at mast height which enabled them to read the names of the vessels as they sped past! The missing *Bat Galim* was not located until the Egyptian port of Sharm al-Sheikh at the entrance to the Gulf of Suez was reached.* It transpired that the vessel had been arrested and the crew of ten held in custody; they were released four months later following international protest. The Egyptians had effectively closed the Strait of Tiran to

---

* Although the B-17 had proved its value during the 11-hour search for the missing *Bat Galim*, all three B-17s were put into reserve and were subsequently flown to Lod, where they were to be maintained by Bedek Aviation.

Israeli shipping and, to enforce their will, had positioned a battery of heavy guns at Ras Nasrani, opposite the island of Tiran, which was officially Saudi Arabian territory although defended by Egyptian forces.

With the international community apparently turning a blind eye to Egypt's move, the IDF General Staff discussed ways and means of taking by force the eastern coast of the Sinai Peninsula, from Eilat to Sharm al-Sheikh, to ease the immediate problem, although such action would undoubtedly cause others. Since no road existed between Eilat and Sharm al-Sheikh, a small party of six IDF surveyors was taken by a fishing boat, operated by the Israeli Navy, to Dahav on the western coast of the Gulf of Aqaba, where they were to be supported by Dakotas of 103 Squadron and Piper Cubs of 100 Squadron. But one day into the operation it became clear that an Egyptian Army unit was following the tracks of the surveyors and it was decided to evacuate them the following day, using a fleet of six Piper Cubs to airlift the party to Eilat. For various political reasons the planned military operation to capture Sharm al-Sheikh did not materialise, although the information gained during the brief survey was to prove to be of immense value when the Sinai War erupted the following year.

During the winter of 1954/55 the Egyptian Furies at al-Arish were replaced by Vampire FB52s, and although the Vampire's performance overall was inferior to that of the Israeli Meteor F8s and FR9s, it was more manoeuvrable. However, its faster top speed in comparison to the Fury meant that it needed to spend less time in Israeli airspace during reconnaissance incursions across the border, making interceptions even more difficult. One aircraft intercepted over Israeli airspace during December was Syrian Airways Dakota YK-AAK, which was forced to land at Lod by a pair of Meteors. It was later allowed to return to Syria.

With the disbandment of 107 Squadron, a buyer was sought for the unit's redundant Spitfires and, following refurbishment by Bedek Aviation at Lod, 30 were sold to Burma for £8,000 each including spares. The Burmese government

In December 1954 Syrian Airways Dakota YK-AAK was intercepted by Israeli fighters and forced to land in Israel. (*GPO*)

The five Burmese pilots who graduated from the Spitfire OTU early 1955: (rear) Lts Tin Hlaing, Tin Maung Htway, Aung Than, Aung Chit Han, Than Kye; (front, left to right) IDF/AF instructors Akiva Presman, Moshe Tadmor, Ran Sharon. (*Aryeh Fredlis*)

required urgent delivery because of border skirmishes and would not wait for them to be delivered by sea. Since Israeli pilots were not permitted to ferry these aircraft, a British company – Field Air Services of Croydon – was contacted to undertake the operation, and were to collect the aircraft in batches of three or four from Cyprus, to where they were to be flown by Israeli pilots in mufti. In the meantime, the Spitfires selected were completely overhauled, repainted in Burmese Air Force markings, allotted serial numbers UB421 to UB450 and were fully air-tested before being flown to Cyprus, as Buck Feldman, the IDF/AF's chief maintenance pilot, recalled:

> "During the period 1949–55, I carried out several hundred maintenance test flights on Spitfires, including those on aircraft to be purchased by the Burmese Air Force. This was to experience one exciting ferry flight to Nicosia, Cyprus – a very close call, indeed. During this period of time I had flown just about every type of aircraft on the IAF inventory."

In the meantime, six Burmese pilots arrived in Israel to gain experience on the Spitfire and, during their training flights on Harvards and Spitfires, several aircraft were lost or damaged, with a few casualties which included the death of one of their number, Lt Than Win. The remaining five pilots – Lts Tin Hlaing, Tin Maung Htway, Aung Than, Aung Chit Han and Than Kye – eventually graduated from the Spitfire OTU at Ramat David early in 1955.

Meanwhile, Field Air Services applied for and was granted permission to use the RAF bases at Habbaniya, Bahrain and Sharjah as refuelling stops for the ferry to Burma and, subsequently, three civilian pilots arrived at Nicosia, Cyprus, having ferried from England Vampire jets for the Indian Air Force. One of the three was South African-born Mrs Jackie Moggridge, a former Air Transport Auxiliary and RAFVR pilot who had amassed in excess of 3,000 hours ferrying aircraft for the RAF during the Second World War. After a delay of almost two weeks, the first three Spitfires arrived from Israel on the morning of 27 September 1954, including UB421 flown by Buck Feldman. The following morning the trio of ferry pilots set out on the first leg, but had to return when one aircraft developed a fuel problem. Another attempt was made the next morning, the leader flying UB427, reaching Habbaniya without problem, but when they departed Shaibah the next day, Jackie Moggridge's aircraft again developed engine problems, necessitating a return to the RAF aerodrome, where one of the Spitfires crashed on landing as the pilot had forgotten to lower his undercarriage. The remaining two eventually reached Burma safely, via Karachi-Jodhpur-Cawnpore-Calcutta-Rangoon, from where they returned to Cyprus aboard a BOAC aircraft.

Two new pilots from England arrived to join Jackie Moggridge and the other pilot for the second ferry flight. When the four Spitfires involved in this flight landed at Calcutta, the leader damaged his aircraft. Determined to push on, he took Mrs Moggridge's aircraft, leaving her with the unserviceable machine. However, she was recalled to Cyprus before the aircraft could be repaired. Meanwhile, three Spitfires of the third ferry flight had progressed no further than Beirut. Whilst flying over Iraq they had been intercepted by Iraqi fighters and escorted back to the Iraq-Lebanon border. One developed engine trouble en route and all three landed at Beirut, where they were promptly impounded. As a result of this latest setback, Field Air Services pulled out of the operation, following which the Burmese Air Force threatened to cancel the order for the remaining 24 Spitfires.

Bedek Aviation was requested to find a solution. Thus, four volunteers were co-opted, two of whom had served with Chel Ha'Avir during the Arab-Israeli war: Leo Gardner (an American) and Gordon Levett, a former RAF Squadron Leader who had flown fighters for the Israelis during the closing stages of the war; the other two were Jackie Moggridge and 57-year-old Sonny Banting. With the RAF having closed its bases to the Israeli aircraft, the route chosen took them via Diyarbekir (Turkey), Kermanshek, Abadan and Bandar Abbas (Iran), and then across the Indian sub-continent to Rangoon, where they were handed over to the Burma Air Force. During the course of the next seven months, the four pilots delivered all 24 aircraft safely, although not all the flights were uneventful. Gordon Levett's aircraft was damaged when landing at Bandar Abbas, which necessitated a replacement propeller; this was delivered by road and he was eventually able to continue the journey without further problems. On his return to Israel, Levett rejoined his companions for the next ferry flight which, however, had been delayed owing to the death of an Israeli pilot (Arye Ostrof) while testing one of the Spitfires.

Up to the end of 1954 the Egyptian military authorities in the Gaza Strip had managed to stop almost all Palestinian incursions across the Israeli border, though not all. The new Israeli government of Ben-Gurion adopted a policy of what it called 'active defence', though this was interpreted as blatant bullying and aggression by Israel's Arab neighbours. As a result, a number of skirmishes occurred along the Gaza border between Israeli patrols and Egyptian troops, which culminated in an attack by 50 Israeli paratroopers on an Egyptian Army camp between Gaza and al-Brayr; 40 Egyptians including two civilians were killed, as were eight Israeli soldiers. The Gaza raid caused General Edison Burns, the Canadian commander of the United Nations Observer force in the Middle East, to exclaim:

> "This was the most serious clash between Egypt and Israel since the armistice had been signed six years before. It was a critical event in [the] dismal history [of the Middle East]."

This attack on the Gaza Strip by Israeli commandos also led the Egyptian authorities to let loose the Palestinian guerillas (fedayeen). Tension between Israel and Egypt had thus intensified and, in many ways, the countdown to the Sinai War of 1956 had begun. During a skirmish in early December, between Israeli and Syrian soldiers on the Golan Heights, five Israelis were captured. Several days later, when Israeli radar picked up what was believed to be a Syrian airliner off the Israeli coast, Serens Yoeli and Alon were scrambled in Meteors with instructions to force it down. It was to be used as a bargaining counter to free the prisoners, but the aircraft turned out to be Lebanese.

The IDF/AF lost one of its Mosquito FB6s during a rainy winter night, when Seren Ya'acov Shalmon's aircraft was struck by lightning while on its landing approach. The stricken aircraft fell in flames and crashed beside the runway. Despite the flames and danger from exploding ammunition, a young nurse, 18-year-old Esther Arditi, rescued both injured crew members: the citation to the subsequent award of the Tzalash, one of Israel's premier awards for gallantry, stated:

> "The ambulance became bogged down in the mud. Without losing any time she jumped out and ran to the plane without paying any attention to the flames and the continually exploding ammunition in the plane. She rendered first-aid to one wounded man and freed the pilot, who was strapped into his seat by his safety harness, and dragged him out of the plane. A few seconds later the fuel tanks caught fire."

The diminutive nurse, barely five feet tall, had somehow managed to extricate the pilot from almost certain death. Despite severe burns to her body, she remained sufficiently conscious to administer blood to the two wounded flyers. Although the navigator, Seren Shlomo Hertzman, succumbed to his injuries a few weeks later, Seren Shalmon eventually made a complete recovery, and returned to his squadron.

By the summer of 1955 tension along the border had reached a new peak and pilots of the Meteor detachment at Hatzor waited with keenness for the inevitable meeting with the EAF's Vampires. On 21 July, during talks between Israeli and Egyptian military officials on the Gaza frontier, four Israeli aircraft flew low over Gaza itself. The leader flew lower than the rest and was engaged by anti-aircraft fire but was not hit. Members of the Egyptian negotiating team felt that this was an intentional provocation by the IDF/AF to sabotage the talks. In Cairo this act was seen as evidence of renewed Israeli military pressure.

International tension mounted when, on 27 July, Bulgarian MiG-15s shot down El Al Constellation 4X-AKC en route from London to Tel Aviv via Paris and Vienna, apparently in mistake for an American spyplane. The route from Vienna took the airliner down a narrow corridor over Yugoslavia near the Bulgarian border. It was flying at almost 18,000 feet in early morning twilight when the fighters appeared and ordered it to lower its undercarriage and proceed to the military base at Sofia. 4X-AKC's pilot, Captain Stanley Hinks (ex-RAF), complied and descended to 2,000 feet in preparation for a landing when, suddenly and without warning, the MiGs opened fire. The crew of seven, which included co-pilot Pinchas Ben-Porat (a 1948-49 War veteran), and all 51 passengers on board were killed when the aircraft crashed north of Petrich.

Then, on 22 August, a local skirmish on the ground developed into a battle when an Egyptian strongpoint opened fire on an Israeli patrol. Retaliation was immediate and the strongpoint was taken, together with the capture of 25 Egyptian soldiers. The Israelis followed this with an operation aimed to destroy the Khan Yunis police station south of Gaza, which served as a local military headquarters. The Egyptians were aware that something was afoot and despatched a flight of four Vampires to reconnoitre the area on 29 August. These encountered two Meteors from Hatzor over the Israeli settlements of En Ha'shlosha and Kisofim, just east of the Gaza Strip. The Meteors, flown by Serens Mordechai Lavon and Yehuda Peri, engaged in a short, sharp combat and Lavon managed to fire a telling burst at one of the Vampires which was last seen shedding parts of its fuselage as it dived into cloud. The remaining three Vampires headed for the safety of Sinai while the Meteors returned to Hatzor. Lavon was unable to claim a definite victory, although next day the Egyptians apparently admitted that they had lost an aircraft while on a training flight. In reality, almost all Egyptian reconnaissance flights across the border into Israel were recorded as training flights. This was because on several, if not most, occasions such incursions were only authorised at local level, without clearance from the more cautious authorities at the Ministry of Defence in Cairo.

Two days later, on 31 August, a pair of Meteors scrambled from Hatzor too late to catch another flight of Vampires in Israeli airspace but, early next morning, there was a further clash in the air. At Hatzor, 117 Squadron's Meteor detachment was at readiness when the call to scramble came just before 0700 and Serens Yoeli and Tsiddon speedily intercepted two EAF Vampires which had crossed into Israeli airspace. Because of the early hour the Meteors were still configured for night operations and the sight adjusted to a range of only 100 yards. Yoeli, flying a Meteor FR9 (s/n 36), recalled:

"We took off and headed south and were told that there was a bogey consisting of two aeroplanes flying southbound below us at two or three o'clock. I made a left turn so they couldn't see me because I would be in the sun and two minutes later my No.2 said – 'I see them' – and I turned my head and saw them. We simply pulled up and started to come down behind them. No.2 was behind me. My sight was on night brightness, I had no time to mess with it. I saw one aircraft at about 500 yards' range, opened the safety cover, and slowly closed line astern behind the Vampire. At 200 to 250 yards I opened fire. My tracers moved from the left to the wing, and I simply shifted them to the centre and I didn't finish until I saw the bubble explode. We were at

61

about 3,000 feet and I was flying at about 460 knots. Bang, the aeroplane broke up but didn't explode and I pulled to the left."

The Vampire's port wing snapped off and the spinning aircraft (s/n 1569) crashed and burst into flames in a corn field near kibbutz Carmia, some 5km north of the Egyptian border. The other Vampire (s/n 1567) turned immediately into the Meteors, then performed several manoeuvres; Yoeli's report continued:

"[My] No.2 was following; he warned me that the Egyptian No.2 was behind me. Then I saw him. The second Vampire turned southbound and started to dive toward a sandy area at 1,000 feet. When I was straight behind him, he started to roll with his nose down, so I missed a chance to shoot him. He made another roll and I closed in. I headed the gunsight up front as I used to do when shooting targets in training. I pulled the trigger and hit the cockpit – bang – unbelievable – the aeroplane exploded! That was that. I went back and made two victory rolls over the base, and I landed."

Wreckage and debris from the second Vampire fell near kibbutz Yad Mordechai, a few kilometres from the scene of the crash of the first Vampire. Both Egyptian pilots were killed. The award of the Tzalash to Yoeli was announced on 7 September 'for carrying out combat duty with exemplary speed and efficiency'.

Remains of one of the two Egyptian Vampires (probably s/n 1569) shot down by Aharon Yoeli on 1 September 1955 while flying a Meteor FR9 of 117 Squadron. (*Authors' collection*)

On 27 September 1955, Egypt announced that it had concluded an arms deal with Czechoslovakia, though this was really a front for the Soviet Union. The Western powers were shocked and dismayed, while Israel feared again for its very existence. The infusion of Soviet equipment gave the Egyptians the confidence to announce in September that any ship wishing to sail through the Strait of Tiran must inform them of its intentions at least 72 hours before it was due to arrive in the area. The same applied to air traffic and, as a consequence, El Al had to cancel its flights to South Africa.

Egypt's actions brought an intensity in Israeli retaliation. IDF forces carried out an attack on an Egyptian outpost at Kuntilla about 50km north-west of Eilat, while three Piper Cubs of 100 Squadron operated from Beersheba flying in

The wreckage of the other Vampire shot down near Gaza by Yoeli. Its Arabic s/n 1567 can still be seen between the dark stripes on its tail-boom. (*IDF*)

Another view of the wreckage of Vampire s/n 1567. (*Authors' collection*)

supplies and evacuating casualties. When the action was concluded, the Egyptians had suffered a dozen killed, six wounded and 29 taken prisoner for two Israeli dead and two wounded. As the IDF force withdrew with the prisoners, the EAF arrived and attempted to attack the column, but were prevented from doing so by patrolling Israeli fighters.

The Western powers had declared that neither Israel or Egypt should get the upper hand in the arms race and, in this respect, almost all the nations in the Middle East had received arms from Britain including jet fighters, but these were Meteors, Vampires and Venoms, obsolete by mid-1950s standards when the British Hunter, the French Mystère and the Russian MiG-19 were making their service debuts. Against the handful of Meteors in the IDF/AF's inventory, the MiG-15 enjoyed not only a quality superiority but was in a class of its own in the Middle East, its potential potency causing alarm amongst the British commanders, particularly at a time when the RAF's Middle East Air Force was equipped mainly with Meteor FR9s and Venom FB4s. Israel's government and her military commanders decided they had three options: (a) to procure aircraft and other weapons of a similar quality; (b) to launch a pre-emptive strike to deny Egypt the possible use of any of its new weapons when they arrived; or (c) wait for an Egyptian attack. However, the Israelis believed they had time on their side, since arms deals normally took many months to fulfil, while pilot conversion from one type of jet to another, particularly one of higher performance, could not be accomplished quickly and certainly not in the numbers required for the EAF's proposed new fighter force to achieve full operational status.

With Nasser supplying munitions and training for the Front de Libération Nationale (FLN) in their fight against the French in Algeria, Israel found a friendly ear amongst influentials at the French Ministry of Defence and were offered the latest Mystère II fighter, which was effectively a swept-wing version of the Ouragan. At the same time the Swedish government offered the new Saab J29 jet interceptor. An Israeli technical delegation, accompanied by Seren Binyamin Peled, was sent to Europe to evaluate the two fighters, and Peled became the first Israeli pilot to break the sound barrier, while flying a Mystère II. A decision was made in favour of the French aircraft owing mainly to its longer range and its ability to carry bombs. As the IDF/AF was about to complete the deal for the Mystère, Canada unexpectedly offered the Israelis the licence-built Canadair F-86 Sabrejet, which was superior to the French aircraft. An order was placed immediately for 24 of the Sabrejets but the Americans, on learning of the agreement, banned the deal. Thus the Mystère remained the only valid option and on 19 August 1954 a contract had been signed, with initial deliveries targeted for late 1955. Although the Americans approved the deal, these developments caused Britain concern since the Mystère II outperformed anything the RAFMEAF possessed; and the RAFMEAF, under the terms of the Anglo-Jordanian Treaty, faced the possibility of finding itself the Israelis' opponent in any future conflict between Jordan and Israel. Britain's Ambassador to Israel grumbled that France lacked political responsibility.

Seren Peled, the Mystère squadron commander-designate, had been sent to France with a small number of pilots for conversion to the new fighter. However, the Mystère II's development was prolonged and problematic to such an extent that the Armée de l'Air decided to opt for a totally different version with a new fuselage, a modified wing, a new tail section and a different engine – the Rolls-Royce Tay built under licence in France by Hispano-Suiza. Although named Mystère IV, it was a completely new design which bore only superficial resemblance to its predecessor. This switch left the IDF/AF two options: to proceed with the planned procurement of the Mystère II, in spite of its obvious deficiencies, or wait for the Mystère IV. Many senior IDF officers, including

Rav-Aluf Dayan and Aluf-Mishne Weizman, newly promoted commander of Ramat David air base, opted for the immediate purchase of the Mystère II, although the commander of the IDF/AF, Aluf Tolkowsky, was prepared to wait for the Mystère IV, and proposed that a small number of Ouragans be procured as an intermediate safeguard.

Nasser's announcement of the Czech arms deal, while coming as a shock to the Israelis, caused decisions to be taken. Tolkowsky argued that it would take the Egyptians many months to become proficient on the new Russian aircraft, by which time the superior Mystère IV would be in Israeli service, and added that the Ouragan, aided by the Meteors, would prove more than a match for the EAF's Vampires in the meantime. Having won the argument, Tolkowsky duly signed a contract for a dozen Ouragans, to be diverted from Armée de l'Air deliveries. Five Israeli pilots flew to France to collect the first batch. Led by a French pilot, the first six aircraft were ferried to Israel via Rome and Athens on 6 October. On arrival at Rome the Ouragans parked alongside a single Bristol Freighter and several Provost trainers which were on their way to Iraq. The remaining Ouragans were ferried to Israel six days later. With the arrival of the new aircraft, Shimon Peres, Director General of the Israeli Defence Ministry (and future Prime Minister), thereupon declared that, "we have provided Israel with superiority over Arab states", and that these new modern aircraft "gave us a new air superiority". This view was apparently the same as that held by British Foreign Secretary Eden who, in a speech to the British Parliament, declared that 'Israel is not in my belief at a military disadvantage today in relation to any Arab state, or indeed to any combination of Arab states who are on her frontier.'

The Ouragans were flown to Hatzor where they became the nucleus of 113 Squadron under newly promoted Rav-Seren Peled. Meanwhile, a further order had been placed for more Ouragans and subsequently another 12 aircraft arrived at Hatzor on 23 November. Although the Ouragan was not in the same class as the MiG-15, it was an excellent introduction to French equipment and enjoyed several innovations including a G-suit for the pilot, which enabled forces of up

Ouragan 5642 was ferried to Israel as 4X-FRB. (*IAF Magazine collection*)

to 7G to be tolerated. The first aim of the new Squadron was to convert as many pilots as possible to the Ouragan, and these included veterans and youngsters alike.

Although suggestions were put forward for a paratroop assault on Sharm-al-Sheikh and a pre-emptive strike against EAF air bases to destroy some of Egypt's new aircraft, approval was not forthcoming from the government. The undertaking of a successful strike depended on suitable aircraft being available, which the Israelis currently lacked, as can be seen by the IDF/AF's Order of Battle, as it was by the end of the year:

100 Squadron, Ramleh	Piper Cubs
103 Squadron, Tel Nof	C-47 Dakotas, Noratlases
105 Squadron, Ramat David	Spitfires
107 Squadron, Ramat David	Mustangs
109 Squadron, Hatzor	Mosquitos
113 Squadron, Hatzor	Ouragans
117 Squadron, Ramat David	Meteors
115 Flight, Tel Nof	Mosquito PR16s
Flying School, Tel Nof	Harvards

101 Squadron had been disbanded at Ramat David in November and its Mustangs handed over to the re-formed 107 Squadron, a reserve unit commanded by Rav-Seren Eli Eyal, but this was a short-lived arrangement. In addition, the Stearman PT-17 Kaydets at the Flying School could be used for internal liaison and communication duties in an emergency, while the three B-17s, together with a number of Mustangs, Spitfires and Mosquitos, were held in storage by Bedek Aviation at Lod. 110 Squadron had earlier been disbanded and its aircraft put into the reserve. 103 Squadron had three twin-boom N2501 Noratlases on charge, while ten of its Dakotas were leased from the Armée de l'Air. Among its 31 pilots was Seren Ya'el Finkelstein, the only female pilot to serve with the Squadron.

Tension between Israel and Egypt grew from day to day during the winter of 1955-56. Meanwhile, tension had also been building along Israel's northern borders, most obviously along the ceasefire lines between Israel and Syria on each side of the narrow UN-designated demilitarised zone. Tit-for-tat raids and shelling became more serious following Israel's plan to divert a large proportion of the headwaters of the River Jordan down a large pipe to irrigate newly settled regions of the Negev Desert in southern Israel. Unfortunately, water being such a precious resource in the Middle East, any such diversion meant that other people lower down the river would have their water supplies reduced. The people down river were largely the Arab inhabitants of Jordan, whereas the new settlers in the Negev were Israelis. Not surprisingly, any such attempts to tamper with the existing flow of water added a further dimension to Israel's quarrel with its Arab neighbours; and within a short time also led to shooting. Israeli and Syrian troops made incursions a short distance inside the others' territory and any prisoners taken were used by both sides as hostages for the release of their own men. The most serious clash occurred on 22-23 October, in what the Syrians came to call the Battle of Lake Tiberius, following which the editor of the *Jerusalem Post* wrote:

"We hope that the Israeli raid has convinced many Syrians that the military pact with Egypt has increased the danger to Syria instead of guaranteeing Syria's defences."

Syria's reaction was to the contrary, and the raid succeeded only in strengthening the Egyptian-Syrian alliance while, at the same time, virtually destroying any prospects of Syria (and Jordan) joining the British- and American-supported Baghdad Pact, a defence treaty initially between Turkey and Pakistan and soon to be joined by Britain, Iraq and Iran. Instead, Syria turned to the Soviets for arms and support. However, unlike the confrontation between Israelis and Egyptians in the south, the relatively minor clashes between Israelis and Syrians during 1955 did not involve the air forces of either side, though both had to remain in readiness in case things got out of hand.

Chapter Five

EGYPT'S FAILED HONEYMOON WITH BRITAIN 1953–55

"I have no doubt that the Bear is using Nasser, with or without his knowledge, to further his immediate aims. These are, I think, to dislodge the West from the Middle East . . ."

Prime Minister Eden to US President Eisenhower.

Following the 1952 Revolution, the new Egyptian government had hoped to improve its relations with Britain and the West in general. There was also the hope that a just peace could be achieved with Israel. At the same time Egypt's patriotic new leadership intended that their country should take its natural place as a leader of the Arab world. But relations with Britain did not improve as the British authorities were still not prepared to treat Egypt as an equal. Peace with Israel also failed to materialise, partly because an influential group within the Israeli ruling establishment believed that Israel needed to win overwhelming military superiority before making peace with its Arab neighbours. The continuing state of war between Israel and the Arab states in turn overshadowed Egypt's relations with the USA and other Western countries.

The REAF, or EAF (Egyptian Air Force) as it was soon to become, remained essentially pro-RAF, if not pro-British, and clearly hoped for better relations following the Revolution. Despite its support for the Revolution, the EAF was a conservative force and looked to the RAF as a model of the technical competence it hoped to achieve for itself. Nevertheless, the British Air Attaché in Cairo recognised that London would have to do something quickly about the Egyptians' supply problems or, as he said, "the rot would set in" with "bitterness towards us". Even in the Canal Zone there had been a marked improvement in Anglo-Egyptian relations after RAF units stepped down from the state of readiness to which they had been brought during the Revolution.

British Foreign Secretary Eden (soon to become Prime Minister) attempted to negotiate with Egypt over the Canal Zone bases, where 80,000 British servicemen were then based. Eden suggested that Britain would be prepared to evacuate provided she would be allowed to occupy the base in any future war, and for Britain and the United States to provide military and economic assistance. However, Colonel Nasser wanted British forces to leave Egypt before any deal be considered, while the Americans refused to act with Britain without an invitation from Egypt. A stalemate ensued. Prior to this, Britain had given the impression that it wanted to build a better relationship with the new Egyptian government and permitted the sale of a dozen Meteor F8s, the most up-to-date fighters so far purchased by the REAF. Yet the reality was far less sympathetic, particularly following the breakdown in negotiations between Eden and Nasser. The attitude to Egypt's defence needs, adopted by many leading British politicians of the time, was illustrated in a secret cypher sent by Prime Minister Churchill from the liner *Queen Mary* to Eden in London on 27 January 1953. It read:

> "Please do not let these jets go to Egypt until you and I have talked it all over together, I hope at noon on Thursday. Necessary technical hitches should be made to occur."

Nevertheless, four of the Meteors (s/n 1415–1418) – the lead aircraft flown by Sqn Ldr Bill Waterton – did reach Egypt in February, though with ballast instead of cannons in their gun ports. Britain then again imposed an embargo on further deliveries of new weapons to Egypt and five of the remaining F8s from this order went to Brazil and three, with cruel irony, to Israel. Meanwhile the Egyptian and British forces continued to co-operate, though at a low level. There were no more full-scale joint manoeuvres but late in March 1953 Egyptian anti-aircraft units joined the RAF Regiment in a three-day air defence exercise, while Egyptian Air Force officers took part as observers.

There was also some confusion over what to do with the deposed King Farouk's private air force. Some of the aircraft could clearly serve as transports once their extravagant internal fittings had been removed, although others like the two Mallard amphibians were of little use, but since they were of some value Air Force technicians were ordered to overhaul them. Once they were brought up to perfect condition, the retired Air Vice-Marshal Mikaati was asked to negotiate their sale on behalf of the government, but this proved impossible since their logbooks had been lost or stolen during the confusion of the coup.

EAF C-46 Commando s/n 1001 which crashed near the Cairo to Suez road in February 1953. (*EAF*)

Severe problems with lack of spares and inadequate training soon became apparent. In February 1953, C-46 Commando s/n 1001 of the EAF's 7 Squadron, en route from al-Arish to Almaza, crashed near kilo 53 on the Cairo to Suez road in the worst accident in EAF history (to date). One of the survivors, Army NCO Abd al-Wahab Mugahid, walked 4km to the nearest police post at Ribeiqi, following which a Dragonfly helicopter of the EAF arrived at the scene of the crash and rushed the first of 11 injured to Almaza Military Hospital. The Commando pilot, Sqn Ldr Ahmad Massud Ahmad, was among the 30 killed, mostly soldiers returning on leave from the al-Arish garrison. A few weeks later, on 15 March, another EAF transport aircraft crashed on its return from a training flight to Iraq, Bahrain, Pakistan and India; seven officers and seven men were killed.

Negotiations on the future of British military bases in the Canal Zone continued and prospects of an agreed British withdrawal looked quite good. On one hand the entire global strategic situation had changed following the Soviet Union's acquiring nuclear weapons, which made the Canal Zone bases very vulnerable; on the other, Stalin was dead and there had been a slight thaw in the Cold War relationship between East and West. The United States hoped to bring Egypt into a pro-Western regional alliance and discussions about this possibility were already under way. On the problem of the Canal, Air Marshal Sir Robert Saundby CB MC DFC AFC, former Deputy AOC-in-C RAF Bomber Command, offered a solution but not one that would find acceptance among Egyptians:

"The only permanent solution is an international base in the Canal Zone, situated in the strip of territory through which the Canal runs, alienated from Egypt and brought under international, possibly NATO, control. The strip, including the Canal itself, might be purchased from Egypt under a system of long-term payments, financed by allocating a portion each year of the receipts from Canal dues on shipping. Britain should announce in the clearest possible terms that she is no longer prepared to bear, single-handed, the responsibility for the defence of a waterway used by almost every nation.

Every effort should be made to obtain Egypt's willing consent to these proposals, but if she will not agree they may have to be imposed on her. It is wrong that an accident of geography should give any country the power to make itself an intolerable nuisance to the nations of the world, by blockading an international highway, and holding them to ransom at its pleasure."

In London, British military planners and diplomats finally seemed to have realised that it was counter-productive to hang on to the Canal Zone bases which simply fuelled Egyptian hostility. Two plans were consequently drawn up by Foreign Minister Eden. Plan A, which Britain hoped Egypt would accept, provided for 7,000 uniformed British troops to be stationed in the Canal Zone to maintain the bases and reactivate them in case of an attack on any Arab state, Turkey or Iran. These ideas included a joint Anglo-Egyptian air defence system. Plan B, which most planners considered more realistic, placed the Canal Zone bases under Egyptian control though with a small number of uniformed British or allied technical staff to supervise their maintenance. Plan B also envisaged the EAF being solely responsible for the air defence of the Suez Canal. Again EAF capabilities and operations were placed at the heart of Egyptian foreign policy decision-making.

Negotiations between Britain and Egypt began in Cairo on 28 April 1953, with Wg Cdr al-Bughdadi, Nasser's leading trouble-shooter, leading the Egyptian team. A week later these talks collapsed as Egypt refused to allow any uniformed British troops to remain on Egyptian territory, while Britain similarly refused to pull out all such uniformed personnel. Meanwhile, Egyptian leaders put great effort into improving relations with other Arab states. Here the EAF was used as an instrument of foreign policy. For example, Saudi Arabian Air Force pilots were invited to train in Egypt in 1953 and several EAF Vampires were also handed over to the Saudis. The British Foreign Office, on learning of Egypt's new training programme, expressed concern about the possible indoctrination of the Saudi, Jordanian and two Nigerian students (Cadets Abdel Shaffar and Abdel Rahman Dabiri) then receiving instruction at Bilbeis.

Following the riots and fire-bombings in Cairo in 1952, and before his subsequent removal from power, King Farouk had negotiated a secret five million dollar arms deal with the US for armoured cars, machine-guns and the like, suitable for dealing with civil unrest. Colonel Nasser only learned of this secret deal in May 1953, and immediately contacted the Americans to change the order to tanks and aircraft, artillery and ships instead. In October of that year he was requested to produce a list of requirements, which was given to the American Military Attaché. Egypt required: one armoured divison with tanks, transport, artillery, anti-tank guns and three squadrons of jet fighters. When the US Assistant Secretary for Defence arrived in Cairo at the beginning of November, he suggested an Egyptian Military Mission should visit the United States to tour bases and arrange for deliveries.

Internally, things went well for the new Egyptian government until July 1953, when the monarchy was finally abolished and Egypt was declared a Republic. General Mohammed Neguib took over as the country's first President although Colonel Nasser retained real power as head of the governing Revolutionary Council, while Colonel Amr succeeded Neguib as Commander-in-Chief of the Egyptian Armed Forces, promptly being promoted to Maj-General. This caused considerable resentment among many other officers who saw it as a political promotion. Air Commodore Hassan Mahmud was one of those who felt that political loyalty was being confused with professional competence and so resigned as head of the Air Force. Wg Cdr al-Bughdadi is then believed to have taken over as nominal commander of the Air Force, but as he was soon also to become Egypt's Minister of Defence, day to day command of the EAF was in the hands of Air Commodore Muhammad Sidqi Mahmud, the EAF Chief of Staff.* Already there had been those in the Air Force who felt unfairly treated by the revolution. Among senior officers obliged to resign from their posts in the Ministry of War were men like Air Commodore Gazerine, who felt strong sympathy for Egypt's new government and whose patriotism had never been doubted. Yet they were denied the opportunity of serving their country, or even of offering their experience in organisation during the many crises that Egypt and her Air Force were soon to face. Such men were the innocent victims whom the Free Officers felt obliged to sacrifice so as to cement the loyalty of more junior ranks.

The years from the end of the 1948–49 War to the declaration of an Egyptian

---

* Air Commodore Sidqi Mahmud became commander of the EAF following the Suez War, a position he held until the disastrous June War of 1967.

Republic in 1953 saw huge political changes in the country. Economic and social upheaval would come later. For the Egyptian Air Force it had been a time of high hopes, almost all of which had been dashed on the rocks of political corruption and incompetence at home and of blinkered British intransigence abroad. The EAF had grown considerably in size but had declined in competence. Egypt's new revolutionary government hoped for a new relationship with the outside world, even of an honourable peace with Israel, although when it was learned that two German formerly high-ranking Nazi officials had been appointed by Cairo – one as an economic adviser, the other as chief adviser to the War Ministry – its motives were questioned. The general Arab ignorance about the Nazi Holocaust and the slaughter of European Jewry by the Nazis during the Second World War frequently led some Arab governments to misunderstand how certain of their own actions would be seen by the outside world. This ignorance and naivety was not itself based on anti-Semitism, which was virtually unknown in the Semitic Arab world. Nevertheless, Arab preoccupation with the suffering of the Palestinian Arabs and with what looked in Cairo, Damascus and elsewhere like Israeli bullying of its Arab neighbours, resulted in a blinkered inability to foresee the results of seeking military advice from former Nazi officers. Similarly, Syrian recruitment of former Luftwaffe pilots as air force instructors led some Israelis to see the Syrian Air Force as a successor to the Luftwaffe – with all the highly emotive and, from a Syrian point of view, disastrous propaganda consequences which that entailed.

Egyptian nationalist excitement reached a high point in the summer of 1953 and there were many clashes between British troops and Egyptian military personnel and civilians. Continuing arguments over the Canal Zone led to a British arms embargo being reimposed. In September, in the midst of the Anglo-Egyptian crisis, Israeli forces unexpectedly occupied a demilitarised zone on the Negev-Sinai border, further increasing tensions within Egypt as well as causing deep concern to Egyptian military leaders. The following month, after three Israeli civilians had been killed when their home was attacked at Yehuda, Israeli commandos raided the Palestinian village at Qibya and bombed 45 homes, during which 66 villagers were killed and 75 wounded. It was the most serious incident among many border clashes during this period.

Friction between British troops in the Canal Zone and Egyptian military personnel and civilians continued, highlighted by an incident when three EAF corporals were shot and seriously injured in their car by a British patrol who suspected they had been cutting barbed wire barriers; subsequent investigation showed that it had been a misunderstanding, as was often the case, but the incident led to very bad feeling in the EAF.

1953 had been a bad year for the British in the Middle East in general and in Egypt in particular, not least of all for the RAF based in the Canal Zone. The year had started badly with the loss of nine crew and passengers aboard a Transport Command Hastings which crashed three miles west of Shallufa on 12 January, although of the dozen or so 205 Group aircraft lost in accidents (with a further eight written off) during the year, there occurred only four further fatalities. These were the two crew members of Auster AOP6 TW580 of 651 Squadron which crashed at al-Ballah during an exercise on 28 April, and the pilot and pupil aboard Harvard KF329 of 107 MU which crashed three miles south of Geneifa on 11 August.

There were only two fatalities relating to Canal Zone-based aircraft in 1954, and these occurred in February when Auster AOP6 TW509 crashed during a fighter evasion exercise; a total of 15 aircraft were lost or written off as a result of accidents during the year. The main RAF units based in Egypt with 205 Group during the period 1953–54 were:

13 Squadron, Kabrit	Meteor PR10 (to Abu Sueir 12/54)
32 Squadron, Deversoir	Venom FB1 (to Kabrit 9/54)
39 Squadron, Kabrit	Mosquito NF36/Meteor NF13
208 Squadron, Abu Sueir	Meteor FR9
213 Squadron, Deversoir	Vampire FB9 (disbanded 9/54)
219 Squadron, Kabrit	Meteor NF11/13 (disbanded 9/54)
249 Squadron, Deversoir	Vampire FB9 (to Amman 6/54)
70 Squadron, Fayid	Valetta C1
78 Squadron, Fayid	Valetta C1 (disbanded 9/54)
84 Squadron, Fayid	Valetta C1
114 Squadron, Fayid	Valetta C1
204 Squadron, Fayid	Valetta C1 (disbanded 2/53)
216 Squadron, Fayid	Valetta C1
651 Squadron, Ismailia	Auster AOP6

Detachments of Bomber Command Lincolns and Mosquitos from the United Kingdom continued to use Shallufa during this time. These could be flown out at short notice and thereby enabled RAFMEAF to have on call a heavy strike force without the need to have bomber units stationed permanently in the Canal Zone.

Possibly a composite photograph portraying REAF Lancasters of 9 Squadron flying over General Neguib as he addressed a crowd immediately after the 1952 Revolution. (*EAF*)

Colonel Nasser, who quietly succeeded General Neguib on 14 November 1954 as President of Egypt, meanwhile declared his government's support for various anti-colonial liberation movements, particularly that in Algeria where the French Army was fighting a singularly savage war against the guerilla organisation which was struggling to free this Arab country from French rule. In turn the French government sided with Israel as a way of retaliating against Egypt and, as a result, France agreed to supply arms to Israel. Nevertheless, talks between Egypt and Britain had restarted and an agreement was finally signed in October 1954. The old Anglo-Egyptian Treaty of 1936 was ended by mutual consent and Britain agreed to withdraw all her troops from Egypt within 20 months. Thereafter Britain would be allowed to station 2,200 civilian technicians in Egypt and to maintain several bases near the Suez Canal for a further seven years.

EAF Vampires over the Citadel of Cairo, probably in the early 1950s. The nearest aircraft is s/n 1514 which appears in Arabic within the tail-boom stripes. (*EAF*)

Although President Nasser achieved much popularity among his own people, there were still those who did not agree with his philosophy and ideals. Certainly the Moslem Brotherhood believed he had been too compromising by allowing the British almost two years to depart and, subsequently, on the evening of 27 October 1954 shots were fired at Nasser as he was addressing a mass rally in Alexandria. Although he was not injured, the Sudanese Minister of Education was wounded in one hand and another member of the delegation sustained injuries to his shoulder. The would-be assassin was seized by police and almost one thousand members of the Brotherhood were rounded up and imprisoned. Six members, including the gunman, were tried and sentenced to death, although they were later reprieved. However, Wg Cdr al-Raouf, an early member of the Free Officers' Movement, was implicated in the plot and consequently fled the country. Nasser further alienated himself from Israel and the West when he confirmed death sentences on two of 13 young Jews arrested in Cairo who had been convicted of spying and planting bombs in Cairo and Alexandria.

Nevertheless, both Britain and Egypt genuinely seemed to want to build a new relationship and in this new spirit of co-operation Britain resumed arms sales to Egypt. In early 1955 the EAF received eight further Meteor F8s (s/n 1419–1426) and six ex-RAF Meteor NF13 night fighters (s/n 1427–1432) delivered between June and August 1955. The EAF had plans for four fighter-bomber squadrons to be equipped with Vampires. One squadron still flew Meteor day fighters and another flight was struggling to reach operational status with Meteor NF13 night fighters. When these aircraft arrived in the middle of 1955 the unit had few trained crews and very little of the support equipment needed to maintain a night fighter's complex radar system. A single heavy bomber squadron worked hard to keep three Lancasters and three Halifaxes flying. The three transport squadrons were in better shape and operated a fleet

Trio of Meteor F4s over Egypt; the nearest aircraft, s/n 1410, survived the 1956 conflict. (*EAF*)

of about 40 C-47s, C-46s, Ansons, and Doves. These deliveries finally enabled the EAF to transfer its piston-engined fighters to the advanced training role. Several RAF squadrons were still stationed in the Canal Zone, but now that a timetable for British withdrawal had been agreed, confrontation was replaced by the co-operation seen in earlier years. Thus, the RAF's 208 Squadron, with its advanced Meteor FR9s, worked closely with the EAF's jet conversion unit of Vampire FB52s and T55s which, under the terms of the new agreement, had moved into the ex-RAF base at Fayid. This EAF jet conversion unit is believed to have been 5/6 Combined Squadron.

The Egyptians had only just converted to Vampires and were very much in need of air-to-air gunnery practice, so pilots of 208 Squadron towed banner targets for them. According to British personnel, the Egyptian pilots certainly needed some instruction, as Flt Lt Michael Bradley* commented:

> "After one or two bad frights from ricochets and other zero degree angle-off incidents, we were asked to send our squadron Pilot Attack Officer [PAO] down to Fayid to check their gunsight harmonization and give them any other possible help. Legend has it that the first Vampire our chap climbed into and switched on the sight, it wound itself up its slide and fell off the top into his lap!"

The PAO in question, Flt Lt Chris Bushe, added:

> "I was not at all keen to show the EAF how to shoot accurately, but it was suggested by higher authority that a refusal was not in my best interests. As we were specifically banned from making any passes at EAF aircraft, should we even see one, we had little idea about them or how they flew. After two

---

* Flt Lt (later Wg Cdr AFC) Michael Bradley was one of a handful of RAF pilots who later flew the American U-2 spyplane on operational sorties over the Soviet Union.

---

days of lectures at EAF Deversoir, attended by pilots from other units, we got down to the practical bit and harmonization was high on the priority list. That was when the gunsight ended in my lap. Most amusing around the bar afterwards, but it caused me some concern about their maintenance. It also raised the point about who was in command when I flew with one of their pilots in their machines. They would not concede so, begrudgingly, I had to give way.

Their flying generally was of a standard accepted as being 'average' with us. The whole thing was rather slap-dash with checklists not carried out on occasions. When one pilot, on a run-in and break, dropped the undercarriage instead of the airbrakes I thought the Vampire T11 would break up. That convinced me that being killed by one of them was not in my plan, and I asked to be taken off the project. I must admit that they were very keen about the cine gunnery that we did, and enthusiastic that 208 [Squadron aircraft] should mix it with them if ever we met in the air. This point was made by other squadrons that attended. In my innocence I took them at their word and some days later bounced a section of [Meteor] NF13s – just one pass. No more than 15 minutes later after landing, the CO [Sqn Ldr T.F. Neil DFC] and I were summoned to the Station Commander's office for me to be given a dressing down for that one pass. When I was withdrawn there was no further contact with the EAF by 208 [Squadron], social or otherwise. Being the only PAI [Pilot Attack Instructor] left in the Zone I doubt if there were other contacts."

Once again it was clear that EAF aircrew were keen to keep up contacts, both professional and social, with their RAF counterparts, but senior Air Force and political leaders were far less enthusiastic. Notwithstanding, one of the EAF's foremost fighter pilots, Sqn Ldr F. Zaher, was sent to the RAF's Empire Test Pilots' School at Boscombe Down in England early in 1955, but he lost his life when the Hunter F1 he was flying crashed on 18 July of that year.

More than 50 Canadian- and British-built Chipmunks were in service with the EAF in the early 1950s but would gradually be replaced by the Egyptian-built Gomhouriya primary trainer. Intermediate flight training was undertaken on the Harvard aircraft. Applicants for entry into the Egyptian Air Force Academy at Bilbeis could be up to 24 years of age (the maximum for entry into the Army's Military College being 2½ years) if the applicant already had a university degree. Before being sent for flying training, EAF cadets spent two years at the Military College. In the third year they were thrown headlong into flying training, when they were expected to learn to fly within 20 hours or so. These fledgling pilots were then plunged into an intensive programme on Chipmunks and Gomhouriyas, when they were taught by EAF pilots, most of whom only had a few hundred hours' flying experience themselves. In the advanced training phase pilot candidates flew Spitfire F22s, Fiat G55s and Fury piston-engined fighters before advancing to Meteor T7 and Vampire T55 trainers, while future navigators attended hundreds of hours of classes and then trained on C-47s and other transports. It was a demanding programme and if a cadet failed to master the art of flying after 20 hours in the air he was considered to be of below average ability. EAF cadets were, in fact, rushed through their training. Those who made the grade flying Harvards were then sent straight on to the jet conversion course located at Fayid, an air base near the shore of the Great Bitter Lake.

Here student pilots flew piston-engined Fiat G55 and Spitfire fighters and then Vampire T55 or Meteor T7 jets. Few student pilots were assigned to bomber or transport units as these positions were filled by older, more experienced pilots.

The EAF was, however, having trouble training a new generation of experienced aircrew and support personnel. There were plenty of volunteers and training aircraft, though these again included a wide variety of types. The chief difficulty lay in a lack of support equipment, outdated methods and inexperienced instructors. The EAF was well aware of these limitations and in 1955 the Egyptian government advertised for 20 ex-RAF instructors to join its flight training programme. Only six British instructors accepted the Egyptian offer and when they arrived at Bilbeis in October 1955 they were surprised by what they found. The condition of training aircraft and base facilities was poor and even flying clothes were in short supply, although the EAF was making a determined effort to improve this situation and many changes were already under way to upgrade the base and its training equipment. Two of the British instructors, Flt Lts Sidney Brisk and David Larcombe, recalled:

"When we got to Bilbeis we found a fairly reasonable assembly of training aircraft: about 15 Gomhouriyas, some 25 Chipmunks and 20 Harvards. We were told: 'Whatever you do, don't try to spin the Chipmunk, we have already lost three of them in spins; it is an impossible manoeuvre.' This intrigued us, and so, of course, as soon as we got into the air in one we duly spun it. No trouble at all. The Egyptians were horrified. In fact, so convinced were they that there was something basically wrong with all Chipmunks that they called for the de Havilland representative from England to 'put it right'. After a searching investigation he reported: 'There is nothing wrong with the Chipmunk; it is the Egyptian pilots. They never get into a spin properly and they have no idea how to get out of one.' We set to work to try and instil a little basic knowledge into our new pupils. They were nice enough fellows on the whole – mostly spoke English – were polite, kind, and very eager to get into a class under a British instructor. 'Now we will really learn to fly,' they said. Unfortunately they never did. Their intelligence was not on a level with their keenness, and their retentive powers were almost nil. They forgot tomorrow what they had been taught today. And above all was their stubborn indifference to the niceties of flying; they didn't care whether they executed a manoeuvre well or badly as long as they somehow got the machine into the air and got down again in one piece."

Cadet Abd Moneim al-Tawil (who later rose to the rank of Maj-General) was a nephew of Air Commodore Muhammad Farag, a former Second World War pilot, and attended Bilbeis at this time. He commented that the two RAF instructors, Brisk and Larcombe, were not regarded with such awe by their Egyptian pupils as they themselves seemed to think. In fact, they were both regarded as 'a bit crazy', a story going around that one had been obliged to retire from the RAF after rolling a Lancaster bomber. Another student pilot of this period was Cadet Nobil Shoarky (one of the few Egyptians to shoot down an Israeli Mirage during the June War of 1967, who rose to become Chief of EAF Training), while Flt Lt Hosni Mubarak (elected President of Egypt in 1981) had graduated as a pilot in March 1950, but returned to Bilbeis as an instructor two years later, a role in which he served for seven years before taking command of a jet bomber squadron in January 1959.

The Egyptian Armed Forces were themselves demanding new weaponry and their increasing frustration had been noted by the British Air Attaché in Cairo. In a secret message to London he warned that anger was spreading through the EAF as a result of the slow and intermittent delivery of British-built combat aircraft. An increasing number of Egyptian officers also believed that such British delaying tactics reflected support for Israel. Rumours were rife, obligating President Nasser on one occasion to send for the British Ambassador, demanding to know why Britain was supplying the Israelis with 100 Super Sherman tanks. Subsequent enquiries revealed that the tanks were, in fact, being supplied by the French, who had been secretly breaking the 1950 Tripartite Arms Control agreement. The French had bought the Shermans from Britain ostensibly for scrap, but on arrival at Cherbourg 75 of the tanks had been re-routed direct to Israel. Nasser sent a message to Eden stating that unless he could obtain arms from Britain or the US he would have to get them where he could.

The British made it clear that any substantial arms supplied to Egypt would depend on a more co-operative attitude by Nasser towards the Baghdad Pact. In February 1955, the United States had turned down an Egyptian request for 27 million dollars' worth of arms on the grounds they could not pay cash for them. On one occasion, when President Nasser was entertaining a visiting CIA agent in Cairo, an Israeli aircraft droned high overhead, causing Nasser to comment:

"I have to sit here and take this, and your government won't give me arms."

Not surprisingly the Egyptian government continued to look for other sources of supply. These efforts became much more serious than before, but they were still directed towards other Western countries. And when the right-wing Israeli Herut political party began proclaiming the doctrine of territorial expansion in the Israeli press, concern in Cairo turned into outright alarm. Egypt's new leaders felt that they had to counter Israel's growing power and increasingly aggressive actions with an all-out effort to strengthen the Egyptian Armed Forces, above all the Air Force. Egypt had asked the Americans for F-86 Sabre jet fighters in 1953 but were refused. Israel also asked for these top-line fighters but was similarly refused. In 1954 Egyptian military buyers negotiated with Sweden to purchase Saab B18B bombers, Norway for ex-Norwegian Air Force Vampire jets and Britain to buy various miscellaneous aircraft. Another Egyptian mission visited Spain. None of these discussions was to pay off and Britain even refused to provide Egypt with drop-tanks for EAF Meteors and Vampires on the grounds that this would turn defensive aircraft into offensive weapons. Italy was the only country to respond favourably to Egyptian requests for assistance.

British-designed Vampire jets, built by Aer Macchi and ordered in 1952, were delivered to the EAF in a secret programme during 1955. The total number involved has never been officially released but was clearly enough to equip two squadrons. After considerable pressure from the British government, Italy announced that 13 Vampires had been sold to Syria, 45 to another unidentified Middle Eastern country, and that 25 would go to Saudi Arabia, although another source mentions 58 aircraft were supplied to Egypt, of which 43 were flown to Almaza via Brindisi and Athens, with the balance despatched by sea in crates marked 'Fragile – Murano Glass'. Dr Cattaneo of Aer Macchi confirms the latter:

"Aer Macchi signed three contracts with the EAF, through the good offices of the Syrian Air Force, between March 1954 and September 1955. These resulted in 58 ex-Italian Air Force Vampire FB52As, fully overhauled to zero hours flying time, being delivered to Egypt at a time when other deliveries of Vampires were severely disrupted by the British government's on-off embargo on the supply of military aircraft to Egypt. After considerable political problems, the first contract was signed by Aer Macchi for 13 Vampires on 23 March 1954. This was done with the discreet approval of both the Italian and British governments. Subsequent sales were made easier because of the rumoured and actual supply of more advanced Soviet aircraft to Egypt; in fact it was seen as a way of maintaining links with the Egyptians.

A discreet political compromise was found by selling the Vampires to the Syrian Ministry of Defence which was in reality acting on behalf of the Egyptian government. Syria then passed on the aircraft to the real customer. A further compromise was found within Italy whereby these second-hand machines were replaced by new ones. The new aircraft also carried the same serial numbers as those which had been supplied to Egypt. The second Egyptian order was for 15 aircraft early in 1955, and another in mid-1955 for 30. These aircraft were delivered directly to Cairo from Malpena via Brindisi and Athens, without going to Damascus. At Cairo they had their markings changed. The aircraft on the first contract went in three batches, each led by the Aer Macchi test pilot Guido Carestiato. The other delivery pilots were Italian Air Force personnel on special secondment. Only six machines from the second contract were flown out in August 1955, again led by Carestiato, while the other nine went on merchant ships in September and October 1955. Of the third contract, six went by sea and the rest flew in four batches, each led by Carestiato. The final batch of eight Vampires landed at Cairo a few weeks before the Anglo-French invasion of 1956.

During the whole course of these deliveries, flight testing was carried out in Italy without any problems by Italian and Egyptian personnel. The only accident was when one aircraft (s/n MDN29: Syrian Ministère de la Défense Nationale 29) was severely damaged in an emergency landing as a result of engine failure during acceptance trials by Flt Lt Baghat Hassan Helmi on 27 December 1955. Helmi's emergency landing was considered highly skilful under the circumstances. This machine was subsequently repaired and delivered some months later in September 1956."*

Egypt did conclude a semi-secret deal with Canada for the sale of reconditioned Harvard trainers and 15 of these aircraft left Halifax, Nova Scotia, aboard an

---

* The serial numbers given to these aircraft by the EAF appear to have included some numbers already applied to Vampires previously supplied by Britain. This was either an attempt to confuse Israeli intelligence services or it included the numbers of Vampires already written off in Egyptian service. MDN (Syrian) 1–13 became 1524–1540 in the EAF; the EAF s/n given to MDN14–58 are unknown but clearly included those shot down in border clashes with the Israelis shortly before the Sinai War.

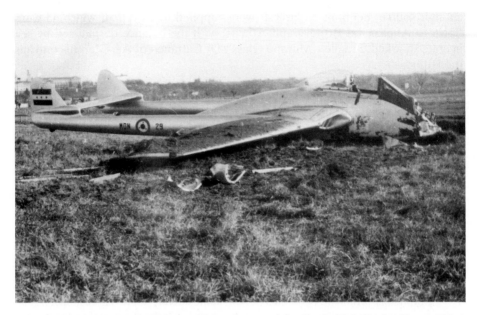

Italian-built Vampire in false Syrian markings, after a crash-landing by Flt Lt Baghat Hassan Helmi in December 1955. (*Dr Ing. Gianni Cattaneo*)

Egyptian ship, the *Star of Aswan*, in November 1955. But since Harvards could be armed with light bombs and machine-guns even this sale caused a controversy in Canada. The problem was finally laid to rest in 1956 when the Canadian Prime Minister announced that the Egyptian order for Harvards had first been discussed with Britain and the USA, and neither country had raised any objections. The Egyptians were no longer interested in building obsolete Vampires and reportedly attempted to sell the jigs and other specialised tooling at the Helwan factory back to de Havilland. At this time German technicians were welcomed to Egypt and put to work on various defence projects. This was the start of a massive effort to enhance Egyptian prestige, technical expertise and business experience through the establishment of domestic jet fighter, missile and other defence programmes.

Despite all these strenuous efforts to diversify its sources of military supplies, Egypt felt increasingly frustrated and trapped by arbitrary embargos and the political whims of foreign suppliers. Anger within the EAF officer corps was reaching a serious level and President Nasser's government may well have felt threatened by this rising chorus of discontent. The Egyptian Armed Forces clearly felt threatened by Israel's new aggressive policies and humiliated by their apparent inability to defend the nation's borders.

The Soviet Union was clearly aware of all these feelings inside Egypt. Soviet support for Israel during that country's War of Independence in 1948 had not given the USSR any political influence in Israel, which instead had rapidly declared its pro-Western sympathies in the Cold War. The Soviet Union therefore started to court Arab states which it had previously been describing as reactionary, feudal puppets of the British Empire. The new revolutionary and enthusiastically anti-imperialist government in Cairo was an obvious target for the new Soviet political offensive. The short-sighted and in some cases clearly unsympathetic policies that so many Western governments pursued in their relations with Egypt made the Soviet task much easier. There was plenty of resentment for the Soviets to seize upon, though as yet there was little real anti-Western feeling among the educated officer class of Egypt. Of this period, future Soviet Premier Khrushchev recalled:

> "When we first began to take an active interest in the affairs of Egypt, our attitude was cautious and our optimism was guarded. When Nasser came to power after the Revolution in Egypt, we were not convinced by his policies that he was going to do what was necessary to reform the social-political structure of his country. For a certain period after the coup and Colonel Nasser's emergence as Chief of State, we couldn't be sure what direction this new government of army officers would take, either in foreign or in domestic policies. We had no choice but to wait and see what would happen. We liked what we saw. The Egyptians began to pursue a policy that had considerable merit. They started actively to put pressure on the English [sic] to pull their troops out. The English were left with no alternative, and they complied with the Egyptians' demand. Now we respected Nasser and realised that his wasn't just another in a series of new governments that seize power and then follow old policies."

As a result, Egypt turned to the Soviet bloc for military and political support, further damaging its relations with the West, so that within four years of the Revolution Egypt was widely perceived as an increasing 'threat' to Western interests. Beginning in June 1955, President Nasser met several times with the Soviet Ambassador in Cairo to discuss trade co-operation and possible arms sales. Khrushchev continued:

> "Soon after the coup, when the Egyptians decided to try to oust the English [sic], Nasser's representatives came to us with a request for military aid. They said they needed to have their own army in order to put pressure on the English. We agreed. We gave them weapons ranging from rifles to regular artillery, but as I recall, we didn't give them any planes at first. We did, however, give them tanks and naval equipment. Nasser said he particularly needed torpedo boats. I think we gave them military aid on a commercial basis, but at a reduced price."

When the British government discovered these secret discussions they tied any future Anglo-Egyptian arms deals to Egypt's participation in an alliance against the Soviet Union – the Baghdad Pact. The United States also refused Egyptian requests for arms unless it signed the Baghdad Pact and allowed an American military mission into the country. This would have meant that Egypt replaced the military subordination to Britain, from which it had so recently escaped, with a new military subordination to the United States. The whole situation was also seen as a case of blatant political bullying by the West. When the British Ambassador protested about Egypt's courtship with the Soviets, Nasser retorted:

> "You are a free country; you can do as you like. We are a free country; we can do what we like."

81

The American Ambassador received similar short shift from Nasser:

> "France bargained with us, saying she would only supply us with arms if we refrained from criticising her attitude in North Africa . . . The United States only gave us promises . . . The United Kingdom said she would readily supply us with arms, but she has only sent us very small shipments."

On receiving these latest reports, US Secretary of State Foster Dulles told senior members of Congress:

> "We are in this present jam because the past Administration had always dealt with the Middle East from a political standpoint and had tried to meet the wishes of the Zionists in this country. That had created a basic antagonism with the Arabs. That was what the Russians were capitalising on."

The Americans secretly, and quite accurately, blamed Britain and France for continuing to harbour colonial views, thus forcing Egypt and other Arab countries to look towards the Soviet Union for assistance and protection. Secretary of State Dulles' aggressive manner and anti-British quips did not endear him to British politicians: Foreign Secretary Eden found him unfriendly, while Prime Minister Churchill had cause to comment: "Foster Dulles is the only case I know of a bull who carries his china shop with him." But perhaps Dulles had an ulterior motive. According to the Egyptian Foreign Minister, Dr Mahmoud Fawzi:

> "When an Egyptian military delegation arrived in the United States in the hopes of purchasing arms, Dulles saw them in a room in which on one wall hung a map of the world. All over Europe and Asia little stars and stripes had been stuck where American troops or airfields were planted. Dulles waved at the blank area of Egypt and the Gulf: 'What we need are some flags here,' he told the Egyptians."

Most Egyptians, while they felt a far greater cultural sympathy with the West than with the Soviet bloc, did not wish to have their country cleared of the British only to have it occupied by American troops, and earnestly wished to remain neutral in the Cold War. The idea of a Third World of neutral countries standing aloof from the East/West confrontation was already taking root. As far as the Egyptian government was concerned this also meant that Egypt would have equal dealing with East and West. It would purchase arms from whichever side offered to sell, particularly from the side which attached fewest conditions to such deals.

When information about Cairo's delicate negotiations on the Baghdad Pact appeared in the world's press, President Nasser believed that the information had been leaked by the British government in order to embarrass him. Furious, he announced in a speech at the Egyptian Armed Forces exhibition in Cairo an arms deal with Czechoslovakia in exchange for rice and cotton. The Soviet Union was, in reality, the power behind this deal and Czechoslovakia was basically just used as a front. The announcement of what the Western press called the 'Czech Arms Deal' caused a diplomatic flurry in London, but did not influence the gradual evacuation of British troops from the Canal Zone as

this process had already been agreed. In Israel, President Nasser's announcement caused much more excitement. There, it seemed to have been assumed that Egypt would not dare to make a final break with its Western arms suppliers, at least not in such a sudden dramatic fashion. On a diplomatic level co-operation between Israel and France, which was still bogged down in a savage colonialist war against the Arab population of Algeria, was stepped up. More immediately the Israeli government took aggressive military action to demonstrate its displeasure along the frontier with Egypt.

Israeli jets had been violating Egyptian airspace over Sinai for some time, but had always avoided interception. On the morning of 1 September 1955 the Egyptians retaliated and four EAF Vampires crossed the Israeli frontier. These were engaged by a pair of IAF Meteors and two Vampires were shot down (see Chapter Four). On the ground, the Palestinian guerillas in Gaza traded raids with Israeli commandos. Late in August one such Israeli incursion left 39 Egyptian soldiers, police and civilians dead, and 16 wounded, which further fuelled Egyptian demands for proper modern equipment with which to defend their country.

Following a state visit to Amman by the Turkish President in November, King Hussein let it be known that Jordan might consider joining the Baghdad Pact if Britain provided her with more arms. Whitehall's response was to send the Royal Jordanian Air Force ten Vampire FB52 fighters. Despite this gesture, among the Arab states there was a growing feeling that they were at a military disadvantage and that the gap between Israel and themselves was growing. Certainly Israel's new Ouragan fighter-bombers out-performed the EAF's Meteors and Vampires, but the Egyptians hoped that newer Russian MiGs would redress the balance.

Jets and other military equipment secured through the new arms deals with the USSR, using Czechoslovakia as a diplomatic front, certainly appeared to shift the military balance very quickly. The first crated aircraft arrived in Alexandria on 1 October 1955 aboard the Soviet freighter *Stalingrad*. More heavily laden vessels followed, while Il-14 transport aircraft subsequently delivered military supplies from Bulgaria, though at least ten of these flights were refused over-flying permission by the Greek authorities. These deliveries included 86 MiG-15 jet fighters and MiG-15UTI conversion trainers, 39 Il-28 jet bombers, 20 Il-14 transports and 25 Yak-11 primary trainers. In addition, the Egyptian Army and Navy also received large amounts of Soviet weaponry. When quizzed by an American journalist about the military build-up, Nasser retorted:

> "I am thinking of Israel's army not as it is today but what it will be tomorrow. Now we will be meeting Mystères with MiGs. This is better than meeting Mystères with nothing."

According to the Annual Report drawn up by the British Air Attaché in Cairo, the EAF adjusted rapidly to the massive influx of Russian-built equipment. The EAF Order of Battle as at the end of the year was assessed by the Air Attaché to be as follows (although clearly he had no idea of the scale of the Russian deliveries):

Unit and Location	Aircraft	Serviceable	U/s	Comments
1 Squadron		0	0	Furies in store, awaiting MiG-15s
2 Squadron, Kabrit	Vampire FB52	15	3	Day-fighter/ground attack
3 Squadron, Almaza	C-47 Dakota	8	3	Transport
4 Squadron, Alexandria	Beechcraft Expeditor	7	0	Used for navigator training
7/12 Squadron, Almaza	C-46 Commando	10	9	Transport/paratroop
9 Squadron, Cairo West		0	0	Lancasters in store, awaiting Il-28s
10 Squadron, Heliopolis	Bonanza	1	1	HQ Communication Squadron
	Dove	0	4	
11 Squadron, Almaza	C-47 Dakota	4	0	Communication Squadron
	C-46 Commando	1	0	
	Mallard	2	0	
	Sikorsky S-51	1	1	
20 Squadron, Dekheila	Meteor F4	7	3	Day-fighter/ground attack
Deversoir	Meteor F8	7	3	
30 Squadron, Deversoir		0	0	Vampires to Fighter Training Unit, converting to MiG-15s
31 Squadron, Almaza	Vampire FB52	16	3	Ground attack
Fighter Training Unit, Almaza	Meteor T7	5	0	Jet conversion unit
	Meteor NF13	5	1	
	Vampire FB52	17	8	
	Vampire T55	4	0	
	Harvard	6	0	
Air College, Bilbeis	Harvard	19	18	Basic training
	Chipmunk	37	14	
	Gomhouriya	13	0	
Health & Agricultural Squadron	Vultee BT13	5	0	Anti-malarial spraying unit
	Super Cub	1	0	
	Magister	2	20	
	Mraz Sokol	8	9	
	Morane 502	2	0	
	Hiller 360	0	2	(helicopter)

The EAF had a manpower strength of about 400 aircrew plus 3,000 support personnel. It possessed almost 100 combat aircraft, over 75 per cent of which were operational, with various obsolete aircraft held in store. In addition there were a little over 200 training and support aircraft, this equipment being almost entirely of Western manufacture. The picture was about to change dramatically with the arrival of the MiG fighters, Ilyushin bombers and Yak trainers. Most

One of the first MiG deliveries, 1955: a MiG-15 at Abu Sueir, possibly photographed from a passing car using a telephoto lens. (*Authors' collection*)

of the new aircraft came to Egypt by ship and were reassembled then tested at Dekheila air base near Alexandria. Wg Cdr Labib (EAF historian) wrote:

> "At the time of the Czechoslovakian-Egyptian arms contract, Egypt possessed what was left of the 60 or so Meteor and Vampire jet fighters supplied by Britain. The EAF also had sufficient pilots for these aircraft. Now, however, the urgent need for additional pilots and, of course, to train them on the new fighters, bombers and other aircraft arriving from the Soviet bloc meant that existing pilots would have to be withdrawn from front-line service to help in any training programme. Such training would also take time. This problem was aggravated by the fact that bringing new types of aircraft into operations required ground maintenance personnel as well as aircrew."

The EAF's first two MiG-15 squadrons were established at Almaza in December. Soviet bloc instructors, Russians and Czechs, had already given Egyptian pilots hurried conversion courses using MiG-15UTI trainers at the Kabrit air base. The Il-28 bombers then moved to Cairo West while the MiG fighters flew to Almaza. By early 1956 the EAF had five fighter and ground-attack squadrons though only three were operational while the others converted to their new Soviet equipment. The EAF's single bomber squadron was similarly out of service as it converted to new aircraft, though the five transport, communications and navigation-training squadrons were all operational. In addition, there was the jet conversion unit, the Air Academy, plus health and agricultural spraying units. Although many changes were made to improve the quality of Egyptian pilot training, the EAF refrained from dramatically altering its programme because this would have slowed down the pace of training. At that time numbers were more important than quality and Egypt needed pilots quickly to

85

EAF Il-28 at Almaza, believed one of the first to be delivered. (*EAF*)

fly the large numbers of new aircraft arriving. The process of suddenly converting from essentially British equipment, training and organisation to Soviet equipment and ways of doing things inevitably caused problems but the EAF coped with these remarkably well. Once again the Egyptians demonstrated their adaptability and flexibility. According to the British Air Attaché there were no immediate changes in the command structure although the EAF did acquire a new Canal Zone HQ once the British had finally evacuated this area.

Years of British unwillingness to supply new equipment had meant that no new squadrons had been formed in the EAF until the arrival of some additional Meteors and Vampires in mid-1955 had permitted a modest expansion of its front-line strength. This growth was nothing, however, compared to the massive expansion programme that new Soviet supplies allowed. Some units were changing straight from piston-engined fighters to high-performance jets: 1 Squadron EAF, for example, finally gave up its very popular Hawker Furies for MiG-15s. Others, like 30 Squadron EAF, already had considerable jet experience flying Vampires before converting to MiGs. The conversion of 9 Squadron from a heavy-bomber unit flying antiquated Lancasters to high-speed Il-28 jet medium-bombers seems to have caused fewer problems than might have been expected. Though this unit was short of pilots it was expected to draw some from the transport squadrons, but the British Air Attaché predicted greater difficulty if the EAF wanted to form a second bomber squadron. There was an overall shortage of trained aircrew, yet the shortage of qualified ground-staff and mechanics was, as it always had been, much more serious. The work of the Fighter Training Unit (FTU) at Almaza was regarded as the most vital during this period of change. At the same time Egypt's political relationship with other Arab states was considered so important that Syrian as well Egyptian Air Force personnel were trained there by Czech and possibly also Russian instructors. Even so, the new high-performance Soviet jets were difficult to master; two MiG-15s and an Il-28 had been damaged in accidents at Almaza by mid-January 1956.

For decades the RAF had remained responsible for the defence of the Canal Zone and Britain had not allowed Egypt to establish an independent network of radars, anti-aircraft guns and fighters. Without direction and control from a ground-based radar network, modern jet fighter pilots would be lucky to find an intruder, let alone shoot it down. So far Egypt could only field a few French and British radar sets but these were not tied together in a network and there were huge gaps in their coverage of the Egyptian frontiers. At the end of 1955 Egypt had the following radar equipment:

12 ESV2 (six early warning plus six GCI)
2 Marconi MWT XXI (for high/low cover)
20 SFR VUXY (radar-acquisition)
20 WAXY (gun-control for light anti-aircraft guns)

Under Russian direction the beginning of a co-ordinated air defence network, using both existing radars and new systems supplied by the Soviet Union, was gradually put in place. This was to include radar sites located along the Mediterranean coast from Alexandria to Port Said and down the length of the Suez Canal to the Red Sea.

The EAF's turning to Soviet equipment and organisational systems had resulted from Egypt's inability to obtain what it considered to be its essential needs from the West; after years of fruitless efforts it had turned to the East. Once such a decision had been made it seemed at first to bear considerable fruit and the EAF was able to modernise and expand at a remarkable rate. The long-term results would be far less happy. Soviet equipment, Soviet training and Soviet organisation never gave the Egyptian Air Force the success it expected. Meanwhile the political price that Egypt would pay for turning to the Soviet Union would eventually prove to be very high indeed.

Appreciating that its days were numbered, the RAF's 205 Group had reduced its strength considerably during 1955, when the following units were based in the Canal Zone:

13 Squadron, Abu Sueir	Meteor PR10
32 Squadron, Kabrit	Vampire FB9 (moved to Shaibah 1/55)
39 Squadron, Kabrit	Meteor NF13 (moved to Luqa 1/55)
208 Squadron, Abu Sueir	Meteor FR9
84 Squadron, Fayid	Valetta C1 (moved to Abu Sueir 12/55)
114 Squadron, Fayid	Valetta C1 (moved to Abu Sueir 12/55)
216 Squadron, Fayid	Valetta C1 (moved to UK 11/55)
651 Squadron, Ismailia	Auster AOP6 (disbanded 11/55)

During the year 205 Group had suffered the loss of six aircraft in accidents, although the only fatalities (two) occurred when Auster TW621 of 651 Squadron crashed near Jebel Ataqa on 27 August. 205 Group effectively ceased to exist in October 1955 when Air Vice-Marshal Barnett moved his rear headquarters to Cyprus, although disbandment would not come into effect until April 1956, when the last Canal Zone airfield still under RAF control, Abu Sueir, was handed over to the Egyptians. Until then, a token force would remain to oversee the British military withdrawal under the terms of the 1954 treaty.

The ceremonial raising of the EAF standard over a Canal Zone airfield following the British withdrawal; these ceremonies were highly significant to the Egyptians. (*EAF*)

THE SYRIAN AIR FORCE

Among the first 15 cadets at the SAF's Air Academy in 1953, only recently expanded from a mere flying school, was a young Lt Hafiz al-Asad (destined to become the country's President), who came top of his class in his first two years of training and won a trophy for aerobatics on graduation. In 1955 he was posted to al-Mezze for advanced fighter training and a conversion course on Fiat G59Bs.

During the summer of 1954, six ex-RAF Meteor NF13 night fighters (s/n 471–476) were supplied by Britain, although a further seven refurbished Meteor F8s and two FR9 fighter-reconnaissance aircraft were not delivered until 1956. Hardly surprisingly, the stop-start unpredictable nature of arms supplies from the West, coupled with the growing European and North American partiality for Israel, encouraged Syria, like Egypt, to turn to the Soviet Union for modern combat aircraft and other weaponry and, in 1955, 25 MiG-15 fighters plus a small number of MiG-15UTI conversion trainers were ordered. A training mission composed of Russian and Warsaw Pact personnel was sent to Syria to instruct the SAF to fly and maintain the new jets. The Syrian MiGs were actually shipped to Alexandria and trucked to Almaza where they were assembled. Meanwhile, Syrian aircrew and maintenance personnel trained alongside the Egyptians at courses in the USSR and Eastern Europe, while others attended a six-month course in Egypt. Initially intended to be given fighter training on the Spitfire F22, the Syrian pilots progressed to the Meteor despite the death of one of their Egyptian instructors while involved in aerobatics in a Spitfire over the training field.

THE LEBANON AIR FORCE

The Lebanon Air Force was slowly expanding and had entered the jet era when it ordered five Vampire FB52s and four T55 trainers (s/n L151, L154, L159–L160) from the British early in 1953. The first of the trainers was delivered to Kleyqate in August 1953, followed by the first FB52 in October of the same year.

THE ROYAL IRAQI AIR FORCE/THE RAF AT HABBANIYA, 1953–55

It was in 1953 that Iraq decided to adopt jet aircraft and the RIrAF chose the Vampire T55 to convert experienced pilots to jet propulsion techniques and seven trainers (s/n 333-335, 367, 386–388) were supplied; the first arrived in May of that year. A training system was established whereby newly trained pilots would proceed to jet squadrons without first having to serve on Furies. There followed an order for 15 ex-RAF Venom FB1s, the first of which was delivered in May 1954, and a dozen Vampire FB52s. An order for the more powerful

Venom FB50 followed, of which the first of 15 (s/n 352–366) arrived in April 1955.

1 Squadron	Fury FB11s and T61s
2 Squadron	Auster AOP6s and T7s
3 Squadron	Devons, Ansons, Freighters, 2 Dragonfly helicopters
4 Squadron	Fury FB11s and T61s
5 Squadron	Vampire FB52s, Venom FB50s
6 Squadron	Vampire FB52s, Venom FB50s
7 Squadron	Fury FB11s and T61s

Provost T53 intermediate trainers were on their way from the UK.

During this period, several RAF units were based intermittently at Habbaniya, including 6 and 73 Squadrons with Venom FB1s. The two squadrons lost four Vampire FB9s during 1953, although no pilot casualties were sustained. On 23 December 1954, 73 Squadron lost four of its aircraft in a sandstorm although all were abandoned successfully; in addition two others crash-landed. These losses brought the Squadron's total write-offs for the year to ten. 6 Squadron lost Venom FB1 WE428 and its pilot on 2 April 1955, a month before Habbaniya was finally handed over to RIrAF. 73 Squadron withdrew to Akrotiri, Cyprus, although 6 Squadron remained until April 1956 when it also moved to Akrotiri, having received Venom FB4s in July 1955. Although the RAF had finally withdrawn from Habbaniya, a small British team of officers and men remained to serve in an advisory capacity on Brigadier Abadi's staff, in the Flying College and with individual squadrons. Additionally, 32 Squadron was based at Shaibah in southern Iraq between January 1955 and November 1956, after which it moved to Amman, Jordan.

THE ROYAL JORDANIAN AIR FORCE/
THE RAF AT AMMAN AND MAFRAQ, 1953–55

By early 1953, the Royal Jordanian Air Force (formerly the Arab Legion Air Force), commanded by Wg Cdr Jock Dalgleish, seconded from the RAF, had obtained several ex-RAF Austers and a twin-engined Dove for the use of King Hussein, who had expressed a wish to learn to fly. Dalgleish became his tutor and his first flights were accomplished in an Auster, before he progressed to the Dove, on which he eventually soloed.

The British government authorised the presentation of ten Vampire FB9s to Jordan in December 1955, these being allocated RJAF serial numbers F600–F609. In 1955 the RJAF acquired two ex-RAF Vampire T11s (minus ejector seats) to convert pilots to fly the FB9s. One of the pilots converted to jet flying in a T11 at this time was young King Hussein himself; in his autobiography, the King wrote of an incident in which he was involved:

"Dalgleish and I had just landed one [Vampire T11] and were halfway down the runway when the port wheel collapsed. The aircraft slewed round and we slithered to a stop on our drop tank. I had often anticipated a moment like this and wondered how quickly it would take me to react. I need not have worried. We were out of that aircraft in a matter of seconds. The damage was not serious."

89

The young King Hussein with Wg Cdr Jock Dalgleish and a Vampire T11 of the RJAF. (*Uneasy Lies The Head*)

A Jordanian pilot boarding RJAF Vampire FB9, s/n F605. (*Authors' collection*)

The young King enjoyed flying and took every opportunity to take to the air. On one occasion, when an RAF aircraft was reported missing near Amman, he went out with Dalgleish on a dawn search for it.

The RAF maintained a presence during this period, using both Mafraq and Amman, 249 Squadron being the resident unit with its Vampire FB9s, and later Venom FB1s, having taken over from 6 Squadron in June 1954. The Squadron lost five of its aircraft through accidents during its first six months at Amman, although all the pilots survived. A further five Vampires and Venoms were lost the following year, one pilot being killed when WK472 crashed east of Amman on 23 March 1955. The Squadron took charge of a former RJAF Tiger Moth (s/n T-20) in 1955, this being allocated the registration TJ-AAG. Many of the RAF pilots enjoyed the change of charge, spending off-duty hours cavorting under Jordan's clear blue skies.

Chapter Six

THE BLOODY ROAD TO SUEZ
January to October 1956

"He who is the enemy of my enemy is my friend."

Arab proverb

The early months of 1956 were relatively quiet in the Middle East and only towards the spring did activity return to its normal level. The Israeli assumption that the Egyptians would require several months to absorb the influx of the new Soviet equipment proved correct and, during that period of transition, the EAF suffered a number of accidents. At the time these were described in the British press as 'alarming', but a more recent analysis shows that they were proportionately much the same as those suffered by Western air forces while making similar transition to high-powered second-generation jet combat aircraft. It was claimed by US intelligence that by May 1956 there had been at least six and possibly ten accidents involving MiG-15s, and a further three accidents involving Il-28s. The EAF's two MiG squadrons, established at Almaza in December 1955, received Soviet bloc instructors, apparently both Russian and Czech, who had already given Egyptian pilots hurried MiG conversion courses using MiG-15UTI trainers at Kabrit air base.

On 15 January 1956 a flight of MiG-15s flew over Cairo to display the EAF's new jets. At the time the Western press assumed that these were flown by Czech and Russian instructors, though this probably was not the case. The following day Egyptian pilots flew over Bilbeis Air Academy in a formation representing the Egyptian flag for the benefit of President Nasser. On the last day of the month, the Czech Ambassador in Cairo presented the President with a five-seater Mraz Sokol to cement the supposed Czech arms deal. For its part, the Soviet Union presented Nasser with a new Il-14 transport (s/n 1101) as his personal aircraft, which replaced the weary Dakota (s/n 113) he had inherited from the former Royal Flight. Meanwhile, the EAF was in the midst of a full-scale publicity campaign to make young Egyptians more air-minded. The *Armed Forces* magazine advertised: 'Fly in a MiG from Cairo to Alexandria and back', applicants being advised not to eat breakfast prior to the flight! The aircraft in question were obviously MiG-15UTI trainers.

In addition to their more normal defence duties, personnel of the EAF were sometimes called upon to help in those emergencies that were bound to occur in a country like Egypt, situated as it was at the crossroads of international civil aviation. At 0500 on 20 February, a Douglas DC-6B (F-BGOD) of the French airline Transports Aérien Intercontinentaux, on a flight from Paris to Saigon, crashed 33 miles south-east of the Cairo to Suez road. When the first distress call was received, Sqn Ldr Niyazy of the EAF immediately took off from Almaza to locate the wreck. He reported it to be burning in the desert and on returning to Almaza, set out for the crash site in a Dragonfly helicopter and picked up four survivors. Two Cessna light aircraft flown by TWA pilots based in Cairo then joined in the rescue attempt. The two Americans and Niyazy, who made a further six flights in the Dragonfly, brought back a dozen more survivors to the French Hospital in Cairo. The injured pilot of the DC-6B proved to be Capitaine Billet, who at the time held the world long-distance record for civil aircraft.

Despite turning to the Soviet Union for arms, the Egyptian government still hoped to remain genuinely neutral. Early in 1956 another request to purchase British military equipment was made to London. Egypt was particularly interested in Bristol Sycamore helicopters, Lincoln heavy bombers and the latest Hawker Hunter jet fighters. The British government, however, was not prepared to see a neutral Egypt and refused these requests in the hope that Egypt would eventually be obliged to return to the British sphere of influence and to Britain as its main source of defence purchases. Partly as a result of this, as well as other British and American political actions, Egypt fell out of the pro-Western orbit altogether.

By early April, with political obstacles cleared, the first six Mystère IVAs for the IDF/AF were ready for ferrying from France to Israel. A few weeks earlier, a small group of Israeli pilots, under the command of Rav-Seren Peled who had just handed over 113 Squadron to Rav-Seren Hod, had arrived at the Armée de l'Air's Cambrai air base, for a conversion course on the Mystère, and it was these pilots who undertook the long flight to Israel with only a single refuelling stop at Brindisi in southern Italy. They were accompanied by a Noratlas of 103 Squadron flown by Seren Uri Yaffe. Although the French had offered one of their pilots to lead the way, the offer was refused and when all six aircraft arrived safely at Hatzor, the pilots were welcomed by Prime Minister Ben-Gurion, the Treasury Minister, the French Ambassador, and Aluf Tolkowsky, commander of the IDF/AF. A further 18 Mystères followed in May and by the end of the month 101 Squadron, which had been disbanded the previous November as a Mustang unit at Ramat David, was officially re-formed at Hatzor on 1 April as the first Mystère squadron, with Peled in command.

The arrival of the Mystères fulfilled Tolkowsky's requirement for an advanced fighter roughly equivalent to the MiG-15, although it was feared that the MiG had the ability to outclimb the French fighter. An intensive period of training commenced, with a number of Ouragan pilots converting to the Mystère while still serving with 113 Squadron. The pool of pilots who were able to fly both the Mystère and Ouragan would serve to good effect during the Sinai campaign. Gradually the IDF/AF was phasing out of service the veteran piston-engine types. During May the Spitfires were withdrawn from use and replaced in the OTU role by the Mustangs, while at Tel Nof a new Mustang unit was formed, 116 Squadron. This emergency squadron was manned by the Flying School's instructors under the command of Rav-Seren Itshak Yavneh. The days of the Mustangs in the OTU role were numbered, however, since it was decided to convert pilots from the Harvard direct to the Meteor.

Throughout the spring of 1956 there had been repeated clashes along the Sinai

Ouragan s/n 29 of 113 Squadron; an aircraft from this unit accounted for an EAF Vampire in April 1956. (*IAF Magazine collection*)

and Gaza Strip borders. On 5 April, an Israeli patrol encountered at the Gaza border caused the Egyptians to open fire, following which the Israelis returned fire, using mortars against Gaza town centre, where 56 civilians were killed and 103 wounded. The Egyptian authorities retaliated by permitting a number of Palestinian fedayeen raids across the ceasefire lines. A dozen Israelis were killed. This action heightened aerial activity, Egyptian and Israeli jets continuing to violate each other's frontiers collecting reconnaissance information. An inevitable skirmish occurred at dusk on 12 April when a pair of EAF Vampires was intercepted near Sde Boker (the kibbutz of which Ben-Gurion was a member) by two Ouragans led by Segen David Kishon, on his first operational sortie. The Vampires were seen near Ramon Crater. The sun was quite low and Kishon was able to pull the Ouragan (s/n 323) up and turn into the Egyptian jets. He fired a long burst at one, s/n 1584 flown by Flt Lt Lufti, and it caught fire, although the pilot was able to carry out a crash-landing near Abdat, a few kilometres south of Sde Boker. The second Vampire turned to face the attack but, after several inconclusive manoeuvres, retreated west to Sinai. Israeli troops arrived on the scene and arrested Lutfi who, as a consequence, would spend almost a year in captivity.

The IDF/AF's Order of Battle by the early summer months included three jet fighter units: 101 Squadron with Mystère IVs and 113 Squadron with Ouragans at Hatzor, plus 117 Squadron with Meteor F8s and FR9s at Ramat David. One of the new Ouragans was lost during the early part of the year when French pilot Lt Claude Foloun, who was on an air-to-air combat training demonstration flight, crashed at Hatzor, losing his life. Numerically the strength of that force was in excess of 60 fighters, but when compared with the combined jet fighter strength of the EAF (100 MiG-15s), the RIrAF (with several squadrons of Vampires and Venoms), the Syrian Air Force (a squadron of Meteor F8s) and the RJAF (with a squadron of Vampires), it was far from adequate to fulfil its role. Thus, an additional 36 Mystère IVs were ordered from France in an effort to balance the shortfall. For political considerations, the secrecy of numbers of aircraft included in the new procurement was of the utmost impor-

The wreckage of the EAF Vampire shot down by Segen David Kishon. (*IAF Magazine collection*)

tance, but how to preserve secrecy while staging through Italy was the problem. In the event, this was overcome by Israeli HQ advising the Italian authorities that 18 of the original batch of Mystères supplied by the French had to be returned to France for repairs following the discovery of technical problems. Thus, following the arrival at Hatzor of the initial 18 aircraft of the new order on 18 and 19 August, the remaining 18 still in France staged through Brindisi on 22 August, posing as the repaired aircraft and bearing the same serial numbers of aircraft from the original delivery. The bluff worked without hindrance, but, as Rav-Seren Bar, who performed two ferry flights from France to Israel, commented: "I am in doubt whether the Italians did not know the truth . . ."

At about the same time six further Ouragans arrived from France, together with three of six ex-RAF Meteor NF13 night fighters on order from Britain; the latter carried ferry registrations 4X-FNA (ex-WM366), 4X-FNB (ex-WM334) and 4X-FND (ex-WM309) and became s/n 50, 51 and 52 in IDF/AF service. Both Egypt and Syria received a similar small number of Meteor NF13s* to preserve the balance in the Middle East and Britain's interests in the area. All three air forces clearly needed night fighters, Israel in particular fearing that the EAF's new Il-28s would be able to penetrate her airspace at night without any effective opposition. A night fighter unit, 119 Squadron, was formed at Ramat David under the command of Seren Tsiddon, who, together with his navigator, was despatched on a night fighting course with the RAF. A second pilot and navigator followed.

Although the EAF's main priority was to train and expand its ranks, and to bring the new Soviet jets into service, air defence remained a major worry for

---

* The EAF's six Meteor NF13s were numbered 1427–1432, while the SAF's became S471–476, and were formerly WM330, WM332–333, WM336–337 and WM341. The Syrians also received two ex-RAF Meteor FR9s (WB133 and WX972) during 1956, which became S480 and S481.

Egyptian military planners and the weaknesses were fully recognised within the EAF. These included poor flying discipline and occasionally bad techniques. According to the British Air Attaché many EAF pilots also suffered from a lack of alertness and were in no position to take on the Israelis. During 1956 the nucleus of a fighter control system was already taking shape under the command of Air Marshal Ali Attia, who had until recently been the Egyptian Air Attaché in London. Meanwhile the EAF's main role was expected to remain the close support of Egyptian ground forces, as it had been during the 1948–49 War. By the summer of 1956 Egypt appeared to have a relatively strong attack force, though air defence remained a weakness despite the addition of new MiG fighters.

On 13 June 1956 the last British troops left Egyptian soil under the terms of the Anglo-Egyptian Agreement of 1954. They slipped quietly away from Port Said to avoid any embarrassing publicity. Five days later, President Nasser, 'with tears in his eyes', hoisted the Egyptian flag to the masthead over the Port Said Navy House, the former British Naval HQ. As jet fighters flew overhead and an Egyptian frigate fired a 21-gun salute, Nasser told the vast cheering crowd:

"This is the most memorable moment of a lifetime . . . We have dreamed of this moment which had been denied to our fathers, grandfathers and our brothers who have fought for years to achieve this moment and to see the Egyptian flag alone in our skies. Citizens, we pray God no other flag will ever fly over our land."

With the departure of the last British troops, celebrations were held to mark the end of foreign occupation of Egyptian soil. During the same period a nation-wide plebiscite was held to agree a new constitution. A wave of patriotic fervour spread across the country and the Revolutionary government had no difficulty in claiming the credit for Egypt's long awaited liberation from British interference. The Revolutionary Council formed during the coup of 1952 was dissolved and its military leaders mostly gave up their uniforms, while Nasser was elected President in a landslide victory. Throughout Egypt there was a general feeling that a new age of true independence had dawned for the country. But in some other countries things were seen very differently.

The Israeli government was clearly alarmed by Egypt's new political independence, its growing influence throughout the Arab world and above all by its apparently growing military power. In Britain old attitudes remained deeply entrenched. The British government also deeply resented what many saw as her political humiliation by a small country led by a man the British press largely characterised as a military dictator. France could not accept Egypt's loudly proclaimed support for the independence of French-ruled Algeria and was quite prepared to use a growing if unofficial alliance with Israel as a means of punishing what it saw as Egyptian interference in French affairs.

In response to impassioned pleas by Egypt and Israel for more arms, both Britain and America refused to budge from their position of intransigence. However, in an attempt to temper the potentially volatile situation, US Secretary of State Dulles advised Dag Hammarskjöld, the United Nations Secretary-General, of a scheme that had President Eisenhower's approval, whereby (a) 24 F-86 Sabre jets were to be based on Cyprus and available to Israel, and (b) a cargo vessel loaded with tanks, recoilless rifles and grenade launchers (to be attached to the US Sixth Fleet in the Mediterranean) for delivery to Egypt or another Arab state 'in the event of war, to whichever side was deemed to be the victim of aggression'. It seems that Hammarskjöld was not enthusiastic with the idea of additional arms being sent to the Middle East, and the suggestion was allowed to fade away without either of the protagonists being aware of the proposal. Quite how the armed forces were expected to use such a sudden donation of military hardware for which they would presumably not be trained was also never explained.

Egypt's purchase of large quantities of Russian military equipment was seen in America as evidence that Egypt was drifting into the Soviet sphere of influence. Naturally enough this fear was played upon by those sympathetic to Zionism and Israel. As a result Britain and America withdrew earlier offers to help finance the building of the Aswan High Dam, President Nasser's prestige development programme and a symbol of Egypt's desire to modernise its economy. Western governments seemed to have failed to understand just how important the High Dam project was to the entire Egyptian nation, not simply to Nasser. When Western offers of financial help were withdrawn for clearly political reasons, this was again seen by the Egyptians as an example of the West attempting to pressure them into adopting a pro-Western position. Such pressure was, however, intolerable to the Egyptians in their present highly patriotic and even nationalistic mood. As a result, Nasser's declaration on 26 July that he would finance the High Dam project by nationalising the Suez Canal was greeted with considerable enthusiasm by the Egyptian people. The President argued that while Egypt received an annual income of £1 million ($3 million) from users of the Canal, the owners – the Compagnie Universelle du Canal Maritime de Suez – collected a revenue in excess of £30 million (approaching $100 million). Nasser's impassioned proclamation over Cairo Radio to his people ended with the words:

> "The Suez Canal belongs to us. The income will be ours in the future. The Canal was built by Egyptians. One hundred and twenty thousand [sic] Egyptians died digging it. A new Suez Canal company will be formed. From now on we will rely on our own strength, our own muscle. The Canal will be run by Egyptians, Egyptians, Egyptians! Do you hear me? Egyptians!"

London and Paris immediately denounced Nasser's action as a flagrant violation of international law; the United States promptly put a block on Egyptian assets, while Khrushchev warned, wagging a finger at Britain and France, that the Suez affair must be settled peacefully. Not only was the idea of nationalising the Canal very unwelcome to many Western governments but it was seen as a direct threat to a vital international waterway, although Nasser gave assurances that it would remain open, despite the offices of the Canal Company being occupied by Egyptian troops. Declarations in the Western press that the Egyptians would also be unable to operate the Canal properly were, however, not taken seriously as it had been run largely by Egyptian personnel for many years.

The London Conference on the Suez Canal opened on 16 August, with the Americans and Russians using delaying tactics, whereas the French were on the offensive. Britain's delegates hesitated, the Labour Party showing signs of dissent. The conference ended on 23 August with a decision to send a committee of five members (headed by Mr Robert Menzies, Prime Minister of Australia) to Egypt, where they were to demand that Nasser hand over the Canal to a new international company. Mr Menzies and his committee duly arrived in Cairo on 2 September, but President Nasser totally rejected the Anglo-French proposal. Four days later, Prime Minister Eden wrote to President Eisenhower announcing his intention of referring the matter to the United Nations Security Council in order to justify launching a military operation, hoping to force the issue, adding:

"The seizure of the Suez Canal is, we are convinced, the opening gambit in a planned campaign designed by Nasser to expel all Western influence and interests from Arab countries. He believes that, if he can get away with this and if he can successfully defy 18 nations, his prestige in Arabia will be so great that he will be able to mount revolutions of young officers in Saudi Arabia, Jordan, Syria, and Iraq. We know from our joint sources that he is already preparing a revolution in Iraq, which is the most stable and progressive. These new governments will in effect be Egyptian satellites if not Russian ones. They will have to place their united oil resources under the control of a united Arabia led by Egypt and under Russian influence. When that moment comes, Nasser can deny oil to Western Europe and we shall all be at his mercy . . ."

Despite Eden's undisguised appeal to Eisenhower, American assistance was still not forthcoming.

The darkening political crisis was, naturally enough, seen very differently in Egypt. The Egyptians regarded themselves as victims of outside interference. They also felt that their country was being used by the Great Powers as a political pawn in the Cold War between the West and the Soviet bloc. This interpretation was summed up by Dr Abdel-Kader Hatem, head of Egypt's information services during the 1956 crisis:

"Egypt replied [to the British and American withdrawal of offers to finance the Aswan High Dam] on 26 July by nationalising the Suez Canal. At the same time she made it clear that she would respect accepted international practice by paying compensation to the concessionaries, the large French-controlled Suez Canal Company, and the President also made good his intention to keep the Canal open to international shipping. The Great Powers had no real grounds for complaint, while, in terms of Egypt's own development, the nationalisation was necessary to provide funds for the construction of the High Dam. Therefore no reasonable case existed for outside intervention on the plea of keeping the Canal operational. The only country whose interests were badly effected by the new state of affairs was Israel, which suffered from the fedayeen raids in the Gaza area and from Egypt's blockade of the Strait of Tiran, burdens for which she had only herself to blame, for they were the consequences of her own infringements of Egyptian territory."

Nasser's nationalisation of the Canal was certainly a bold political move, but it would have grave consequences. Israel had little direct interest in the Canal and the Egyptian government was correct in assuming that Israel would not go to war over the issue. Cairo was also correct in believing that Israel would not attack Egypt on its own, and in expecting the United States to mediate if the dispute between Egypt and Israel did lead to war. What the Egyptian government failed to recognise was the extraordinary possibility that Israel would form an anti-Egyptian alliance with both France and Britain. This miscalculation was based on a misunderstanding of the depth of French resentment over Egypt's support for the Algerian independence movement, of British emotional investment in the Suez Canal, or of the depth of Prime Minister Eden's personal animosity towards Nasser. Indeed, as early as April, the first of a series of secret Franco-Israeli conferences had taken place in France, when the initial discussions concerning the invasion of Egypt were aired, and further orders placed for Mystère IVs, tanks, mobile guns, ammunition and radar. An agreement was signed, this time without the approval or even the knowledge, of the Americans or the British.

To be on the safe side, however, Egypt did halt organised Palestinian guerilla incursions into Israel and moved troops towards the border in Sinai. Half of the Egyptian Army was stationed in Sinai and the Canal Zone. Reserves were mobilised and plans to change the national guard militia into a better equipped part-time Army of National Liberation were speeded up. In September all British and French Suez Canal pilots were ordered to leave the country. Then, as some people felt that popular morale was weakening, President Nasser delivered another of his fiery speeches, this time to EAF cadets at the Bilbeis Air Academy, announcing that Egypt would certainly fight if attacked. Clearly aspirations outpaced performance at this stage. As if to symbolise this fact, two of the EAF's new Yak-11 trainers, the first dozen of which had arrived less than a month before, were damaged while rehearsing for the flypast that followed Nasser's speech, as Flt Lts Brisk and Larcombe, two of the British instructors, recalled:

"The Egyptians did not get on very well with the Yak. At a rehearsal for a grand flypast to be reviewed by Colonel Nasser, even two of the Egyptian instructors crashed in their Yaks on a low-level run. Five were written off or damaged out of the twelve."

An EAF Yak-11 trainer (s/n 524) photographed at Almaza. In EAF service the Yak was painted sky-blue overall with yellow fuselage and wing bands. (*Authors' collection*)

An Egyptian pilot also recalled that his colleagues found the type very sluggish when compared to the Harvard they had previously flown. In addition to the loss of a number of the original batch of Yaks in training accidents, another of the trainers had been impounded by the British in Cyprus following engine trouble during its delivery flight from the Soviet bloc, although this was released later.

Tension along the borders reached new heights. On the night of 10/11 September, the Jordanian police station at al-Rahwa, south of Hebron, was attacked by Israeli forces while a Piper Cub of 100 Squadron acted as an airborne observation post. Two nights later the target for Israeli attack was the Jordanian police station at Gharandal, 70km north of Eilat, when five Piper Cubs participated in the operation, mainly in the role of air ambulances. In the event no Israeli casualties were suffered, although 16 Jordanians were killed. A third assault against a Jordanian police station occurred on the night of 25/26 September, Hossan near Bethlehem being targeted, four Piper Cubs taking part in another successful action for the Israeli forces. These operations were justified as retaliation for earlier attacks by Palestinian guerillas, in which nine Israeli citizens and seven Israeli soldiers had been killed and many others injured. In fact they themselves led to Arab counter-raids in which five civilians were killed at Sodom on 4 October and two agricultural workers killed near Tel Mond (east of Netanya) five days later, followed by a further Israeli strike in which the IDF/AF became involved. The target on this occasion was the Jordanian police station at Kalkiliah east of Tel Mond, which was attacked on the night of 10/11 October.

As with the earlier operations, Piper Cubs provided communication relays and observation services as the police station was blown up by ground forces, but Israeli troops blocking the road from Azun to the police station were then engaged by Jordanian reinforcements and desperately required help. The seriousness of the situation led to a pair of Mustangs from the emergency unit at Tel Nof being scrambled, together with two others from Ramat David. The

Mustang s/n 71 of 105 Squadron was an ex-Swedish Air Force example. It was written off in a forced-landing near Yeroham on 4 September 1956 due to loss of oil pressure. The pilot was Eldad Paz. (*Eldad Paz*)

four aircraft were able to make only low-level passes over the area since the pilots were unable to distinguish friend from foe in the darkness, but their presence enabled the Israeli survivors to withdraw. Segen Ze'ev Sharon, who flew with Segen Ami Hativa from Tel Nof, recalled:

> "We were at [Segen David] Kishon's wedding. It was two a.m. when we returned and we went to sleep. After an hour or so they woke us up, a scramble to . . . Azun. Take-off and [Lt Yonatan] Atkes (the air/ground co-operation officer) will guide us . . . but he guided us nowhere, nothing came of this. We jettisoned our bombs in the sea and landed at Tel Nof. I was so tired . . . landed heavily and some five rockets fell off my wing."

Meanwhile, Seren Lavon and Segen Aryeh Tse'elon arrived over the area from Ramat David, as the latter reported:

> "They scrambled us and told us there was a problem with the paratroopers and we had to help them. We flew over Kfar Saba so that the air/ground co-operation officer would guide us. Lavon had a problem with his aircraft and he returned to base. I told him I saw something, he said: 'drop it there.' I dropped two 250kg bombs and the mission was over."

It had been a costly operation for both sides: 18 Israeli soldiers killed and 68 wounded, against 88 Jordanians killed and 15 wounded.

As a result of the serious nature of the Israeli assault and severe casualties inflicted, King Hussein of Jordan asked the British to invoke the Anglo-Jordanian Treaty and send the RAF from Cyprus to help his country. Britain's response was for the British Chargé d'Affaires in Tel Aviv to advise Prime Minister Ben-Gurion that Britain would be obligated to go to Jordan's aid if Israel took further military action against her neighbour. Indeed, British Prime Minister Eden implied that 'our aircraft were on the point of going up', while agreeing in principle to the entry into Jordan of an Iraqi Army division to 'bolster Jordanian defence'. The latest British ultimatum prompted Rav-Aluf Moshe Dayan, Commander of the IDF, to comment:

> "I must confess to the feeling that, save for the Almighty, only the British are capable of complicating affairs to such a degree. At the very moment when they are preparing to topple Nasser, who is a common enemy of theirs and Israel's, they insist on getting the Iraqi Army into Jordan even if such action leads to war between Israel and Jordan in which they, the British, will take part against Israel."

He added:

> "I do not know if the Royal Air Force would in fact have attacked our planes if the battle had continued after daylight; but the general view among us is that since the Jordanians sacked Glubb [General John Glubb, former British commander of the Jordanian Arab Legion], Britain is anxious to show them that this was a mistake, and that she is their only faithful prop upon whom they can depend for defence against Israel."

Thus, at the eleventh hour, Britain was seemingly girding its loins in a show of strength against both Israel and Egypt; the former, an ally by treaty although a former enemy, the latter, an enemy although a former friend! The British Lion appeared to be biting its own tail. Britain's dilemma was further deepened by the increasingly hostile exchange of correspondence between Prime Minister Eden and Soviet Premier Marshal Bulganin who, aware of the Anglo-French military build-up in the Mediterranean, reminded Eden that:

> "The United Nations Charter directly forbids the employment of force against any state except in cases of self-defence."

And he went on to make the following salient points:

> "Can all these actions by Britain and France be regarded as compatible with their participation in the United Nations? The British and French governments evidently intend to seize the Suez Canal, which passes across the territory of Egypt and is under Egyptian sovereignty. But, Mr Prime Minister, I beg you to consider what this could end in . . . Neither Egypt nor Algeria can be subjugated. Attempts to do so are inevitably doomed to failure . . . It is said sometimes that the Russians are inciting Egypt. But such statements are utterly groundless . . . How can the Soviet Union support an unjust cause . . . and threats against Egypt? How can the Soviet Union fail to regard Egypt's position favourably if she is defending her sovereignty? Under such circumstances, how can one fail to be on the side of Egypt, if one is guided by the noble principles of the United Nations? It is evident that both in Britain and France there are certain circles which are instigating hostilities against Egypt . . . I must tell you that the Soviet Union, as a great power interested in the maintenance of peace, cannot hold aloof from this question."

Bulganin's letter ended with an ominous caution:

> "We want to warn you in a friendly way."

A similar letter was sent to the French Prime Minister, M. Guy Mollet. In his reply to Bulganin, Eden continued to emphasise that the Anglo-French agreement actually called for a peaceful solution to the problem, and that both Britain and France were acting within the terms of the United Nations Charter to protect the independence of the Suez Canal as an international waterway. Eden went on to condemn President Nasser as a militarist, citing the seizure of the premises of the Canal Company by armed troops, when British and French civilian employees were threatened, as a point in question. Mollet's response, as to be expected, was in a similar vein.

However, to add to Eden's worries, President Eisenhower's letter of similar vintage contained the following passage:

> "The use of military force against Egypt under present circumstances might have consequences even more serious than causing the Arabs to support Nasser. It might cause a serious misunderstanding between our two countries . . ."

With both the United States and the Soviet Union clearly showing their hands, commonsense should have demanded that a halt be called to any intended use of force against Egypt by Britain and France, even at this late stage, but commonsense did not prevail.

With daylight on 22 October, a French Navy P2V-6 Neptune of 21F Flotille arrived off the Israeli coast en route from Karouba via Bizerte (Tunisia). Its pilot, Ens deV Le Chalony, having failed to make contact with Israeli air traffic control, landed the aircraft at Hatzor air base, where its arrival was not expected. While taxiing to nearby hangars, the Neptune was followed by four armoured cars and, having disembarked, Le Chalony explained to an Israeli officer that he was acting on orders issued directly from the French Prime Minister. The crew was led away and it was not until Aluf-Mishne Weizman arrived that the situation was clarified. Once fed, watered and rested, Le Chalony was advised that he and his crew were to return to Karouba at 1900, with five passengers embarked aboard his aircraft. After an eight-hour flight, the VIPs disembarked at Karouba where they boarded an SO-30P Bretagne transport, which flew them to Paris. Although the French crews were unaware of the identities of their passengers, they were in fact the Israeli delegation (including Rav-Aluf Dayan and Mrs Golda Meir) on their way to France to finalise an agreement with representatives from Britain and France for a co-ordinated assault on Egypt.

All three members of the secret alliance wished to strike a blow at Egypt's growing military power and political influence. Each of the protagonists had its own reasons for this drastic action: Egypt had bloodied Britain's nose; Algeria had bloodied France's nose and Nasser openly supported the Algerian nationalists in their struggle; while Israel was happy to receive support from such unexpected sources in her continuing struggle against Egypt. In Anglo-French eyes it was Egypt's turn to be the whipping boy. Militarily, Egypt's fate was sealed with the signing of the document, which took place at the Sèvres villa of the French Minister of Defence, and which became known as the Treaty of Sèvres.

> "For the British, their ends were twofold: to preserve freedom of traffic on the Canal and to reaffirm their position in the Middle East, if necessary even with the help of Nasser. The French aims were twofold also, but far from the same: France wanted to maintain freedom of the Canal and to crush Nasser flat, as an enemy of France in North Africa. The Israeli government for its part was against the Anglo-French landing and would much rather have acted alone."

The agreed plan was for Israel to launch an attack in the Sinai Peninsula, as near to the Suez Canal as possible, with an airborne operation, hoping that the Egyptians would think that this was just another retaliation operation, albeit unexpectedly daring. The British and French would claim that a major conflict so near to the Suez Canal – an international sea lane – was a severe risk to shipping in the area and would present both Israel and Egypt with an ultimatum to withdraw from the Canal Zone. Israel would obviously respect the ultimatum but Egypt would naturally reject it, thus giving Britain and France the excuse required to land their forces at the northern entrance to the Canal, near Port Said and Port Fuad. To ensure that the Egyptian Air Force would not interfere with these landings, EAF bases were to be attacked. It was hoped that Nasser's inevitable defeat and the loss of the Canal Zone would lead to his overthrow in favour of a Western-affiliated regime. The secret document stated:

> "On the afternoon of 29 October 1956 the Israeli forces will launch a large-scale attack on the Egyptian forces, with the object of reaching the Canal Zone on the following day. Having been informed of the event, the Governments of Great Britain and France will on 30 October 1956, separately and simultaneously, address appeals formulated in the spirit of the following essential points:

> "To the Egyptian Government:
> – Absolute ceasefire.
> – Withdrawal of all forces to 15 kilometres from the Canal.
> – Acceptance of the occupation by Anglo-French forces of key positions on the Canal, so as to guarantee the free passage of vessels of all nations until the conclusion of a definite agreement.

> To the Israeli Government:
> – Absolute ceasefire.
> – Withdrawal of forces to 15 kilometres from the Canal.
> – The Israeli Government to be notified that the French and British Governments have required the Egyptian Government to accept the temporary occupation by Franco-British forces of the key positions on the Canal.

> Should either government reject the appeal, or not give its consent within twelve hours, the Anglo-French forces would be in a position to take the steps necessary to ensure that their demands were met.
> In the event of the Egyptian Government not accepting the conditions in the appeal it has received, it will not be required of the Israeli Government that it should meet the conditions of the appeal. If the Egyptian Government does not accept the conditions presented to it within the stipulated period, the Anglo-French forces will launch an attack against the Egyptian forces in the early hours of 31 October 1956.
> The Israeli Government will send forces to occupy the west bank of the Gulf of Aqaba, as also the islands of Tiran and Sunagrin, so as to ensure freedom of navigation in that gulf. Israel will not attack while the operation against Israel is proceeding. But if Jordan attacks Israel during that period the British Government will not come to Jordan's assistance."

The final paragraph, whilst it brought relief to Prime Minister Eden – who apparently destroyed his copy of the agreement in the futile hope that his collusion with Israel would not be established – contravened the Anglo-Jordan Treaty and caused Lord Louis Mountbatten, First Sea Lord, to observe:

> ". . . if Israel attacked Jordan and the United States went to Jordan's aid against Israel then we and the United States would be fighting on opposite sides. We should be the unwilling allies of Israel and our forces in Jordan would be hostages to fortune."

Eden himself endeavoured to play down any suggestion of collusion with Israel:

> "We must face the risk that we should be accused of collusion with Israel. But this charge was liable to be brought against us in any event, for it could now be assumed that, if an Anglo-French operation were undertaken against Egypt, we should be unable to prevent the Israelis from launching a parallel attack themselves; and it was preferable that we should be seen to be holding the balance between Israel and Egypt rather than appear to be accepting Israeli co-operation in an attack on Egypt alone."

Such were the stakes, with the Americans being left in the dark; meanwhile the possibility of the Soviet Union intervening on the side of Egypt does not appear to have been afforded serious consideration at this stage of the conspiracy. Those who made this secret agreement also seem to have ignored or discounted the way their proposed military operation would be presented in the world's press, not least in Arab newspapers. Even in its most simplistic form it could, and indeed would, be shown as an Israeli conquest or occupation of the entire Sinai Peninsula, one of Egypt's largest and historically most significant provinces. Not only would Egypt, and by extension the entire Arab world, lose this strategically and emotionally vital stretch of land, but the Egyptian Armed Forces would be obliged to withdraw into the Nile Delta, the very heartland of Egyptian civilisation. The idea that maps showing such a situation could appear on the front pages of newspapers from Marrakesh to Muscat without causing an explosion of anger was naïve to say the least. In fact the British and French governments' lack of concern about such a looming propaganda disaster merely reflected their negative attitude towards the Arab people in general, reinforcing the feeling that they and their opinions counted for little to the Western powers. A vicious circle was about to be closed: alienation, fear, paranoia, ignorance and prejudice soon becoming the common currency of relations between the West and the Arab world.

But the die was cast and plans for the Israeli invasion of Sinai were urgently finalised. It was agreed that during the initial stage of the conflict, defined as the first two days, the aim of the IDF/AF was to minimize air activity in order to deny a possible EAF attack on Tel Aviv and other Israeli towns. An attack by Egyptian Il-28s was so feared that Israeli pilots were instructed not to fly over Tel Aviv while anti-aircraft units were in action, as the gun crews had orders to fire on all aircraft passing over, thus eliminating the identification stage and reducing the reaction time of the gun crews to the minimum. However, if the EAF were to react against Israeli towns, the IDF/AF were to attack EAF bases including those west of the Suez Canal. During the second stage, from the third day onwards and following the proposed elimination of the EAF by the RAF and the Armée de l'Air, the IDF/AF was to support its ground forces, defend its airspace, and be ready for the possible intervention of Syrian and Jordanian forces, since both countries had mutual defence agreements with Egypt. The question of what might happen should Eastern bloc volunteers come to Egypt's aid was raised, prompting Rav-Aluf Dayan to reply:

> "The shorter the campaign, the greater the chances that no 'volunteers' will come. If they do come, they are likely to be Czechs or Poles but not Russians. Such 'volunteers' are likely to be not infantry units or tank crews

The EAF's first operational unit of Il-28s, 8/9 Squadron, during a flypast at Bilbeis in September 1956 (*EAF*)

but pilots, so that we shall meet them only in the air. I have no doubt that this will be less pleasant than facing Egyptian pilots, but after all, Poles and Czechs are no more than Poles and Czechs."

Amidst great secrecy, Bedek Aviation was instructed to make ready for operations the many aircraft held in storage at Lod, these to either augment existing units or to form new ones. The three B-17s were de-mothballed and placed under the command of Sgan-Aluf Ya'acov Ben-Chaim, a former commander of 69 Squadron, while Rav-Seren Yehezkiel Somekh was ordered to re-form 110 Squadron at Ramat David. The serviceable Mustangs were divided between 105 OTU Squadron under Rav-Seren Moshe Tadmor and the Flying School's emergency 116 Squadron, commanded by Rav-Seren Yavneh, while the Reconnaissance Flight was expanded into 115 Squadron under Rav-Seren Eli Eyal, a veteran of the 1948–49 War. Even the Flying School's Harvards were rendered operational, becoming 140 Squadron and manned by instructors, while the Stearmans were to operate as 147 Squadron at Ramleh under the command of Seren Meir Shefer. With the arrival of the three Meteor NF13 night fighters, a new unit, 119 Squadron, had been formed at Ramat David under the command of Seren Tsiddon, but because of the anticipated campaign looming, air and ground crews were returned to operational units. With tension mounting, three other experienced fighter pilots – Serens Shmuel Shefer, Amnon Halivni and Yoel Dan – were hurriedly called back from Canada, where they had been flying the F-86, since it was hoped that the United States would finally approve its export to Israel.

Away from the political arena, probing by Israeli units continued and, on the afternoon of 6 October, a Mosquito PR16 was despatched to reconnoitre the Mitla Pass through the Jebel Heitan mountains, some 40km west of the Suez Canal, a key point in the Sinai Desert where it was proposed that a force of paratroopers were to be dropped on Day One of the invasion. The photographs acquired by the Mosquito crew clearly indicated a small tented camp at the western approach to the Mitla Pass, where the paratroops were to be dropped. Mosquito sorties continued, increasing towards the end of the month, and one such flight on the eve of the invasion revealed that the camp at the western approach to the Mitla Pass had expanded to three huts and up to 29 tents, and was assumed to be occupied by Egyptian troops. As a consequence, the dropping zone for the Israeli paratroops was moved to the eastern entrance of the pass. The Egyptian Air Force apparently made no attempt to intercept these Israeli reconnaissance flights, Cairo perhaps hoping that information about the strengthening of Egyptian positions in the area would be sufficient to deter an Israeli attack.

To encourage Israeli participation in the secret alliance, and at Ben-Gurion's insistence – France had pledged to defend Israel from possible air attack by Egyptian jet bombers. Thus, two squadrons of Armée de l'Air fighters comprising 18 Mystère IVs from the 1/2 Cigognes and 3/2 Alsace squadrons of EC2 from Saint-Dizier via Cyprus, together with 18 F-84Fs of EC1 (the 1/1 Corse, 2/1 Morvan and 3/1 Argonne) under the command of Cdts Ladouce and Juillot, also via Cyprus, secretly flew to Israel in late October to fulfil this promise, together with additional Mystère pilots and ground personnel for a third squadron. The latter group of pilots were to fly Israeli Mystères, although Aluf-Mishne Weizman initially refused to allow the French pilots to fly his aircraft, such was his confidence in the ability of his own pilots. On landing – the Mystères at Ramat David and the F-84Fs at Lod* – the French fighters were repainted with Israeli insignia and their pilots and ground crew were issued with Israeli identity cards written in Hebrew. The French Mystères were granted the spurious IDF/AF identification '199 Squadron', the F-84Fs became '200 Squadron', and when French pilots later flew Israeli Mystères, the unit was referred to as '201 Squadron'. Colonel Maurice Perdrizet was in overall command of the French contingent, with Cdt Perseval in charge of fighter operations at Lod. The French also loaned the IDF/AF a number of Dakotas and provided the services of eight Noratlas transports (allocated the IDF/AF identification '203 Squadron'), in addition to supplying ammunition, fuel and ground equipment. Of this period Weizman noted:

"When we received the planes [Mystères] in March and April, we were supplied with small amounts of ammunition [30mm], far less than what was needed for the most modest war. Only a day or two before the operation, a French transport plane landed at our base and unloaded eight small crates containing 20,000 30mm shells. We didn't have any bombs for the Mystère, and we scarcely had any 68mm rockets. The plane was not fitted for carrying bombs – a most serious defect in what was then our most advanced plane, which was only corrected later."

---

* According to one source, the USAF had 'obligingly' airlifted from America to France extra fuel tanks for the F-84Fs and Mystères, to enable them to be flown direct to Israel without refuelling, although this was undertaken without the apparent knowledge of President Eisenhower.

F-84F 1-NX of '200 Squadron' at Lod, wearing Israeli markings in addition to Sinai stripes. (*Albert Grandolini*)

A line-up of French Mystères of EC3/2 which operated in Israel initially as '199 Squadron' of the IDF/AF. (*Albert Grandolini*)

On the night of 25 October, Ens deV Le Chalony and his Neptune crew, who had been involved in the clandestine flight from Tunisia to Israel three nights earlier, were instructed to fly three passengers from Karouba to Tel Aviv, returning empty on this occasion. The same crew was asked to make a third flight to Israel four nights later, this time carrying a French diplomat. The Neptune was followed by two Bretagnes from 31S Escadrille loaded with ammunition and captained by OE1 Buhot Launay and Lt deV Jean Courtois respectively; the latter recalled:

> "The flight must be done with the watch, the compass and the stars. Unfortunately, the weather staff at Karouba made a mistake for the winds, which drove us near the Egyptian coast. Our surveying on various VHF frequencies warned us that Egyptian fighters were up. This mistake increased our flight time. We contacted the Israeli airfield but they are under alert,

and in total blackout. They asked our origin, but we had been told not to do this."

With fuel dangerously low, the Bretagne circled off the Israeli coast awaiting permission to land, but Courtois was warned by the Israeli controller that if he did not declare his aircraft's origin in three minutes, a fighter would be sent to shoot him down:

"The choice was clear – I gave them my origin: Bizerte. [The controller replied] 'OK, we have an alert, Egyptian planes are in the area. We'll lead you to the landing strip and we'll switch on the landing lights for just one minute.' "

The Bretagne landed safely at Hatzor, the last of the trio to arrive, and the crew was taken to the Mess, where they were greeted by Rav-Aluf Dayan, who had just returned from France. Having discharged their respective cargoes, all three aircraft were airborne again before dawn, the Neptune returning to Karouba with only a few gallons of fuel remaining, while the Bretagnes flew to Cyprus.

Israel prepared for the battle with a little over 100 serviceable operational combat aircraft including 50 Mystère, Ouragan and Meteor jets and 42 Mustang and Mosquito fighter-bombers. Moreover, since the Israelis were supported by the two French squadrons, the IDF/AF could concentrate on supporting the invasion of Sinai.

IDF/AIR FORCE ORDER OF BATTLE, 29 October 1956
(serviceable aircraft only)

Ramat David

69 Squadron	2 B-17s	(an emergency reserve unit)
105 Squadron	13 Mustangs	(a unit about to be disbanded)
110 Squadron	13 Mosquito FB6s and T33s	(an emergency reserve unit)
119 Squadron	2 Meteor NF3s	(forming, with just one crew)
199 Squadron	18 Mystères	(a French unit flying French aircraft)
201 Squadron	12 Mystères	(a French unit flying IDF/AF aircraft)

Ramleh

147 Squadron	25 Kaydets	(the Flying School's Primary training squadron, normally based at Tel Nof)

Lod

200 Squadron	18 F-84Fs	(a French unit)

Tel Nof

103 Squadron	3 Noratlases, 16 Dakotas	
115 Squadron	3 Meteor T7s, 2 Mosquito PR16s	
116 Squadron	16 Mustangs	(staffed by Flying School QFIs)
117 Squadron	11 Meteor F8s and FR9s	(normally based at Ramat David)

(serviceable aircraft only)

Hatzor

101 Squadron	16 Mystères	
113 Squadron	22 Ouragans	

Beersheba

100 Squadron	11 Piper Cubs	(normally based at Ramleh)
140 Squadron	17 Harvards	(the Flying School's basic squadron normally based at Tel Nof)

Eilat

100 Squadron	4 Piper Cubs	(a detachment)

NB: Two Sikorsky S-55 helicopters had arrived from the USA in crates shortly before the start of hostilities. Rav-Seren Yehuda Arbel, commander of 103 Squadron, was in America on a helicopter conversion course, as was Seren Uri Yarom, just prior to the outbreak of the Sinai war and both were immediately recalled to fly the S-55s.

French Noratlas 63-LL in Israel during the Sinai Campaign. These transports were operated as '203 Squadron' of the IDF/AF. (*Chaim Niv*)

OTHER SIDE OF THE COIN

Although the Egyptian government had come to expect savage raids by Israeli commandos along the border and military leaders had debated the possibility of a sneak attack by British forces to seize the Suez Canal, the idea that Britain, France and Israel would join forces and simultaneously invade Sinai, bomb Egyptian military positions and assault the Suez Canal, was not seriously considered. However, such a huge build-up of military forces could not obviously remain undetected by the Egyptian intelligence services, as President Nasser's confidant Mohamed Heikal noted:

"Egypt had good friends in Cyprus. We had helped the EOKA rebels, giving them arms and money and facilities. They had returned the help by taking photographs inside the radio stations set up on Cyprus to attack Nasser. Now Egypt's intelligence service asked the EOKA rebels to report on what forces the British had on the island. They also asked Egypt's friends in the Labour movement on Malta for a similar report. Egypt had contact with all the rebels in the area. EOKA and Egypt's supporters in the Maltese Labour movement sent news of large troop, air and shipping movements based on the two islands. EOKA sent photographs of the French Noratlas transports arriving at RAF bases on Cyprus."

As a result, President Nasser and General Amr, Commander of the Egyptian Armed Forces, ordered several Army units back from the Sinai Peninsula to protect the Suez Canal and Nile Delta. This left approximately 30,000 troops and about 200 tanks to face an Israeli strike force which included around 45,000 men and in excess of 300 tanks. The main Egyptian force consisted of two divisions concentrated in north-eastern Sinai. They occupied a triangle formed by the towns or oasis villages of Rafah on the frontier, al-Arish with its air base close to the Mediterranean coast, and al-Qusseima 70km to the south. Near the centre of this triangle was the main Egyptian strongpoint around the oasis of Abu Aweiglia. While Rafah and al-Arish covered the main coastal road from Israel to al-Qantara on the Suez Canal, Abu Aweiglia covered the equally vital road from the Israeli frontier to Ismailia on the Suez Canal; and al-Qusseima covered the third road across Sinai which led back to Suez itself. Further south there were, at this time, only desert tracks, most of which converged on the central Sinai oasis of Nakhl. The coastal route around southern Sinai, following the coasts of the Gulfs of Aqaba and Suez, was not only far longer but was still little more than a difficult track. Ahead of the main Egyptian forces, the Gaza Strip was held by some 5,000 Palestinians and Egyptian National Guard militiamen. The rest of the long frontier between the Egyptian Sinai and the Israeli Negev deserts south of al-Qusseima as far as the Gulf of Aqaba was patrolled by 1,500 lightly armed but motorised troops of the Frontier Forces. These, however, were an élite paramilitary police rather than an Army unit. As far as the southern tip of the Sinai Peninsula, the strategic village and military outpost of Sharm al-Sheikh was garrisoned by 1,200 reservists who, despite the fact that they were regarded as second-line troops, would prove to be amongst the most effective and determined Egyptian soldiers in the forthcoming conflict.

The Egyptian Air Force had established a number of forward dispersal strips since the first Arab-Israeli War of 1948–49, some of which had in fact first been used during the closing stages of that conflict. But the only airfield in Sinai which could yet be described as an air base remained at al-Arish. Nevertheless, considerable effort had gone into improving these and other dispersal bases in the Nile Delta in the months preceding the Sinai War, since a British aerial attack on the Canal Zone remained an obvious possibility. The primary responsibility for the defence of airfields fell to anti-aircraft batteries as the EAF High Command clearly recognised their Air Force's limitations in aerial combat. Instead, Egypt's limited air power was to be focused on the direct support of its ground forces. Heavy AA batteries ringed the airfields near Cairo, as well as communications centres and major fuel dumps. Naval ships were expected to defend their harbours. According to copies of military orders issued at the time, Unit 1 of the Egyptian Army's anti-aircraft regiments covered the Cairo sector with 31 heavy and 11 light guns; Unit 2 covered the Northern Sector of Alexandria and the Nile Delta with 19 heavy and 14 light guns; and Unit 3 covered the Eastern Sector of Sinai and the Suez Canal with 13 heavy and nine

An unusual view of a MiG-17 of the EAF's 1 Squadron being serviced at Almaza. The construction number 8047 is stencilled beneath the tailplanes. (*Mustafa Shalabi al-Hinnawi*)

light guns. A few French-built radars of unspecified type were operational in the Canal Zone and the huge Fayoum oasis south of Cairo, a British-supplied radar being based at al-Arish, while the more recently supplied Russian radars were not yet fully operational as their crews were still under training. EAF squadrons were similarly divided into operational zones, though in this case only two: the Eastern Zone covering Sinai and the Canal Zone, and the Central Zone encompassing Cairo, the Delta and perhaps the Nile Valley. The western part of Egypt, from the Nile to the Libyan frontier, does not appear to have had an air defence zone as no threat was seen in this direction.

While still trying to adjust to the flood of new Soviet-built equipment, Egypt's military services were soon to fight a war against enemies that were not only numerically superior, but far more experienced and better trained. While the Army was the largest and politically most powerful military service in Egypt, the EAF also had considerable influence. President Nasser was very proud of his Russian-supplied Air Force and frequently employed it as a political and public relations tool.

Just before the conflict erupted, the estimated strength of the EAF was about 150 jet fighters, 24 jet bombers and 20 piston-engined fighters used in the training role. The EAF's Order of Battle included three MiG-15 squadrons (apparently 17 MiGs had been damaged or lost in accidents by September), three Vampire squadrons, one Meteor squadron, two Il-28 jet bomber units, plus five squadrons of transport and support aircraft. In addition, the first batch of MiG-17s (one source states the number to be 12) had arrived by early October, and were based initially at Almaza where a flight of six aircraft was attached to 1 Squadron EAF.

EGYPTIAN AIR FORCE ORDER OF BATTLE, October 1956

The Eastern Zone: HQ at Ismailia

5 Squadron, Fayid	12 Meteor F4s and F8s
20 Squadron, Kabrit	15 MiG-15s
30 Squadron, Abu Sueir	15 MiG-15s
31 Squadron, Kasfareet	18 Vampire FB52s (probably only 15 operational)
40 Squadron, Fayid	10 Vampire FB52s
(Fighter Training Unit)	7 Meteor F4s, 7 Meteor F8s
MiG OTU, Kabrit	6–12 MiG-15UTIs
Il-28 OTU, Luxor	20 Il-28s

The Central Zone: HQ at Almaza

1 Squadron, Almaza	15 MiG-15s, 6 MiG-17s
2 Squadron, Cairo West	14 Vampire FB52, 1 Vampire T55
3 Squadron, Almaza	20 C-47 transports
4 Squadron, Dekheila	Beechcraft & light aircraft
7 Squadron, Almaza	20 C-46 transports
8 Squadron, Inchas	12 Il-28 bombers
9 Squadron, Inchas	17 Il-28 bombers
10 Squadron, Almaza	5 Meteor NF13s
11 Squadron, Almaza	20 Il-14 transports

All serviceable Lancasters were recalled from retirement, together with eight Fury FB11s and a handful of Spitfire F22s.

There was, as would be expected, much movement of units between bases, particularly once operations commenced. Numbers were one thing, operational readiness quite another. The Sinai/Suez War caught the EAF at a very difficult time, as many fighter units were in the process of transitioning from Furies, Meteors and Vampires to MiG-15s and some 200 EAF aircrew and technicians were away in Poland and the Soviet Union attending training courses. Adequate numbers of fully trained aircrew and qualified ground personnel had always been the Egyptian Air Force's greatest weakness, and would remain so for several decades. The primary mission of the EAF in the event of war was protecting Egyptian airspace and defending army units in Sinai. By the autumn of 1956 the EAF had a personnel strength of 6,400 including some 400 officers, 3,000 enlisted and 3,000 civilians. While the force included some 440 pilots, only about 100 were judged by the EAF High Command to be combat ready. Of these, only a handful had actual combat experience.

FIRST BLOOD

During late October, General Amr, together with members of his staff, flew to Amman, there meeting delegations from both Jordan and Syria. An agreement was soon reached whereby Amr would assume the role of Commander-in-Chief of the new Egyptian/Jordanian/Syria military force in the event of a crisis with Israel. Discussions included aid to the RJAF and, as a token gesture, seven EAF Vampires – apparently surplus to requirements – flew to Amman on 25 October and were handed over in a ceremony following a flying display by these aircraft (which became F610–F616 in the RJAF). General Amr and his delegation had planned to fly to Damascus from Amman but instead went by road because of the need to fly close to the Israeli border. They travelled in convoy on 26 October and were greeted by large crowds and great excitement in Damascus.

When Israeli intelligence sources learned that the Egyptian delegation was due to return to Cairo by air from Damascus on 28 October, following the well-publicised visit, a plan was speedily hatched to shoot down the delegation's aircraft. The IDF Command hoped to eliminate Egypt's military commander and members of his staff in one fell swoop before the fighting started, as recalled by navigator Segen Elyashiv Brosh, who was then serving as a staff officer at Air HQ:

"Ramat David was instructed to prepare two fully armed Meteor NF13s in a maximum fuel configuration. I was flown in a Stearman to Ramat David while [Seren] Yoash Tsiddon was called from 117 Squadron. At Ramat David I met the ground crew – mechanics and radar technicians who prepared the two aircraft. I checked the radars and both were serviceable. I sat in one aircraft and practised operating the radar as it was six months since I last flew a similar aircraft on a course in England. When Yoash arrived we got a Harvard [on which] to calibrate the radar. The Harvard pilot was briefed and we took off for a 15-minute flight."

As darkness fell, Tsiddon and his navigator were placed on immediate alert in Meteor s/n 52. They were scrambled in the early evening hours and, after take-off, established radio contact with the controller. They were then vectored in the general direction north-west. At that time the Egyptian Presidential Il-14 (s/n 1101) was in the area of Beirut on the international air route to Cairo. The pre-interception phase lasted about 25 minutes. Segen Brosh continued:

"We were flying at about 15,000 feet but still we had no target data. At that stage Yoash realised that he could not transfer fuel from the external wing tanks. Then the controller suddenly began to give us directions towards the target, so we ignored the fuel problem and concentrated on the interception. At a range of three to four miles I acquired the target, which was flying in the general direction south-west with navigation lights on, which eased velocity synchronisation and positioning. We reported to the controller and were instructed to definitely identify the target as an Il-14. At that stage we were some 45–50 miles west of Atlit. The identification phase lasted about eight to ten minutes. We were flying in close formation with the Ilyushin which was on our starboard side. In addition to its navigation lights, the passenger cabin lights were on. I immediately identified the target but our report to control was not decisive. It was not clear to me why Yoash delayed the report. I was quite relieved when we were allowed to open fire.

When permission to open fire was granted, we slipped back and performed the first firing pass. The rounds included tracers which disturbed Yoash's aim but helped us to observe hits. At the end of the pass, Yoash reported a possible jam in one of the starboard cannons. We then positioned ourselves alongside the Ilyushin and observed a small flame in the area of its port engine. The navigation and cabin lights were off. The second pass was on a target which was still flying more or less straight and level, but at a lower speed. We observed hits on the fuselage and wings as we broke to the left,

113

and the burning Ilyushin commenced a shallow dive to its end. As it hit the water a large flame erupted."

On reporting the result of their attack, the Israeli crew was instructed to fly to Hatzor where the lights were switched on to facilitate a safe landing. There they were greeted and congratulated by Aluf-Mishne Weizman before being driven to Air HQ at Ramleh.

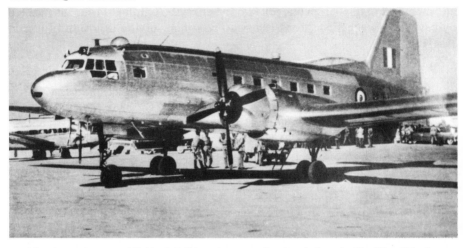

President Nasser's personal Il-14, s/n 1101, at Amman a few days before the Sinai/Suez War began. It was shot down by an Israeli Meteor NF13 on the night of 28/29 October 1956. (*EAF*)

The Ilyushin was totally destroyed and all 16 passengers and crew of two (Sqn Ldr Mustafa Mahmud Helmi Ismail and Sqn Ldr Kamal al-Din Ahmad Abu'l Rahim) were killed. But, in the event, General Amr and his staff were not aboard this aircraft. Instead its passengers consisted of journalists from the Egyptian and foreign press corps covering the Egyptian Army commander's visit to Jordan and Syria. The General was in fact flying in the other aircraft of the Presidential Flight, Dakota s/n 113. This aircraft, piloted by Sqn Ldr Sa'ad al-Din Sherif, returned safely to Cairo later that same evening.

The Israelis kept their secret from their allies and enemies alike, since the following morning the Egyptians requested help from the British air-sea search and rescue services at Cyprus, from where two Valettas and a Meteor were joined by a Royal Navy Gannet and a Shackleton from Malta, but to no avail, even though the crew of a USAF Constellation had earlier reported sighting oil patches in the area.*

---

* Although on this occasion General Amr escaped with his life, fate had decreed that he would not live out his three score and ten; in August 1967, when Deputy Supreme Commander of the Egyptian Armed Forces, he was arrested following the disastrous Six Day War with Israel and, as a consequence, committed suicide a few weeks later.

Chapter Seven

OPERATION KADESH*: The Sinai War
29 October to 6 November 1956

". . . the decisive element which brought about the speedy collapse of the enemy was the Air Force. The Egyptians had neither effective weapons nor the spirit to withstand the air attacks."

> Rav-Aluf Moshe Dayan, IDF Commander-in-Chief,
> following the capture of Sharm al-Sheikh

Following the unprovoked shooting down of the Egyptian Il-14, and fearful of the possible repercussions as a result, Israeli Prime Minister Ben-Gurion sent a cable to US President Eisenhower, the gist of which could have been construed as Israeli justification for the impending but undeclared invasion of Sinai; the communication stated:

> "With Iraqi troops poised in great numbers on the Iraq-Jordan frontier, with creation of joint command of Egypt, Syria and Jordan, with decisive increase of Egyptian influence in Jordan, and with renewal of incursions into Israeli territory by Egyptian gangs, my government would be failing in its essential duty if it were not to take all necessary measures to ensure that declared Arab whim of eliminating Israel by force should not come about. My government has appealed to the people of Israel to combine alertness with calm. I feel confident that with your vast military experience you appreciate to the full the crucial danger in which we find ourselves."

DAY ONE – 29 OCTOBER

In the event, the first day of the Sinai campaign was not an indication of the intensive fighting which was to follow. During the morning hours only a few operational sorties were flown by the IDF/AF and those were all reconnaissance flights. Two of the flights were carried out by Mosquito PR16s to what had been the Canal Zone where most of the EAF's jet fighters were based. The photographs obtained revealed no unexpected activity in spite of the massive build-up of British and French forces on Cyprus and in the Mediterranean, and

---

* Kadesh, near Beersheba, was a cluster of oases on the frontier of Canaan, the biblical 'Promised Land', favoured by the Israelite tribes during their nomadic wandering after leaving Egypt. It became known as the Crossroads of Final Decision where the tribes ultimately decided to invade Canaan.

the mobilisation of reserves in Israel. A pair of Mystères from 101 Squadron, flown by Seren Ya'acov Nevo and Segen Zoric Lev, were despatched at 0935 for a low-level visual reconnaissance of the Mitla Pass, which up to then had only been surveyed by high-flying Mosquitos. On their return the Mystère pilots reported that the camp at the western approach was occupied by civilian road workers and was not a military installation, as had been feared. Nevertheless, it was deemed to be too late to change again the proposed dropping zone.

Activity intensified in the early afternoon, with a third reconnaissance sortie being flown by a Mosquito PR16 to the Canal Zone. The aircraft departed from Tel Nof at 1415, just 15 minutes after a pair of Mustangs from 116 Squadron, specially adapted for cutting telephone wires, set out from the same base. In an effort to disrupt Egyptian communications in the area, some of the Mustangs had been fitted with a special attachment behind the tailwheel which consisted of a 25-metre length of cable, complete with lead weights. The idea was that this would be trailed behind the aircraft during attacks on Egyptian installations. The device had been tested successfully by Seren Ze'ev Tavor and Segen Amitai Chason, both instructors from the Flying School but, under operational conditions, the 'cable cutters' proved less effective than had been hoped. The two Mustangs (flown by Serens Dan Barak and Aryeh Tse'elon) were followed 20 minutes later by another pair flown by Rav-Seren Yavneh (s/n 73) and Segen Chason. The target for the first pair was the telephone line linking Kuntilla via the Mitla Pass to Suez, the two cutting points being located between the al-Thamed to Mitla road and the al-Qusseima to Nakhl road. The Mustangs flew at very low altitude to avoid detection but, when well into Sinai, Tse'elon's steel cable became detached. Nevertheless, he continued to fly in lose formation with Barak's aircraft until the target area was reached. Barak made the planned low pass but lost his cable in the process. Uncertain whether he had brought down the telephone line, he made several passes at low-level, barely 12 feet above the desert floor, before he succeeded in cutting the line with his propeller; meanwhile, Tse'elon (s/n 2329) made a total of six passes before he, too, successfully brought down the other line:

> "I was No2 and I followed him [Barak] . . . I flew too low, the cable hit the ground and was torn . . . I felt some kind of a hit and he [Barak] signalled me that I no longer had the [cutting] devise. At first he cut with his devise – it was torn after the first pass . . . and in the second pass he cut with his propeller and I did the same. In fact, we had discussed it earlier – if the devise failed we would try to cut with the propeller."

The second pair of Mustangs also lost their cables without bringing down the lines, although Yavneh eventually used his propeller and Chason his wing-tip, thus the mission was successfully concluded in spite of the difficulties.

As the four Mustangs flew back towards Tel Nof they passed a formation of 16 Dakotas heading into Sinai, on their way to the Mitla Pass, flying at about 100 feet above ground level in four formations of four and carrying a total of 395 paratroopers of the 890th Parachute Regiment. The lead aircraft was flown by Rav-Seren Avishar, whose co-pilot was Segen Finkelstein, one of two female pilots to see service in the campaign. The Dakotas were escorted by ten Meteors of 117 Squadron led by Rav-Seren Yoeli. The much faster jet fighters flew at between 5,000 and 10,000 feet, zig-zagging as they kept an eye on the vulnerable transport aircraft below. The crossing point of the border was west of Ramon Crater and was reached at 1630, barely five minutes before the departure of six Ouragans led by Rav-Seren Hod which were to relieve the Meteors and cover the dropping of the paratroops. Simultaneously, a dozen Mystères also departed from Hatzor and headed for Kabrit, where they were to circle at high altitude and attack any MiGs that might attempt to take off. However, no airborne MiGs were observed, the Israeli pilots noting only that a number were seen to be dispersed around the airfield whereas, in the past, they had been parked closely together. One unofficial Egyptian source suggested later that this was because the EAF feared a British aerial attack from Cyprus rather than a sudden Israeli assault from the east.

At the same time as the Dakotas had lifted off from Tel Nof, a pair of unarmed Meteor T7s, which were to act as a diversionary force by flying along the northern coast of Sinai, also departed, but that flown by Rav-Seren Eyal was soon obliged to return to base. His wingman, Segen Meir Livne, continued alone with the risky mission of flying the trainer as a decoy to detract the EAF's radar operators, although in the event the Meteor apparently failed to attract any attention. The other part of an intended bluff – the dropping of dummy parachutists near Ismailia by a lone Dakota – was cancelled due to the high risk involved, combined with the general inactivity in the Canal Zone as witnessed by the latest reconnaissance photographs. The Dakota commander had stressed to his crews the importance of the mission and that if the formation was broken for any reason, by Egyptian fighters or technical malfunction, each aircraft had to press on individually to the dropping zone. However, there was no such occurrence and all aircraft arrived over the dropping zone safely but, although the dropping of the paratroopers began on time, due to a navigational error they were dropped 4km east of the intended dropping zone and, as a consequence, had to walk for about two hours to reach their planned destination. With the completion of the air drop, six more Ouragans arrived to replace the first formation, but these were unable to locate the returning Dakotas due to the failing light. One Dakota remained in the area to act as a communication relay aircraft until fuel exhaustion necessitated its return to Tel Nof.

103 Squadron's three Noratlases joined three Dakotas in conveying more paratroops, supplies and 120mm mortars to the area. Following the drop, French Noratlases from Tel Nof, to where they had flown earlier from Cyprus to take on board Israeli navigators, arrived in the area. Although two of the aircraft were unable to locate the dropping zone, the others disgorged eight jeeps, four 106mm recoilless guns and two 120mm mortars to the Israeli invasion force.

At the same time as the Dakota drop, several Israeli armoured columns from 202 Brigade crossed the border near Kuntilla and pushed into Sinai, where they were to link up with paratroops. Thus, the first phase of the invasion was accomplished with a sizeable Israeli force firmly established some 40km east of the Suez Canal, Israel having fulfilled its obligation under the secret agreement with Britain and France. The whole operation had been shrouded in such secrecy that many within the IDF/AF had not been aware of the imminence of the invasion, as witnessed by an incident that had occurred earlier in the day. During the morning Seren Tavor, an instructor at the Flying School, was asked to take up a PR Mosquito on a test flight, oblivious to the fact that the invasion was under way:

"I went off to fly, alone . . . and while climbing I noticed mushrooms of AA fire. The border was close so I said to myself 'Well, the Jordanians are celebrating'. I turned left [into Israeli airspace] and saw it [AA fire] coming (from Israel) at my altitude. I yelled on the radio. No one answered me. I descended. I escaped. I landed and came to [Rav-Seren Eyal] and said 'Are you crazy?' He did not say a word. All the call-signs had been changed, all the frequencies replaced. He did not tell me anything – only after they had parachuted at Mitla [did] that wise guy come to me to tell me what happened. There was an instruction at Tel Aviv to live fire at any aircraft."

During the night of 29/30 October, the IDF Command focused its attention on the 890th Regiment spending its first night almost 200km deep into Egyptian territory. Once landed, the paratroopers had constructed a small landing strip from which wounded and injured could be evacuated; a Dakota and eight Piper Cubs were placed on standby to respond to such calls. First to arrive was a Piper Cub in the hands off Samal (Sgt) Moshe Aven from Kuntilla, which then took off again to carry out a nocturnal reconnaissance of the roads in the area before it departed for Eilat. A second Piper Cub, despatched from Eilat, flew to the Mitla Pass to evacuate a paratrooper who had broken his leg, but its pilot, Rav-Torai (Cpl) Amnon Lolav, became lost and was forced to land in the desert, where he spent the night alone.

With the political tension surrounding the new Arab military alliance between Egypt, Syria and Jordan – as well as the closing of the Gulf of Aqaba to Israeli shipping – Egyptian military leaders expected an Israeli response, but they did not anticipate a full-scale invasion. The Israeli moves had not gone undetected by the Egyptians but were initially thought to be another of the frequent commando raids, and Egyptian Army headquarters ordered units to respond accordingly. When Cairo learned of the Israeli action, President Nasser called a meeting at the Joint Military Headquarters in Misr al-Jadida at Heliopolis. Among those present was Wg Cdr al-Bughdadi, administrative commander of the EAF, who recalled:

"[Air Commodore] Muhammad Sidqi Mahmud, the Air Force Chief-of-Staff, arrived. He had received orders according to which our air force was to immediately bomb the [Israeli] forces which had parachuted in the [Mitla] Pass, as well as the enemy's airfields. Faced with this order, it was discernible that he [Sidqi Mahmud] was uneasy and embarrassed. He said that several difficulties arose which prevented our bomber planes from carrying out these missions at once. His excuse was that there wasn't enough fuel for the planes at the airport of Cairo West, which was the airfield for the bombers. As the general regulations were to refuel the tanks of the planes at the end of their daily flights, I suggested to him, after he mentioned this obstacle, that the planes could execute the orders that same night by using the fuel which was already in their tanks. Simultaneously, means would be taken to supply the needed quantities of fuel for the base in the morning . . ."

There were no raids by Egyptian bombers that night.

DAY TWO – 30 OCTOBER

With the arrival of dawn, three Piper Cubs including that flown by Lolav, who had spent the night in the desert, dropped in at the paratroopers' makeshift

The Israeli answer to the Egyptian MiG: IDF/AF Mystère IV s/n 630. (*SHAA via Albert Grandolini*)

landing strip. A pair of 'cable cutting' Mustangs were also out early, Seren Tse'elon leading Segen Aryeh Fredlis (s/n 06), who recalled:

"I did not practice, it was pretty secret. An operational order arrived and Tse'elon and I were the only ones available. [When informed he was to fly a cable cutting mission, Fredlis remarked] 'I do not know what you are talking about' [Tse'elon replied] 'It will be alright, you will follow me, you will do exactly what I do.' He explained the idea, there was not much time to discuss it . . . we had to go. As we came in for the first run to cut the lines . . . I felt the aircraft suddenly stop in the air. I was thrown forward. It happened three or four times and then I understood that the cable had hit the ground. Suddenly it was released. I thought the aircraft was crashing. Then [Tse'elon] said 'OK, now let us try and cut the lines in a different method.' "

Seren Tse'elon (s/n 2329) added:

"It was south of al-Arish . . . at first we cut with the devise and then with the propeller."

Both Mustangs returned safely.

Meanwhile, pairs of 101 Squadron Mystères departed Hatzor at 40-minute intervals, to patrol over the paratroopers who had by then made contact with advanced units of the Egyptian 2nd Brigade which had been sent to investigate. As Jew and Arab clashed, the Mystères remained at high altitude, eyes peeled for the sight of EAF fighters but for about only ten minutes at a time – the limit of their endurance – which meant that the ground forces were devoid of cover for up to 30 minutes between change-over. The Israeli pilots were ordered not to become involved in the ground battle. Their task was aerial cover in case Egyptian jets appeared on the scene. Similarly, the fear of the EAF's response

The Egyptian answer to the Israeli Mystère: one of the EAF's first MiG-17s taxying at Almaza. (*Mustafa Shalabi al-Hinnawi*)

to the invasion deterred IDF/AF commanders from releasing their Mustang ground attack fighters into the fray.

The first signs that the Israelis saw of the Egyptian Air Force came at 0730, when four Vampires of 2 Squadron EAF on a reconnaissance mission from Fayid overflew Mitla and the Israeli armoured column moving from Kuntilla to Nakhl. Of this period, Wg Cdr Labib (Operations Officer at Cairo West) wrote:

"On the night of 29 October the war began when Israeli parachutists equipped with light weapons were dropped at the eastern end of the Mitla Pass. Egypt was surprised by this attack as it seemed to have no obvious military purpose. The weakness of the assault meant that it posed no real threat and it appeared to be pointless. As a result the Egyptian military command (in Cairo) was confused and unable to make any operational decisions until the following morning when sufficient information had been gathered."

IDF officers inspect the wreckage of a Piper Cub after it was shot down by EAF MiG-15s on 30 October 1956. (*Israel Ben-Shachar*)

120

Once the Egyptians realised the size of the Israeli assault, the EAF was ordered into action and the first air attack was made by four MiG-15s, two of which attacked the paratroopers at Mitla at 0900. A Piper Cub (s/n 47) on the ground was destroyed and four Israelis wounded, including the regimental doctor, Major Moshe Agmon, who had been tending an injured soldier when the MiGs struck with cannon fire. The Piper's wing and fuel tank were hit, fragments of shrapnel wounding the doctor in the chest. Meanwhile, Samal (Sgt) Moshe Bokai, the pilot, had jumped clear of the burning aircraft but, on seeing the wounded doctor trying to free the patient, leapt into the flames to help; between them they succeeded in extricating the soldier and dragged him clear of the inferno. The doctor then fainted. All three were airlifted back to Israel (together with the other two wounded soldiers), where the severely burned pilot was later decorated for his bravery.* Meantime, the other two MiGs strafed the 202 Brigade column near al-Thamed, setting six vehicles ablaze and causing three further casualties.

Another pair of MiGs which tried to repeat the attack at about 1000 were distracted by a surveillance Piper Cub flying ahead of the column. The Cub was piloted by Seren Binyamin Cahana, a veteran of the War of Independence, who succeeded in leading the fighters away from the vulnerable transport column. However, after 15 minutes of weaving and bobbing, the Piper Cub was shot down with the death of the pilot but, by then, the MiGs were low on fuel and returned to their base without attacking the military column. The first air combat success of the Sinai War had therefore been achieved by the EAF, but this pattern was not to continue. At 1100, four Egyptian Vampires from an

Seren Uri Yarom, in Sikorsky S-55 s/n 02, lifts Piper Cub s/n 47 which was set on fire by EAF MiGs on 30 October 1956; the Cub was airlifted to Tel Nof air base. (*Uri Yarom*)

---

* The IDF/AF's new Sikorsky helicopters were later sent to the scene of the action, from where Seren Yarom (in S-55 s/n 02) airlifted the damaged Piper Cub all the way back to Tel Nof, with a single refuelling stop at al-Arish. He was accompanied by Rav-Seren Arbel in the second S-55 (s/n 03).

---

unspecified unit followed up the MiG attack on the Israeli column at al-Thamed and destroyed a number of vehicles. Shortly afterwards, four Vampires from 2 Squadron EAF escorted by a pair of MiGs returned to the Mitla Pass, while Meteor F8s from 5 Squadron EAF at Fayid were similarly in action.

In response to these damaging raids, the IDF/AF ordered two patrolling Mystères, flown by Seren Alon and Segen Ohad Shadmi, to attack an Egyptian column – elements of the 5th and 6th Battalions of the 2nd Infantry Brigade from Fayid – on its way to the Mitla Pass, while Meteors of 117 Squadron and 113 Squadron's Ouragans were despatched to support Israeli ground forces. First off were eight Ouragans which departed in two flights from Hatzor at 1325. The first quartet headed for the Mitla Pass but the pilots reported on return that they could not identify friend from foe. The second flight was more successful and attacked Egyptian forces at Bir Hasana, strafing some 20 vehicles and a tented camp. Later, three more Ouragans set out for the Mitla Pass, with Alon leading an attack against an Egyptian 120mm mortar battery which had been engaging the paratroopers. Two trucks loaded with crates were reported destroyed by Seren Ran Sharon, using rockets, having released his two bombs against other vehicles pulling field artillery. Though practically all their vehicles were destroyed, the Egyptian 5th and 6th Battalions suffered only light casualties during the Israeli air attacks, the dispersed troops having taken up positions in the eastern half of the Heitan Defile.

At 1530, near Jebel Libni, some 60km west of Nitzana, there occurred an engagement between six MiG-15s and two Israeli Meteors, the first such meeting between MiG and Meteor since the end of the Korean War in 1953. One of the Israeli jets was able to evade the interception and return to base, but the other attempted to engage, although Seren Hilel Elroee was unable to release one of his auxiliary fuel tanks, which resulted in an unexpected spin and his attackers apparently lost sight of him. The Meteor recovered stability at low level and the

Dramatic view of an EAF MiG-17 of 1 Squadron taking off from Almaza with full afterburner. (*EAF*)

relieved Israeli pilot was able to return to Hatzor. The MiGs had been escorting two Meteor F8s of 5 Squadron EAF, which carried out a strafing attack on Israeli ground forces without hindrance and succeeded in blowing up an ammunition wagon, inflicting severe casualties; over 60 wounded Israeli soldiers were evacuated during the afternoon by half-tracks.

In response to an Israeli intelligence warning of what was expected to be a 'massive aerial attack' planned by the EAF against the paratroopers at Mitla Pass for the late afternoon, 101 Squadron scrambled six Mystères to the area. As the first trio – Seren Nevo, Segens Shai Egozi and Yoseph Tsuk – approached Kabrit at 20,000 feet, they noticed six MiGs taking off (there were in fact seven MiGs) and immediately dived at them, opening fire almost simultaneously. Nevo and Egozi missed their targets but Tsuk (with just 12 hours' experience of flying the Mystère) was more successful:

> "Yak [Nevo] headed down first, then Egozi, then I. It was a mess. No tactics.
> No organisation. We just followed Yak down in single file like a bunch of
> Indians. At first nobody hit anything. We were going too fast. But then I
> put my air brakes on, and shot one of the MiGs."

The MiG was seen to emit black smoke, spin and was believed to have crashed. By then a further six MiGs had joined the fight although the other flight of Mystères also arrived on the scene – flown by Seren Dror Avneri, Segens Dan Gonen and Shabtai Gilboa – and there ensued a series of dogfights. Tsuk meanwhile managed to manoeuvre on to the tail of another MiG and was about to open fire when one got on to his tail. The Mystère received a 37mm shell through its starboard wing although he was able to return to Hatzor safely, though his engine cut due to lack of fuel just as he was landing. Avneri, before being forced to disengage due to lack of fuel, claimed hits on a second MiG. The EAF admitted the loss of one MiG in this action but in return claimed two, possibly three, Mystères shot down. This was presumably the action to which President Nasser referred when he later told an American reporter:

> "Nobody knew we had any MiG-17s until one day early in the fighting, when
> three of them were surprised near an airfield in the Canal Zone. The MiGs
> turned, shot down three Mystères and drove off five others with no losses."

At approximately the same time as the Mystères and MiGs were fighting over Kabrit, an unarmed, camera-equipped Israeli Meteor T7 was despatched on a reconnaissance sortie over the Mitla Pass, escorted by a Meteor fighter from 117 Squadron. On approaching the battle area, the Meteor pilots observed five of 113 Squadron's Ouragans low down, busily attacking Egyptian mortar batteries. Espying the two intruders above, the Ouragan pilots checked with the controller as to their identity and were informed that no friendly aircraft were in the area! Fortunately the Meteor pilots heard the radio transmission and realised an error had been made. Yelling excitedly over the R/T as the Ouragans climbed to engage, they were able to avert an error in communication from turning into possibly a tragic incident.

These first air battles had demonstrated that Israeli pilots and the new Mystère fighters were a match for the EAF's MiG-15s, but had equally shown that the Egyptians were more competent in their new aircraft than had been expected. The Mystère was fast and could go supersonic in a dive but the MiG could climb faster and was more manoeuvrable. In air combat the Mystère had two important advantages: power-assisted controls allowed Israeli pilots to turn more quickly at high speeds, while the French jet was armed with two 30mm cannon which had a higher rate of fire than the MiG's mix of two 23mm and one 37mm cannon. On the other hand, a shell from the MiG's larger cannon did huge damage, proving particularly effective in the ground attack role.

On this first day of fighting proper, the EAF had flown more than 50 fighter and attack sorties over Sinai, and these air raids had disrupted Israeli operations at Mitla Pass and inflicted casualties on several convoys advancing into Sinai. The Israelis admitted the loss of 20 vehicles during these attacks, while the EAF claimed the destruction of 23. On the other side, Israeli air attacks also caused losses among Egyptian reinforcements coming in from the west.

On the evening of 30 October, according to plan, Britain and France demanded that both Egypt and Israel stop fighting. The ultimatum addressed to the Israeli government read:

"The Governments of the United Kingdom and France have taken note of the outbreak of hostilities between Israel and Egypt. This event threatens to disrupt the freedom of navigation through the Suez Canal on which the economic life of many nations depends.

The Governments of the United Kingdom and France are resolved to do all in their power to bring about the early cessation of hostilities and to safeguard the free passage of the Canal. They accordingly request the Government of Israel:

(a) to stop all warlike action on land, sea and air forthwith;

(b) to withdraw all Israeli military forces to a distance of ten miles east of the Suez Canal.

A communication has been addressed to the Government of Egypt, requesting them to cease hostilities and to withdraw their forces from the neighbourhood of the Canal, and to accept the temporary occupation by Anglo-French forces of key positions at Port Said, Ismailia and Suez.

The United Kingdom and French Governments request an answer to this communication within twelve hours. If at the expiration of that time one or both Governments have not undertaken to comply with the above requirements, United Kingdom and French forces will intervene in whatever strength may be necessary to secure compliance."

The wording caused Israel's Ambassador to the United Nations to muse, "since we were nowhere near the Canal, we would have to remove ourselves forward in order to obey!" Egypt, as expected, rejected the demand since she was not only defending her own territory, but was as yet doing so very effectively. When news of the severity of the situation reached Egypt's military allies, Jordan offered immediate help, as recalled by King Hussein:

"We had been the first to stand by him [Nasser] when the Suez Canal was nationalised, and the first to call the Arab world to stand united in support of him after the attack by Israel and the Western powers. In fact, it was

Jordan that played a leading part in bringing the Arab world together at the time of the Suez invasion. We had even agreed earlier that the armies of Jordan, Saudi Arabia, Egypt and Syria should be united under one command."

Meanwhile, Israeli forces continued their air and ground attacks despite the call to end the fighting. As a direct result of these air battles, and in the light of the obvious fact that the invasion was no ordinary Israeli cross-border raid, the EAF High Command was ordered to attack Israeli airfields, although permission to bomb major Israeli population centres was, however, neither requested nor received. Thus, Israel's fear of night air attacks was realised when at least one EAF Il-28 (one source says four) crossed the border, at about 2000, to bomb IDF/AF air bases at (according to Egyptian sources) Tel Nof, Eilat and Ramat Rachel, although the latter was not an airfield but a kibbutz west of Jerusalem. Of the nocturnal bombing, Wg Cdr Labib wrote:

"Ilyushin bombers attacked targets inside Israel itself. These attacks continued all night and inflicted losses, as proved by huge fires caused by the bombardment."

Despite the claim, there were no Israeli casualties as a result of the raids. It seems that Tel Nof and Eilat were not in fact attacked. However, explosions were reported near Ramat Rachel, where, next morning, the fragmented remains of Soviet bombs were found. From Tel Nof, 119 Squadron's lone night trained crew – Seren Tsiddon and Segen Brosh – flew two missions in the evening hours of 30 October, both in Meteor NF13 s/n 52. The first was a fruitless one-hour patrol over the battle fields and the second was to intercept intruders over Hatzor, but no enemy aircraft were encountered. Some reports suggest that Sqn Ldr Mustafa Hilmi's bomber failed to return to its base, its loss presumably due to technical malfunction or navigational error. This, however, remains unconfirmed.

DAY THREE – 31 OCTOBER

Under cover of darkness two Mosquitos of 110 Squadron, including one flown by the Squadron commander, Rav-Seren Somekh, took off from Ramat David to attack Egyptian vehicles reported in northern Sinai. The column was located and attacked but results were difficult to assess. Further supply drops were made to the paratroopers at Mitla Pass during the night, although several Dakotas were unable to locate the dropping zone owing to low cloud over the area. One of the transports became lost, the disorientated pilot having turned in the opposite direction, thereby straying over Saudi Arabia and Jordan for a couple of hours before realising his mistake; the aircraft eventually returned safely to its base. Piper Cubs were also kept busy evacuating soldiers wounded during the day's fighting.

The war was again brought home to Israel at 0330, when an Egyptian destroyer, *Ibrahim al-Awal* (formerly HMS *Cottesmore*), having slipped undetected along the northern Sinai and Israeli coast from Port Said, opened fire on the harbour at Haifa, seeking to destroy shipping, oil tanks and military bases. Although a total of 220 four-inch shells was directed at the harbour, only minor damage was caused to the quay, the navy compound and the shipyard area. The French destroyer *Kersaint* (part of the Anglo-French Task Force allocated to the defence of Israel) which was in the vicinity of Haifa, engaged and fired 64 shells at the Egyptian vessel. Although no damage was inflicted, the action forced the intruder out to sea. However, the French captain at this stage was not absolutely certain of the identity of his opponent and advised the Task Force commander accordingly.

Meanwhile, the Egyptian vessel, commanded by Lt Cdr Hassan Rusdi Tamzan, set course for Port Said closely pursued by two Israeli destroyers, *Yaffo* and *Eilat* (ex-HMS *Zealous*). Shortly before 0530 they engaged and fired in excess of 400 rounds although the only damage came from near misses. Lt Cdr Tamzan signalled Alexandria (HQ of the Egyptian Navy) his plight, to be advised that the EAF would provide air cover and bombers were on their way from Syria, but the promised help did not materialise.

On being alerted of the skirmish at sea, Tel Nof despatched a Dakota of 103 Squadron to reconnoitre the area. On receiving the pilot's report, a flight of 110 Squadron's Mosquitos was ordered to stand by at Ramat David. Meanwhile, two rocket-armed Ouragans from Hatzor were scrambled to assist in the attack, Seren Ya'acov Agasi leading Segen Kishon. Agasi reported later:

> "When we got near the area, Ground Control directed us to a ship which I was about to attack when it seemed to me that it was a merchant ship. I reported this to Ground Control, but Control ordered me to attack it. Three times I reported it was a merchant ship, and three times Ground Control said that it was the *Ibrahim*. Then a Dakota came and pinpointed the target for us. The weather was cloudy, and we were flying at 5,000 feet. The wake of the ship showed that she had been turning from west to due east, but at the time of our attack she was on a course of 120° (south-east)."

The Ouragans approached the destroyer at low level. Each pilot released his full load of armour-piercing rockets in a single pass, while firing their cannons to keep the Egyptian gunners' heads down, as Agasi recalled:

> "I attacked out of the sun and made my run along the ship from bow to stern. I dived and released all 16 rockets, at about 500 yards from a height of 700

Ouragan 59 of 113 Squadron. (*IAF Magazine collection*)

feet. I broke from the ship before I could see the hits, but I saw pieces of metal in the air. I broke high and to the left and saw my No2 leaving the ship after releasing the rockets. After this attack by my No2, the ship was hidden in smoke. There were two kinds of smoke, some black and some very white. All this time the Dakota was watching."

The *Ibrahim al-Awal* suffered four direct hits, including one on the bows which disabled the anti-aircraft gun; others damaged the forward part of the ship, affecting its steering, electricity supply and ammunition elevator. Tamzan again radioed Alexandria at 0650 to report that the ship had been brought to a standstill, only to be reassured that help was on its way from Beirut, but by then the fight was already lost. A lifeboat launched from the disabled vessel at 0730 capsized owing to damage inflicted during the attack and 53 members of the crew, included two with wounds, were fished out of the sea by the Israelis. When the destroyer was eventually boarded by Israeli sailors, two bodies were found, while a further 98 Egyptian sailors were taken prisoner, of whom six were wounded. One of the dead was a Syrian naval lieutenant who had been sent to Egypt for training shortly before the war broke out. Ironically, the stricken vessel was towed by the *Eilat* to Haifa harbour, where it was repaired and later entered service with the Israeli Navy as *Haifa*.

Of the failure of the promised air support for the Egyptian destroyer in its hour of need, President Nasser stated later that the Syrian government had offered to enter the conflict but that he, Nasser, had asked them to stay aloof for the time being. Indeed, Sabri al-Assali, Syria's Prime Minister, stated later:

"We were unhesitatingly on Egypt's side from the first moment danger arose on the horizon. We mobilised all our material and moral means for Egypt's help. When we received directives from the Combined Command to wait and watch developments, because the battle ground shifted from Sinai to facing attempts from aggressive Britain and France to land forces in [sic] the Suez Canal, we were about to start speedy action."

Shortly before the surrender of the *Ibrahim al-Awal*, a second pair of Ouragans had scrambled from Hatzor, one piloted by Rav-Seren Hod, the other by Aluf-Mishne Weizman, who wrote:

"Each of these excellent planes carried 16 rockets and we were eager to give the ship a taste of them. Then we were stopped short: ground control informed us the ship had surrendered. We requested permission to return to Sinai. When we reported that we had enough fuel, permission was granted. Moti and I headed south. At al-Arish we saw Egyptian Vampires parked on the runway. We reported this, and two of our planes [Meteors from Ramat David] went up to attack, scoring good hits – unfortunately, it transpired that the planes had been dummies. We continued southwards and discovered an Egyptian column on its way up from the Canal hauling cannon. We swooped down, rocketing, strafing and scoring good hits."

All told during the day the Meteors of 117 Squadron carried out six sorties against al-Arish, where a Mraz Sokol trainer (s/n 311) was strafed and damaged, in addition to the wooden dummy Vampires.

EAF Mraz Sokol s/n 311 severely damaged during an Israeli stafing attack on al-Arish and was subsequently captured. (*Authors' collection*)

One of the remarkably realistic wooden mock-up Vampires destroyed on the ground at al-Arish. Its s/n, 1582, is ficticious. (*Authors' collection*)

Meanwhile, over Sinai at dawn, four unescorted Vampires of 2 Squadron EAF from Fayid had flown in to strike at Israeli forces near the Mitla Pass. They had hoped to make their attack before the Israeli standing patrol arrived but were bounced by two Mystères which had been patrolling at 36,000 feet. As Segens Egozi and Aharon Shavit lost altitude in response to the ground controller's instructions, they saw the four Vampires flying in pairs in a tight vic formation at about 15,000 feet. Shavit recalled:*

---

* Aharon Shavit later commanded a Super Mystère squadron and, during the 1967 Six-Day War, shot down a MiG-21 on the first day of hostilities.

"I saw four points glittering like mirrors from the sun. Four Egyptian Vampires had taken off from a base near the Suez Canal and were flying at 1,500 feet, which was above the morning clouds . . . We crossed the speed of sound and we put the engines on idle . . . We levelled off at about 2,000 feet . . . I picked up one and put the cross on him . . . and saw the bullets miss him. So I took a deflection, fired a short burst and one or two bullets hit him . . . I pulled up and went up to 10,000 feet with my speed. [Egozi] did an S turn and got one and then I saw him shooting at another. The fourth one ran away, and I got him with a short burst as he ran towards the Suez Canal and he exploded in the air. We climbed up to 36,000 feet in order to save fuel and headed back to base."

Three of the Vampires crashed in the desert, with the deaths of Flt Lt Bahgat Hassan Helmi and Plt Off Mahmud Wael Afifi, while the third pilot baled out

Italian-built Vampire FB52 s/n 1563 after delivery to Egypt, probably serving with 31 Squadron EAF. (*EAF*)

Scramble! Mystère s/n 81 in Sinai campaign stripes takes off. (*IAF Magazine collection*)

and was taken prisoner by Israeli forces. The fourth aircraft, badly damaged, crash-landed near Kabrit. According to Egyptian accounts, the Israelis broke off combat when six MiGs arrived on the scene. Nevertheless, it had been an expensive sortie for the EAF. Operations by the clearly outclassed Vampires were reduced, though not halted, and the remaining flights of 2 Squadron EAF were dispersed to forward strips inside Sinai, towards the advancing Israelis, at Bir Gafgafa and Bir Rod Salim. Wg Cdr Labib commented:

> "In consequence, it was decided that Vampires should only fly combat missions when protected by MiG-17 fighters. The Mystères then fell into a trap formed by this MiG air cover and as a result high losses were inflicted upon them, despite the fact that the MiG-17 pilots had only been flying their jets for a short time."

This claim is not borne out by the facts, however, although Vampires of 31 Squadron EAF continued to carry the fight to the invaders. For example, one of this unit's newest members, Plt Off Adel Nass, who had only gone through the Vampire OTU course in February and March that year, flew three sorties before the Anglo-French assault wiped out the Squadron's remaining aircraft on the ground (see Chapter Ten).

The Egyptian armoured column moving eastwards from Ismailia similarly hoped to make Bir Gafgafa the centre of Egyptian resistance in north-western Sinai, but how far this EAF forward disposal plan was carried through remains unclear. At 0800, four Harvards from the improvised 140 Squadron departed from Sde Teman airstrip near Beersheba to attack Egyptian strongpoints at Om Kattef south of Nitzana, where they came under heavy ground fire. With rocket rails installed beneath their wings, each Harvard could accommodate 16 rockets, although on this occasion each was armed with eight 50lb bombs since they were to carry out dive-bombing attacks on Egyptian artillery. As they dived in single file, the aircraft flown by Seren Moshe Ashel was shot down and crashed in flames with the death of the Squadron commander, while a second also failed to return, having crash-landed in a field close to an IDF tank unit, from where the pilot was recovered. The remaining two Harvards also suffered damage but were able to limp back to Beersheba. A second flight of four survived undamaged although the pilots had been unable to locate their target. Following the loss of Ashel, Seren Ovadiah Nachman was appointed to lead the Squadron. Two Meteors from 117 Squadron joined in the attacks at Om Kattef, both of which suffered damage from ground fire although they were able to return to Tel Nof safely.

While the Harvards were involved at Om Kattef, the first formations of Mustangs went in to action in the ground attack role. Rav-Seren Yoffe led six bomb-laden and rocket-armed aircraft from 116 Squadron from Tel Nof at 1000. A former 101 Spitfire pilot but then an Operations Officer at IDF/AF headquarters, Yoffe longed for action. He took the formation out to sea and along the coastline before recrossing into Sinai and following the Ismailia road, there meeting the intended target, an Egyptian convoy, part of 1st Brigade of the 4th Armoured Division. One of the pilots was Segen Eliezer Cohen who reported seeing six blazing tanks after the initial attack, which was followed by another when a further six tanks were claimed destroyed. Although there was intense light ground fire, none of the Mustangs sustained serious damage but, as the

Harvards of the Flying School were pressed into service during the Sinai campaign. (*Israel Ben-Shachar*)

formation sped across the desert on its way back to Tel Nof, Seren Uri Schlessinger's aircraft was struck by gunfire from an unseen location. The pilot, apparently severely wounded, called his leader over the R/T before he started to lose altitude, although he was able to cross the border into Israel, closely accompanied by Cohen, who watched the Mustang carry out a crash-landing in sand dunes at Chalutza. Having himself landed at the nearest emergency airstrip, Cohen notified the controller of the location of Schlessinger's aircraft. A Piper Cub with a doctor on board took off immediately but, on arrival at the scene of the crash, Schlessinger was found to be dead in the cockpit.

Mystères and MiGs again clashed over the Mitla Pass at about 1030 when two of the former, returning to Hatzor at the end of their patrol, encountered seven of the latter, although only three stayed to fight. These engaged Seren Nevo's aircraft. Nevo was able to out-turn his attackers although his one operable cannon made combat difficult, while his wingman, Segen Tsuk, kept a close eye on the action from above, which was broken off by the MiGs after about ten minutes. As the pair of Mystères continued their homeward journey they were joined by two others, both of which had exhausted their ammunition ground strafing in the Mitla Pass area. Without warning, all four were bounced by more (or the same) MiGs, but surprisingly, none of the Israeli aircraft was hit. Nevo promptly gave chase and caught one at which he fired, closing to 200 metres, after which the MiG started to pour white smoke, indicating a fuel leak. As Nevo closed in again to finish it off, he found his ammunition expended, as he related later:

"I attacked the MiG and apparently hit him. The Egyptian pilot started to slow down and headed for his base. My buddy [Segen Zoric Lev] and I pursued him but, as we got close and I shot my cannon, I ran out of ammunition. The MiG started to lose altitude. We continued the pursuit and flew in front of him, under him and behind him in order to stretch out his flight. For a full minute I flew alongside the Egyptian. I could see his face. He was powerless. I doubt that he reached home."

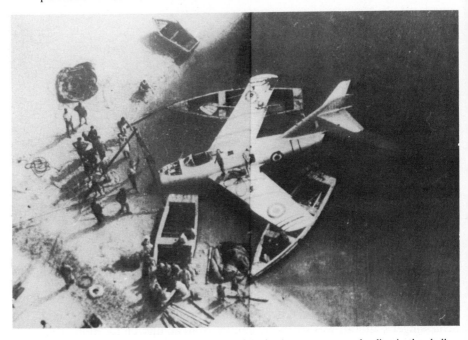

The unknown pilot of this MiG-15 made a successful wheels-up emergency landing in the shallow waters of Lake al-Bardawil following a combat with Israeli Mystères; severe combat damage to the MiG's starboard wing is clearly visible. (*IDF*)

Unable to land at al-Arish, the MiG continued flying westwards while still losing height although the Mystères, low on fuel, declined to follow. The MiG was eventually force-landed on the edge of the Sabhket al-Bardawil lagoon, virtually intact. The aircraft had, in fact, been struck in the starboard wing and aileron. That the Egyptian pilot managed to make a successful emergency landing in this condition says much for his skill and nerve. The pilot survived, evaded capture and was presumably recovered by Egyptian forces before returning to his unit.*

While the Mystères were thus engaged, a pair of 113 Squadron Ouragans were searching for suitable targets along the Bir Hasana to Jebel Libni road when several swept-wing fighters were seen above. Believing the newcomers to be Mystères, the Israeli pilots continued with their task, only realising their mistake when they came under attack from astern. Both pilots immediately jettisoned their bombs, rockets and wing-tip fuel tanks, and broke hard to find at least five MiGs bearing down on them. Seren Ran Sharon, the Ouragan leader, pulled round in a tight turn:

---

* Following the end of the Sinai War, Israeli forces salvaged the MiG and conveyed it by barge to open sea west of al-Arish, from where barge and MiG were towed to Haifa by the Israeli motor ship *Rimon*. It remains at Hatzor on display to this day.

The MiG-15 was taken back to Israel where IDF/AF pilots examine the damaged wing. (*Authors' collection*)

"I broke left and saw that my No2 had three MiGs on his tail. I warned him and told him to break harder. I noticed that tracers were passing close to my wing and I broke harder myself. I broke right and saw a MiG followed by my No2 and two MiGs following him – everybody shooting. When I broke right there was a MiG on my wing breaking left. We criss-crossed each other several times, passing each other at about ten metres. After this, because I was slower, I found myself on the MiG's tail and, when he saw that he was losing, he started to pull away, and I was in a good position for firing. As I was about to fire, I saw tracers coming from behind on both sides of me. I looked in my mirror and saw a MiG filling in. We were at 3,000 feet. I did a split S – a wing turn towards the ground – hoping that the MiG would follow me and crash. I had difficulty in pulling out myself, but unfortunately the MiG stayed upstairs. Then my No2 shouted again, and again I saw tracers. I flew very low, throwing my plane all over the place to try and avoid the MiGs. I looked right and left and in the mirror, but could see no MiGs, so I straightened the plane and started to fly level and very low."

The Egyptian fighter had broken off the attack when two Mystères appeared. Perilously low on fuel, Sharon was just able to reach the frontier before being forced to carry out a belly-landing, also on the sands near Chalutsa. The aircraft was undamaged and Sharon clambered out to await rescue, which arrived within half an hour, when a Piper Cub landed and took him back to Hatzor. There he found that his wingman had returned safely, although his aircraft had suffered some damage inflicted by two 23mm cannon strikes.

Meanwhile, the two Mystères, flown by Nevo and Tsuk, were busily engaged with the MiGs – believed to be the more powerful MiG-17s from Almaza. Tsuk had spotted two MiGs at 18,000 feet but was unable to open fire at the one he selected since the angle of attack was too great, although Nevo was more successful:

133

Pilots of 113 Squadron with an Egyptian flag and Ouragan s/n 29 just after the Sinai campaign. Rav-Seren Dani Shapira is extreme right. (*IAF Magazine collection*)

"The MiGs broke and got separated. One of them went home. My No2 was in a favourable position to shoot, but, on account of his turn, it was a high angle-off. Since I was in an even more favourable position, I told my No2 to break and I closed in. The MiG pilot made a mistake which a lot of them seemed to make . . . They think they can get away by changing direction with full power and making a climbing turn. They can't do this, because although the MiG can climb faster, the higher speed of the Mystère when it starts to climb cancels it out. I didn't lose at all on the climb and I was able to cut in and close to 250 yards. I opened fire, a fairly short burst, and saw the MiG go into a very fast spin. I followed him down about 8,000 feet and saw him straighten out of the spin and use his ejector seat. Unfortunately his parachute didn't open. The Mig went into a great blaze before it hit the ground."

The EAF did not admit losing a pilot in that sector at that time but it seems probable that Nevo's victim was Plt Off Hafiz Mohammed Iwais, although his death was officially recorded as having occurred on 4 November. Nevertheless, ejection from the early MiG-15s and MiG-17s did cause problems. For example, when Plt Off Abdel Moneim al-Tawil had to bale out from a MiG-15 following a training accident shortly after the war, he landed with a badly broken arm – though no one could tell why. Having read some Martin-Baker* publicity literature, he came to the conclusion that his arm had snatched in the slipstream as he left the aircraft, since the early Russian ejection seats incorporated no means of securing the pilot's arms. The pilot also had to bend down in the cockpit and pull a lever to operate the ejection seat, all of which made it more difficult to escape from a damaged, perhaps violently tumbling and burning aircraft.

The Egyptian fighters had been flying top cover for four Meteor F8s of 5 Squadron EAF from Fayid which had been attacking Israeli forces at Bir

---

* The British Martin-Baker company was amongst the forerunners in the design of the ejector seat, its product being fitted to most RAF high-performance aircraft.

Wreckage of EAF Meteor F8 s/n 1424 apparently shot down by ground fire on 31 October 1956. (*IDF Archive*)

Hasana, when seven soldiers were killed and 20 wounded. One of the Meteors (s/n 1424) was apparently shot down by ground fire although it is believed the pilot survived and evaded capture. Some 45 minutes later, at 1330, another pair of Ouragans was despatched to the Mitla Pass for ground attack and these, too, were bounced by two MiGs only one of which pressed home an attack. With plentiful fuel and facing only a single MiG, Seren Agasi took advantage of the fact that the Egyptian pilot was chasing his wingman:

> "I saw an aircraft on my No2's tail, but I wasn't sure if it was a MiG or a Mystère, though I thought it was a MiG. I told him to break left and jettison his bombs and wing tanks. I did the same. I saw the MiG shooting in the turn and of course missing because of the very high angle-off (deflection) and because of the high G. I made the same mistake myself – I fired one short burst in the turn and missed. I knew of course that there was another MiG somewhere above, but I couldn't see it. I was anxious about it. Anyway, I could see that the first MiG was closing the turn on my No2, and if he changed the bank it would save him, so I told him to do so. Then I saw some more MiGs above. This change of direction brought me into a favourable position to fire on the first MiG, and I gave him a long burst and saw pieces fall off him. He immediately pulled up and straightened his wings. I shot at him again, hit him again and saw a big hole in his left wing and something burning and a lot of white smoke. I shot again but only one cannon fired, but I hit him near his jet pipe. After that, there was black smoke coming from his jet pipe. Because my cannons were not working any more, I came home."

The Ouragans' opponent was probably the MiG-15 flown by Flt Lt Farouke al-Gazawy, who reported:

Ouragan s/n 28 of 113 Squadron in flight shortly after the end of the Sinai campaign. (*Chaim Niv*)

"We were briefed to fly with three sections of two in an open battle formation and to patrol over Sinai at 6,000 metres (almost 20,000 feet). I picked up a target which was flying low on a reverse course heading south-west. I told my Squadron mates about the target and they said, 'You lead and we will follow'. It was my first engagement with an enemy aircraft so I should have checked whether my leader was following me or not but all I remember was how excited I was. I kept my eye on the enemy aircraft and started to close and prepared the guns. Then I discovered that I was alone but I kept my gunsight on the plane and fired one, two, three bursts. He was from time to time changing direction to throw off my aim. All of a sudden I heard two booms, then nothing. I thought it was a bump from flying through his slip-stream. My target reversed his steep turn and then I felt a severe crash and I was at a high angle of attack, perhaps 40°, and the stick was jammed. I put on full throttle, there was no afterburn in the MiG-15, and I climbed to 6,000 metres and found myself all alone. It was calm, not a word on the radio. I had taken a bullet through the canopy so I was losing pressurisation but luckily I could fly straight and level. I moved the stick and it jammed in a slight upward position. I came close to the Suez Canal and I was still losing height and I was worried because there was a big hole in the wing. I was worried that the enemy fire had damaged the undercarriage. But luckily I came in and landed OK."

During the early afternoon the Israeli Harvards were back in action when four aircraft attacked Egyptian vehicles on the al-Arish to Abu Aweiglia road; all returned safely. At 1400, six Mustangs of 105 Squadron from Ramat David attacked with napalm bombs Egyptian armoured forces near Bir Gafgafa, almost midway between the Israeli border and the Suez Canal, but lost one aircraft to ground fire. Its pilot, Seren Eldad Paz, recalled:

"I felt a strong shock, I smelled glycol . . . at first I thought to jump but I saw a field suitable for a belly-landing and I figured it would be better to clear the Egyptians that got my napalm. I did an emergency landing. There is no control after the aircraft touched down, you just pray that it would stop."

He climbed out of the Mustang (s/n 19) and crawled to a nearby wadi, where he remained until nightfall since Egyptian forces were in the area, although once on the ground he did not see any. As soon as darkness fell, he started walking eastwards in the direction of Bir Hasana but on arrival found it still occupied by Egyptian troops, so he headed north-eastwards towards Jebel Libni where he finally met an Israeli patrol after having covered 60km in 37 hours.

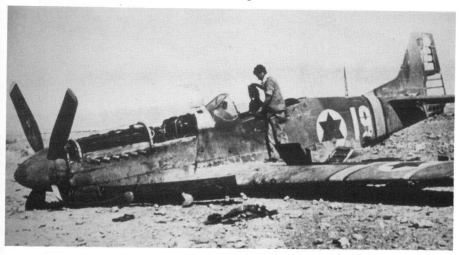

Seren Eldad Paz of 105 Squadron was obliged to force-land Mustang s/n 19 when it was damaged by ground fire on 31 October 1956. (*Eldad Paz*)

Meteors of 117 Squadron flew ten sorties against the Egyptian 1st Armoured column on the Bir Gafgafa to Jebel Libni road and a further eight sorties against lesser armoured vehicles along the al-Arish to Abu Aweiglia road. Four of the jets were damaged by ground fire during these attacks, of which two made emergency landings: one, with a damaged engine, at Hatzor, and the other, flown by the unit's commander Rav-Seren Yoeli, at Tel Nof. The port engine of Yoeli's aircraft had been hit while strafing near Bir Gafgafa and Yoeli himself wounded in the left hand. However, with a tourniquet wrapped round his arm and only one engine working, he arrived at Tel Nof to find that his port wheel would not come down:

> "I landed safely on the nose wheel and one side wheel [but] the fire crews nearly killed me with their axes, trying to get me out [until] I pulled out my pistol and threatened to shoot anybody who got near."

Taken to hospital for treatment to his wounded hand, Yoeli discharged himself three hours later to fly another sortie.

More and more Mustangs were being thrown into the battle, these ranging far and wide looking for targets. However, the Mustang, because of its lower speed and exposed radiator, was proving vulnerable to ground fire, and several returned to base carrying the scars of battle damage. The tanks of the Egyptian 1st Armoured Brigade remained a prized target although contact had temporarily been lost, as recalled by Seren Tse'elon of 116 Squadron:

> "We were ordered to search for an armoured column. I searched for about two hours in the area of Abu Aweiglia . . . and not just us but also other

Camouflaged Meteor F8 carrying Sinai campaign stripes. (*IAF Magazine collection*)

formations were searching, Mosquitos and Mustangs, and nobody found it. Finally, I decided to fly towards Bir Gafgafa and suddenly I located the advancing column. I asked for a jet fighter at high altitude to notify ground control. We attacked it and they [HQ] sent all the formations to that place. They stopped the column."

One Mustang attacked an ammunition truck which exploded with such force that the fighter-bomber was tossed upwards like a leaf. After the action the lucky pilot, Segen Zvi Kohorn, reported:

"Suddenly we spotted an armoured column on the central axis. Things became lively. Truck after truck and tank after tank went up in flames. It seemed at first like a practice range in peacetime; but after bullets began exploding all round us, it got more serious. [Seren] Gelbard and [Segen] Fredlis, their windshields covered in oil, swooped blindly on where they expected the targets to be, and the rest of us tried to fill in the gaps. Gelbard and I went in to attack a concentration of tanks. I suddenly saw puffs of exploding 40mm shells flicking into the air near us. In a second I located the firing gun and began diving on it. The gun crew tried to keep their barrel trained on me, but when they found they were too late, they jumped and started crawling on the ground. A short burst from the .5 Browning took care of them. A similar incident almost led to a crash, when I fired on an ammunition truck and it exploded. The blast lifted me into the line of flight of another plane, and we nearly collided. All but one of us ran out of ammunition, and [Segen] Sharon stayed behind to finish his rounds after our five other planes turned for home."

Despite the graphic account, the Mustangs on this occasion were credited with the destruction of only two tanks and two trucks. Of the six Mustangs that took part in this action, five returned with damage inflicted by ground fire or debris. Seren Tse'elon was back in action that evening:

138

". . . that evening I returned to attack it [the Egyptian armoured column]. While I was diving in a rocket attack, a shell exploded above my wing and blinded me. I could not see for a couple of seconds. I pulled out slowly so that I would not hit the ground, because I could not see . . . they [the Egyptians] had an excellent firing discipline, they shot from all their weapons."

One of his flight, Seren Ya'acov Rafaeli, crash-landed his Mustang near the Bir Hama road after being hit by ground fire while attacking tanks and vehicles. All told, 14 Mustangs suffered damage during the day, and five of these failed to return, including that flown by Rav-Seren Tadmor, commander of 105 Squadron, who was killed when shot down near Abu Aweiglia; Seren Shlomo Hagani, a Reservist, took his place as temporary commander of the Squadron. Segen Asaf Ben-Nun's Mustang was hit while attacking an armoured column on the al-Arish to Abu Aweiglia road, although the pilot was able to crash-land the crippled aircraft near Be'erot Itshak.

By the end of that day (31 October), Israeli fighters had flown almost 150 sorties over Sinai. The Ouragans had been particularly active and alone notched up 48 sorties in support of the ground forces. Tragically, on one occasion, a flight of four aircraft mistook their own forces for those of the Egyptians and carried out a strafing and bombing attack on units of the 7th Brigade at Jebel Libni, during which seven Israelis were wounded. The Meteors contributed a further 30 sorties, including an attack by four aircraft on an Egyptian radar station.

Fighting for control of the Mitla Pass had been particularly bitter. However, for the Egyptians the battle had demonstrated the high degree of effective co-operation between ground forces and ground-attack aircraft achieved by the Army and the Air Force, since the often chaotic days of the first Arab-Israeli War of 1948–49. On several occasions EAF Meteors and Vampires flew into this deep desert valley in support of Egyptian troops holding positions in caves and along the cliff on either side. Though the MiGs usually flew top cover, they also strafed Israeli vehicles trapped in the valley, joining Meteors and Vampires in raking exposed Israeli troops who were attempting to scale the cliffs to flush out the Egyptian defenders. On one particular occasion, an Israeli patrol was pinned down by Egyptian aircraft in the narrow Heitan Defile within the Mitla Pass and suffered serious casualties in killed, wounded, loss of support weapons and transport. Because the Egyptian defenders were in prepared positions and under very determined leadership, the EAF was able to attack the more exposed Israeli troops, whereas the IDF/AF found it difficult to separate friend from foe in this close fighting for the control of the Pass. The Egyptian squadrons also had the added advantage of operating closer to their Canal Zone bases, enabling them to loiter over the target and make repeated strikes whereas the Israelis were operating from very long range.

EAF pilots at the Fighter Training Unit at Fayid also flew a number of attack missions against Israeli forces. Flt Lt Tahseen Zaki,* an instructor assigned to

---

* Flt Lt Tahseen Zaki had previously flown Spitfire F22s with 2 Squadron at Helwan and al-Arish; later he became the leader of the EAF aerobatic team and commanded the Air Force's first squadron (55 Squadron, 1st Air Regiment) of Su-7 ground attack aircraft in 1967.

Tahseen Zaki, seen here as a newly qualified pilot in front of one of 2 Squadron's Spitfire F22s, probably at Helwan, flew a Fury during the Sinai War. (*Authors' collection*)

Plt Off Ali Sharmi was still on the EAF's jet conversion course when the war started. He flew one or two missions in a Spitfire F22 and a Fury in the early days of the war. (*Authors' collection*)

this squadron, on one occasion flew a Hawker Fury over Sinai and strafed several Israeli targets. One of his students, Plt Off Ali Sharmi, also made at least one attack sortie flying a Spitfire F22, though the precise time and locations of these missions has not been released. During the second day of fighting, EAF aircraft flew more than 100 strike and patrol sorties against Israeli forces in Sinai. As the fighting grew in intensity, so the EAF's response became more determined, its sortie rate increasing dramatically. Only the Anglo-French blitz effectively removed the Egyptian Air Force from the Sinai War.

In an effort to buy time and conceal from the Egyptian public news of the increasingly serious situation faced by their forces in Sinai, Cairo Radio and newspapers spoke only of the great victories being achieved:

"The story was that a small Israeli force had crossed the frontier at a point guarded only by a narcotics patrol mounted on camels; that the Israeli soldiers were chopped down as fast as they came in contact with the Egyptian Army; that most of the Israeli Air Force was destroyed in the first 24 hours; that everywhere the Egyptian Army was victorious."

Despite these extravagant claims, President Nasser ordered a general withdrawal of Egyptian forces from eastern Sinai during the evening of 31 October, those based in the Gaza Strip in northern Sinai – a coastal strip of land bordered on two sides by Israeli territory, and on the third by the Mediterranean – being told to surrender if they were unable to escape so as to avoid civilian casualties. The Gaza Strip was crowded with refugee camps inhabited by Palestinian Arab refugee families who had been forced out of what had been southern Palestine prior to 1948. But part of the indigenous Palestinian Brigade based at Khan Yunis refused this order and were determined to fight on regardless. Although most of the aerial activity was centred on the Mitla Pass and Om Kattef to al-Qusseima regions, considerable Egyptian forces were based within the Gaza Strip, mainly in the locality of

Mosquito FB6 in Sinai campaign stripes being refuelled. (*Andy Thomas*)

Rafah, and comprised fortified emplacements to the south of the town occupied by elements of the Egyptian 5th Infantry Brigade, whose task was to prevent Israeli forces gaining access into Sinai through the al-Arish axis.

In an attempt to soften up the Egyptian defences for an assault by IDF ground forces, plans were put into operation for a naval and air bombardment of the well prepared emplacements. Mustangs from 105 Squadron and Mosquitos from 110 Squadron were called in initially. The first strike by four Mosquitos was launched against the hangars at al-Arish which were being used for tank ammunition storage. Seren Shimon Ash's aircraft, an FB6 s/n 69, sustained 15 strikes, one bullet piercing the hydraulics system, necessitating a belly-landing. Another of the Mosquitos (s/n 68, a T33) was flown by Segen David Gatmon, a Reservist who had just started a career as a civilian pilot with El Al; he also flew on a second strike by four Mosquitos, accompanied on this occasion by navigator Yair Alber:

"I was leading the second pair, my wingman was Amram Shemer. After the second or third pass my cannon jammed. I waited for him [Shemer]. I saw how he was diving and attacking and I remained above to watch over him, when I was hit by 20mm fire. I told him I was hit and injured, so he aborted the attack and accompanied me to base. There was a huge mess in the air traffic control (there were many British and French aircraft in the air) so I did not try to land at Hatzor or Tel Nof – I did not know the codes – and I had to drag myself to Ramat David. I did not know the extent of the damage to the aircraft but I was seriously injured in my [right] leg and also had a wound in my hand."

Despite his wounds, Gatmon made a safe landing at Ramat David from where he was rushed to hospital; he was discharged a month later.

The EAF launched a second nocturnal intrusion into Israel's skies during the night of 31 October/1 November, though this was also unsuccessful even though at least one Il-28 penetrated Israel's airspace. Hatzor was the intended target, but bombs fell harmlessly in fields near Gezer, east of the air base. Seren Tsiddon and Segen Brosh flew a one-hour sortie in the Meteor NF13 (s/n 52) but again no encounter occurred. It was, however, to be the last Egyptian air raid during the Sinai campaign as, at 1900, the RAF's Canberras and Valiants belatedly commenced their attack on the EAF's air bases (see Chapter Nine), causing the Egyptian Command to immediately evacuate some of its aircraft to Syria and Saudi Arabia, whilst up to 24 Il-28s were flown to Luxor in southern Egypt, thus effectively surrendering the skies over Sinai to the IDF/AF. The presence of the Ilyushins at Luxor had been confirmed by an Israeli Mosquito from Tel Nof, crewed by Seren Tavor and his navigator, Seren Elisha Gal-On, who had used binoculars from a safe distance to observe the bombers, and thereby avoided activating Egyptian anti-aircraft defences.

DAY FOUR – 1 NOVEMBER

Despite the air attacks around Rafah, Israeli troops were unable to penetrate the Egyptian defences and asked the French for help, who in turn ordered the cruiser *Georges-Leygues* to bombard the fortifications but, as she neared the Egyptian coast, a flight of jet fighters appeared and started making mock attacks on the cruiser. French gunners' fingers 'twitched on the triggers' until the identity of the 'attackers' had been established as US Navy aircraft from one of the Sixth Fleet carriers.

At 0200 the *Georges-Leygues* opened fire, shells allegedly 'crashing on the blockhouses, and disembowelled the system of trenches and wire', although the actual damage inflicted was later admitted to have been minimal. The proposed air attack by two B-17s and four Harvards, three of which carried flares for illumination of the target, revealed the limitations of the improvised strike force, as noted by a somewhat scathing Rav-Aluf Dayan:

> "For various reasons, the naval shelling could not begin before 0200 and lasted half an hour. The air bombing followed, from 0230 to 0305. The first was a complete flop, and the second a disaster. We all expected that the pounding would be carried out on a European scale . . . a total of 150 shells were fired on the Rafah camps, less than the number of rounds any self-respecting artillery battery of ours would have laid down for such an attack. As to the Air Force, our pilots managed to drop their parachute flares right on our own units, exposed them, and started bombing them. We immediately signalled them to stop."

Sgan-Aluf Ben-Chaim led the two B-17s back to Ramat David, their bomb loads intact. However, when two hours later Israeli ground forces moved into the attack, supported by Ouragans and Mustangs from 105 Squadron, the two B-17s returned to the battle area as dawn approached but, with cloud covering the target area, the crews were forced to release their bombs, somewhat ineffectively, on the northern and southern suburbs of Rafah. During the early morning strikes, a Mustang of 116 Squadron was hit by ground fire and crash-landed near Rafah, from which the pilot, Seren Barak, was recovered unhurt. As the Israeli ground forces advanced, some Egyptian units were ordered to withdraw to al-Arish, while others were told to 'fight to the last', which many did, but Rafah's fate was effectively sealed. By 0900 Rafah had fallen, and when the Israelis entered the town they found hundreds of Molotova trucks, field guns, machine-gun carriers – and hangars stocked with mountains of mines and Czech ammunition. Despite the Israeli success at Rafah, Gaza itself and most of the Gaza Strip remained in Egyptian hands, defended by a relatively small force of Egyptian troops supported by the large but poorly equipped Palestinian local defence force.

With the onset of the Anglo-French attack against Egyptian airfields, armoured and other units which had been resisting the Israeli invasion with some success, were ordered to abandon the Sinai front and return to defend the Egyptian heartland, where they were required to confront the new threat. Few EAF incursions were made over Sinai following the start of the Anglo-French attacks, although one was undertaken at dawn by a quartet of MiG-17s from Almaza, led by Sqn Ldr Shalabi al-Hinnawi, the Squadron commander:

> "At first light I led a flight of four MiG-17s in a strafing attack against an Israeli position near Mitla Pass. The Israelis were dug in and well camouflaged, exactly like sand and were very difficult to see. We started firing and caused several explosions. We finished our ammunition and turned back."

Sqn Ldr Shalabi al-Hinnawi, commander of the EAF's first MiG-17 squadron in the cockpit of his aircraft shortly before the Sinai/Suez War. Note construction number 8044 on an engine inspection hatch. (*Mustafa Shalabi al-Hinnawi*)

Later, during the afternoon, three long-nose Meteors – apparently Egyptian NF13s – were reported flying westward over Sinai, presumably being withdrawn after the EAF's brief attempt to disperse some of its aircraft to forward bases in eastern Sinai; the Meteors remained at high altitude and were not intercepted. However, a French RF-84F pilot operating from Cyprus reported sighting a Meteor going into land at an unspecified airfield and noted that it was "probably returning from Sinai", adding that the aircraft "exploded before reaching the ground". Possibly the Egyptian aircraft had suffered battle damage.

Before the onset of the Anglo-French assault, the Egyptians had remained confident of holding the western part of the Sinai Peninsula and of stopping the

Pilots of 116 Squadron pose in front of a Mustang during the Sinai campaign (from left to right, front): Itshak Yavneh (CO), Dan Barak (IO), Eliezer Cohen, Aryeh Fredlis, Amnon Bloch; (left to right, rear): Israel Borstein, Ami Hativa, Shlomo Gelbard, Aryeh Tse'elon, Zvi Kohorn, Ze'ev Sharon. (*Itshak Yavneh*)

Israelis from reaching the Suez Canal. Their forces were making an orderly withdrawal from positions further east where, in fact, they had blunted a series of Israeli attacks on Abu Aweiglia until that position's flanks were turned by IDF thrusts into central Sinai and towards Rafah. Meanwhile, the men defending the Mitla Pass had still barred the Israeli paratroopers, and the light desert column sent to support them, from breaking through to the Canal. Apparently the Egyptian Army planned to make a stand at the northern end of the Sinai mountains, straddling the main road which led to Ismailia and the Egyptian heartlands west of the Canal. It also appears that the EAF intended to support this stand by sending flights, if not full squadrons, to the Sinai airfields of Bir Gafgafa and Bir Rod Salim. The imminent Anglo-French landings at the northern end of the Canal and their drive southwards towards Ismailia behind these positions would, of course, soon have made them untenable. Only then did an Egyptian evacuation of the entire Sinai Peninsula become inevitable. But even before the Anglo-French landings, it seems that the EAF had decided on a radical change of plan, reversing the dispersal of some aircraft forwards into Sinai. Large numbers of machines were flown out of harm's way to Saudi Arabia and Syria, or to the false security of southern Egypt. Others were sent singly or in pairs to emergency dispersal strips in the Nile Delta.

At 1030, eight Mustangs of 116 Squadron set out from Tel Nof to bomb and strafe Egyptian units at Om Kattef, where they were keeping up a stiff rearguard action. Segen Cohen recalled:

> "At the moment I dropped the napalm bomb, a chill passed through me as I saw a machine-gunner sitting on the cannon firing – at my 04 [his aircraft].

French Mystère 2-EL of EC1/2 which operated initially as '199 Squadron' IDF/AF. (*Chaim Niv*)

The cannon erupted in flames, perhaps incinerating its gunner as well, and my 04 began to spill blood. The machine-gunner's bullets had pierced the oil-filled radiator. Black liquid gushed out, spraying the cockpit canopy, turning day into night."

Cohen was able to carry out a creditable crash-landing. He was followed down by Segen Fredlis, who pinpointed the location of the crash, and recalled his eventual return:

"He returned with the aircraft's radio! We had an instruction to extract the crystal . . . after he had landed he searched for the crystal but did not find it so he dismantled the complete radio (then the radios were big, heavy boxes); he met an Arab with a donkey, so took the donkey and returned to the Squadron with the radio."

Fortunately Cohen had come down well clear of the Egyptian positions he had been attacking and, after carefully surveying the area, set out eastwards towards the frontier. He reached the al-Qusseima to Abu Aweiglia road just after noon, where he eventually 'surrendered' to an IDF tank crew. Having convinced his captors of his identity, he was returned to Tel Nof. A second Mustang of 116 Squadron was also shot down during the attack and the pilot, Seren Shlomo Gelbard, similarly survived the subsequent crash-landing.

While the Anglo-French attacks on EAF bases reduced the air threat over Sinai, IDF/AF sorties against the retreating Egyptian ground forces intensified; Mustangs, Meteors and Ouragans were joined by Mystères and Mosquitos in this role. F-84Fs and French Mystères of EC2 from Ramat David also made an appearance during the day, ground crews having reinstated the French cockade for the Mogan David during the preceding night, the need for secrecy having passed. By the end of the day, the F-84F pilots alone claimed 38 Russian-built T-34 tanks destroyed. Other targets included Egyptian units withdrawing towards what the Egyptian High Command planned as a second line of defence running from the Mitla Pass, through Bir Gafgafa and Bir Rod Salim, towards Lake al-Bardawil on the Mediterranean coast. A total of 62 sorties were flown by the French fighters during the day against the armoured column on the Bir

Gafgafa road, and against convoys and vehicles on the roads between al-Arish to al-Qantara, and Abu Aweiglia to Ismailia. All Mystères and F-84Fs returned safely from these sorties, some showing signs of minor battle damage. However, two of the latter were lost in an accident at Lod. Due to a fog over the main runway, the two F-84F pilots decided to use the short strip reserved for piston-engined aircraft, only to run out of runway which resulted in both aircraft careering across the grass, out of control. Both pilots were able to scramble clear before the jets exploded in balls of flame, causing the crew of a nearby parked DC-4 to rapidly evacuate their aircraft.

Ouragans of 113 Squadron were also in action at Om Kattef where 30 tanks of the Egyptian 4th Armoured Brigade were attacked, three of which were left in flames. One of the Ouragans returned to Hatzor with no fewer than 60 bullet and fragment holes in its wings and fuselage, a tribute to its ruggedness and reliability; another, flown by Seren Shefer, suffered a fuel malfunction but was able to return to Hatzor on completion of its sortie. Two more rocket-armed Ouragans departed Hatzor on an unofficial sortie, one flown by the base commander Aluf-Mishne Weizman, the other by his operations officer, Seren Yeshayahu Bareket, who had complained to his commander that he felt he was missing out on the action. En route to the road separating al-Arish from Port Said, Weizman's aircraft developed a leak in its starboard fuel tank, although it did not prevent him from leading a rocket and strafing attack on an Egyptian train encountered on the railway track leading to Port Said.

Mustangs launched an afternoon strike against Egyptian tanks retreating from al-Arish, the airfield and military depot having been abandoned just as it had been during the 1948–49 War. Units of the IDF's 27th Brigade arrived at al-Arish and occupied the base, which was soon made ready to receive IDF/AF Dakotas and Piper Cubs, including one of the liaison aircraft conveying Rav-Aluf Dayan. The Israelis found several dummy Vampires, expertly constructed mainly from wood (including one bearing the s/n 1582) and two abandoned Mraz Sokol trainers, one of which was severely damaged. Dayan noted:

"Al-Arish was evacuated without being destroyed or sabotaged. A few military stores had been set on fire, but these formed only a trifling part of the huge quantity of military equipment which was left. It was apparent that when the withdrawal order was given, everyone simply left his post and rushed to join the convoys leaving the city. I took off from the al-Arish airfield in my Piper to return to GHQ. I asked my pilot to circle the city, but we quickly had to climb to get beyond the range of rifle and machine-gun fire being directed at us; the sand dunes east, south and west of al-Arish were studded with Egyptian soldiers, singly and in groups, taking cover among bushes and in folds in the ground."

At least 20 Russian T-34 tanks, six Russian SU100 self-propelled guns, dozens of Zil trucks, hundreds of Czech 82mm recoilless guns and thousands of anti-tank mines were captured intact. The T-34s were immediately taken into action by the IDF, although problems with identification soon arose, particularly for the French pilots who on one occasion attacked the Israeli column. Following this incident, the French requested that white crosses be painted on Israeli vehicles to avoid a repetition but there were a few orthodox Jews who, initially, refused to fight under the sign of the cross. To avoid further confusion, the

The end of Mosquito PR16 s/n 90 in November 1956 following a recce flight to Syria by Ze'ev Tavor (pilot, right) and navigator Rafael Sivron. (*IAF Magazine collection*)

French Mystères were ordered not to cross the Canal, since Allied pilots from Cyprus and the aircraft carriers stationed off the Egyptian coast were experiencing difficulty recognising each other, let alone having to distinguish between MiG and Mystère.

Mosquitos of 110 Squadron were despatched to support the IDF's 9th Brigade's advance that evening against Ras Nasrani and Sharm al-Sheikh, at the southern tip of the Sinai Peninsula, in an attempt to achieve one of Israel's original aims – to open the Strait of Tiran to Israeli commercial shipping. The 9th Brigade rested at Eilat until total air superiority over Sinai was secured, since it was to advance some 200km over very difficult terrain. To aid the Brigade in its movement, 100 Squadron despatched several Piper Cubs to Eilat, their crews tasked with local reconnaissance.

That night the Egyptian frigate *Domiat* (formerly HMS *Nith*), bringing reinforcements to the Sharm al-Sheikh garrison, was sunk when she failed to answer a signal and exchanged shots with the Royal Navy cruiser HMS *Newfoundland*, part of the British squadron patrolling the Gulf of Aqaba; 68 survivors were rescued later by other vessels of the Squadron and held as prisoners of war. *Newfoundland* suffered minor damage in the one-sided action, although one sailor was killed and five wounded.

Darkness brought with it a further night sortie for the 119 Squadron crew, Tsiddon and Brosh flying Meteor NF13 s/n 50 on this occasion, as recalled by the latter:

"We probably intercepted a British Canberra . . . apparently the British were
for once close to our southern coastline and we intercepted the Canberra,
but it saw us and it evaded. The skies were very cloudy and it was very easy
to evade."

Meteor NF13, s/n 50, intercepted an RAF Canberra on the night of 1/2 November 1956. (*Adam Tsivoni*)

DAY FIVE – 2 NOVEMBER

As IDF forces made final preparations for an assault against Khan Yunis, the centre of the southern sector of the Gaza Strip, Meteors were called in to soften up the Egyptian defences. Operating in pairs, three separate strafing attacks were carried out, the Meteors joined in the task by the ubiquitous Mustangs from Tel Nof. All aircraft returned safely from these operations.

During the morning, Mustangs continued to support the Israeli 37th Brigade in its attack on Om Kattef, where pilots reported that the Egyptian strongpoints appeared to be deserted. However, although the report was accurate, elements of the 37th Brigade advanced so rapidly that they were mistaken for Egyptians by the IDF's 7th Brigade, which opened fire and destroyed eight of the nine tanks in the leading company before the mistake was realised; there were many casualties including the company commander, who was killed. 37th Brigade called for help and two Meteors were scrambled to the area to investigate. The pilots identified the ambushing force as another IDF unit and tried to stop the fight by buzzing the opposing forces. Their action was not wholly successful and it was not until a Piper Cub flown by Samal (Sgt) Paltiel Sirotkin arrived and landed nearby that the incident was brought to an end.

Focus of attention was now turned to the difficulties facing the Israeli 9th Brigade in its advance down the eastern shores of Sinai. To speed up the capture of Sharm al-Sheikh, intensive air attacks were planned against the Egyptian forces still defending the area. These included a unit equipped with 88mm and 30mm anti-aircraft guns. In addition to the air attacks, it was decided to drop two forces of paratroopers: one at Sharm al-Sheikh and the other at al-Tor on the western coast, some 70km north of the objective. The paratroopers were to advance from the latter to the former to expedite its capture.

Almost every type of aircraft available to the IDF/AF was thrown into the battle to soften up the Egyptian defences at Ras Nasrani and Sharm al-Sheikh. Both targets were relatively small and well defended against air raids and could only be attacked from north to south or vice versa, since they were located between the Gulf of Aqaba and the mountainous central Sinai. Although it was

148

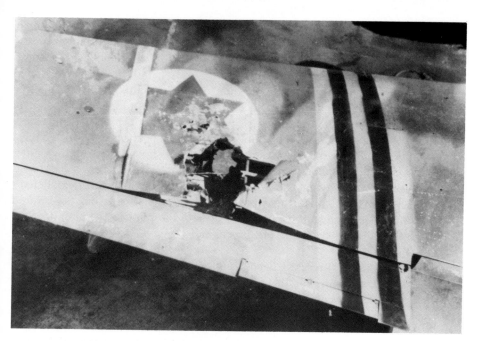

The port wing of Rav-Seren Itshak Yavneh's Mustang, s/n 53 of 116 Squadron, was damaged by a 30mm AA shell on 2 November 1956. (*Itshak Yavneh*)

possible to bomb from high level, accuracy was surrendered for equally dangerous risks, as witnessed when two of the B-17s were sent to bomb the anti-aircraft guns located there. The aircraft flown by Rav-Seren Nachom Efrat, a former commander of 69 Squadron, escaped damage but that flown by Sgan-Aluf Ben-Chaim suffered a direct hit in its port wing. Ben-Chaim ordered the bombs to be jettisoned, shut down the damaged engine and headed for Ramat David, where a safe landing was made. Mustangs from both squadrons operated against the defenders of Sharm al-Sheikh; Rav-Seren Yavneh of 116 Squadron returned to Tel Nof from one sortie with his aircraft (s/n 53) having been damaged in the port wing by a 30mm AA shell. One of his pilots, Segen Atkes, was not so fortunate and his Mustang (s/n 73) was brought down north of Ras Nasrani. Segen Fredlis remembered:

"We were ordered to bomb and strafe from high altitude, not to get close so that nobody would be hit, but Atkes decided to descend. We lost contact with him and his wingman . . . I saw that he made an emergency landing. The aircraft was completely covered with dust and it disappeared; you could not observe it any longer, it was the colour of the desert."

Badly wounded, Atkes managed to extricate himself from the aircraft but then passed out. He was found by Egyptian soldiers and taken prisoner.

At noon, two formations of Mystères were despatched to the area, where Rav-Seren Shapira's aircraft suffered damage from ground fire; the other formation was tasked to strike at Ras Nasrani and was led by Rav-Seren Peled. During the second or third pass at the target, intense ground fire hit Peled's Mystère and, with his aircraft gushing black smoke, the Squadron commander climbed to 5,000 feet before ejecting from his crippled machine – the first Israeli pilot to save his life by this means. With burns to his exposed arms and face, he landed heavily some three kilometres from the Egyptian strongpoints, and then, having discarded his parachute with some difficulty, he hobbled on a fractured ankle westwards towards the mountains to avoid capture, as Mustangs and Mosquitos circled overhead. One quartet of Mosquitos, led by Rav-Seren Somekh, dived down to low level and strafed three armoured vehicles that were probably searching for the downed pilot. Peled kept himself concealed, confident of rescue, and at 1500 he saw a Piper Cub approaching, which circled several times before departing again. However, two hours later another Piper Cub was seen and its pilot, Segen-Mishne Avraham Greenbaum, a Reservist, soon spotted Peled waving part of his parachute. Having confirmed Peled's identity, Greenbaum landed the Piper Cub about 200 yards from the injured pilot's hiding place and sent his observer to help the pilot to the aircraft, then followed himself after switching off the engine:

> "He [the observer] reached Benny, and only then did I understand that Benny had been hurt. Together we shuffled to the plane, Benny between us with his arms over our shoulders. He was limping heavily. We placed him on a stretcher on the Piper's back seat."

It was dark by the time the Piper Cub reached Eilat, from where Peled was flown by Dakota to Tel Nof. Greenbaum was decorated later for the rescue.

During the day French Mystères had again been in action. Armed with rockets, the aircraft of EC2 attacked a train and a number of trucks between Kabrit and al-Qantara. Late in the afternoon, two formations of Dakotas totalling seven aircraft set out for the airborne assault on Sharm al-Sheikh and al-Tor. The plan called for two companies to be parachuted at dusk, one to each target. However, it was appreciated by Air HQ that anti-aircraft emplacements at Sharm al-Sheikh had not been suppressed, and a decision was made against risking the slow and vulnerable Dakotas in this location. Instead, all the paratroopers were to be dropped over al-Tor, but by the time the change in plan had been agreed, the Dakotas were already on their way and could not be contacted by radio as they were flying at 300 feet to avoid possible detection by radar and high-flying EAF fighters.

In an attempt to make contact with the three Dakotas flying to Sharm al-Sheikh, a Meteor flown by Seren Lavon was sent to overtake them, which he managed to do, and was able to advise the leader of the change of plan by short-range radio. Consequently, all the paratroopers jumped over the deserted al-Tor airfield at dusk, aided by the lights of torches from the ground. Several suffered injuries including the battalion commander, who fractured an ankle and had to be evacuated for treatment. The airfield was rapidly made serviceable and during the course of the night a total of 25 flights were made to al-Tor – 23 by Dakotas and Noratlases and two by an El Al Constellation pressed into service, in which a complete infantry battalion was conveyed to the new battle front, together with weapons and ammunition for the paratroopers.

DAY SIX – 3 NOVEMBER

With total air superiority over Sinai in the hands of the IDF/AF, Rav-Aluf Dayan and his staff were able to fly, on the morning of 3 November, firstly to al-Tor, then to the Mitla Pass and on to al-Arish via Bir Hama, the Dakota

Noratlas 4X-ALH in El Al colours seen at Sharm al-Sheikh on 6 November 1956 wearing the Sinai campaign stripes. (*GPO*)

completely unescorted. However, fighting continued as Israeli forces closed in on Sharm al-Sheikh, with close support provided by the Piper Cubs of 100 Squadron. Towards the afternoon, IDF forces were nearing the Egyptian garrisons and further air strikes were ordered. At 1600, Mustangs from Tel Nof were despatched to the area, but as these were unable to make contact with the ground forces they were ordered to search for suitable targets and discovered a frigate sailing east of Ras Nasrani. Believing this to be the Egyptian *Domiat*, the Mustangs attacked in a single pass, firing their guns and rockets before releasing their napalm bombs. Their target was in fact HMS *Crane* (commanded by Capt B.S. Pemberton RN), part of the Royal Navy squadron that had sunk the Egyptian frigate two days earlier. The British vessel was struck by a small number of rockets which failed to inflict much damage since they were not armour-piercing, while all bombs missed.

However, *Crane*'s troubles were not yet over, since she had been spotted by rocket-armed Mystères, part of a larger formation that had just sunk a small Egyptian cargo vessel in the Gulf of Aqaba. The formation leader, Rav-Seren Bar, recalled:

"Following intelligence information, we were despatched to Ras Nasrani beach in a quartet armed with rocket pods and indeed we sunk the [cargo] ship. We were not informed of any other ship but, as we finished our attack, we observed a much larger ship off Sharm al-Sheikh. I informed about the ship over the radio."

Rav-Seren Shapira's element made a single pass but each of the pods contained regular, not armour-piercing, rockets. Nonetheless, four British sailors were killed during the attack. Able Seaman R.B. Loader, a Bofors gunner, was later awarded the DSM for continuing to fire at the attacking aircraft by manual control after the weapon controls had been damaged, and the ship's gunners believed they had hit one of their attackers. Indeed, an official communiqué claimed that an Israeli jet had crashed; however, this misinformation had been confused with the shooting down by Egyptian anti-aircraft fire of Rav-Seren

Peled's Mystère the day earlier. Commenting later on the incident, Aluf-Mishne Weizman wrote:

> "When we found out that it was a British destroyer, four of whose men were killed in the attack, we could only – and inadequately – express our regrets."

THE FINAL DAYS – 4 to 6 NOVEMBER

During the night of 1/2 November, a force of RAF Canberra bombers from Cyprus had raided Luxor in southern Egypt, where up to two dozen Il-28s were reported to have taken refuge, this raid being repeated the following night (see Chapters Ten and Eleven). Little damage resulted from these raids and the Egyptian jet bombers remained a threat. Cdt Perseval requested permission for his F-84Fs to carry out a low-level strike. Hence, shortly before 0600 on 4 November, 13 fighter-bombers of EC1 took off and headed for Luxor, the flights led by Perseval and the two escadrille commanders, Cdts Ladouce and Juillot. Fitted with long-range fuel tanks, the F-84Fs crossed the Egyptian border near Quseir and approached Luxor from the south, finding the Ilyushins drawn up in two neat rows either side of the runway. After a rocket and strafing attack lasting five minutes, the French fighter-bombers raced away in a north-easterly direction.

The attack was repeated by six more F-84Fs at about midday. High above the airfield taking photographs was Cdt Gerard Lapiche in an RF-84F (RF285) of ER4/33 from Cyprus. Although a subsequent press communiqué reported that 18 burning wrecks were seen on the airfield by the departing pilots, Lapiche's more precise report reveals that of the "17 aircraft including ten Beagles [Il-28s]" observed at Luxor, "one . . . was probably undamaged".

The Sinai campaign was rapidly drawing to a close. Mustangs continued to support the battle raging around Ras Nasrani and Sharm al-Sheikh during 4 November. The pilots reported a decrease in the intensity of AA fire from the defenders. At midday, five Mustangs showered the Egyptian defences at Ras Nasrani with napalm bombs but the defenders had already withdrawn to Sharm where, later that afternoon, two Mustangs rocketed an outpost from which

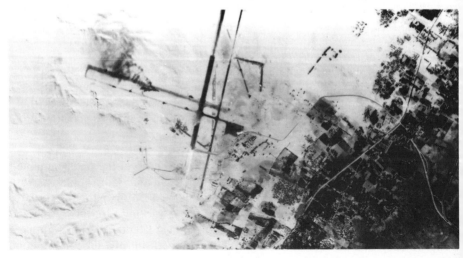

Cdt Lapiche's photograph of Luxor following the F-84F strikes on 4 November 1956; one Il-28 is seen burning. (*SHAA via Albert Grandolini*)

152

heavy fire had been pinning down the advancing Israeli troops. By nightfall the end was nigh and Egyptian casualties (plus the wounded Israeli pilot prisoner, Segen Atkes*) were evacuated by sea, but next morning saw continued fierce resistance by the gallant survivors despite further attacks by Mustangs and Ouragans, until the garrison finally surrendered at 0930; the Egyptians had suffered about 100 killed and 31 wounded, many of whom were casualties of the incessant air strikes, while a further 864 were taken prisoner. The Israelis suffered ten killed and 32 wounded.

At 1130 on the morning of 5 November, Mustangs and Ouragans armed with rockets and napalm bombs attacked the small island of Sunagrin, two miles off Tiran, after which Israeli forces landed. The island was deserted, its small garrison having been evacuated during the night.

At the very moment victory was in their grasp, the IDF suffered a severe blow when Aluf-Mishne Assaf Shimhoni, commander of the Southern Army, was killed during the night of 6 November. He was aboard a Police Piper Pacer (4X-AEQ) piloted by 22-year-old Samal-Rishon (Police Flt Sgt) Binyamin Gordon, on its way back from Sharm al-Sheikh when it strayed into Jordanian territory near Nablus and was shot down.† It crashed into a mountain; Gordon was also killed, as was Shimhoni's aide, Sgan-Aluf Asher Dromi. Their bodies were recovered and handed over to the United Nations who transported them to Jerusalem, where they were received by Israeli forces for burial.

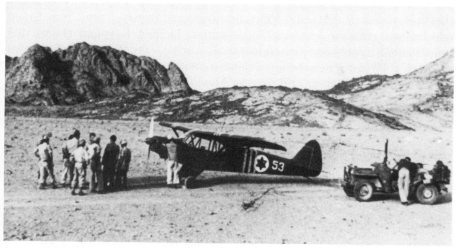

Piper Cub s/n 53 in a typical Sinai campaign scene. (*IAF Magazine collection*)

THE BALANCE SHEET

The IDF/AF flew a total of 1,846 sorties during the Sinai campaign, of which a staggering 831 were flown by the Piper Cubs and Kaydets, their tasks covering observation, liaison, casualty evacuation, pilot recovery and transportation; three Piper Cubs had been lost: one shot down by MiGs, one destroyed on the ground by MiGs, and one shot down over Jordan. A further 192 sorties were

---

* Segen Yonatan Atkes was transferred to Egypt from Sharm al-Sheikh aboard a small sailing vessel, and remained a prisoner of war until released on 31 January 1957.
†The Jordanians reported that the Piper was shot down, while the Israelis claim that it was an 'unfortunate' accident.

flown by the Dakotas and Noratlases, during which 1,200 casualties were evacuated to hospitals in Israel; there were also 42 reconnaissance sorties by Mosquitos and Meteors.

Mystères, Ouragans, Mustangs, Meteors and Harvards flew a total of 489 combat sorties, losing nine Mustangs, one Mystère, and two Harvards – all to ground fire; in addition at least five Mustangs suffered battle damage, as did two Meteors, one Ouragan (inflicted by a MiG), one Mystère and two Harvards; five pilots were killed and one taken prisoner. The vulnerable Harvards had in fact been withdrawn from operations on 1 November, 140 Squadron having flown 24 sorties by that date during which a total of 320 80mm rockets and 1,000 rounds of .5 ammunition had been expended.

In return for these losses, the IDF/AF claimed the shooting down of four Vampires, three MiG-15s and the Il-14, and was also credited with the destruction of 22 tanks, 17 armoured vehicles, three half-trucks, eight Bren carriers, four 40mm gun carriers, and 254 soft-skin vehicles. Although records are not available for the Armée de l'Air detachment, it is known that the F-84Fs at Lod logged a total of 101 operational sorties during *Operation Kadesh*. Apart from the two F-84Fs written off in accidents, no Israeli-based Armée de l'Air aircraft was lost although eight, including Mystères, suffered damage from ground fire.

Egyptian fighters and bombers flew more than 200 sorties during the initial phase of combat against Israel in Sinai, fighter-bomber pilots flying many effective ground attack sorties which destroyed and damaged numerous Israeli vehicles and inflicted considerable casualties. Despite Egyptian claims, the Israelis admitted only one aircraft lost in air combat – the Piper Cub shot down by MiGs; EAF losses were believed to have comprised three MiG-15s, probably one MiG-17, four Vampire FB52s, two Meteors (at least one of which was an F8), plus at least two Mraz Sokols on the ground at al-Arish, one of which (s/n 322) was captured virtually intact and flown later to Tel Nof by Rav-Seren

The IDF captured this EAF Sokol (s/n 322) at al-Arish. The grinning pilot with an Uzi sub-machine-gun is Rav-Seren Yeshayahu Gazit who had just flown the Sokol from al-Arish to Tel Nof. (*Israel Ben-Shachar*)

Israeli pilots pose in front of the wing of a shot-down Egyptian MiG. The black wingtip stripes are clearly visible. (*IDF*)

Gazit. Although the EAF over Sinai had fought well, once its bases in the Egyptian heartland had been attacked by the Anglo-French forces, it did not reappear in any numbers over this theatre of operations.

The EAF was proud of its performance in action against Israel; the command staff, pilots and support crews aggressively contested the Israeli invasion. Clearly the EAF had shown itself much more effective in the ground attack role, particularly in the close support of the Egyptian Army, than in air combat, just as it had in the 1948–49 War. This pattern would, in fact, remain for many more years. Nevertheless, it was the Israelis who celebrated victory at the conclusion of the brief Sinai War. In summing up the successful *Operation Kadesh*, Rav-Aluf Dayan wrote:

"The military victory in Sinai brought Israel not only direct gains – freedom of navigation, cessation of terrorism – but, more important, a heightened prestige among friends and enemies alike."

Chapter Eight

THE ANGLO-FRENCH BUILD-UP
August to October 1956

"We can stop them [the Anglo-French Task Force] but we will have to blast hell out of them. We can defeat them. The British, the French, the Egyptians, and the Israelis."

Admiral Ardleigh Burke,
US Chief of Naval Operations, to US State Department

During the autumn of 1956, Britain and France had 'secretly' called up reserves, assembled an invasion fleet and flown dozens of fighters and bombers to bases in Malta and Cyprus for the proposed attack on Egypt, codenamed *Operation Musketeer*. The initial plan called for an air assault to neutralize the Egyptian Air Force, followed by a joint air–sea assault on Alexandria, then a break-out along the road to Cairo and an advance across the Delta to the Canal, but this had been discarded in late August for political reasons based partly upon the fear of causing heavy civilian casualties. The revised plan fell into four distinct phases: Phase I – the neutralisation of the EAF; Phase II – air attacks against selected key points, combined with a psychological warfare campaign designed to reduce the Egyptian will to resist, thereby leading to the overthrow of President Nasser and his government; Phase III – a joint Anglo-French airborne assault against Port Said and Port Fuad to secure the coastal airfield at Gamil, to the east of Port Said, and the bridges leading to Suez; Phase IV – a seaborne landing at Port Said by Royal Marine commandos and French commando units, followed by a break-out down the length of the Canal.

To deal with all aspects of assembling the force and operational planning, the British and French governments established a joint military planning committee. Air Marshal Denis Barnett, former AOC of 205 Group in Egypt, was appointed Air Task Force Commander, with Général d'Brigade Aérienne Raymond Brohon of the Armée de l'Air as his deputy. French officers who attended the committee meetings in London included Colonel Maurice Perdrizet (see Chapters Six and Seven), who acted as Général Brohon's representative, Lt Colonel Jacques Le Groignec (in charge of the deployment of the Armée de l'Air's F-84F fighter-bombers), Lt Colonel Gueguen (responsible for transport planning), and Lt Colonel Vallet (in charge of aerial reconnaissance). The French delegation expressed a preference for Phase I of *Operation Musketeer* to be followed by a total attack on Egyptian ground forces, but the British were more concerned with efforts to break Egyptian morale. In addition to eliminating the EAF, the British wanted to strike at power stations, the railway network, bridges and communications, and also planned to drop leaflets to incite a revolt against Nasser's government. They hoped that the subsequent invasion of Egyptian territory would be seen as a liberation. The proposed psychological phase of *Operation Musketeer* posed serious problems for the French command. Having been obliged to accept that the initial aerial assault would be reduced to three nights and two days, they believed that ten days of psychological warfare demanded by their British opposite numbers would enable the Egyptian Army to regain its balance and establish defences against the Allied invasion. In the event the French insisted on more prompt action and a speedy invasion.

One particular problem faced by the French military chiefs was to assemble an effective force without weakening the French military effort against the insurgents in Algeria. To cover all eventualities in case Egypt should be able to retaliate, the French drew up a contingency air defence plan in case of attacks on the French mainland or French possessions in North Africa by Egyptian Air Force Il-28s and Lancasters. Hence, Mystère IICs and Mistrals (French-built Vampires) were placed on alert at Istres, Nice and Ajaccio (Corsica), and sections of Mistrals from EC6 and EC7 were similarly prepared in Algeria at Boufarik and Telergma.

By 19 September, London realised that the military movements in the Mediterranean had been recognised by the United Nations Security Council as a threat towards Egypt. There was a great deal of indecision before the final plan of attack was agreed upon but, even then, much was left to chance. An insight into the political and military uncertainty was given by Air Marshal Sir Harry Broadhurst GCB KBE DSO DFC AFC, AOC-in-Chief, Bomber Command:

> "I was sent for by the Secretary of State who asked whether I knew about the plan. I said it wasn't a Commander-in-Chief's job to know plans; that I merely supplied the bombers. He then said 'But they'll be shot down, won't they?' and I said, 'What by?'; and he said 'Well, the Russians are there, you know, they've got instructors.' I said, 'Yes, but they haven't got any night fighters, and we're not going by day, but by night.' He then said, 'Well, they've got very good radar.' And I said, 'I know. It was installed by Marconi, and I have had a personal briefing which said that there are no technicians left and there are no spares. I doubt if the radar will be working.' He then said, 'Do you know the plan?' I said, 'No,' so he took me across to the blackboard and showed me the plan and I started to laugh. He said, 'What are you laughing at?' I said, 'The plan.' He said, 'What's the matter with it?' I said, 'It's a typical Army plan! I reckon you can wipe that lot out with an airborne set-up and a good tactical air force support.' He then threatened to put me under arrest! I couldn't believe it. I brushed out of the room and went along to see the CAS [Chief of Air Staff] and said, 'What the hell's going on in this place? He threatened to put me under arrest.' He [the CAS] said, 'Not to worry. It happens to me before breakfast every morning!' "*

---

* Air Marshal (later Air Chief Marshal) Sir Harry Broadhurst, a Second World War fighter ace and commander of the famous Desert Air Force, added retrospectively: 'If we had had Maggie Thatcher [British Prime Minister 1979–91] in charge of this operation we'd have gone through the Suez Canal like a dose of salts!' Sir Harry died in 1995.

Sqn Ldr Peter Ellis of 6 Squadron with Akrotiri's commander, Grp Capt J.C. Macdonald. (*Grp Capt P.C. Ellis*)

Among the first aircraft arrivals at Nicosia, as British military forces began to build up in Cyprus, were two RAF Canberra PR7s (WH775 and WH801) of 58 Squadron, followed by two more in September (WH799 and WT540) under the command of Flt Lt B.L. Hunter (a former fighter pilot), to augment 13 Squadron at Akrotiri which was in the process of converting from Meteor PR10s to the type. Due to their short range which rendered them unsuitable for operations over Egypt, the Meteor FR9s of 208 Squadron at Akrotiri had moved to Takali, Malta, in early August, to make room for the 15 Venom FB4s (and two T11s) of Sqn Ldr J.R. Maitland's 249 Squadron which arrived from Amman on 27 August. Jock Maitland, recipient of the US DFC and Air Medal, had flown with the USAF in Korea, where he had shot down one and possibly two MiG-15s, but then his mount had been an F-86 Sabrejet. Akrotiri was also the current base for 6 Squadron's Venom FB4s, the unit having arrived from Habbaniya in April, commanded by Sqn Ldr Peter Ellis DFC who had flown Mosquito fighter-bombers during the closing stages of the Second World War.

Two dozen of Fighter Command's new Hunter F5s of the Tangmere Wing (1 Squadron under the temporary command of Flt Lt H.J. Irving, and 34 Squadron commanded by Sqn Ldr Alastair Wilson DFC, the latter a Second World War ace) were next to arrive. The detachment was under the command of Wg Cdr Peter Simpson DFC (Tangmere's Wing Leader and Second World War fighter ace) whose personal aircraft (WP144) bore his initials, PJS, in place of the usual individual aircraft code letter. However, Simpson soon returned to the UK, tour-expired, and command of the Hunter Wing was assumed by Sqn Ldr Wilson until the arrival of Wg Cdr E.W. Wright DFC DFM, another wartime

158

Pilots of 8 Squadron digging trenches at Akrotiri for protection against possible air attack (left to right): Flg Off Dave Power, Flg Off Dai Jones, Flg Off Jock Munroe (with pick), Flg Off Nick von Berg. (*Sqn Ldr R.K.J. Hadlow*)

ace. Flt Lt F.W.T. Davis temporarily took over 34 Squadron and, at about the same time, Sqn Ldr R.S. Kingsford arrived to take over 1 Squadron. Two of the Hunters (WP124 and WP132/T) were soon lost to 34 Squadron following accidents at Nicosia, where the former crash-landed on 29 August and Flt Lt A.R. Satow was injured. 1 Squadron also suffered damage to one of its aircraft when an oleo leg collapsed on landing. Two replacement Hunters arrived for 34 Squadron on 12 September, their pilots being attached to the Squadron. However, the Hunters were found wanting when the shooting war started, with insufficient endurance for offensive operations, and were thus used mainly in the defensive role as it was feared that Cyprus would be a possible target for Egypt's jet bombers, should she have the opportunity to retaliate.

More Venom FB4s had arrived at the beginning of October, when 8 Squadron flew to Akrotiri from Habbaniya, to where it had flown three weeks earlier with 16 aircraft from its normal base at Khormaksar in Aden, ostensibly to undertake an Air Practice Camp but in reality to locate the Squadron north of Suez for easy transfer to Cyprus; one of the Venoms had been fitted with a replacement canopy, courtesy of the Iraqi Air Force, following a last-minute accident. The unit was under the command of Sqn Ldr Colin Blyth DFC AFC (known to his friends and contemporaries as Joe), who had flown Meteors during the Korean War. Of the brief stay at Habbaniya, one of 8 Squadron's pilots, Flg Off Nick von Berg, a South African-born Kenyan of German ancestry, recalled with amusement:

"The Iraqis were also using the facilities [at Habbaniya] and had a Venom squadron based next door to us at the same time. Consequently, we could not help noticing that they were openly cheating on their air-to-air scores by failing to cancel hits on the banner before it was reused! They [the Iraqi pilots] said quite aggressively that if we ended up on the opposite sides we, the RAF, would get hacked out of the sky!"

Soon after its arrival at Akrotiri, 8 Squadron scrambled two standby Venoms to investigate an unidentified aircraft approaching Cyprus from the south, Sqn Ldr Blyth (WR405) leading Flg Off von Berg:

"It turned out to be a Curtiss C-46 Commando with strange markings. Apparently an American pilot used to buy these machines from war surplus in India and fly them single-handed to South America, where he no doubt made a handsome profit. I gather that he had large quantities of four-gallon fuel cans on board and, when required, would engage the autopilot and go back and pump these into the fuel tanks. Anyhow, he refused to speak to us and slowly started to turn to the west. When our fuel got low, another pair of Venoms arrived on the scene and saw him off towards Malta!"

Sqn Ldr Blyth added:

"Apparently he [the American pilot] was navigating with the aid of an old atlas. Rather him than me!"

Of the build-up period, Flg Off Tony Gronert, one of 249 Squadron's senior pilots, remembered:

"During October the [Venom] Wing was flying a large number of Alert Patrol sorties, with security tightened up considerably. Escape and evasion techniques and procedures were taken more seriously than previously. Escape kits were issued with button magnetic compasses, saw blades, knives, maps and the usual paraphernalia stitched into flying suits and underwear. We were also given a pile of 'goolie chits' which valued us at about a fiver each! We also had a sealed rubber bag reputed to contain five gold sovereigns: they must have been there because they were very insistent on them being returned afterwards. Apart from the standard water bag which was integral in the ejector seat, we all took another couple of bottles. Together with our Smith and Wesson .38s strapped to our waists, it was with some difficulty we managed to fit into the cockpit."

In the meantime, the Hunters were engaged in a variety of air defence exercises against Venoms from Akrotiri, and mounted a Battle Flight to investigate incursions into Cypriot airspace by unidentified aircraft, a role undertaken during the hours of darkness by the Meteor NF13s of 39 Squadron. During the last ten days of October the night fighters flew an average of 12 sorties a night, making many interceptions of 'unidentified' aircraft, the majority being Allied aircraft – Constellations, Yorks, Dakotas and Vikings – which had strayed from their flight-planned routes. On one occasion (20 October) a French civil DC-6 was forced by the Hunters of 34 Squadron to land at Nicosia after it had strayed into a prohibited zone while on its way from Athens to Karachi. 34 Squadron's diarist noted:

"The [DC-6] captain proved to be most unco-operative even when informed

160

Hunter F5 WP136/N of 34 Squadron ready for take-off, Akrotiri. (*Sqn Ldr R.K.J. Hadlow*)

that he was flying outside his allotted air corridor, but eventually did land after being 'shadowed' by three pairs of Hunters and jettisoning all his overload fuel.''

During the daylight hours of 29 and 30 October, pairs of Hunters operating from Nicosia intercepted not only a Syrian Dakota and an Egyptian Convair in Cypriot airspace, but also four Canberras, a Viking, a Washington (apparently an aircraft of 192 Squadron), a French Noratlas, a DC-3, and two USAF aircraft – a C124 Globemaster and a Dakota. Egyptian sources claim that the EAF carried out a number of reconnaissance missions prior to the Suez invasion, though there is no evidence of any penetrating Cypriot airspace. However, an Israeli B-17, which had apparently been photographing Egyptian coastal military defences and shipping movements, did stray into Cypriot airspace and was ordered to land. The B-17 duly arrived over the island and began its landing approach but, when near to the airfield, the pilot reported that he was unable to lower the starboard undercarriage, and therefore would have to go around again in an attempt to free the offending wheel. This he did, but again reported the same problem and offered to belly-land the big aircraft. Fearful of the consequences, the RAF controller ordered the Israeli pilot to leave Cypriot airspace forthwith and return whence he came. Whether the aircraft had genuinely experienced undercarriage malfunction, or that the Israeli pilot had simply bluffed his way out of an awkward situation, is not known.

Early in October, the seizure by French forces of a cargo vessel from Cairo carrying arms intended for the Algerian insurrectionists had revived anti-Egyptian feeling in France, followed later in the month by the capture of an aircraft carrying the Algerian rebel leader and several of his aides which raised the war fever to the highest pitch. French air units began arriving towards the end of October, and for the most part came from the Commandement Aérien Tactique and the Groupement des Moyens Militaires de Transport Aérien (Tactical Air Command and the Military Transport Group). These were brought together as the Groupement Mixte no.1 which was created on 23 October with its own operational command, integrated with the Anglo-French command,

F-84F 1-NF (s/n 23068) of EC1/1 complete with long-range tanks at Akrotiri. (*Sqn Ldr R.K.J. Hadlow*)

although the logistical structure remained under French control. There were detachments from five fighter-bomber squadrons: the EC1/1 Corse (1-N series codes), EC2/1 Morvan (1-8 codes), EC3/1 Argonne (1-P codes), EC1/3 Navarre (3-H codes) and EC3/3 Ardennes (3-V codes), with a total of 54 F-84Fs, although only EC1/3 and EC3/3 remained at Nicosia (with 36 aircraft), the other three units flying to Israel. A further six F-84Fs from EC2/3 Champagne (3-I codes) arrived at Nicosia on 31 October. The pilots were drawn from all six squadrons of the 1re and 3e Escadres de Chasse based at Saint-Dizier and Rheims; there were also ten RF-84Fs of a reconnaissance unit temporarily known as the ER4/33, drawn from two escadrilles, the ER1/33 Belfort and ER3/33 Moselle, under the overall command of Colonel Gabriel Gauthier, commander of Rheims air base. An additional five RF-84Fs from ER2/33 Savoie arrived on 31 October. Flg Off Gronert of 249 Squadron remembered the arrival of the French pilots at Akrotiri:

> "I do not recall the squadron number but they were a PR squadron flying the RF-84F. The three [Venom] squadrons gave them a good welcome with an invitation to a hooley in the Officers' Mess which went down very well with everyone until it was discovered that most of the French pilots had the equivalent rank of Corporal, but we didn't care. We got on very well with them."

Flg Off Tom Lecky-Thompson, also of 249 Squadron, added:

> "We struck up a very good liaison with the French at Akrotiri and by some magical means we found ourselves a plentiful supply of red wine and spare petrol to run our Squadron cars."

By the time the Suez war finally got under way, Cyprus had assembled a total

Bréguet 761 of Air France taking off from Nicosia having delivered troops and supplies. (*Sqn Ldr R.K.J. Hadlow*)

of 34 RAF transports (Hastings and Valettas), while the Armée de l'Air made available 40 Noratlases, including two HQ machines, and a few Dakotas, to deliver paratroops and support forces on the ground. The French transport element was drawn from ET1/61 Touraine, ET3/61 Poitou and ET2/63 Sénégal from Orléan's 61st Transport Wing, plus a detachment of six aircraft from ET1/62 from Maison-Blanche in Algeria. To convey the 2,950 officers, NCOs and men of the three French parachute regiments to Cyprus, together with almost 700 vehicles and trailers and a great deal of technical equipment, French civil airlines had been requested to make available aircraft to supplement Armée de l'Air transports. An air bridge between France, Algeria and Cyprus was maintained by a fleet of aircraft comprising Bréguet 761S/763s of ET2/61 Maine and Air France, Sud-Est Armagnacs of SAGETA, DC-4s of Air France, TAI, Air Algérie, UAT and SGACC, and DC-6s of TAI and UAT, and eight troop-

Bréguet 761S 61-PD of ET2/61 at Nicosia, Cyprus. (*Sqn Ldr R.K.J. Hadlow*)

163

carrying flights were undertaken by Air France and Air Algérie Constellations. The first aircraft arrived at Nicosia on 26 October, involving DC4s, a DC-6 and a Bréguet. Only one aircraft (Armagnac F-BAVF) broke down during the 52-sortie, four-day operation.

On the eve of hostilities, units based at Cyprus included:

RAF AND ARMÉE DE L'AIR ORDER OF BATTLE (CYPRUS), October 1956

RAF Akrotiri:

6 Squadron	16 Venom FB4	Sqn Ldr P.C. Ellis DFC
8 Squadron	16 Venom FB4	Sqn Ldr C.I. Blyth DFC AFC
249 Squadron	15 Venom FB4	Sqn Ldr J.R. Maitland DFC(US)
1 Squadron	12 Hunter F5	Sqn Ldr R.S. Kingsford
34 Squadron	12 Hunter F5	Sqn Ldr A.S. Wilson DFC
13 Squadron	7 Canberra PR7	Sqn Ldr J.L. Field
39 Squadron	8 Meteor NF13	Sqn Ldr A.J. Owen DFC DFM
EC1/3 Navarre	18 F-84F	Cne Payen
EC3/3 Ardennes	18 F-84F	Cne
ER4/33	10 RF-84F	Cdt Lapiche

NB: a further six F-84Fs and five RF-84Fs arrived on 31 October

RAF Nicosia:

10 Squadron	8 Canberra B2	Sqn Ldr G. Sproats
15 Squadron	8 Canberra B2	Sqn Ldr A.R. Scott DFC
18 Squadron	8 Canberra B2	Sqn Ldr A.H. Chamberlain
27 Squadron	8 Canberra B2	Wg Cdr P.W. Helmore DFC AFC
44 Squadron	8 Canberra B2	Sqn Ldr J.W. Barling DSO DFC
61 Squadron	10 Canberra B2	Sqn Ldr N.L. Hartley
139 Squadron	12 Canberra B6	Sqn Ldr P. Mallorie AFC

RAF Tymbou:

30 Squadron ⎤		Sqn Ldr P.G. Coulson
84 Squadron ⎬	20 Valetta C1	Sqn Ldr F.L. Spencer
114 Squadron ⎦		Sqn Ldr D.B. Delany AFC
70 Squadron ⎤		Sqn Ldr W.K. Greer AFC
99 Squadron ⎬	14 Hastings C1/C2	Sqn Ldr D.R. Ware DFC AFC
511 Squadron ⎦		Sqn Ldr G.W. Turner
ET1/61 Touraine ⎤		Cne Muller
ET3/61 Poitou ⎬	40 Noratlases	Cdt Latour
ET1/62 Algérie ⎪	and 5 Dakotas	Cdt Guillou
ET2/63 Sénégal ⎦		Cne Marrill

The Cyprus Bomber Wing was under the command of Grp Capt G.C.O. Key DFC (OC RAF Upwood), while Grp Capt J.C. Macdonald DFC AFC, Station Commander at Akrotiri, effectively took control of the Venom Strike Wing, although Wg Cdr J.C. Button DFC was Wing Commander (Ops). Grp Capt Macdonald, known to his contemporaries as 'Black Mac', had served with Bomber Command during the Second World War and had, until recently,

Transports at Tymbou: 23 Noratlases and four Dakotas can be seen dispersed around the airfield. (*SHAA via Albert Grandolini*)

commanded RAF Habbaniya, where he had regularly carried out inspections from the saddle of his horse!

Meanwhile at Malta, where the British Task Force was being assembled, four Hunter F4s of 111 Squadron arrived from the UK to share day fighter duties with the Meteor FR9s of 208 Squadron. Earlier, on 22 September, the first of 29 Canberra B6s had arrived at Luqa from RAF Binbrook, and these were followed two days later by four of Bomber Command's new four-engine Valiant bombers, three from 214 Squadron and the other from 207 Squadron, both RAF Marham-based units. A single Valiant of 49 Squadron arrived from RAF Wittering on 1 October, but this departed four days later. Sea Hawks from HMS *Bulwark* carried out practice interceptions of the incoming bombers on 11 October but, as noted by 810 Squadron's diarist, 'they were eventually intercepted but not with a very high degree of success', although next day Valiants were successfully intercepted at between 40,000 and 45,000 feet, despite poor radar reception. The main body of Valiants arrived on 26 October, six from 138 Squadron, three more from 207 Squadron, two more from 214 Squadron and five from 148 Squadron, followed by two more (from 138 Squadron) four days later. The Malta Bomber Wing was under the command of Grp Capt L.M. Hodges DSO, commander of RAF Marham.

RAF ORDER OF BATTLE (MALTA), October 1956

RAF Luqa/Hal Far:

138 Squadron	8 Valiant B1	Wg Cdr R.G.W. Oakley DSO DFC AFC DFM
148 Squadron	5 Valiant B1	Wg Cdr W.J. Burnett DSO DFC AFC
207 Squadron	6 Valiant B1	Wg Cdr D.D. Haig DSO DFC
214 Squadron	5 Valiant B1	Wg Cdr L.H. Trent VC DFC
9 Squadron	7 Canberra B6	Sqn Ldr L.G.A. Bastard
12 Squadron	7 Canberra B6	Sqn Ldr W.L. Donley DFC DFM
101 Squadron	8 Canberra B6	Sqn Ldr B. Moorcroft DSO DFC
109 Squadron	7 Canberra B6	Sqn Ldr J.L. Causton
37 Squadron	Shackleton MR2	
38 Squadron	Shackleton MR2	

Wg Cdr Walter Burnett's 148 Squadron Valiant, XD815, at Luqa. (*Wg Cdr A.E.G. Woods*)

To make room for the influx of bomber aircraft at Malta, the Venom FB1s of 32 Squadron, commanded by Sqn Ldr A.H.W. Gilchrist DFC, had moved to Amman (Jordan) thereby giving the RAF a presence on the eastern flank of the troubled area. Following their arrival, the Commander of the Royal Jordanian Army, Maj-General Ali Abu Nuwar, announced that 'Venom aircraft at this Station were alerted in case of any Israeli border attacks'. Clearly the Jordanian authorities had no idea that other RAF squadrons would soon be attacking Jordan's Arab ally, Egypt*. One of 32 Squadron's Venoms soon became a casualty, when WR337 stalled on approach, hit a bank and crashed, killing its pilot. A section of Hunters from 1 Squadron, on detachment from Cyprus, led by Flt Lt Jimmy Mansell who had flown F-86s during the Korean War while on attachment to the USAF, also arrived at Amman to provide an additional deterrent should the Israelis turn their attention to their near neighbour, although an RAF spokesman, commenting on the arrival of the Hunters on Israel's border, refused to be drawn into discussion and simply stated "Hunter detachments are part of normal MEAF procedure to send its aircraft on visiting flights to airfields in this area." Nevertheless, Abu Nuwar went as far as to suggest that the RAF fighters could be called upon to assist Jordan at very short notice if the need arose. But, as late as mid-October, the British were still contemplating having to send the RAF to bomb Israel in the event of a conflict with Jordan, under

---

* Following the opening rounds of the Anglo-French assault on Egypt, Jordan warned Britain that the RAF bases at Amman and Mafraq could not be used for operations against Egypt, which was the reaction that had been anticipated by the British.

Ready for action! Aboard HMS *Eagle* can be seen seven Wyverns of 830 Squadron, a Skyraider of 849/A Flight, 16 Sea Hawks of 897 and 899 Squadrons, and seven Sea Venoms of 892 and 893 Squadrons. (*Authors' collection*)

the terms of the Anglo-Jordan Treaty, even though British diplomats were then also on the verge of signing the secret Treaty of Sèvres agreement with France and Israel. With an intensification of the crisis, the RAF contingent in Jordan was ordered to concentrate its forces at Mafraq and 32 Squadron flew its 15 Venoms there at the end of the month, two of which remained at readiness, fully armed.

When fully assembled and ready for war, the Anglo-French Task Force commanded by Vice-Admiral D.F. Durnford-Slater CB would include the aircraft carriers HMS *Eagle*, HMS *Albion* and HMS *Bulwark*, plus the light helicopter carriers HMS *Ocean* and HMS *Theseus*, the former carrying six Whirlwind HAR2s and six Sycamore HC14s of the Joint Helicopter Unit (JHU), flown by RAF and Army pilots under the command of Lt Colonel J.F.T. Scott, and the latter with ten Whirlwind HAS22s of 845 Squadron. Apart from the five carriers, the Royal Navy provided four cruisers, 13 destroyers, six frigates and five submarines, of which one cruiser, one destroyer and two frigates were stationed in the Red Sea. The French naval contribution, in addition to the two light carriers *Arromanches* (formerly HMS *Colossus*) and *La Fayette* (formerly the USS *Langley*), comprised one battleship (the *Jean Bart*), two cruisers, four destroyers, eight frigates and two submarines, plus transports and supply vessels. On board the carriers were a total of 163 aircraft, of which 117 comprised Royal Navy Sea Hawks, Sea Venoms, Wyverns (the world's first military turboprop aircraft) and Skyraiders. *Eagle* was the only one of the three Royal Navy strike carriers on station in the Mediterranean when the call came to prepare for operations, and was equipped with two Sea Hawk squadrons (897 Squadron with FB3s and 899 Squadron with FGA6s), 892 Squadron with Sea

Lt Cdr Bruce Clark (right), CO of 899 Squadron, with his Senior Pilot Lt Cdr Pete Newman. (*Capt A.B.B. Clark*)

"My own squadron had formed and worked up at Lossiemouth in preparation for a commission in *Ark Royal*. We were diverted to *Albion* for the Suez operation. After some time in Malta with all the squadrons training hard and learning to work together, the COs were called to a briefing in the flagship the day after the Fleet sailed. The general feeling in the Fleet, culled from the radio and the press, was that we were going to confront the Israelis who were seen to be aggressing as they pushed towards Egypt. We were very surprised to find that the opposite was the case! Most of my age group had seen active service in World War II but the realisation that the Egyptians had MiGs made for a certain amount of apprehension."

Lt Cdr Eveleigh came close to missing the Suez operation when, on the night of 24 October, his Sea Hawk (WM922/131) crashed into the sea shortly after take-off from *Albion*'s deck:

"On this particular day the Squadron had received orders from Admiralty saying that to improve the turn-round time between sorties, the metal retaining straps over the main fuel tank filler cap were to be removed from the aircraft. My colleague, CO of the other Sea Hawk squadron on board *Albion* [Lt Cdr Des Russell of 800 Squadron], and I objected, but we were overruled, and the straps removed. An accident involving this procedure had caused the loss of a Sea Hawk of another squadron, and we did not want to

---

170

Sea Hawk FB3s of 802 Squadron prior to embarking on HMS *Albion*, including WM963/136 and WN118/137. (*Capt R.L. Eveleigh*)

repeat it. I therefore said I wished to be first off after the straps had been removed. I was, with the following result on a night take-off. My No2, an exchange RAF officer, Flt Lt George Black, was on the second catapult waiting to follow me. As I accelerated down the catapult a glaring light, which reminded me of the light from the old-fashioned flares at a fairground, lit up the deck. I left the catapult with the feeling that the throttle was not fully open. I pushed 'white knuckled' on the lever, but the power still fell away and I realised that the light came from the aircraft and that I was on fire. I crashed into the sea ahead of the carrier, which swerved to avoid colliding with the burning and sinking Sea Hawk.

I always took off on the catapult with my hood open and in spite of the crash it remained open. I remember hitting the sea, seeing the windscreen crack but not shatter. I took some time extricating myself from the machine as my dinghy strap fouled something and I had to get back into the cockpit, from being halfway out, to clear the strap. By this time the plane (or rather, my part of it) was well down in the sea. I struck out for the surface, bursting for breath, and found that in the dark I was not going up at all. Negative buoyancy begins at a remarkably shallow depth. Fortunately, the carrier had released a flare as near as it could to where the plane ditched as it passed by. The light from the flare penetrated the water sufficiently for me to see a glow and to realise that I was swimming parallel with the surface and not 'up'.

When I broke surface I grabbed the tailplane and rear fuselage, which was still afloat, but as I did so it decided to sink. I was swimming in a lot of aviation fuel but I felt the flare must be illuminating me, and I assumed that I would be picked up by the SAR destroyer, HMS *Daring*. I swam around for half an hour wondering why they couldn't see me. Suddenly it dawned on me that my Mae West light was not working. I had a pen-torch in my flying overall pocket given me by my wife Gwen before we left the UK. I pulled it out and it worked in spite of the dunking. The carrier immediately

Four pilots of 802 Squadron prior to leaving the UK: (left to right) Sub Lt Carl Clarke, Lt Cdr Roy Eveleigh, Lt Peter Miller, Lt John Carey. (*Capt R.L. Eveleigh*)

spotted the light, beamed its searchlights on to me and a boat arrived within minutes."

Immediately following the accident Flt Lt Black was ordered to shut down his engine and, consequently, before any further flights were undertaken, the safety straps were refitted to all Sea Hawks. The reason for the fire was known and had occurred before. Lt Cdr Eveleigh continued:

"The main fuel tank in the Sea Hawk is just abaft the cockpit. Due to the expansion of fuel in hot climates an air space has to be left when fuelling. The G exerted on a catapult take-off meant that the fuel surface was thrown up against the filler cap with some force. It appeared that the clip on the filler cap could become worn and if not carefully secured could come adrift with this impact, and allow fuel to run down into the plenum chamber of the engine. As a result all our aircraft had been fitted with the metal straps over the filler cap to prevent it being opened by the force of the fuel."

Three weeks earlier (on 5 October) the Squadron had lost Sea Hawk WM971/ 133 off Malta, when Lt John Bridel ejected over the island, as recalled by Lt Cdr Eveleigh:

"John and I went off over the northern half of the island [Malta] to have an aerobatic 'chase-me'. I gave him the lead as we had had some time in close formation, and he led into a loop. We had been having one or two instances of the fire-warning light coming on in the Sea Hawks. If it was functioning correctly this was the signal for the pilot to eject. However, there had been some cases of malfunction of the light and we were always left in a quandary. John called me to say his light was on. He continued to climb and abandoned the aerobatic. From my position in line-astern I watched and almost immediately some silvery pieces appeared to be coming from his jet-pipe, so I called him to eject, which he did forthwith. Fortunately we were approaching the coast, although Malta is fairly narrow at the northern end. His parachute developed and I followed him down and pinpointed his landing. When he was picked up he was suffering from minor injuries as he had landed astride a Maltese stone wall. He recovered in time for the Suez operation. The Sea Hawk crashed into the sea about a mile to the north-west."

Aboard *Albion*, 800 Squadron's Senior Pilot was Lt Cdr Maurice Tibby, who had previously served with the Squadron as a 19-year-old Hellcat pilot towards the end of the Second World War:

"800 Squadron re-formed at Brawdy in South Wales in the early part of May 1956 and was equipped with 12 Sea Hawks. The work-up went to plan and there was nothing to indicate the fun and games that lay ahead, and we continued the working-up procedure throughout the summer. During that time the CO was Lt Cdr Des Russell.* We were, around July, planning our summer leave when we were told leave was cancelled. We were not told the reason why, we were simply told we had to concentrate on training, especially on the air armament side, so we concentrated on rocket-firing, bombing and night firing. We carried out quite a large number of sorties from Brawdy involving night strafing and dummy deck landings.

On 14 September we flew to Ford in Sussex, and from Ford we embarked in HMS *Albion*. We carried out a number of sorties from *Albion* in September until setting off for the Mediterranean. At this stage we had no idea what we were in for, but thought we were to take part in a special exercise in that area. It became apparent when off Malta that other carriers were in the vicinity. We then did a number of exercises involving a great deal of air-to-ground communication with army units, and it became apparent that something was in the wind but still had no idea what it was."

The Royal Navy Carrier Task Force was commanded by Vice-Admiral Manley Power CB CBE DSO, much respected by his officers and men alike. The French Navy's *Arromanches* was equipped with two squadrons – 14F and 15F Flotille with a total of 36 F4U Corsairs, and *La Fayette* had a squadron (ten aircraft) of TBM-3 Avengers, half of which were radar-equipped, although once operations got under way Corsairs would also use *La Fayette*. Normally based at Karouba in Tunisia, 14F Flotille flew its Corsairs out to the *Arromanches* on 23 October, after which the carrier returned to Bizerte (Tunisia) to await events. Ens de V Philippe de Gaulle, son of the wartime leader of Free France and former French President, was an observer with the Avenger unit, 9F Flotille. The French Task Force commander had requested the light helicopter carrier *Dixmude* but she was at the time shuttling between the United States and France carrying helicopters for Algeria. Consequently, it was 7 November before six French Army Bell 47G helicopters of GH3 were made available for service with the Task Force, although each carrier carried two Piasecki HUP-2 Pedro helicopters for planeguard and ASR duties. 897 Squadron's Senior Pilot, Lt Cdr Keith Leppard, who had suffered a broken leg in an accident aboard *Eagle* – sustained

---

* In 1958 newly promoted Cdr Des Russell was killed during a deck landing accident when commanding 803 Squadron, the first Scimitar squadron.

Corsairs of 14F Flotille aboard *Arromanches*. (*SHAA via Albert Grandolini*)

'during after dinner games' – was therefore unfit for flying duties and found himself attached to the French carriers as Air Liaison Officer, as he recalled:

> "Admiral Caron (to whose staff I was attached) was in command of *Arromanches* and *La Fayette*. I am not sure what the Admiral and his staff

Quartet of 830 Squadron Wyverns led by the CO, Lt Cdr C.V. Howard, in '371'. (*Cdr W.H. Cowling*)

thought of the arrival by helicopter on board *Arromanches* at first light of their Royal Navy Liaison Officer, speaking only schoolboy French and with one leg in a plaster cast! I was sent at very short notice. I spent a few days in each carrier but was closest to 14F Flotille. The Squadron CO was a friendly and experienced pilot, Jean-Pierre Cremer. The Squadron deck-landed the Corsairs very well – a notoriously difficult aircraft. Ship's discipline was high. I remember being surprised when all the sailors jumped to attention as I walked along the passage ways through their mess-decks. I was impressed with the French carrier operations. Although equipped with piston-engined aircraft, their general standard was comparable with our own, and morale was high."

FLEET AIR ARM AND AERONAVALE ORDER OF BATTLE, October 1956
British Carrier Task Force (Vice-Admiral M.W. Power DSO)

HMS *Eagle*

830 Squadron	Wyvern S4	Lt Cdr C.V. Howard
892 Squadron	Sea Venom FAW21	Lt Cdr M.H.J. Petrie
893 Squadron	Sea Venom FAW21	Lt Cdr M.W. Henley DSC
897 Squadron	Sea Hawk FGA6	Lt Cdr A.R. Rawbone AFC
899 Squadron	Sea Hawk FGA6	Lt Cdr A.B.B. Clark
849A Squadron	Skyraider AEW1	Lt Cdr B.J. Williams
SAR Flight	Whirlwind HAR3	Lt Cdr J.H. Summerlee

HMS *Albion*

800 Squadron	Sea Hawk FGA4	Lt Cdr J.D. Russell
802 Squadron	Sea Hawk FB3	Lt Cdr R.L. Eveleigh
809 Squadron	Sea Venom FAW21	Lt Cdr R.A. Shilcock
849C Squadron	Skyraider AEW1	Lt Cdr D.A. Fuller
SAR Flight	Whirlwind HAR3	

HMS *Bulwark*

804 Squadron	Sea Hawk FGA6	Lt Cdr R.Von T.B. Kettle
810 Squadron	Sea Hawk FGA4	Lt Cdr P.M. Lamb DSC AFC
895 Squadron	Sea Hawk FB3	Lt Cdr J. Morris-Jones
Ships Flight	Avenger AS5	
SAR Flight	Dragonfly HR3	

HMS *Theseus*

845 Squadron	Whirlwind HAS22	Lt Cdr J.C. Jacob

HMS *Ocean*

JHU	Whirlwind HAR2,	Lt Col J.F.T. Scott
	Sycamore HC14	Sqn Ldr D.C.L. Kearns AFC
		(deputy commander)

French Carrier Task Force (Admiral Yves Caron)

Arromanches

14F Flotille	F4U-7 Corsair	Lt deV Cremer
15F Flotille	F4U-7 Corsair	Lt deV Degermann
23S Escadrille	HUP-2 Pedro	

La Fayette

9F Flotille	TBM-3 Avenger	Lt deV Bros
23S Escadrille	HUP-2 Pedro	Lt deV Sarreau

There had not been such naval activity in the central and eastern Mediterranean since the heady days of the Second World War. Steaming from the west were the French light aircraft carriers *Arromanches* and *La Fayette*, together with their attendant destroyers and refuellers; at and around Malta were the Royal Navy carriers *Eagle*, *Bulwark* and *Albion*, and a profusion of smaller vessels, while *Theseus* and *Ocean* were on their way from Gibraltar; also operating in these waters, around Cyprus, was the mighty American Sixth Fleet led by the heavy cruiser USS *Salem*, with the carriers USS *Coral Sea* and USS *Randolph*. The skies above the fleets were just as busy, with an assortment of British Sea Hawks, Sea Venoms and Skyraiders; French Corsairs and Avengers; and American FJ-3 Furies, F9F-8 Cougars, F2H Banshees and AD-2 Skyraiders.

Comparative Aeronavale/Royal Navy ranks:	
Second Maître	= Petty Officer 2
Maître	= Petty Officer 1
Officier des Équipages 1ere (OE1)	= Midshipman
Enseigne de Vaisseau (Ens deV)	= Sub Lieutenant
Lieutenant de Vaisseau (Lt deV)	= Lieutenant
Capitaine de Corvette (Cne deC)	= Lieutenant Commander

Although the British and French Task Force commanders were wary of the US Sixth Fleet's intentions, it transpired that Vice-Admiral Charles R. Brown, its commander, had instructions only to evacuate American citizens from Egypt should fighting break out, and to deploy his ships in such a way so as to defend them against possible attack. However, the US Chief of Naval Operations, Admiral Ardleigh Burke, had warned Brown to be ready for anything, and advised the State Department:

> "We can stop them [the Anglo-French Task Force] but we will have to blast hell out of them. If we are going to threaten, if we're going to turn on them, then you've got to be ready to shoot. We can do that. We can defeat them. The British, the French, the Egyptians, and the Israelis."

Clearly the American government's policy of remaining neutral in the looming crisis was not reflected among the ranks of some of its senior military men.

The carriers *Eagle*, *Bulwark* and *Albion* sailed from Malta between 0730 and 0845 on 29 October, ostensibly for security purposes to carry out a communication exercise, codenamed *Operation Boathook*, in conjunction with Air HQ Cyprus. Unfortunately, on the first morning, *Eagle*'s starboard catapult collapsed due to a design weakness or material failure, remaining unserviceable for the whole operation. The failure occurred as Sea Hawk XE441/198 of 897 Squadron was about to be launched at 0915. All went well until the aircraft started to move forward, when the pilot, Lt Lin Middleton (a former member of the South African Air Force), became aware that the movement was not uniform but rather jerky, and was also aware of a high-pitched noise coming from the catapult. Almost immediately there was a jerk and Middleton realised that the catapult had failed in some way. As the Sea Hawk left the bows its speed was only between 70 and 80 knots, obliging the pilot to ditch immediately

---

176

Lt Cdr Jim Summerlee in the cockpit of one of *Eagle*'s SAR Whirlwind helicopters, with crewmen L/Air Mitchell and Hazel. Note side arms about which Lt Cdr Summerlee commented: "I could not hit a bull in the arse at five paces!" (*Lt Cdr J. Summerlee*)

ahead of the carrier. Having had previous experience of ditching a Sea Hawk, Middleton knew the procedure and was able to rapidly vacate the sinking aircraft; in a very short period of time he was picked up by one of *Eagle*'s Whirlwinds flown by Lt Cdr Jim Summerlee, and was soon back on board having suffered a slightly strained left shoulder. His bonedome, which had cracked, had saved him from more serious injury when he hit his head on the side of the carrier while surfacing. A grateful Lt Cdr Rawbone (CO of 897 Squadron) presented Lt Cdr Summerlee with a Squadron tie in recognition of the rescue of one of his pilots.

All three carriers refuelled from the Fleet Tanker *Olna* during the afternoon of 30 October, after which the destroyer screen rendezvoused and set course for the area of intended operations 50 to 60 miles north of Egypt, when aircrew were briefed on possible targets, opposition and tactics, while aircraft were painted with black and yellow identification stripes. Of the final hours before the launch of *Operation Musketeer*, Lt Cdr Rawbone, remembered:

"Three days before the operation, squadron commanders were briefed on the intended strike. Officers and ratings were not informed at that stage but the order to paint black and yellow identification stripes on aircraft left little to the imagination.* On 31 October all personnel were informed that we were intending to strike at first light the following day. This allowed little time for the final briefing of aircrew and subsequent essential preparations, i.e. intelligence bulletins, escape and evasion (sewing compasses into flying suits, blood chits, etc.). Nevertheless, we were ready to strike at first light as planned."

One of his pilots, Lt Don Mills, wrote later:

"We had been issued with khaki trousers and shirts with rank badges so there could be no accusations of being a spy if we had to bale out in enemy territory. We also had escape kits with maps and a little packet of golden sovereigns to bribe the Bedouin tribes in the desert, and we carried .32 Webleys in belt or leg holsters to defend ourselves, with the option of a Sten gun as well."

800 Squadron's Senior Pilot, Lt Cdr Tibby commented:

"When the decision was taken for us to participate in an operation, we found ourselves sailing east in the Mediterranean and we were ordered to paint white stripes on our aircraft. Although we spend a lot of money on camouflaging our aircraft, in times of war we paint stripes on our aircraft so our own side can recognise them! But it was not until we were clear of Malta and had a general aircrew meeting that we were told what we were going to do and whose side we were on."

Ships of the French Carrier Task Unit sailed from North African ports on 26 and 27 October. Having refuelled on 30 October from French tankers east of Crete, they took up their designated positions within about 15 miles of the British force. As the capital ships took up station, a signal was sent from the Commander-in-Chief Mediterranean to All Ships' Companies:

"We are now to carry out the operations for which you have trained and prepared with such spirit and enthusiasm. I am very proud to have such a large fleet under my command manned by a highly efficient and cheerful team of officers, ratings and Royal Marines. I have full confidence that you

---

* The markings consisted of three yellow and two black 12-inch stripes encircling the wings outboard of the wing-fold (Sea Hawk, Skyraider, Wyvern) or outboard of the booms of the Sea Venom. Similar bands were painted round the rear fuselage.

Armourer aboard HMS *Eagle* walking between Sea Hawks of 899 Squadron. (*Authors' collection*)

will all carry out your duties with the same determination and courage for which the Royal Navy is famous, and that we shall with the other Services and our French allies bring these operations to a successful conclusion. May all go well with you."

It was considered that, in the event of hostilities, the most likely threat to the Anglo-French Task Force would be from the air, with relatively lesser threats from surface and submarine attacks. Therefore, unit formations, Combat Air Patrols (CAP) and anti-submarine patrols were based on this assumption. At this stage, the New Zealand destroyer HMNZS *Royalist* was ordered to retire northwards, much to the chagrin of her crew, as the New Zealand government showed its disagreement with Britain's Suez policy. Canada was also unhappy with the situation and as a result ordered Lt D.A. Muncaster of the RCN, a helicopter pilot with 845 Squadron aboard *Theseus*, be withdrawn from operational duties.

A mighty force had by now been assembled at Cyprus and all three airfields were bulging at the seams with fighters, fighter-bombers, bombers, reconnaissance aircraft and transports, the latter continuing to fly in supplies, stores, equipment and ammunition. The runway at Tymbou, once a satellite of Nicosia, had been hastily brought up to standard in short time, 800 tons of bitumen having been transported to the island by a variety of means: 100 tons had been flown in using Beverleys of RAF Transport Command; 200 tons arrived from Tobruk (Libya) aboard a tank landing craft, and the remaining 500 tons came from Benghazi and Spezia using commercial shipping. The resurfacing had been completed by the end of February, and the airfield became the base for RAF Transport Command's Hastings and Valettas, and also for the Noratlases of the Armée de l'Air which had arrived on 29 October.

The British, historically, have always had a peculiar knack of upsetting their

Valetta C1 VW196 of 84 Squadron at Nicosia. (*Chris Thomas via Andy Thomas*)

friends and allies, particularly it seems in times when their support is needed most, and British appreciation of their French allies was clearly lacking, as Général Andre Beaufre, commander of the French Task Force, had cause to remember:

> "I arrived in Cyprus late in the afternoon of 29 October. We were made to land at Akrotiri whereas we were expected at Nicosia. On arrival I was surprised to note, although I myself had a room, no provision had been made for my staff. I had to manifest ill humour in order to obtain a few rooms in a building."

A message from an anxious Prime Minister Eden to President Eisenhower, outlining what he intended to say to the United Nations Security Council, was despatched to Washington only three hours before the issuing of the Anglo-French ultimatum to Israel and Egypt. Eisenhower, in the meantime, had learned of the ultimatum from newspaper reports and the angry President immediately sent Eden a formal response:

> "I have just learned from the press of the 12 hour ultimatum which you and the French government have delivered to the government of Egypt requiring under threat of forceful intervention the temporary occupation by Anglo-French forces of key positions at Port Said, Ismailia and Suez in the Canal Zone. I feel I must urgently express to you my deep concern at the prospect of this drastic action even at the very time when the matter is under consideration as it is today by the Security Council. It is my sincere belief that peaceful processes can and should prevail to secure a solution which will restore the armistice conditions as between Israel and Egypt, and also justly settle the controversy with Egypt about the Suez Canal."

The rebuff fell upon deaf ears. This was one occasion when Eden believed the sword mightier than the pen. Besides, the wheels of war were already in motion. However, it would be naïve to believe that the Americans were not aware of what was about to unfold in the eastern Mediterranean. The mighty Sixth Fleet was omnipresent, its aircraft constantly flying surveillance missions, as were the

UN Navy's P2V-5 Neptunes of VP-24 based at Malta. French Général Robineau, in his *Histoire de l'Affaire de Suez*, commented:

"Phrases like 'without the knowledge of the Americans' really fooled nobody. It was impossible that 36 aircraft passing through Akrotiri [the Mystères and F-84Fs on their way to Israel], and the daily liaison flight by Dakota from Tel Aviv, were really 'unnoticed'. It was equally impossible that the US Sixth Fleet which was in the immediate area, and whose reconnaissance aircraft sometimes accompanied the raids to Egypt, did not give the Pentagon as precise information as that which reached the War Room at Episkopi.

All the evidence suggests that the Americans knew exactly what was going on. This was particularly so considering the number of French aircraft and all their huge amount of support services and supplies, especially as so much of it came directly from French NATO bases in Germany which had been working alongside the 4th ATAF. Also, the American liaison officer at Saint-Dizier said 'Good Luck' to the 1st Squadron as it left, and added, 'You don't know where you are going, but I know . . .' It is most likely that the US knew exactly the movements of French forces [likewise, those of the British] throughout their transfer to the eastern Mediterranean."

The Americans were also making good use of their new Lockheed U-2 spyplane, operated by the CIA from the USAF's Incirlik base at Adana, Turkey, not only to observe movements in the Mediterranean but also to reconnoitre military installations in both Egypt and Israel. During one such flight in late October, the U-2's cameras recorded a large number of Mystères in Israel, causing President Eisenhower to remark that the aircraft had a 'rabbit-like capacity for multiplication' in view of the fact that the number seen exceeded that admitted as having been supplied to Israel by France. A U-2 pilot also reported and photographed British convoys assembling at Malta and Cyprus, and military supplies being loaded on to French ships at Marseilles and Toulon. Eisenhower, fearful of the Soviet reaction to the Anglo-French build-up, placed the USAF's Strategic Air Command on alert, including the B-47 jet bombers of 306th Bomb Wing based in Morocco. These were joined on 26 October by RB-47s of the 70th Recon Wing.

It was not only the Americans who were involved in aerial spying. To monitor Egyptian activities and prepare for the assault, RAF Canberra reconnaissance jets kept watch on the Egyptian armed forces. Most reconnaissance sorties were flown just outside Egypt's territorial limits but on several occasions Canberras penetrated Egyptian airspace, keeping an eye on the airfields and movements of military traffic, seemingly unobserved by Egyptian fighter controllers, the first such flight having been carried out by Flt Lt G.J. Clark in WJ821. Mohamed Heikal, Nasser's confidant, wrote:

"In Cairo, the first indication that some larger design was unfolding came on Tuesday morning. By 11 o'clock reports had begun to come in of Canberra aircraft carrying out reconnaissance missions over Lake al-Bardawil in Sinai, Suez and Port Said. These were obviously British planes."

A Canberra (WT540) which departed from Akrotiri at 1150 on 29 October,

French paratroopers disembarking from Armagnac F-BA?C of SAGETA. (*Sqn Ldr R.K.J. Hadlow*)

flown by Sqn Ldr John Field and Flg Off D.J. Lever, was able to complete its reconnaissance although fired upon by 'ineffectual AA', returning safely at 1600. Next day, four RAF Canberra PR7s from Cyprus flew along the Suez Canal at an altitude of 35,000 feet to monitor Egyptian reaction to the Israeli assault, while others made incursions into Syria's airspace. Apparently one of the eight RF-84Fs despatched during the morning was intercepted by an EAF MiG, as recalled by Lt Joseph Bertin-Maghit of ER4/33, who wrote:

> "This is it! We are going to war! The lucky ones – Capitaines Rieuneau and Renault, and Lieutenants Saget, Delarche [in RF326, who reconnoitred Inchas and Bilbeis] and Willay – go down the runway. At eight o'clock three new different missions arrive. No other missions that day. Everyone returns safe and sound and the heroes of the day are bombarded with questions the moment they touch down. Maxime made his film run at 30,000 feet and had seen tracer [from behind], which immediately made him turn, and he returned at top speed."

Meanwhile, in Eastern Europe, an entirely separate crisis was brewing. In July 1956 the hated Stalinist President Rákasi of Hungary was dismissed in disgrace. This was done on the promptings of Soviet Secretary-General Khrushchev in an attempt to improve Soviet relations with Yugoslavia whose leader, Marshal Tito, had a personal quarrel with Rákasi. Unfortunately, the Hungarian President was replaced by the equally unpopular Ernö Gerö, who made it clear that, as far as Hungary was concerned, a change at the top did not mean a change in hard-line communist policies. But change was in the air in Eastern Europe, the Poles having already attempted to challenge Soviet domination during the spring and summer of 1956. The simmering political crisis in Hungary boiled over on to the streets of Budapest on 23 October, with a huge march by students demanding redress of various political and other grievances. They found widespread and perhaps unexpected popular support. The gatherings were noisy though still peaceful but then the police fired into the crowd and what had been a political demonstration erupted into a full-scale revolution. The Hungarian Army joined the revolutionaries as did the bulk of the peasantry in the countryside. Imre Nagy, the reformist communist leader who had governed Hungary for a short time from July 1953 to spring 1955, found himself reinstated. In fact, events were moving so fast that Nagy soon found himself at the head of a coalition government in which communists only formed a small part. In the face of this turmoil the Soviet occupation troops withdrew across the frontier, either into the USSR, Czechoslovakia and Romania, or remained in barracks. Most significantly, all, or at least the overwhelming bulk, of Soviet tanks left Hungary, though they remained just beyond the borders.

With the threat of the latest Middle East conflict spreading to mainland Egypt, and forewarned by both Radio Cyprus and Radio Cairo of the impending attacks to enable Egyptian civilians to evacuate intended target areas, Soviet and Czech instructors and technicians flew some 20 MiGs and 20 Ilyushins, destined for the Syrian Air Force, to the safety of Riyadh in Saudi Arabia. A variety of Egyptian Air Force machines followed, including at least 20 MiG fighters and trainers, together with ten Il-14 transports. All were then flown to Syria, although a further 20 Il-28s of the EAF reached only as far as Luxor in southern Egypt, where they were deemed to be out of immediate danger (although, as recorded in Chapter Seven, most of these were subsequently destroyed by French F-84Fs operating from Israel). Among those leaving Egypt at this time were the families of British diplomats in Cairo, including Lady Trevelyan, wife of the British Ambassador, who told reporters on her arrival in London 30 hours later:

> "We were ordered to leave at six a.m. on Tuesday [29 October], and were given only a few hours to pack. The atmosphere in Cairo is calm."

A calm about to be shattered.

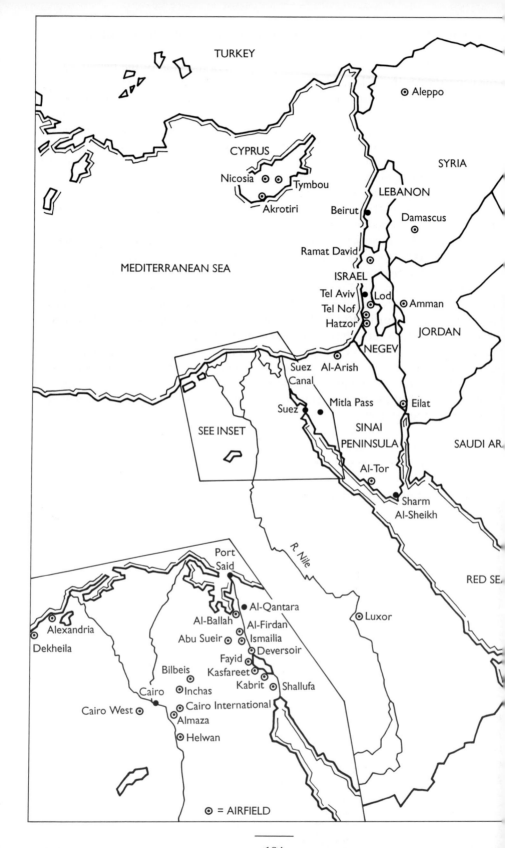

184

Chapter Nine

THE BOMBERS STRIKE THE FIRST BLOW
31 October 1956

"The affairs of Britain seem now to be in the hands of a madman."
The *Egyptian Gazette*, 31 October 1956.

As the mighty Anglo-French naval armada manoeuvred to maintain position off the Egyptian coast, the carriers launched sections of fighters on CAP, while Royal Navy Skyraiders and French Avengers flew anti-submarine patrols and kept an eye on the movements of Egyptian naval craft, as well as those of the American Sixth Fleet. Two Avengers from *Arromanches*, armed with depth charges and rockets, encountered two US Navy destroyers at dawn, while a later patrol also sighted an Egyptian Navy Skoryi class destroyer (the Egyptian Navy possessed two such ex-Soviet vessels, renamed *al-Nasr* and *al-Zafr*) and two minesweepers. The next pair of Avengers, launched from *Arromanches* at 0800, similarly sighted two destroyers and a frigate, again undoubtedly Egyptian since the Avengers were then intercepted by a pair of Egyptian Spitfire F22s almost certainly flown by instructor Flt Lt Tahseen Zaki and Plt Off Ali Sharmi which, although they carried out an attacking pass, did not however open fire, as the Anglo-French assault against Egypt was yet to commence.

Apart from the possibility of air attack, the Allied commanders feared that Egyptian MTBs might attempt an attack on vessels of the Task Force, particularly in view of the naval activity observed during the morning. Although not part of the *Operation Musketeer* plan, a dawn strike against the Egyptian Navy located at Alexandria was hurriedly arranged for the morrow. The Corsairs of 15F Flotille were allocated the mission, even though the French pilots had received no training for attacks against naval vessels. Nevertheless, a plan was devised which called for half the attacking force to neutralise harbour defences with rockets, while the other flight would attack at low-level with 1,000lb delayed-action bombs. Air cover was to be provided by FAA fighters.

With such large numbers of aircraft assembled at Cyprus, the fear of attack against the poorly defended airfields was uppermost in the minds of those responsible for the security of the Anglo-French air force. The possibility of such an attack had been discussed in some detail prior to the commencement of hostilities, as revealed in a note written by the Chief of Air Staff, Air Chief Marshal Sir Dermot Boyle GCB KCVO KBE AFC:

"Consider use of Suez airfields by Egyptian aircraft totally unacceptable...

the risk of only one attack [on Cyprus] is unacceptable, especially now there is even greater concentration of aircraft in Cyprus. The essential point is that once one attack, which might be flown by volunteer pilots, had been mounted, the damage would have been done."

Thus, sections of Hunters and Venoms were on constant alert and two of the latter from 8 Squadron were scrambled during the morning of 31 October, when radar picked up approaching aircraft. Flying No2 to Flt Lt Will Scarlett was Flg Off Dick Hadlow (WR480):

"Tension was mounting and I was scrambled as wingman to intercept, supposedly, unknown aircraft. The swift scramble left me struggling to keep up with my experienced leader and I remember taking off not properly strapped in. During the course of an hour we intercepted three aircraft, namely a French AF Dakota, a USAF C-119B Packet and a TWA Constellation. Having satisfied ourselves as to their non-aggressive identity by flying close enough to report serial numbers and registrations, we returned to base."

Pairs of Hunters were also busy during the day and intercepted two US Navy Banshees from the Sixth Fleet, a US Navy DC-4, a Canberra and an F-84F. Of his feelings as to the imminence of operations, 8 Squadron Venom pilot Flg Off Hadlow added:

"I suppose for any young man, contemplating battle for the first time must be more or less traumatic. On the one hand is the desire to put into practice all that one has striven to learn – for, after all, that is the whole purpose of military training, to operate a weapon. On the other hand there is a healthy fear of failure or even worse. The well trained military mind will concentrate on the first hand as it were. I was fortunate having just achieved operational status and the reasonably secure position as wingman to one of the

Flg Off Dick Hadlow of 8 Squadron. Venoms were shared during the Suez operation. (*Sqn Ldr R.K.J. Hadlow*)

Deputy Flight Commanders. Thus, I expected to fly regularly if the balloon went up. Our main operational concern had to be how the Egyptian Air Force would react to any raids over and against their territory. Suddenly, as an aircraft recognition pundit, I became very popular as the other pilots brushed up their aircraft recognition skills! One had to remember that Egypt was in the grip of 'Nasser Fever' and nationalistic identity was the name of the game now that the hated British had left. That we might be back within months would surely be as red rag to a bull.

We knew the EAF had MiG-15s, either flown by themselves or their Russian advisers. We knew the Venom was much slower than the MiG and that the standard of flying would be an unknown quantity, depending on which pilots flew against us. The Venom was quite slow but very manoeuvrable. We would be able to out-turn them comfortably but at some stage would have to set off back to Cyprus, or run out of fuel somewhere along the route. They would then be able to easily catch us. A low-level dash right on the deck, weaving irregularly, seemed likely to be the best defence, presenting a difficult target. If they stayed to dogfight, our manoeuvrability would give us a good chance to shoot them down."

To obtain up-to-date intelligence during the afternoon of 31 October, RAF Canberra and French RF-84F jets penetrated into Egyptian airspace, the Canberras flying four sorties, the RF-84Fs a further seven sorties. One of the latter was flown by Lt Tiseire in RF327 to Port Said, his task to locate American destroyers of the Sixth Fleet reported to be in harbour. Another sortie, flown by Lt Willay in RF321, was a reconnaissance of the al-Qantara to Ismailia road looking for the movement of military vehicles; convoys containing at least 100 lorries were observed. However, the principal targets of these missions were EAF airfields and the photographs revealed the strength of the EAF to be 110 MiG-15s, 14 Meteors, 44 Vampires and 28 Il-28 jet bombers, dispersed as follows:

Abu Sueir	35 MiG-15s
Kabrit	31 MiG-15s
Inchas	20 MiG-15s
Almaza	24 MiG-15s, 4 Meteors, 21 Vampires, 10 Il-28s
Fayid	9 Meteors, 12 Vampires
Cairo West	9 Vampires, 16 Il-28s
Luxor	22 Il-28s
Kasfareet	1 Meteor, 2 Vampires

However, less than half of this total was operational and ready for action because only a limited number of pilots and support personnel had yet been trained to fly and maintain these aircraft. Since the aim of the secret Anglo-French-Israeli plan was to break Egypt's military power for years to come and topple President Nasser, major EAF bases and Egyptian Army centres were priority targets. Lt Colonel Vallet, commander of the French air reconnaissance force, in his assessment of the EAF's capabilities, wrote:

"EAF were most effective in the ground attack role. Pilots of MiG-15s, Vampires and Meteors were well trained in the use of rockets and bombs against ground targets and naval targets. But there was no air support organisation (no co-ordinated actions of Air Force and Army). Because all training on the Il-28 in the Soviet bloc had been done in daytime, the operational standards of these squadrons was low, particularly at night. About 60 per cent of EAF aircraft were operational because of shortage of mechanics, and this was expected to drop below 50 per cent in time of war. The lack of a system to detect enemy aircraft and to control Egyptian fighters, and the lack of Egyptian experience in this field, meant that the EAF's effectiveness here was low, particularly at night. Nevertheless, training in the Soviet Union had improved this capability, at least by day. There were 18 runways capable of taking jets, five of which could take Il-28s. Another 20 or so runways could operate jet fighters, but their combat effectiveness would be greatly reduced here because of a lack of logistical mobility.

Anti-aircraft artillery was entirely under Army control. There were abundant light calibre AA guns but very few heavy calibre. There was virtually no liaison between heavy AA batteries and radar, but the light AA had recently been supplemented by mobile batteries including some of Swiss origin. The maximum altitude the heaviest AA guns could reach was 30,000 feet.

Radar coverage: this was based upon the three centres at Zamalek, al-Mix and al-Firdan, with 12 radars (seven long-range and five GCI) for the respective sectors of Cairo, Alexandria and the Suez Canal. These were French SFR radars, plus British Type 13-14 at al-Arish. The recent departure of French technicians was expected to have a serious effect on the operation efficiency of the radars as there were very few qualified Egyptian technicians. This was recognised by the Egyptian Command and in some cases Russian-supplied radars had doubled up on the coverage supplied by the earlier radars. The Russian radars had a range of 80 and 120 nautical miles. The liaison between operational centres and radars was considered very poor and could soon be saturated under operational conditions. Only the MiGs had IFF.

Conclusions: the EAF has about 300 front-line aircraft, of which fewer than 200 are operational. Egypt's air defences do not constitute a serious obstacle to Allied air operations. But this situation could quickly change if aircrew, mechanics and radar operators arrived from the Soviet bloc along with equipment from this same source."

By the eve of the assault, the British and French were able to field a total of 115 jet bombers – Canberras and Valiants – based at Cyprus and Malta, plus 48 Venom FB4 fighter-bombers, 24 Hunter F5 fighters and 36 F-84F tactical fighters; in addition there were seven Canberra PR7s and 15 RF-84Fs for tactical and photo-reconnaissance duties (all flying from bases in Cyprus), to which could be added the 163 carrier-borne mainly fighter-bomber aircraft of the Anglo-French Task Force.

The opening attack was to be made on Cairo West by Valiants and Canberras from Malta, together with Canberras from Cyprus. However, things went wrong right from the start as recalled by Sqn Ldr Allen Woods of 148 Squadron at Malta:

"Grp Capt Hodges [OC Malta Bomber Wing] received a signal from Bomber Command to prepare for night raid on Saturday, 31 October, but the AOC Malta (which came under Middle East Command) would not give permission for the bomb dumps to be opened as he had received no orders from ME Command, and no one in authority could be contacted as on Saturdays Air HQ was closed! Hodges ordered the gates of the bomb dump to be broken down."

Grp Capt Hodges added:

> "We certainly didn't know up until 24 hours before operations commenced whether we were going to bomb the Egyptians or the Israelis. It was only at the eleventh hour that the plans were unveiled and we discovered that we were going to bomb the Egyptians."

Despite the problems at Malta, four marker aircraft of 139 Squadron departed from Cyprus on time, getting airborne from Nicosia at 1715. The main task of the bombers was to crater the runways of the airfields and thereby deny EAF fighters the opportunity to attack them, or for EAF bombers to attack airfields in Cyprus, where the Anglo-French strike force could effectively be eliminated in one fell swoop.

PLAN OF ATTACK

Malta Bomber Wing/Cyprus Bomber Wing, 31 October/1 November 1956

RAID 1 – Target: CAIRO WEST

From Cyprus

4 Canberra B6s of 139 Squadron (Markers)	Target changed to
2 Canberra B2s of 10 Squadron	Almaza at short
2 Canberra B2s of 15 Squadron	notice but Cairo
2 Canberra B2s of 44 Squadron	International bombed
1 Canberra B6 of 139 Squadron	in error.

From Malta

6 Valiant B1s of 138 Squadron	Raid cancelled at
3 Canberra B6s of 12 Squadron	short notice; Valiants
4 Canberra B6s of 109 Squadron	recalled and Canberras held back.

RAID 2 – Target: ALMAZA

From Cyprus

4 Canberra B6s of 139 Squadron (Markers)
2 Canberra B2s of 10 Squadron
2 Canberra B2s of 15 Squadron
3 Canberra B2s of 44 Squadron

From Malta

5 Valiant B1s of 148 Squadron (2 Markers)
1 Valiant B1 of 214 Squadron
4 Canberra B6s of 109 Squadron
3 Canberra B6s of 12 Squadron

RAID 3 – Target: KABRIT

From Cyprus

4 Canberra B2s of 18 Squadron (Markers)
2 Canberra B2s of 10 Squadron
3 Canberra B2s of 15 Squadron
2 Canberra B2s of 44 Squadron

PLAN OF ATTACK

Malta Bomber Wing/Cyprus Bomber Wing, 31 October/1 November 1956

RAID 3 – Target: KABRIT (continued)

From Malta
5 Valiant B1s of 207 Squadron
7 Canberra B6s of 101 Squadron

RAID 4 – Target: ABU SUEIR

From Cyprus
4 Canberra B2s of 18 Squadron (Markers)
2 Canberra B2s of 10 Squadron
1 Canberra B2 of 15 Squadron
1 Canberra B2 of 44 Squadron
2 Canberra B2s of 61 Squadron   One returned early

From Malta
2 Valiant B1s of 138 Squadron (Markers)
2 Valiant B1s of 214 Squadron
7 Canberra B6s of 9 Squadron   One returned early
1 Canberra B6 of 109 Squadron

RAID 5 – Target: INCHAS

From Cyprus
2 Canberra B6s of 139 Squadron (Markers)
8 Canberra B2s of 27 Squadron
7 Canberra B2s of 61 Squadron   Two failed to take off

The first Canberra to undertake a hostile sortie over Egypt was also among the first to land back at Nicosia. This was WT371 of 139 Squadron captained by Flt Lt John Slater, who guardedly recounted details of his flight to waiting journalists on his return to Nicosia:

> "I can only speak for my own aircraft and not for any others which may have taken part in the operation. Our target was an airfield [Almaza] somewhere in Egypt, east of the Delta. We were in fact 30 seconds late after a 25-minute flight. With other Canberras we flew high over the target. There was no fighter resistance but there was some light flak up to 8,000 feet. It was very wild shooting. We saw the lights of Cairo in the distance. The airfield we attacked was beautifully lit up. There were many planes on it. We came in high, dropped our bombs and watched them explode. As soon as our bombs struck, lights began to go out but we had taken them completely by surprise and the damage was done. As soon as the bombs dropped we turned for home in a perfectly clear night sky."

Eight 4.5-inch flares and two 1,000lb TIs were released by Slater's aircraft, a similar load being carried by a second Canberra from his unit, while two others each carried 12 flares only; the flares were primed to ignite 3,000 feet above the ground. The operation called for Marker 1 (Slater) to drop his flares at 8,000 feet, then break to port and orbit at 4,000 feet, followed by Marker 2 (Flt Lt N.M. North in WT369), who was to orbit at 5,000 feet after releasing his flares, the TIs being dropped when the target was illuminated and identified. On board WT369 was Flt Sgt Mike Heather, a last-minute replacement navigator:

> "We crossed the Egyptian coast as it was getting dark and when we arrived over Cairo all the lights were still on. We had little difficulty in finding Almaza airfield but in spite of this we went through the full procedure of dropping flares over the target and then into a shallow dive to place the TIs. The Egyptian gunners seemed to shoot at the flares rather than us, so marking the target was easy, although by the time we had finished all the lights had been turned off."

The other two marker aircraft, WJ768 and WJ778, also released their flares once the target had been identified, to assist the bombers following: seven Canberras drawn from 10, 15, 44 and 139 Squadrons, which dropped a total of 41 1,000lb bombs. The bomber crews assessed that the marker was on the aiming point and reported bombs straddled hangars, runways and hardstandings, where a dozen transport were observed parked. However, it transpired that the Canberras had attacked Cairo International in error, the airport having been wrongly targeted by one or more of the marker aircraft. One pilot of 139 Squadron admitted later that "he was not certain that the target had been correctly identified". The official report continued '. . . Fortunately, the presence of Russian military aircraft [of the Egyptian Air Force] on Cairo International was later established.' Not a very auspicious start to the night bombing campaign. Air Commodore D.J.P. Lee CB CBE (later Air Chief Marshal Sir David), Secretary to the Chiefs of Staff Committee, wrote later:

> "Although the proximity of Almaza to Cairo International was undoubtedly a contributory factor, the mistake would never have been made by the experienced crews had the normal time for flight planning been available to them. This error was hardly a propitious start to *Musketeer*, but the last minute change of plan had been crucial."

Meanwhile, the first wave of bombers was on its way from Malta. Thus, much was at stake as the first sections of Valiants from Malta climbed into the afternoon sky. However, at the last moment, information was received that American civilians were in the process of evacuating from Cairo West,* the target for the attack, and all six Valiants from 138 Squadron were rapidly and urgently recalled, while the seven Canberras of 12 and 109 Squadrons were held back, their crews having been similarly briefed to bomb Cairo West. Grp Capt Hodges, the Bomber Wing Commander, remembered:

> "I received a personal signal direct from the Chief of Air Staff, Sir Dermot

---

* A fleet of US aircraft evacuated a total of 533 American citizens from Egypt, Israel and Syria, and a further 1,680 departed aboard ships of the Sixth Fleet which had steamed into Alexandria to assist with the evacuation. The presence of the USN vessels caused the planned Aeronavale strike against the Egyptian Navy to be cancelled.

Boyle, saying that on no account was Cairo West airfield to be bombed that night. The first wave of Valiants was on its way to Cairo; this created enormous problems, because there were four or five subsequent waves due to take-off immediately afterwards. I initiated an immediate recall of the first wave on W/T, but in addition the routing of the aircraft was very near to El Adem [Libya] and we were in communication with El Adem to give a verbal instruction by R/T in plain language to recall these aircraft to Luqa. This was successful and the aircraft were recalled but we had a situation where six Valiants were returning to Luqa with full bomb loads and further waves [of Valiants and Canberras] were taking off to go to Cairo. We had to have the bombs jettisoned."

Valiant crew: Wg Cdr Walter Burnett (second from right) checks his aircraft's serviceability log with Chief Tech Vernon Kitt before taking off. Others are, left to right, Flt Sgt Ed Waller, Sqn Ldr Allen Woods and Flg Off David Baldwin, all of 148 Squadron. (*Times of Malta*)

Sqn Ldr Woods, navigator/plotter aboard Wg Cdr Wilf Burnett's 148 Squadron Valiant XD815, remembered:

"Five Valiants of 148 Squadron departed Luqa late afternoon to arrive over Almaza just after dark, following Valiants from 138 Squadron which were to attack Cairo West airport. However, 138 Squadron was recalled when information was received that the Americans were still evacuating US personnel from Cairo West. We expected to be recalled ourselves but we weren't, hence 148 Squadron became the first [Valiant unit] to attack Egypt and I became the bomber leader. The Valiant was loaded with 11 1,000lb bombs and one 1,000lb Target Indicator (TI). We were ordered to bomb from 30,000 feet for supposed greater accuracy, although crews had trained for visual bombing from 40,000 feet."

The 148 Squadron Valiants were joined by WZ377 of 214 Squadron, flown by Sqn Ldr J.H. Garstin, and the first wave of seven Canberras (three from 109

Squadron and four from 12 Squadron). Two of the Valiants were to act initially as marker aircraft, using their ground radar to locate the target. At 30,000 feet, strong 80-knot winds were encountered, which slowed down the armada. Four marker Canberras of 139 Squadron from Cyprus, the crews briefed to be in the area at the same time, were to fly over the target at low level and drop red TIs, and the bombers were to release on these. Wg Cdr Burnett, flying the leading Valiant, recalled:

> "After the take-off from Malta we had a 1,800-mile trip ahead of us. It was uneventful until we came over the target at eight p.m. at a time when the city lights of Cairo were still twinkling."

But not all went to plan, as Sqn Ldr Woods recalled:

> "On approaching Almaza neither we nor our No2 [Sqn Ldr Trevor Ware in the other marker aircraft, XD819] were able to locate the target since our radar failed and, as we could not drop the TIs visually [there was no visual bombsight], we did what was called a racetrack: we carried out a wide sweep of the target in an effort to rectify the problem with the radar and came in again ten minutes later. I was in the bomb-aiming position and could see the lights of Cairo still blazing."

The problem of marking was overcome by the Canberras, as Wg Cdr Burnett explained:

> "Canberra marker aircraft had put down flares on the runway intersections and conditions were ideal for the attack."

From his position in the leading Valiant, Sqn Ldr Woods saw his bombs fall along the runway, followed about five seconds later by explosions from Sqn Ldr Ware's Valiant, before the other three Valiants – including XD816 flown by Flt Lt Dave Blomeley DFC AFC, a Second World War night fighter ace – and the Canberras from Malta and Cyprus came in and hit the airfield with more 1,000lb bombs (a total of 104 being dropped); some fell short and one exploded in the centre of the parade ground of the nearby barracks, as revealed by photographs taken later. Wg Cdr Burnett added:

> "All our bombs were on target. We spent 15 minutes over the target area before turning away and making our way back to Malta."

Egyptian radars detected the high-flying intruders and engaged with heavy anti-aircraft guns, while two or three Meteor NF13 night fighters of the EAF's 10 Squadron were scrambled and one engaged the Valiant piloted by Sqn Ldr Ware, which caused the pilot to take violent evasive action. Ware commented:

> "The night fighter came in to attack firing bursts of tracer. We took swift evasive action and the fighter fell away below us."

The co-pilot, Flt Lt Bob Alexander, confirmed that he, too, had seen 'flashes

Meteor NF13, s/n 1438, of the EAF prior to delivery in 1955; the CO of the EAF's night fighter squadron claimed a Valiant shot down during the RAF's first bomber raid. (*Authors' collection*)

from cannons firing', although the Valiant was not hit.* One of the Canberras was held by a searchlight over the target area but was able to evade successfully. On returning to Malta, one of the 109 Squadron Canberras, WJ781 flown by Flt Lt I.N. Wilson, was found to have a faulty fuel line from its tip tank and, as a consequence, was short of fuel. The controller at Hal Far ordered Wilson to make a direct approach and land without delay, which was accomplished safely with hardly a drop of fuel to spare.

Kabrit was the target for Raid 3, when seven Canberras from Cyprus drawn from 10, 15 and 44 Squadron, plus four from 18 Squadron as marker aircraft, were joined by seven more from Malta (101 Squadron led by Sqn Ldr Moorcroft in Flg Off L.D. Wrapson's WJ758) and five Valiants from 207 Squadron led by Wg Cdr Haig in WZ404. The departure of part of the air armada from Nicosia an hour before midnight was graphically described by journalist George Evans:

> "I stood on an airfield [Nicosia] somewhere in Cyprus tonight and watched part of the bomber force take off at regular intervals of a few minutes. One after another the Canberras roared down the runway, their twin engines emitting an ear-piercing whistle, climbed high into the night sky and set course for the Egyptian coast, which is only about half an hour's flying time from Cyprus. Overhead, silhouetted against a rich canopy of stars, other Canberras, their mission completed, circled the airfield and touched down. They went along the tarmac into the enveloping shadows at the far end. All other sound was drowned by the high-pitched whine of their engines as they took off and landed."

A total of 132 1,000lb bombs was released on Kabrit airfield, all of which were assessed to have fallen within 450 yards of the marker. Many MiGs were seen on the ground, at least three of which were believed to have been destroyed by

---

* Notwithstanding this, BOAC personnel waiting to depart Egypt reported later that they had heard rumours to the effect that the officer commanding the Meteor night fighter squadron claimed a Valiant shot down, and this was apparently repeated on Cairo Radio next day.

194

the marker aircraft. On board WJ761, a 101 Squadron Canberra flown by Flt Lt P.A. Ward, occurred an incident when one bomb failed to release until the bomb doors were closed, when it then caused minor damage. On his return to Malta, the Valiant leader Wg Cdr Haig was asked by waiting reporters about the possibility of accidentally bombing civilian property:

"If there was the slightest shadow of doubt, bombs may not be released."

He then proceeded to talk about the crews under his command:

"Not more than 15 to 20 per cent of our crews are old enough to have seen World War Two service. Most of them are 24 to 27 [years old]. In one respect it could be said we are continuing training. A good many of my men have not dropped a live bomb before."

Canberra B2 XA536 of 15 Squadron, a replacement aircraft, at Luqa, Malta. (*C. Donne via Andy Thomas*)

An hour before midnight, four more Valiants – two each from 138 and 214 Squadrons – took off from Luqa, the first pair (WZ384 and WZ401) to act as primary target markers for the attack on Abu Sueir airfield by the other two Valiants (WZ393 and WZ394) and six Canberras (five from 9 Squadron led by Sqn Ldr George Bastard in WH977, and one from 101 Squadron); a sixth aircraft from 9 Squadron, WH974 flown by Flt Lt J.F.G. Stoneham, had returned early due to undercarriage problems. Sqn Ldr R.G. Collins AFC, captain of Valiant WZ401, recalled:

"The sortie was uneventful and the weather over Egypt perfect for visual bombing. The Egyptians had made no attempt to 'blackout' and the lights of Cairo were visible for miles. The target was located and proximity markers dropped. The markers cascaded at 8,000 feet and indicated the area for low-level Canberra target marking. The two Valiants did a racetrack round from the target and came in in front of the bomber stream. Everything went like clockwork and we left the target satisfied with the job that had been done."

The Malta force was joined in the attack on Abu Sueir by five Canberra bombers

195

from Cyprus drawn from 10, 15, 44 and 61 Squadrons; a sixth aircraft, WH918 flown by Flg Off G.C. Price of the latter unit, had been unable to retract its undercarriage and consequently returned early. Markers were dropped by four Canberras of 18 Squadron.

The final bomber attack of the night was launched from Nicosia at 0500, eight Canberras of 27 Squadron led by Wg Cdr Peter Helmore (WH732) being followed into the still dark sky by five of 61 Squadron (led by Flt Lt G.A. Boston in WJ647), two marker aircraft of 139 Squadron (including WJ774 flown by Sqn Ldr R.S.D. Kearns DSO DFC DFM) having set out earlier for Inchas. Two Canberras of 61 Squadron had failed to take off, Flg Off D.R. Kenyon having retracted WH915's nose wheel, allegedly in error although it was believed that this was a deliberate act of dissent over the Suez operation by the pilot.* The Canberra following Kenyon's aircraft, WH918 piloted by the unlucky Flg Off Price, found itself too close to the incident and Price was unable to re-position the aircraft in time to join the others, so was stood down. All bombers returned safely from the attack on Inchas although one Canberra had been intercepted, but not attacked, by a Meteor NF13 over the target area; the crew watched it circle at distance and then dive away into the darkness.

On returning to Malta, Valiant and Canberra crews urged Grp Capt Hodges to request a change to operating height from 30,000 feet to 40,000 to 45,000 feet since (a) they had trained at that height and were more comfortable and confident, (b) the wind was almost negligible at that height and the aircraft more stable, and (c) there was no threat from night fighters at that height. Hodges gained the necessary permission and subsequent operations were carried out at between 40,000 and 45,000 feet.

The two British instructors at Bilbeis Flying School, Flt Lts Brisk and Larcombe, commented:

"When the British ultimatum came, the first reaction of the Egyptians with whom we were working was one of frank disbelief. They were certain it was a bluff. Then when the RAF bombers appeared the Egyptians were completely shattered. If you ask why the Egyptian Air Force did not take to the air against the attackers, there is one simple answer: the RAF had played an ungentlemanly trick by launching their attack at night. The Egyptians did not like flying in the dark; in fact they never flew the MiGs or Il-28s at night; and when weather conditions were unfavourable, all flying was automatically stopped."

Commenting upon the reaction to the surprise bombing of Egyptian airfields, Wg Cdr Labib wrote:

"The results of this bombardment did not completely stop the movements of Egyptian planes. For example, Cairo West air base continued to operate throughout the night. Nor did the Ilyushin bombers stop targeting Israeli positions, landing back at Cairo West. With the help of Egyptian radar tracking stations, I managed to organise take-offs and landings between each wave of British bombers. On the other hand, the British use of delayed-

---

* The pilot, Flg Off Dennis Kenyon, was court martialled and sentenced to 12 months' imprisonment 'for not carrying out a warlike operation with the utmost exertion'.

action bombs did affect our operations. These were particularly difficult to find and defuse at night."

President Nasser, whose house was located in Heliopolis near Almaza airfield, heard the bombers going over and observed the attack from his roof. Nasser soon left his house and headed to his military headquarters. On the way he was greeted by crowds of civilians who chanted 'We shall fight!' Nasser called together his military commanders and he made several important decisions. He ordered the Egyptian Army to withdraw from Sinai (see Chapter Seven) to defend against the expected Anglo-French invasion and authorised distribution of weapons to civilians to prepare for guerilla warfare against the invaders. Egypt's senior military commanders were surprised by Nasser's decision to evacuate Sinai by midnight. He also took time to broadcast over Cairo Radio, in true Churchillian style:

> "We shall fight bitterly, O compatriots. We shall not surrender. Each one of you is a soldier in the National Liberation Army. Orders have been given for the issue of arms, and we have many arms. We shall fight from village to village and from place to place. Let each one of you be a soldier in the Armed Forces so that we may defend our honour, dignity, and freedom. Let our motto be: We shall fight, not surrender. We shall fight, we shall fight, we shall not surrender."

Chapter Ten

THE DESTRUCTION OF AN AIR FORCE
1 November 1956

". . . if we had been up against an enemy with even a modicum of fighting qualities with the modern aircraft and equipment the Egyptians had, the situation would have been different."

Air Marshal Denis Barnett, Air Task Force Commander

British and French reconnaissance jets soon discovered the RAF's night bomber attack had not been very effective. The results were disappointing and photographs revealed that aircraft parked around the airfields seemed intact, though it was assumed some had probably been damaged by debris. Although some runways were cratered most appeared operational. Two of the Canberra reconnaissance aircraft came under attack by EAF MiGs during these early morning sorties. WH801 flown by Flg Off Jim Campbell and Flg Off R.J. Toseland was intercepted by a MiG-15. The pilot reported:

"[We were] quite disturbed to see explosive shells sailing by the cockpit on both sides from the rear."

Having recovered from the shock, Campbell proceeded to carry out violent evasive action and succeeded in shaking off the MiG with only minor damage having been inflicted on the aircraft's port elevator. The incident led Prime Minister Eden to comment that the interception was "a brillant piece of work by any standards". These interceptions came as somewhat of a shock to the RAF, particularly in view of the memo of assurance received by the Chiefs-of-Staff Committee from the War Office some three weeks earlier:

"If photographic reconnaissance is undertaken by single Canberra aircraft, the chances of detection are very small. Indeed, apart from some misfortune due to engine failure or a fortuitous interception, the risk of interception can be discounted."

Of the disturbing incident, Prime Minister Eden added:

". . . when it was reported to me the next day it gave me grim cause for thought. I kept my own council. In the later fighting the Egyptian Air Force was, by contrast, completely ineffective. I do not know the explanation. Maybe the pilots of another nation were flying the MiGs that dawn."

198

Canberra PR7 WH801 was attacked by an EAF MiG on the morning of 1 November 1956; minor damage was inflicted on the aircraft's port elevator. (*Authors' collection*)

Although little tangible damage had resulted from the RAF night raids, Egyptian morale was shaken according to Flt Lts Brisk and Larcombe, the British instructors at Bilbeis:

> "After the British night attacks had stunned the Egyptians into inactivity, came the renewed daylight offensive at first light of dawn. We saw Egyptian pilots gazing into the sky at the British bombers and remarking wistfully that something should be done about them. But it never occurred to them to take to the air themselves. In fact, so chaotic was the communications system that there seemed to be no one with the necessary authority to order the fighters to scramble."

This was not of course how the situation was seen by their students. When later Maj-General Abdel Moneim al-Tawil (who was then a mere Pilot Officer under training) was told of Brisk and Larcombe's comments, he suggested they were motivated by ill-feeling in the wake of the Suez invasion and by a certain guilty conscience for having helped train 'the enemy' – namely the Egyptian Air Force. Despite the comments of the RAF instructors, the British hope of undermining Egyptian morale by bombing was not fulfilled. In fact, the raids served to strengthen Egyptian morale, much as German bombing stiffened the British will to resist in 1940. As Tameen Fahmy Abdullah, who later rose to the rank of Brigadier-General in the EAF, recalled:

> "As a young boy I lived in Heliopolis and I saw the many flights of jets from the nearby airfields. I was almost 15 years old when, on 31 October 1956, the British attacked. I was taking a shower when the night bombing started and the alarm went off. I had to shut off the shower and get out. The next day I went on the roof of our building and we could see Almaza from there, and I watched the Sea Hawks and Sea Venoms attacking. We could see some anti-aircraft guns, perhaps 37mm, firing back. I was then very enthusiastic about joining the military."

This he did, and he eventually commanded a number of MiG-21 squadrons.

With dawn came waves of British and French fighter-bombers flying from Cyprus and aircraft carriers steaming in the Mediterranean to bomb, rocket and strafe all the major EAF bases in northern Egypt. Akrotiri-based Venoms of 6, 8 and 249 Squadrons were tasked to attack airfields east of the 32° line of longitude – Abu Sueir, Deversoir, Fayid, Kabrit, Kasfareet and Shallufa – and were joined in these strikes by all available rocket-armed F-84Fs of EC1/3 and EC3/3, while the Fleet's fighter-bombers were to operate against airfields to the west of the line – Cairo West, Cairo International, Almaza, Inchas, Bilbeis and Dekheila, the latter a former Fleet Air Arm airfield near Alexandria.

AKROTIRI STRIKE WING

A pair of 249 Squadron Venoms led by Flt Lt Charlie Slade in WR506/W took off from Akrotiri at 0520, followed 15 minutes later by a second pair (including Flg Off Denis Moyes in WR533/F), their pilots briefed to frustrate any possible attack on the aircraft preparing for the day's operations. No enemy aircraft were seen although there was a scare at 0600 when the crew of a returning Canberra of 13 Squadron called up to report it was being pursued by a MiG. Sirens were sounded at Cyprus and defences put on alert, but 15 minutes later radar operators were able to explain that the Canberra was in fact being 'pursued' by a returning French RF-84F. Both aircraft landed safely at Akrotiri.

Venom FB4s of 8 Squadron at Akrotiri. Suez stripes cover serials and Squadron markings; however, nearest aircraft is coded 'C' and was WR485. (*Sqn Ldr R.K.J. Hadlow*)

Meanwhile, eight Venoms of 6 Squadron, with Sqn Ldr Peter Ellis (WR404/X) and Flt Lt Harry Harrison (Venom D) leading the sections, had taken off and set course for Kasfareet and Kabrit. In order to make the return trip, Akrotiri's Venoms were equipped with jettisonable wingtip and pylon fuel tanks. However, the jettisoning of fuel tanks was merely an option which reduced drag and increased range on remaining fuel. Sqn Ldr Ellis remembered:

> "It was rumoured the Egyptians had 'all singing, all dancing' radar-controlled
> guns which could shoot you down from any angle. Some of the chaps were
> a bit wary, so I led the first lot off."

Arriving over the target area at 0604, the Venoms encountered no enemy aircraft in the air and only meagre and inaccurate light anti-aircraft fire. Sqn Ldr Ellis continued:

> "When over the target at 30,000 feet, we barrelled down with the first section, followed by second section. We encountered only light flak."

Flt Lt Harrison, the senior Flight Commander, recorded:

> "The normal flight plan was for aircraft to climb immediately after take-off to 35,000 feet and to descend when 20 miles off the target. Depending on the range from base to the target it was possible to spend ten to 15 minutes over the target area using full throttle at low level. Our aircraft were armed with high-explosive rockets and 20mm cannon. Opposition was confined to light sporadic anti-aircraft fire. Instead of the rehearsed tactics of leaving the target area after the initial attack, we were able to circle the airfield and make several attacks on the dispersed aircraft."

Two MiGs, aircraft of 20 Squadron EAF or the fighter OTU, were destroyed on the ground at Kabrit and an unidentified piston-engine aircraft damaged. One Venom, WR382/C, suffered minor damage to its starboard wing during the strike. While 6 Squadron was thus engaged, eight Venoms from 8 Squadron visited Abu Sueir and Fayid, with Sqn Ldr Blyth (WR509) and Flt Lt Harcourt-Smith (WR480) leading the sections. Sqn Ldr Blyth recalled:

> "Someone at ME HQ had the bright idea of ordering spread harmonisation (probably thought we couldn't shoot). Jock [Sqn Ldr Maitland of 249 Squadron] ordered his lot to ignore it and go for 'spot'. I wish I'd followed suit, but I was new and used to receiving instructions from HQ when with Levant. Nevertheless, we got a lot of MiGs – our four got 11 [the official record shows seven destroyed and two damaged]. I got five of them, but then I was first in. There was a lot of talk about model (dummy) MiGs. Bit of a quirk of mine I suppose, but I pig headedly said no claims unless they went up in flame and smoke."

Flt Lt Harcourt-Smith (WR480) added:

> "At Abu Sueir we saw a lot of MiGs parked in hangars, some with the tails sticking out."

In addition to the MiGs destroyed at Abu Sueir, a Meteor was destroyed at Fayid and a Vampire damaged while a hangar was also destroyed. The Squadron's WR501 suffered minor damage to the leading edge of one wing. Hard on the tails of the Venoms came F-84Fs from Akrotiri, six aircraft having departed for Fayid and Abu Sueir at 0545, followed by a further eight 20 minutes later with Kabrit and Kasfareet as their targets. The first flight claimed two Meteors destroyed at Fayid in addition to damaging a hangar, then damaged three MiGs at Abu Sueir. Although five MiGs were attacked at Kabrit by Cne Payen's EC1/3, no positive damage was observed, while at Kasfareet a number of dispersed MiGs were seen but not attacked. With the safe return to Akrotiri of the first wave Venoms and F-84Fs, three more sections of French fighter-

---

Sqn Ldr Joe Blyth in the cockpit of his 8 Squadron Venom FB4. (*Sqn Ldr C.I. Blyth*)

bombers were sent off, followed closely by two flights of Venoms from 249 Squadron, to continue the series of attacks. One section of F-84Fs visited Abu Sueir, where a MiG had apparently just landed, and attacked anti-aircraft gun positions. The same quartet flew to al-Firdan and finished their ammunition strafing gun emplacements. Abu Sueir was attacked by another four F-84Fs, as was Deversoir where a hangar was rocketed. The third section destroyed a Vampire and a Meteor at Fayid.

Meanwhile, the 249 Squadron Venoms were busily engaged, one section flying to Kabrit and the other striking at Fayid and Abu Sueir, the sections led by Sqn Ldr Maitland (WR499/V) and Flt Lt Doug Dallison (Venom A). Six MiGs were claimed destroyed at Kabrit, as recalled by Flg Off Gronert (WR504/Z):

> "On 249 Squadron we had developed a system for rocket firing which gave more time for target identification and longer tracking time, thus enabling much greater accuracy. This also gave us a longer time flying at altitude, a significant factor due to the distance between Cyprus and Egypt. It involved flying from 30,000 feet and maintaining Mach 0.7 until 300 knots was reached, and this speed was maintained to the target. The formations were drawn up for the squadron shortly before the first day of operations. I was to fly in the formation of four led by Flt Lt Doug Dallison, who was B Flight commander. His No2 was [Flt Lt] Mick Waterhouse with myself as No3 and [Flg Off] Bill Barker as No4. It was a very experienced section and we were first off with our target being Kabrit, which was a MiG-15 base.
>
> Our long dive worked out very well and we all had a good strike on aircraft parked neatly in lines on the dispersal area. Following our rocket attack we flew on to Abu Sueir where we attacked further MiGs and motor

Venom FB4 'G' of 8 Squadron starting up at Akrotiri. (*Andy Thomas*)

transport targets. [Flg Off Gronert claimed a MiG destroyed at each airfield.] It appeared that the Egyptian Air Force was taken completely by surprise and at that time had made no attempt to hide or disperse its aircraft, though some that survived were very skilfully hidden in sunken blister hangars, particularly at Abu Sueir. It is difficult to recall my feelings before and after the first sortie. I suppose it was a mixture of anticipation, apprehension and a fear of the unknown. I recall the debriefing officer wanting to know our mission number but no one could remember it. We didn't want to be bothered with trifles like that, we wanted to tell about the MiGs we had shot up and so on."

At 0800, 6 and 8 Squadrons each despatched four aircraft, the former flying to Fayid where three Meteors were seen but not attacked, though two MiGs at Abu Sueir were strafed and damaged. During the strike Venom WR473/U suffered minor flak damage to its tailplane. The 8 Squadron section struck at Kabrit and destroyed four of 11 MiGs observed on the ground, before flying to Abu Sueir where a dozen apparently undamaged aircraft were seen by the Venom pilots. However, since they had exhausted their ammunition they returned to Akrotiri to report their find.

By 0930, with the return of the latest strike, a total of 58 sorties had been flown by the Venoms and F-84Fs, and it was assessed that up to 30 MiGs had been destroyed or at least disabled, with four Meteors and two Vampires being left in a similar non-operational condition:

SUMMARY OF SORTIES FLOWN BY VENOMS and F-84Fs by 0930

ETA Target	Target	Aircraft	Claims
0604	Kasfareet	4 Venom	2 MiGs destroyed, one u/i
0609	Kabrit	4 Venom	aircraft damaged
0604	Abu Sueir	4 Venom	7 MiGs destroyed, two damaged

ETA Target	Target	Aircraft	Claims
0609	Fayid	4 Venom	Meteor destroyed, Vampire damaged
0624	Fayid	3 F-84F	2 Meteors destroyed, hangar damaged
0629	Abu Sueir	3 F-84F	3 MiGs damaged
0644	Kabrit	4 F-84F	5 MiGs strafed
0649	Kasfareet	4 F-84F	
0704	Abu Sueir	4 F-84F	AA gun destroyed
0709	al-Firdan		
0704	Fayid	4 F-84F	Vampire destroyed, Meteor
0709	Shallufa		destroyed
0709	Abu Sueir	4 F-84F	
0714	Deversoir		Hangar attacked
0734	Kabrit	4 Venom	6 MiGs destroyed
0739	Fayid	4 Venom	
0804	Abu Sueir		
0839	Fayid	4 Venom	
0844	Abu Sueir		2 MiGs damaged
0844	Kabrit	4 Venom	4 MiGs destroyed
0849	Abu Sueir		

Following the initial strikes, RF-84Fs were sent to photograph the damage inflicted on the various airfields. Lt Bertin-Maghit wrote:

"Last night the English [sic] bombers attacked and at dawn the French and English fighters took off to strafe the enemy airfields. As a result we flew eight missions to check on the bombardment, plus two reconnaissance and one photographic mission."

One sortie was flown by Lt Arnaud in RF334, who visited Kabrit at 0930 where he reported seeing 17 MiGs and five single-engine unidentified aircraft, noting that three of the MiGs had suffered damage. At Kasfareet a single Vampire was observed, while Fayid revealed the wrecks of three Vampires and a Meteor, together with two damaged hangars. Three other Vampires seen on the airfield appeared to be undamaged.

Having refuelled and re-armed, the Venoms took to the air for a second series of airfield strikes at 0930, a section from 6 Squadron again led by Sqn Ldr Ellis (WR404/X). As Flt Lt Harrison (Venom H) led his section towards Abu Sueir at about 1000, two MiGs were encountered in the air some 70 miles from Cyprus, heading in the direction of Syria. Apparently the fighter-bombers were not seen by the Egyptian pilots, though the Venom pilots could not have given chase since they were carrying external fuel tanks and a full load of rockets – not that they would have been able to catch the MiGs anyway! During the strike on Abu Sueir a MiG was destroyed and another aircraft damaged, while Venom WR413 suffered a hit in one of its pylon tanks but was able to return to Akrotiri

RF-84F 33-CF, s/n 17019, of ER4/33 at Akrotiri. (*Sqn Ldr R.K.J. Hadlow*)

safely. Eight Venoms from 8 Squadron also carried out a second strike, this time against Kasfareet and Kabrit, as Sqn Ldr Blyth (WR509) recalled:

> "On this occasion I put a few rounds through my old office at Kabrit."

A section led by Flt Lt Harcourt-Smith (WR480) also visited Kabrit, where a number of MiGs were strafed, two being claimed destroyed and a third damaged. Flg Off Bryn Jones flew WR445 on this sortie, Kasfareet also being targeted where a hangar was strafed. Despite the incessant attacks, at least 14 MiGs were believed still to be airworthy at Kabrit. When eight F-84Fs arrived over that airfield at 1100, the pilots reported seeing four MiGs on fire together with three or four burnt wrecks. An apparently undamaged MiG was strafed by the French pilots before they departed for Fayid where a hangar was rocketed.

Pilots and groundcrew of B Flight 249 Squadron: pilots (left to right) Flg Off George Garner, Flg Off Dave Elford, Flg Off Andy Anderson, Flt Lt Tam Syme, Flt Lt Mick Waterhouse, Flg Off Pete Purnell, Flg Off George MacIntosh. (*Sqn Ldr T.S. Syme*)

Shortly before midday, two sections from 249 Squadron arrived over Fayid, one led by Flt Lt Tam Syme (WR531/R) and the other by Flt Lt Slade (WR506/W). A hangar, attacked with rockets, was left in flames and a Meteor was destroyed by cannon fire, with a second damaged. Flg Off Lecky-Thompson's aircraft (WR533/F) sustained some damage during the attack:

> "After firing the rockets I got a hole in the port pylon tank from some ground fire and had to abort, returning before the fuel ran out."

Following the strike against Fayid, the remaining three of Syme's section flew to Kasfareet where a hangar was strafed. On this strike WR504/Z suffered damage to its port pylon tank and tip tank. Nevertheless, the pilot was able to return to Akrotiri safely. Another section – four aircraft from 8 Squadron led by Flt Lt Scarlett – visited Abu Sueir at about the same time and rocketed the main hangar which inflicted damage on a nearby MiG. Flg Off Hadlow (WR432/R) recalled:

> "The brief was rocket projectile attacks on Kasfareet followed by strafing Kabrit with 20mm cannon. Both these airfields were just north of the Great Bitter Lake and about the southernmost extent of our range. One attack and then out to preserve surprise and avoid trouble with AA fire. The most vivid memory is of arriving over Kasfareet to find many of the hangars and buildings on fire, closely followed by the image of just how big a hangar looks when you are diving to attack with R/Ps – practice targets on the range were ten feet square, a slight difference! I damaged a hangar and a MiG-15 at Kabrit. Somewhere along the way I managed to pick up what looked like a rifle bullet through one of the underwing tanks."

A dozen F-84Fs followed the Venoms to Fayid, Abu Sueir and Kabrit. One MiG and another aircraft were strafed at Fayid, and two MiGs at Abu Sueir, one of which was destroyed. Many fires were observed on the airfields as aircraft and hangars continued to burn. An hour later, eight 6 Squadron Venoms attacked Abu Sueir where a MiG and a Vampire were claimed destroyed, while damage

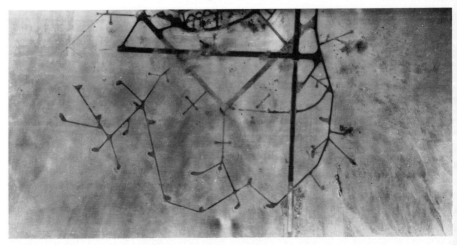

Fayid as seen through the camera of an RF-84F of ER4/33 flying at 30,000 feet; the runways appear to have been badly damaged. (*SHAA via Albert Grandolini*)

was inflicted on another MiG and two Vampires. Two hangars were also rocketed and left in flames. Flt Lt Harrison's section included Grp Capt Macdonald (Akrotiri's Station Commander), as he recalled:

"I remember well the very special briefing that I gave my section after the main brief and without the Group Captain present. I would lead the section with [Flg Off] Brian Hurn [a South African] as my No2, the Group Captain as No3, and with [Flg Off] Chris Preston looking after his tail at No4. After my attack, both wingmen were to stick on the tail of No3 and I would find them. This proved to be good insurance because he never had any idea of where I was after a dive, and I had a hard chase to catch up with the three of them. It was quite a relief to get him home safely!"

By 1330, an additional 62 sorties had been flown by the Venoms and F-84Fs, with the tally of aircraft destroyed and damaged on the ground having risen to an estimated 50 to 60, mainly MiGs:

SUMMARY OF SORTIES FLOWN BY VENOMS and F-84Fs, 0930-1330

ETA Target	Target	Aircraft	Claims
1004	Abu Sueir	4 Venom	MiG destroyed, u/i aircraft damaged
1009	Fayid	4 Venom	
1029	Kasfareet	4 Venom	Hangar strafed
1034	Kabrit	4 Venom	2 MiGs destroyed, one damaged
1054	Kabrit	4 F-84F	MiG damaged
1059	Abu Sueir	4 F-84F	
1149	Fayid	4 Venom	Meteor destroyed, one damaged
1154	Kasfareet	4 Venom	Hangar in flames
1204	Abu Sueir	4 Venom	Hangar rocketed
1209	Kabrit		MiG damaged, hangar rocketed
1219	Fayid	4 F-84F	U/i aircraft damaged
1224	Abu Sueir		MiG destroyed, one damaged
1219	Fayid	4 F-84F	MiG damaged
1224	Kabrit	4 F-84F	Ammo dump damaged
1256	Fayid	3 F-84F	MiG damaged
1310	Abu Sueir	3 F-84F	
1304	Abu Sueir	4 Venom	MiG destroyed, Vampire destroyed
1309	Kabrit	4 Venom	MiG damaged, 2 Vampires damaged

The airfield strikes continued unabated and unchallenged throughout the afternoon. All three Venom squadrons despatched sections at 1330, 249 Squadron leading the way. At 1410, Flg Off Dave Williams' section arrived over Abu Sueir where Williams (WR492/U) claimed a Meteor F8 destroyed; a second Meteor was seen to be afire. A Vampire was also destroyed before the section headed for Kasfareet and inflicted damage on the control tower. The 8 Squadron quartet struck at Fayid and Kabrit, destroying four MiGs at the former and rocketing the main hangar at the latter. One MiG was seen to be burning furiously as the

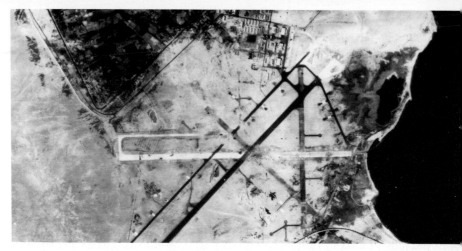

Aerial view of Kabrit taken by an RF-84F of ER4/33 flying at 30,000 feet; note the many bomb craters including damage to the runways. (*SHAA via Albert Grandolini*)

pilots pulled away. Two MiGs were destroyed and three damaged by 6 Squadron as a result of their attack on Kasfareet and Kabrit, where a hangar was also left in flames. Two of the Venoms suffered damage during this strike, WR476 returning with holes in one wing which had also damaged the fuel tank. Although the pilot of WR481 managed to fly back to Akrotiri, the subsequent inspection of his aircraft revealed the necessity for an engine change due to debris damage. The returning pilots reported sighting 11 camouflaged MiGs still apparently intact at Kabrit.

Four Venoms from 8 Squadron struck again at Fayid and Abu Sueir shortly after 1500; the pilots reported further damage to the main hangar at the former and damage to a hangar and the control tower at the latter. Three flights of F-84Fs repeated the strike within minutes, also visiting Kabrit and Kasfareet; two MiGs were strafed at Abu Sueir although one F-84F also sustained damage. A second section strafed aircraft seen at Abu Sueir although no claims were made against the two Masters and six MiGs targeted. An hour later, two sections of 249 Squadron aircraft repeated the attacks on Fayid, Kasfareet and Abu Sueir. Sqn Ldr Maitland (WR506/W) led a rocket strike against hangars and other buildings, while Flt Lt Syme (WR489/D) took his flight to Fayid where he claimed damage to a long-nose Meteor – obviously a NF13 of 10 Squadron EAF – during a rocket attack. The quartet then flew to Kabrit, where Syme strafed a MiG and a Fury but met heavy flak. Flt Lt Dallison's section struck at Abu Sueir and then Fayid, as noted by Flg Off Gronert (WR504/Z):

> "My second sortie was similar to the first except that I was not so apprehensive; this is what we had trained to do and we set about it in a professional way. The targets this time were Abu Sueir for our rockets, and Fayid afterwards with our 20mm cannon [where he destroyed a Meteor]. We were asked on our return about damage to runways and infrastructure at the various airfields, but it was obvious that the damage and disruption caused was minuscule. For all the damage inflicted by the bomber force, they might just as well have stayed at home. On our return the feeling was one of great exhilaration and relief that everything had gone so well; debriefing was a mad affair with everyone wanting to talk at once."

Close up of rocket-armed F-84F (3-VI) of EC3/3 at Akrotiri. (*SHAA via Albert Grandolini*)

Flg Off Moyes participated in this attack and subsequently claimed a Vampire destroyed by cannon fire plus a hangar damaged during a rocket strike. However, his aircraft (WR527/C) suffered flak damage to its tail unit:

> "I remember being apprehensive on the way in, doing as much damage as quickly as possible, then breathing a sigh of relief as we coasted out."

Meanwhile Flt Lt Waterhouse and Flg Off Lecky-Thompson (WR492/U) visited Fayid, Kasfareet and Kabrit in succession:

> "Mick [Waterhouse] and I found aircraft partly dug in and camouflaged around the peri[meter] track of the airfields and we had a field day. We had a mutual agreement with the other squadrons that we would leave a few undamaged so that when we went in – 249 was planned to deploy in Egypt – we would be able to have fun flying the MiG-15s!"

Nonetheless, the pair claimed six MiGs and a Vampire T11 destroyed by cannon fire, although Lecky-Thompson noted that his salvo of four rockets aimed at some parked Vampires missed the target.

A third wave of Venoms departed from Akrotiri at 1545, including a section of 8 Squadron again led by Sqn Ldr Blyth (WR485/C), flying his third sortie of the day:

> "Our target was Abu Sueir again. I managed to do more sorties than the others. I claimed it was how the rotation worked out!"

209

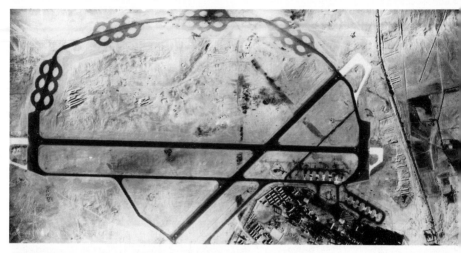

Abu Sueir as seen by an RF-84F of ER4/33 flying at 22,000 feet; the runways appear to be undamaged. (*SHAA via Albert Grandolini*)

Flt Lt Scarlett's section headed for Kabrit, where Flg Off Hadlow (WR405/B) strafed a number of MiGs:

> "It was back to Kabrit [where I managed] to damage two or three MiGs. The last 30 minutes [was flown] in the dark back to Akrotiri. So ended my first day in action. An eventful day with some satisfaction for a job, one hoped, well done."

Meanwhile, Flt Lt Harrison (Venom D) at the head of his 6 Squadron section found a large number of MiGs (presumably including aircraft of 30 Squadron EAF) at Abu Sueir and seven of these were subsequently claimed destroyed and four damaged by the quartet of Venoms; the pilots reported that many more were seen dispersed around the airfield as they completed their attacks. The Venoms returned in the dark to Akrotiri. The final strike of the day was launched from Akrotiri at 1600 when 17 F-84Fs headed for Abu Sueir and Kabrit. A total of ten MiGs were claimed damaged, all but two at Kabrit where AA fire damaged two of the French aircraft. With the safe return of all the French fighter-bombers, a final tally of the day's claims was made. A total of 65 sorties had been carried out during the afternoon period, resulting in 54 further claims of Egyptian aircraft destroyed or damaged on the ground, taking the total for the day by the Venoms and F-84Fs to at least 130, achieved for no losses to the Allies.

SUMMARY OF SORTIES FLOWN BY VENOMS and F-84Fs, 1330–1700

ETA Target	Target	Aircraft	Claims
1409	Abu Sueir	4 Venom	Vampire and Meteor destroyed
1414	Fayid		Hangars damaged
1419	Fayid	4 Venom	4 MiGs destroyed
1424	Kabrit		Hangar rocketed

SUMMARY OF SORTIES FLOWN BY VENOMS and F-84Fs, 1330–1700 (continued)

ETA Target	Target	Aircraft	Claims
1439	Kasfareet	4 Venom	2 MiGs destroyed, 3 damaged
1444	Kabrit		Hangar in flames, 3 damaged
1504	Fayid	4 Venom	Hangar damaged
1509	Abu Sueir		Hangar damaged
1544	Fayid	4 F-84F	Installations attacked
1549	Abu Sueir		2 MiGs damaged
1554	Kasfareet		
1544	Fayid	4 F-84F	Buildings attacked
1549	Kabrit		Hangars attacked
1544	Abu Sueir	4 F-84F	2 Masters attacked
1549	Fayid		6 MiGs attacked
1604	Fayid	4 Venom	Meteor and Vampire destroyed
1609	Kasfareet		6 MiGs destroyed
1634	Fayid	4 Venom	MiG destroyed, hangar damaged
1639	Abu Sueir		MiG destroyed
1634	Shallufa	4 Venom	Buildings attacked
1639	Deversoir		8 MiGs observed under camouflage
1634	Abu Sueir	4 Venom	7 MiGs destroyed, 4 damaged
1639	Kabrit	4 Venom	5 MiGs destroyed, 7 damaged
1639	Abu Sueir	5 F-84F	
1644	Kabrit		6 MiGs damaged
1644	Kabrit	4 F-84F	2 MiGs damaged, hangars attacked
1649	Abu Sueir	4 F-84F	Barracks attacked
1654	Kabrit		Barracks attacked
1654	Abu Sueir	4 F-84F	2 MiGs damaged

By the end of the day the three Venom squadrons had flown 104 sorties and jointly claimed 59 Egyptian aircraft destroyed on the ground, the vast majority of which were MiGs; in addition, claims were made for 11 probables and 37 damaged. During the course of 16 missions, the F-84Fs flew a total of 75 sorties and the French pilots included a dozen MiGs among their claims for 16 aircraft destroyed, nine probables and four damaged. A dozen of the Venoms had suffered minor damage, much of it caused by debris, while three of the French fighter-bombers also sustained minor damage.

Canberra PR7s of 13 Squadron flew eight reconnaissance sorties during the day, and ER4/33's RF-84Fs a total of 11 sorties. All aircraft returned safely. Lt Bertin-Maghit of ER4/33 noted:

"This evening there was a great mood in the tent of the intelligence officer when everyone looked at the latest photographs which had hardly even dried. There was a discussion about what the fighters had hit as the pictures

211

were passed from hand to hand, the whispering, the light-hearted teasing of a group of pilots who were all in the same state of excitement."

13 Squadron lacked processing and interpretation equipment, which meant that photographs taken by the Canberras had to be processed at Episkopi, often taking three to four hours before the results could be studied, whereas the French unit had arrived at Cyprus complete with its processing equipment and could produce results almost immediately.

The morning interceptions by the MiGs gave cause for grave concern. The crews of 13 Squadron, most of whom had been attached from 58 Squadron, recalled that the parent Squadron had carried out trials with a periscope – the early model Canberra had a mounting unit for a periscopic sextant for astro-navigation – by which the navigator was able to observe the area to the rear of the Canberra, and it was realised that contrails of attacking aircraft could be easily tracked by this means. Such periscopes were now fitted to 13 Squadron's aircraft as a local modification, as Flt Lt Hunter recalled:

"One of the problems of flying the [photo-recon] Canberra on operations was that the pilot was involved very much in flying the aircraft as a steady platform for photography. The navigator was 100 per cent involved in taking the photography and making sure the cameras were pointing at the piece of ground or territory that he wanted to take. So we had, as crew members, complained that the PR Canberra was not a good aircraft when it came to looking after your own tail.

Because of the MiG interceptions, HQ decided it would be safer to fly operational sorties in the future with a look-out occupying the navigator's normal position, a third crew member with a periscope mounted aft of the aircraft. He was supposed to be there doing nothing but protecting the tail from attack. It [the periscope] became very much temporary equipment. I think all our aircraft were so fitted, but I think it ran foul of AHQ Levant. HQ Mediterranean were directing the operational set-up through a team of people they had brought out from London. There was a little cell formed, particularly on the recce side, and these people were making the operational decisions regarding the Squadron – AHQ Levant were in fact omitted from the operational chain. Therefore, AHQ Levant was not involved with the operational control of the Squadron during the fracas and the look-out man and a rear-seat periscope, call it what you will, was not with its authority. AHQ Levant felt it should have been informed."

Hunters from Cyprus had been busy throughout the day although all suspects turned out to be British or French aircraft, and included two flights of Venoms, two Canberras, two Shackletons from Malta, and a French Dakota.

**SUMMARY OF GROUND ATTACK CLAIMS AGAINST AIRCRAFT
OF THE EGYPTIAN AIR FORCE
by Venoms and F-84Fs, 1 November 1956**

Missions: Venoms 19   F-84Fs 16
Sorties: Venoms 106 (2 aborts)   F-84Fs 81 (5 aborts)

	Destroyed	Probables	Damaged
Claims for MiG-15s			
Venoms:	48	7	28
F-84Fs:	12	8	4
Claims for other types:			
Venoms:	11	4	9
F-84Fs:	4	1	0
	75	20	41

CARRIER STRIKE FORCE

Two fully armed Avengers of 9F Flotille were launched from the *Arromanches* at 0349 to carry out an anti-submarine patrol, followed by a further two at 0405. The latter pair sighted an Egyptian destroyer, the *al-Nasr*, near Nelson Island but were greeted by heavy anti-aircraft fire as they approached. At 0520 the Aeronavale patrol encountered and attacked with rockets the Egyptian frigate *Tarek*, the French crews claiming two hits. When news of the attack reached *Arromanches*, *La Fayette* was instructed to launch a strike of eight Corsairs, each armed with two 1000lb bombs. The fighter-bombers were launched at 0700, led by Lt deV de Saint-Quentin, the deputy commander of 15F Flotille. After 50 minutes, the wakes of two ships were detected and the leader ordered drop tanks to be released, but first Ens deV Caron (son of the Task Force's Admiral) was sent down to confirm that the ships were not part of the US Sixth Fleet. On observing Caron's aircraft being greeted by AA fire, de Saint-Quentin ordered an attack, having been briefed to bomb from a height of 8,000 feet – far too high to ensure accuracy against moving targets. However, both Egyptian vessels did suffer minor damage during these attacks although they were able to withdraw to Alexandria under cover of a smokescreen. Rocket-armed Corsairs of 14F Flotille were also launched during the morning, Lt deV Cremer (flying 14F-1) briefed to attack any military convoys encountered north of the Nile Delta. Although one such target was located, the pilots were unable to attack without the possibility of inflicting casualties among the many refugees also on the road, so they returned to the carrier having first discharged their rockets into the sea.

At 0520 the Fleet Air Arm commenced its assault, 36 Sea Hawks and Sea Venoms being launched from *Eagle*, *Bulwark* and *Albion* to attack the airfields at Cairo West, Almaza and Inchas, which were the priority targets; a further eight fighters (four Sea Venoms and four Sea Hawks) were sent off to fly protection patrols over their respective carriers and escorts, while Whirlwinds and Dragonflys from the carriers took off to undertake planeguard duties in case of emergencies.

First strike launched at 0520:

	Designated Target/Duty
HMS Eagle	
897 Squadron 6 Sea Hawks ⎤	
899 Squadron 6 Sea Hawks ⎟	
893 Squadron 2 Sea Venoms ⎟	Inchas
892 Squadron 2 Sea Venoms ⎦	
893 Squadron 2 Sea Venoms	CAP HMS Eagle
HMS Albion	
800 Squadron 4 Sea Hawks ⎤	
802 Squadron 4 Sea Hawks ⎬	Almaza
809 Squadron 4 Sea Venoms ⎦	
809 Squadron 2 Sea Venoms	CAP HMS Albion
HMS Bulwark	
804 Squadron 8 Sea Hawks ⎫	Cairo West
810 Squadron 4 Sea Hawks ⎭	
810 Squadron 4 Sea Hawks	CAP HMS Bulwark

Amongst the first aircraft to be launched from *Eagle* were the Sea Hawks of 899 Squadron, led by Lt Cdr Clark (XE457/487):

"I turned on to course for Inchas and climbed to 20,000 feet. They all followed 'the light' and were formed up on reaching the coast without a word being said."

Inchas after a strike by Allied fighter-bombers, as seen by Lt Cdr John Morris-Jones from the cockpit of his camera-equipped Sea Hawk of 800 Squadron. (*Cdr J. Morris-Jones*)

214

The Sea Hawks of 897 and 899 Squadrons reached Inchas without incident, led by the four Sea Venoms of 892/893 Squadrons, as recalled by Lt Cdr Henley (WW193/096):

"I was Strike Leader [with Lt Ian Gilman as observer], which involved four Sea Venoms leading 12 Sea Hawks on a strafing attack against Inchas. The launch and form-up were pre-dawn, the plan being to use the Sea Venom's superior navigation capability (radar, observer) to arrive at the target at first light, closely following the high-level bombing attacks by the RAF [Canberras from Cyprus] – almost too close as a stick of bombs exploded across the airfield as we were on the run-in. Thereafter, the Sea Hawks and Sea Venoms operated separately."

The Sea Hawks rocketed and strafed a number of MiGs and other aircraft seen on the airfield and claimed four MiGs destroyed, five probables and three other aircraft damaged. Lt Cdr Rawbone of 897 Squadron (flying Sea Hawk 201) claimed one MiG destroyed and two possibly damaged:

"There were several craters from RAF bombs but no damage to runways, hangars or airfield primary targets. We strafed aircraft, hangars and the control tower, claiming damage only on those aircraft which actually burnt. Three flamers for Flight."

Another pilot of 897 Squadron, Lt Mills (XE448/191), graphically described his attack:

"We had no trouble in finding the target and started letting down to begin our attack. We could see the hangars and runways with rows of parked aircraft which we attacked with three-inch rockets. As I climbed away from the attack, following the Boss, I suddenly realised the sky was full of little black puffs of smoke, and I thought 'My God, they're shooting at me!' On my second attack, this time using my 20mm cannon, I saw a lot of winking lights coming from the airfield perimeter, but it was much later when it penetrated that these came from anti-aircraft and small-arms fire. Then we re-formed in good order and started the trip back to the ship expecting to be attacked by fighters at any minute. As we crossed the coast, 'tail-end Charlie' turned to make sure we were not being followed, giving away the position of the Fleet, but all was clear and we landed on without incident. At the debriefing, it was clear that we had destroyed or damaged a large number of parked aircraft, but how many was a different matter. I had seen a MiG blow up when hit by one of my rockets, and claimed it, but I think the score was much higher."

As the 802 Squadron section approached Almaza they encountered a flight of MiGs, as recalled by Lt Cdr Eveleigh (WM911/133):

"Almaza was the main operational airfield of the Egyptian Air Force. We were surprised by a flight of MiGs which climbed away from Almaza towards us, and as we were only straight-winged compared with their swept-wing high performance, I can still recall the feeling of my Squadron closing up tight on

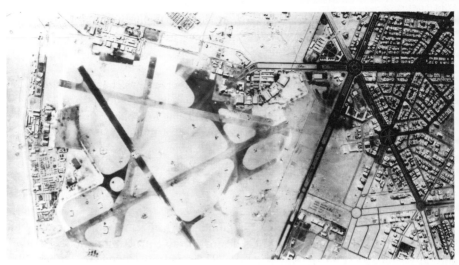

Many wrecked aircraft can be seen scattered around Almaza, where the runways are heavily bomb cratered. (*SHAA via Albert Grandolini*)

me on sighting them. We were apprehensive to say the least, but they swept straight past and did not attempt to mix it with us. We can only assume they were being flown away to some nearby safe haven."

Lt Cdr Ron Shilcock of 809 Squadron led the strike in Sea Venom XG670/220:

"Strafed line of small aircraft – thought to be MiG-15s. Encountered some light flak. Results of strike not observed."

His observer, Lt John Hackett, however noted:

"Attacked Almaza at 0601 – four Sea Venoms. Five MiG-15s damaged on ground."

Another of the Sea Venom pilots, Lt Bob Wigg (in XG620/226, with Lt Eddie Bowman) who had flown operations during the Korean War, recalled the strike in more graphic detail:

"On our way in to the primary target, Almaza airfield, the sun came up, bathing the Egyptian landscape a stunning rose red. We had heard at the final briefing that the Canberras, flying direct from Malta, would bomb the runways at the Egyptian airfields and generally soften them up for us, so that we could get on with destroying the aircraft on the ground with rockets and cannon. As we made our long descent towards the target, it became obvious that the Canberras had not been there ahead of us. Almaza was untouched, apparently still asleep. Apart from a couple of unidentified transport aircraft [which he claimed damaged], there was no sign of the Egyptian Air Force's MiGs and Ilyushins. With the lack of targets, there was no problem in deciding where our rockets would do most good. The hangars on both sides of the runway erupted as 64 assorted HE and AP rockets exploded inside them, and then it was time to switch to cannon and concen-

216

trate on hitting something worthwhile with them and at the same time avoid hitting the ground with the aircraft.

The Egyptian anti-aircraft guns must have been at maximum depression. Sited between the hangars on both sides of the runway we were currently streaking along, all they had to do was squeeze and wait for us to fly through, and that's what they did. The white hot balls of tracer criss-crossed the runway in front of us and I remember shouting a warning, not that any of us could have taken avoiding action. A few more seconds of the sort of terror I hadn't known since Korea and we were all clear."

Sub Lt Tony Yates and his West Indian observer, Sub Lt Charlie Dwarika (XG677/225), observed an Il-28 on the airfield which they duly strafed and claimed damaged. The leader of the Sea Hawks, Lt Cdr Eveleigh, continued:

"However, we did find some MiGs on the airfield, and some Ilyushins, to strafe. We were overflown by RAF bombers who actually bombed through our formation when we were over Almaza at medium level (8,000 to 10,000 feet). Apart from a little friendly barracking there were no problems."

Flt Lt George Black (WN118/137), 802 Squadron's 'tame crabfat' (the Navy's endearing colloquialism for RAF aircrew serving with the FAA), added:

"The flak we encountered had lived up to the intelligence briefs – even in excess in certain areas of the target complex – and we had sighted the first enemy aircraft in the air. I had gone to war and survived my first operational sortie."

The Sea Hawks strafed and one MiG was seen to go up in flames and two more of the jet fighters were damaged, while a Vampire was also hit; strikes were reported on an Il-28 and an Il-14 transport by Lt Jack Worth, who was leading the 800 Squadron flight in XE400/107, while a C-46 of 7 Squadron EAF and a 3 Squadron EAF Dakota were also damaged. On their return to *Albion*, the pilots generally agreed that they had failed to notice any damage to the airfield from the nocturnal bombing attacks.

The last bombs from the Valiant and Canberra attacks were also dropping on Cairo West as *Bulwark*'s Sea Hawks – eight from 804 Squadron led by Lt Cdr Randy Kettle, another Korean War veteran, and four from 810 Squadron – went in. Many Il-28s were seen in their blast pens and a small aircraft believed to have been a Vampire (probably a 2 Squadron EAF machine) was seen on the airfield. Four of the jet bombers were claimed destroyed by 804 Squadron and two more by 810 Squadron; the latter unit also destroyed a Lancaster. Four of the jets and two more of the elderly Lancasters were damaged during the strafing attacks. Lt Cdr Peter Lamb (XE403/238), another veteran of the Korean War, leading the 810 Squadron quartet (one of whom was Lt Graham Hoddinott in WV796), claimed one Il-28 destroyed and a second damaged. One pilot reported:

"Every pilot tensed, concentrated on his own target. The Beagles [Il-28s] and Lancasters took shape and grew larger beneath the fixed centre cross. Fire and fairy lights mottled the silver fuselages in the cold grey dawn. Suddenly a sheet of flame arched skywards, etched with black billowing smoke."

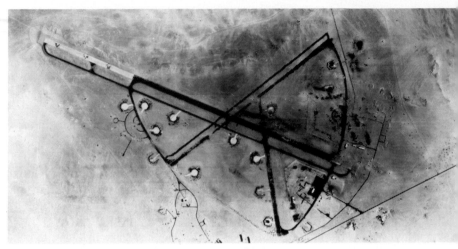

A number of burnt aircraft can be seen at Cairo West following air attack. (*SHAA via Albert Grandolini*)

Two swept-wing aircraft, presumably MiGs, were reported to be over the airfield at 6,000 feet, although the Sea Hawk pilots failed to sight these and they were not attacked. Sqn Ldr Mohammed Nabil al-Messiry,* commander of a MiG squadron at Cairo West, recalled:

"I was in a state of readiness and could take off and get into action if the enemy were to come. However, I was attacked while I was on the ground without any warning. We were at Cairo West. I had only a very narrow chance to jump from my jet and run from the attacking aircraft. The jets were turning to the left toward me so I ran to the right to get away from their guns. I got only 20 or 30 metres before my aircraft was destroyed. We had four aircraft near the start of the runway in an open area. My No2 asked me, 'What should I do?' I yelled, 'Jump!' I didn't see him after I ran and saw that all four aircraft were in flames. After a while I saw this young pilot come out of the flames not touched or burned and he was still struggling with his parachute which was going left and right . . . it was very funny at the time. No one saw us get out and they thought we were killed. There were repeated attacks and most of the aircraft at our base were destroyed on the ground. Some of the Il-28 bombers were able to take off between attacks and escaped but many of the aircraft were destroyed."

Eight Sea Hawks (four from each of 800 and 802 Squadrons) and two Sea Venoms from 809 Squadron repeated the attack on Almaza, departing *Albion* at 0720, while two other Sea Venoms flew CAP. Leading the 800 Squadron quartet was Lt Cdr Tibby (XE435/104):

"We carried out a strike on Almaza and strafed aircraft. Light flak was coming up but it was not very accurate. An interesting experience because it revealed that despite the training you give your young pilots, you can never

---

* Major-General al-Messiry served later as Deputy Commander of the EAF during the Ramadan War in 1973.

Wyvern WN328/374 of 830 Squadron flown by Senior Pilot Lt Cdr Bill Cowling, launching a salvo of rockets. (*Cdr W.H. Cowling*)

be quite sure how they are going to react in an emergency. Leading my Flight in the dive, my No4 suddenly shot right past me and as I was about to press the button to fire my rockets, he was in my line of sight. So that was an aborted attack. He realised that he had panicked and overshot the target. That does show that despite all the training there is no substitute for operational flying. He learnt the lesson pretty quickly after that."

As a result of the strafe of the airfield one Il-28 and one Vampire were claimed destroyed, and two MiGs and two Il-28s damaged. The pilots reported that the north-south runway was in use by MiGs during the strike (although there was no mention of these fighters actually taking to the air), and that Cairo International airport showed signs of being bombed. One pilot wrote:

"Throughout the day the strikes continued on a one-hour-five minute cycle. Eight or twelve aircraft launched; cut out at 20,000 feet; let down on track; attack with cannon; retire on the deck at 400 knots to the coast; then throttle back, up to about 5,000 feet, and back to the ship via the picket. The 'one pass and away' principle was adhered to strictly at first."

Wyverns of 830 Squadron were sent into action at 0800. Seven aircraft from *Eagle*, each carrying a 1,000lb bomb, attacked Dekheila airfield near Alexandria. Three bombs were reported to have exploded on the intersection of the north-east/south-west and east-west runways, and another two on the intersection of the north-south and east-west runways, leaving the north-east/

Pilots of 830 Squadron pose in front of Wyvern 378 aboard HMS *Eagle*; front, left to right: Lt King, Lt Dumphy (AEO), Lt Cdr Howard (CO), Lt Cdr Cowling (SP), Lt Barras, Lt Roddick; rear, left to right: Sub Lt Webster, Lt Humphries, Sub Lt Scott, Sub Lt Parsons, unknown, Lt McCarthy, Sub Lt McKern. (*Cdr W.H. Cowling*)

south-west runway probably still usable. Lt Cdr Bill Cowling*, the Squadron's colourful American-born Senior Pilot, recalled:

> "The first Wyvern strike was against Dekheila airfield; six [sic] Wyverns in two vics attacked with 500lb bombs. We concentrated on runway intersections with a view to the MiGs getting airborne."

As the Wyverns withdrew, 11 Sea Hawks of 895 Squadron arrived from *Bulwark*, the sections led by Lt Cdr John Morris-Jones (XE396/167), Lt Ted Anson, the Senior Pilot in XE375/239, and Lt Eric Palmer; the pilots subsequently reported damage to two Beechcraft Expediters of 4 Squadron EAF seen on the airfield. Two large crates, assumed to hold aircraft, were damaged, as were hangars to the north and east of the airfield. Lt Cdr Morris-Jones noted:

> "No other aircraft seen on airfield, hangars appear empty except for aircraft crates."

A priority non-airfield target was the blockship *Akka*, which was lying in Lake Timsah. She was a derelict craft loaded with 3,000 tons of cement, scrap iron and heavy rubbish. It was hoped to sink it before it could be placed in the Canal. The first strike at 0845 by four Sea Hawks from 897 Squadron armed with 500lb bombs, and eight from 899 Squadron armed with rockets, failed to sink her, as

---

* Lt Cdr Cowling left the USA in 1938 to join the RAF as a pilot but lacked the necessary education, so enlisted as ground crew until sent to Canada for pilot training in 1941. He finally qualified in 1943 and was commissioned but, to his chagrin, was retained as an instructor. With the war over, he transferred to the Royal Navy in 1945.

Dekheila, a former Fleet Air Arm air base, under attack by Wyverns of 830 Squadron. (*Authors' collection*)

Lt Cdr Clark recalled:

"I was briefed to take eight aircraft armed with solid shot anti-submarine rockets to knock holes in the bottom of the blockship. Ray Rawbone was to follow dive-bombing. I objected to attacking with R/P on the grounds that there was only two feet of water under the hull and my rockets would stick in the mud. Or, if they managed to miss the mud they would not penetrate the concrete. I also suggested that dive-bombing was unlikely to damage a hull full of concrete. I suggested an alternative which was to simply take two aircraft and write off the tug using 20mm front guns. I should point out that a small tug was alongside in Ismailia waiting to tow the blockship into position. This suggestion was refused on the grounds that the tug was manned by civilians."

Lt Cdr Rawbone of 897 Squadron (XE448/191) added:

"We hoped to sink it in the lake before it could be moved. Intelligence reports positioned it accurately but we were led to believe it would be heavily defended by AA and patrolling MiG fighters. We therefore planned to attack immediately it was sighted and then re-form as swiftly as possible. On approaching the target there was some broken cloud but we could see the blockship quite clearly. We dive-bombed in succession, had several near misses but no one had a direct hit. We re-formed swiftly but were amazed that there was little AA fire and no enemy fighters!"

221

Lt Cdr Clark commented:

> "The attack was a waste of time. I could see the tug raising steam and again asked (by radio) if I could attack her but was refused."

Although Lt Cdr Rawbone had not sighted any Egyptian fighters, one of his pilots, Lt Mills (XE388), did, but not the feared MiGs:

> "As I pulled out of the dive, I saw two Vampires flash in front of me. I turned after them calling on the radio, but there was so much chat about the attack on the blockship that nobody heard me. Eventually, bearing in mind the strictures about wandering off alone, I gave up the chase and turned to rejoin the Squadron. When we landed on and debriefed, Ray [Lt Cdr Rawbone] said I had almost certainly missed a chance to down two Egyptian aircraft but he was very understanding about my reasons for not doing so."

The Egyptian Vampires were probably returning from a strike against Israeli forces in Sinai, or were involved in the brief attempt to disperse aircraft to forward airfields in western Sinai.

On their return to *Eagle* the 897 Squadron pilots reported the near misses during their attack on the *Akka*, and recommended an immediate restrike. However, they were held at readiness pending a reconnaissance report. Four camera-equipped Sea Hawks of 810 Squadron were sent at 1050 to photograph the *Akka*.

While *Eagle*'s Sea Hawks were involved with the blockship, seven more from *Albion*'s 800 and 802 Squadrons carried out a further strike against Almaza, in company with two Sea Venoms from 809 Squadron led by Lt Wigg (with Lt Bowman) in XG669/224:

> "I believe the idea was to check the damage and to surprise any last-minute aircraft movements. As we started our dive I saw a MiG being towed along the perimeter track. I saw the tractor driver sprinting for cover, and then our 20mm shells began striking the MiG. By the time we had passed overhead, I was sure the MiG would not be bothering anyone for a while. The flak gunners must have been on their tea break because we had a clear run across the airfield and out over the desert. And then I saw something that I believe none of us noticed on the first sortie. The run out was directly over a military camp; khaki-clad figures were running in all directions, except for one small group who were lying on their backs with their weapons pointing upwards – shades of Korea again! A split second of bum-crinkling panic and we were clear again, heading east towards the Canal and our second part of the brief, a recce north along the Canal to see if we could spot any interesting movements along its banks."

During the attack one MiG was seen to burst into flames and another was claimed damaged. One Sea Hawk returned slightly damaged. This attack was followed by another against Inchas by ten Sea Hawks from *Bulwark*'s 804 and 810 Squadrons (two aircraft having failed to join up due to catapult failure). A MiG was damaged during the attack and other aircraft strafed a hangar and the control tower. *Bulwark*'s three Sea Hawk squadrons were now sharing aircraft.

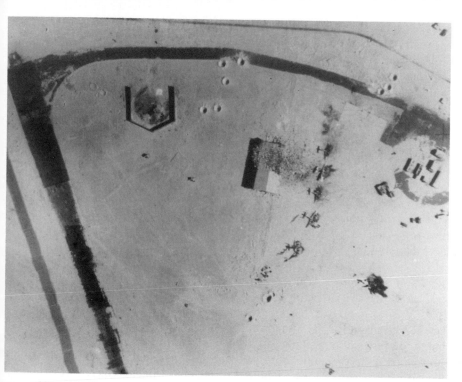

The wrecks of five EAF Lancasters at Cairo West. (*Cdr J. Morris-Jones*)

Cairo West airfield was targeted again at 1035 when seven Sea Venoms drawn from 892 and 893 Squadrons from *Eagle* were launched, led by Lt Cdr Malcolm Petrie, 892 Squadron's New Zealand-born commander. A successful strafe of the airfield was carried out which resulted in claims for the destruction of four Vampires (2 Squadron EAF), one Il-28 and two Lancasters, plus damage to another Vampire and a second Lancaster. The bombers were claimed by 892 Squadron pilots, the Vampires by 893 Squadron. Anti-aircraft fire was slight and none of the Venoms was damaged.

Albion's Sea Hawks (800 and 802 Squadrons) carried out a third strike against Almaza, eight aircraft, plus two Sea Venoms from 809 Squadron, departing at 1045. Flt Lt Black, 802 Squadron's RAF pilot, recalled:

> "I was sent to Cairo West on the second sortie of the day, and I saw Pan-Am DC-4s where I had expected to see Egyptian Air Force aircraft. I therefore flew to the secondary, which was Almaza."

A MiG and a Fury were seen to catch fire during the attack, and of each type plus two Dakotas and an Il-28 were claimed damaged. Flak was light but accurate. Returning pilots reported small-arms fire from a military camp to the south-west of the airfield. Almaza was the base for Egypt's new MiG-17s commanded by Sqn Ldr Shalabi al-Hinnawi (who had earlier that morning led an attack on Israeli forces in the Sinai – see Chapter Seven), who recalled:

> "I was giving a briefing to my pilots and, at this moment, we saw four aircraft – Sea Hawks – come in and strafe. Unfortunately our MiGs were sitting in

the open. The attack met with very weak anti-aircraft fire. Many of our aircraft were wrecked and I remember seeing one Il-28 jet blow up. A shell splinter from the strafing hit me in the leg and I was ordered to go to the hospital for surgery but I refused. Some eight of our MiGs were covered by nets near the hangars and weren't hit in the first attacks. We tried to move the surviving MiGs but we couldn't get approval from headquarters and they were destroyed in later raids. When the Sea Hawks started their attacks the two Soviet advisers to our squadron drove away in their car. Later they came back after the war. When we challenged them they said, 'those were our orders'."*

Midday saw four Sea Hawks of 802 Squadron launched from *Albion*, two of which carried cameras. Led by Lt Cdr Eveleigh (WM996/135), photographic runs were carried out over Almaza and Cairo International, initially at 10,000 feet, then at 1,000 feet:

> "The photo-recce was in response to fear that some other flight might have attacked a civil airliner by mistake. These were not in the target brief!"

Two Il-14 transports of 11 Squadron EAF were seen at Almaza and were immediately strafed and set afire by Lt John Bridel and Lt John Carey, while at Cairo International the two pilots observed and photographed cratered runways and two burning aircraft – one identified as a civil airliner, which was probably Viscount SU-AIC of Misrair, and a transport aircraft, although this may have been SU-AFF, a Fiat G212 of Air Orient, which was also destroyed during an air raid. The damage at the civil airport was presumably inflicted during the night attack by the Canberras from Cyprus.

At midday *Bulwark* sent 11 Sea Hawks from 804 and 810 Squadrons to Inchas, where four MiGs were claimed destroyed, one by Lt Cdr Lamb (flying XE396/167 of 804 Squadron) of the latter unit. Reconnaissance photographs taken by *Bulwark*'s Sea Hawks of the *Akka* reached *Eagle* at midday and these revealed that the blockship, towed by a tug, was moving towards the Canal. 897 Squadron's bomb-laden Sea Hawks were launched again at 1240 – eight aircraft led by Lt Cdr Rawbone (on this occasion flying WV907/190) – and found the blockship still under tow:

> "Such were the political implications, however, that our briefing strongly emphasised that under no circumstances was the ship to be attacked if it was actually in the Canal when we arrived. Much to my dismay, the tug and blockship were just entering the Canal as we approached and when they saw us arriving the tug manoeuvred to turn across the Canal and scuttle our target in the centre of the stream. We were now out of range of *Eagle* on the R/T and I decided to position the Squadron ready to bomb whilst climbing to altitude in the hope of regaining R/T contact with the carrier, thus obtaining

---

* Sqn Ldr Shalabi al-Hinnawi had flown Macchi MC205Vs during the closing stages of the 1948-49 War, and had been shot down by an Israeli Spitfire. Severely wounded, al-Hinnawi would carry a steel strengthening plate in his skull for the rest of his days. During late 1967 he was made Commander of the EAF, tasked with rebuilding this force following the catastrophic June War.

Lt Cdr Ray Rawbone, CO of 897 Squadron, flanked by Lt Lin Middleton (left) and Lt Cdr Keith Leppard, his Senior Pilot. (*Rear Adm A.R. Rawbone*)

further instructions. Clearly it was better to sink the blockship at the edge of the Canal rather than have it scuttled in the main stream. The Squadron aircraft were now nicely poised to attack and there were no enemy fighters. However, my brief had been so specific that I could imagine the outcry if I decided to bomb and any damage to the Canal resulted. In the event I decided to bomb because I could not contact *Eagle*. Sub Lt [David] Prothero was first in position, and his bombs narrowly missed the blockship and blew a large hole in the west side of the Canal! Not very encouraging! But the gods must have been with me as the next bomb (delivered by Lt Mills) was a direct hit and blew the blockship into two halves, each of which sank near the west back of the Canal."*

The successful pilot, Lt Mills (XE379), added:

"For once, I got it right and sent my bomb more or less down the funnel."

With the task apparently completed – although reconnaissance photographs later revealed that the Egyptians had nevertheless been able to move the severely damaged and half submerged vessel across the Canal – Lt Cdr Rawbone led his Sea Hawks to Abu Sueir, their secondary target, where those with bombs remaining attacked the hangars:

"At least two hangars and their housed aircraft were destroyed. We all strafed lines of MiGs parked on the hardstandings and were surprised at the almost complete lack of defensive fire."

One pilot reported seeing an Egyptian soldier, armed with a machine-gun,

---

* Some four years later when newly promoted Cdr Rawbone took his first sea command, the frigate HMS *Loch Killisport*, through the Suez Canal, he was very aware of a large hole in the west bank. It was repaired but obviously there.

standing firmly between two parked MiG-15s, hosepiping at the swooping fighters. Eight MiGs (probably aircraft of 30 Squadron EAF) were claimed destroyed during the attack and a further three damaged, of which Lt Cdr Rawbone claimed two flamers and two possibles. Sqn Ldr Farouke al-Gazawy was at Abu Sueir as the strike came in, and commented later on his experiences:

> "I was at Abu Sueir which was a former Royal Air Force base. It was a lovely place full of beautiful gardens. We were just finishing lunch and I was about to go to the Squadron when we were caught. I remember seeing four Hawker Sea Hawks come in and strafe our aircraft. I was face down in one of the gardens and looked up and watched the jets hitting us."

Syrian Air Force personnel training alongside their Egyptian comrades at Abu Sueir inevitably became involved in the fighting, and a number of SAF training mission MiG-15 fighters and trainers were destroyed on the ground by British and French aircraft. On his return to *Eagle*, Lt Cdr Rawbone was much relieved to have Admiral Power's backing for his decision to attack the *Akka*, which was no doubt vindicated further by the sinking in the Canal of some 50 other blockships later in the operation.

The Wyverns from *Eagle* were off again at 1140, five aircraft completing a second bombing and strafing attack on Dekheila, where the runways were again targeted. Four 1,000lb bombs were seen to straddle both the north-south and east runway, and the east/south-west runway. Additionally, an aircraft observed parked in the centre of the airfield was strafed and damaged. Six Wyverns returned at 1455, when four bombs were seen to explode on or near the runways as a result of their attack.

Avenger crews from *Arromanches* had earlier reported seeing an Egyptian destroyer entering Alexandria harbour and seven rocket-armed Corsairs were despatched, in two flights, from *La Fayette* to hunt for further movement of Egyptian naval units, albeit without success. Another Avenger was sent to identify a vessel detected on the radar of a patrolling aircraft and discovered a US Navy minesweeper which was not displaying its national colours. However, as the Avenger approached, its crew spotted an American sailor hurriedly hoisting the stars and stripes.

Shortly before 1100, *Albion* launched a dozen Sea Hawks (four flown by 800 Squadron pilots and eight of 802 Squadron) to carry out a strike against the EAF Flying School at Bilbeis, where an estimated 100 trainers were observed within the airfield perimeter. Lt Cdr Eveleigh of 802 Squadron, who led the attack in WM938/131, wrote:

> "Bilbeis was a training station but we were asked to destroy planes on the ground in case any could be used offensively."

Flt Lt Black (WN118/137) led one section of four Sea Hawks:

> "To my surprise I can remember going into the dive and seeing a variety of static aircraft types which had all been pushed out of the hangars and left scattered in the centre of the airfield. There were Harvards, Yaks, Chipmunks, a Sea Fury trainer etc. It seemed too good to be true. I sighted on the first target, a Harvard, and opened fire with a short burst down to

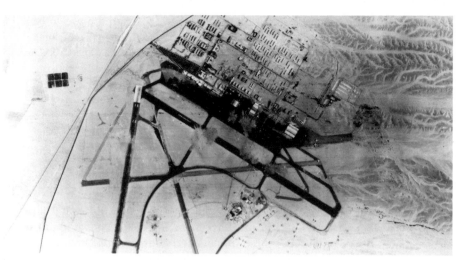

The EAF's Flying School was located at Bilbeis where up to 100 trainers were based, the majority of which were destroyed by air strikes. (*SHAA via Albert Grandolini*)

minimum range. With hindsight, it was exhilarating to experience 20mm cannon shells rip into static aircraft, followed almost immediately by a small explosion as the aircraft fuel tank caught fire. The 20mm ammunition we carried had every third round tipped with an incendiary head, the other being semi-armoured piercing rounds – the effect was quite dramatic as the tracer ammunition showed instantly whether the aiming point was being achieved.

Time did not allow a total count of static aircraft, but I estimate it was in excess of 90 – clearly there was no shortage of targets for all of us to have a field day! This gave us tremendous confidence and I can remember hitting one trainer before inching the sight onto the next target and claiming two more 'flamers'. This type of sortie felt unreal and reminded me of the more mundane range-work which was routine for ground attack pilots. I note that my logbook records I claimed five aircraft destroyed and two damaged on this mission. Ammunition exhausted, we headed north leaving behind large palls of smoke from burning aircraft."

800 Squadron's diarist noted:

"Here [at Bilbeis] a strafing roundabout was set up as pilots made attack after attack on aircraft parked literally nose to tail."

Lt Cdr Tibby (XE435/104) leading the 800 Squadron quartet added:

"We were strafing training aircraft – a bit of a 'turkey shoot' since there was no flak at all. So at one stroke we probably destroyed the training capability of the Egyptian Air Force."

Following the strafing passes, five Harvards, three Chipmunks and two Yaks were claimed destroyed in flames, and a further 15 aircraft heavily damaged, of which Lt Worth (XE411/108) claimed one of each type destroyed. Lt Cdr Eveleigh reported seeing two aircraft on fire and a third obviously damaged as a result of the strike. All aircraft returned safely. Flt Lt Black continued:

"Following the landing back on board *Albion*, the next surprise was to be told to go back to Bilbeis for another strike and finish off the remaining undamaged aircraft! This we duly did, although I can recall the task of finding undamaged machines quite difficult; indeed, I remember opening fire and, as I got closer, noting that the target had already been partly damaged. All in all, the 'turkey shoot' at Bilbeis, as it was subsequently referred to, proved an excellent means of sharpening our aiming procedures whilst adding greatly to the confidence factor for what was to come in the following days. Moreover, I was to add a further three aircraft to my score!"

As a result of the second strike, pilots of 802 Squadron claimed ten trainers and left a dozen others damaged. During the two attacks – in addition to Flt Lt Black's eight destroyed – Lt Paddy McKeown (the Senior Pilot and another Korean war veteran) and Sub Lt Carl Clarke (the Squadron's most junior pilot) each claimed the destruction of three trainers and a further six damaged jointly.

The crew of one of *Albion*'s helicopters, patrolling in case of an emergency ditching by returning aircraft, reported seeing two unidentified aircraft at 1350, described as silver with black star and red stripes, armed with rockets; these were believed to have been USN Skyraiders from one of the American carriers. Six Sea Venoms from *Eagle* – two from 892 Squadron and four from 893 Squadron (including WW154/448, an aircraft of 892 Squadron crewed by Lt Ben Neave and Flg Off Duncan Watson, and another flown by Lt Cdr John Willcox with Flg Off Bob Olding) – followed up the strike on Bilbeis two hours later. The crews reported the destruction of a further nine Harvards and one Chipmunk, and damage to four of each type, of which 892 Squadron's share comprised four Harvards destroyed and three damaged, plus one Chipmunk damaged.

Eight Sea Hawks from *Bulwark*'s 895 Squadron, the sections led by Lt Cdr Morris-Jones (XE394/165) and Lt Palmer, were launched at 1410, this time joined by three more from 810 Squadron (including XE375/239 flown by Lt Hoddinott), the pilots briefed to attack Almaza. On their return to *Bulwark* they reported the destruction of one MiG, two Dakotas (of 3 Squadron EAF) and three C-46s of 7 Squadron EAF, the probable destruction of an Il-28 and a C-46, and damage inflicted on four Dakotas, two MiGs and a Fury. Two of the transports were claimed by the 810 Squadron section, and a further one damaged. A general report of the strike noted that aircraft were seen on the runways and dispersals all over the airfield: on the western side were transport aircraft, and on the eastern side MiGs, Furies and Il-28s, while up to 50 soft-skinned vehicles (referred to as SSVs) were observed to the south of Almaza.

Three 800 Squadron Sea Hawks from *Albion* visited Cairo West at 1500, flying over the airfield at 1,000 feet. The pilots reported seeing six Lancasters on the ground south-east of the airfield, of which four had been destroyed. Near a hangar six Vampires (apparently aircraft of 2 Squadron EAF) were observed, of which four appeared to have been burnt out. A lone Il-28 was seen in the same area, and another of the jet bombers was seen on the ground south of the airfield and was adjudged to have crash-landed. This was strafed and destroyed. The pilots also reported a ditch was being constructed about four miles south of the airfield alongside which appeared to run a light railway. As *Albion*'s aircraft returned, they were passed by four Sea Hawks of 895 Squadron from *Bulwark* – a section led by Lt Palmer – which carried out a further attack on

Cairo West and claimed two Il-28s and five Lancasters damaged. On receipt of this report, *Eagle's* last strike of the day, launched at 1600, was also directed against Cairo West, Lt Cdr Clark (XE457/487) leading eight Sea Hawks of 899 Squadron to destroy one Il-28, one Lancaster and two Vampires. A second Lancaster was claimed as probably destroyed and a third Vampire was damaged. In addition, the control tower was strafed, as were three trucks, anti-aircraft positions and other buildings.

Albion's last strike of the day consisted of a dozen Sea Hawks, six each from 800 and 802 Squadrons being sent to Inchas at 1515, where the pilots reported no sign of life on the airfield. The wrecks of seven burnt out MiGs were observed on the runway and, although wheel tracks were clearly seen leading from the hangar area to a plantation to the north-west, no aircraft could be seen concealed there. Flt Lt Black of 802 Squadron, on his fourth sortie of the day, noted:

> "We were off back to one of the more heavily defended airfield targets near Cairo. Here, life in the Sea Hawk cockpit became much more lively and sporting."

With dusk rapidly approaching, *Bulwark* launched six Sea Hawks flown by 895 Squadron pilots led by Lt Cdr Morris-Jones (XE396/167) and Lt Anson (flying XE378/168) for a final strike against Almaza, where two MiGs were claimed destroyed, one in flames. Aircraft damaged during this attack included a Vampire, a Meteor, a Fury and a Dakota. The Sea Hawks returned at 1720. During one of the raids on Almaza, a Mallard amphibian of the former King's Flight was strafed and destroyed.* Bombs also destroyed the EAF's Museum which housed, amongst other types of aircraft, a Spitfire, a Hurricane, a Tiger Moth, an Avro 626, a Hawker Audax, a Hawker Hart, a Lysander, and a Gladiator.

With the end of the day's carrier operations, the captain of one of *Bulwark's* escorts, HMS *Decoy*, sent a signal to the carrier:

> "I hope you will allow a fish-head [a non-flying naval officer] to say that I have never seen such consistently first class landing-on and flight deck drill as your team have put up today."

However, other signals were not in such a complimentary vein, as witnessed by the one sent by Admiral Durnford-Slater to the Admiralty regarding the activities of the US Sixth Fleet:

> "Sixth Fleet are an embarrassment in my neighbourhood. We have already twice intercepted US aircraft and there is constant danger of an incident. Have been continually menaced during the past eight hours by US aircraft approaching low down as close as 4,000 yards and on two occasions flying over ships."

Sqn Ldr Maitland of 249 Squadron, who had served with the Americans in Korea, had been less perturbed:

---

* The second Mallard of what had been the King's Flight survived, and could still be seen, no longer serviceable, at Almaza in the early 1970s.

DANGER
ECTION

S 4 - V B

Flt Lt George Black, flying with 802 Squadron, accounted for at least eight trainers at Bilbeis. (*Air Vice-Marshal G.P. Black*)

> "The Americans from the Sixth Fleet frequently intercepted us outward bound but never anywhere near the war zone. They would come up alongside, wave and depart."

A view not entirely shared by Flt Lt Black of 802 Squadron, since the carrier pilots were called upon to carry out interceptions of all intruders approaching the Fleet:

> "It was not uncommon for aircraft to be scrambled to intercept US aircraft coming to look at what was going on. This hampered operations because the carriers had to keep turning into wind to launch intercepting aircraft, often at the most inconvenient time."

Lt Cdr Eveleigh of 802 Squadron similarly recalled:

"Knowing the Egyptians had MiGs, we had to intercept all incoming fighters and, until identified, US swept wing fighters appeared as a threat. The wing destroyer of their Fleet even got inside the screen of our own Fleet, occasioning an interchange of signals which probably cannot be repeated. Our Wing CO asked the American whose side he was on. On receiving a rather negative reply, our Wing CO made back in plain language, 'Then why don't you f . . k off!' "

However, at least one American unit had offered its services, albeit without official sanction, as recalled by one particular Fleet Air Arm observer:

"We had been working-up the Squadron at Hal Far in Malta in mid-October, and had become very friendly with the US Navy squadron of Neptune aircraft (Squadron VP-24) which was also based there at the time. If I remember rightly, their Commanding Officer was a Lt Cdr Cook. When we started our strikes on Egyptian airfields, the Neptunes quite unofficially did some high-level spotting for us which was most useful. Their involvement was certainly at the very beginning of the operation either at the time of, or shortly after, the RAF bombers had bombed Egyptian airfields from high level. We were in air-to-air communication with the Neptunes and they gave us information of what targets had been hit. I was personally in communication with one of the Neptunes and reported accordingly. I do not believe they were in the vicinity during the strikes. I understood later that Commander Cook incurred the displeasure of Mr Dulles [the US Secretary of State] and the US Navy, and was relieved of his command. I am unable to corroborate or verify the sequel to this story, but the Neptunes certainly helped us, and Commander Cook was no longer in Malta when we returned there on 30 November."

It is not known if Admiral Power was privy to the information being passed by the American crews, although it seems likely he was since *Albion*'s Operations Officer was almost certainly aware of the intelligence reports.

SUMMARY OF GROUND ATTACK CLAIMS AGAINST AIRCRAFT OF THE EGYPTIAN AIR FORCE by the Fleet Air Arm, 1 November 1956			
	Destroyed	**Probables**	**Damaged**
Claims for MiG-15s:			
HMS *Eagle*'s squadrons	12	5	0
HMS *Albion*'s squadrons	3	0	6
HMS *Bulwark*'s squadrons	7	0	3
	22	5	9
Claims for other types:			
HMS *Eagle*'s squadrons	20	1	15
HMS *Albion*'s squadrons	26	0	38
HMS *Bulwark*'s squadrons	12	3	23
	58	4	76

In addition, *Arromanches*'s Avengers flew 12 sorties and *La Fayette*'s Corsairs a further 15, although none of these was in the ground attack role.

During the course of the day Canberra PR7s and French RF-84Fs continually overflew Egyptian air bases, taking photographs of damage inflicted. An assessment of EAF losses for the first 24 hours of attacks concluded that at least 50 aircraft had been destroyed and a further 40 damaged. Another aircraft operating high in Egyptian skies was the CIA's U-2 spyplane, which also took photographs of the aftermath of the Anglo-French raids on Egyptian airfields. Pictures of the damage inflicted on Cairo West, in particular, were despatched promptly to MI6 and RAF intelligence in London, apparently without the immediate knowledge of the US government.

The British and French pilots were puzzled by the lack of aerial opposition to their attacks, unaware of a decision made by President Nasser. Having earlier aroused the fighting spirit and patriotism of his people, Nasser somewhat paradoxically ordered his air force not to contest the Allied air assault, an act which was interpreted by some in the West as evidence of a lack of *esprit de corps* among Egyptian pilots, but shortly after the ceasefire President Nasser explained his decision to hold back the Air Force:

"We have 120 pilots fully trained for combat, and another 250 to 260 still in training. If I sent these to fight against the combined air forces of Britain and France I would be mad. At some stage the British and French are going to withdraw, probably after a month or two. But we are going to be in a state of war with Israel for years, and we shall need all the pilots we can get. Planes can be replaced overnight, but it takes years to train a pilot."

Nasser had obviously made a wise but painful decision. However, the accusation of a lack of fighting spirit was deeply resented by the EAF. Many Egyptian officers insisted that it was both ill-founded and based upon prejudice rather than any understanding of the situation faced by the Egyptian government. Wg Cdr Labib commented:

"The situation was that all air bases were swamped by enemy fighters from the start of 1 November. This also came after a night of enemy air raids. Although it was true that the enemy force included types of aircraft which were considered rather old-fashioned and included machines comparable to Egypt's Vampires, such as the RAF's Venoms, the majority were much more recent types. These had been withdrawn from NATO's tactical air forces. Apart from their superiority in terms of numbers of aircraft involved, the pilots had long experience with their machines and were highly experienced. On the opposite side, Egyptian jets were few in numbers and were flown by pilots who had little experience on their new aircraft. As a result [Egyptian] pilots would have had limited capability in manoeuvring and in taking advantage of their aircraft's best points. Over and above all these factors, which would alone have justified the decision to take Egypt's pilots out of the one-sided battle, the delayed-action bombs seriously limited our ability to move around the airfields. Such conditions meant that the pilots' lives were in danger even when they were not sent on impossible missions. So it was decided to save the pilots and thus prevent the enemy from achieving his objective of destroying the Egyptian Air Force. Planes could be replaced quickly but the replacement of pilots, who were in any case few in numbers, would have taken a very long time."

Many Egyptian pilots and ground personnel wanted to fight back, despite Nasser's orders, but EAF air bases in northern Egypt had been under almost constant attack for most of the day. Notwithstanding this, Sqn Ldr al-Gazawy stated that his unit had been able to move some of its MiG-15s to safety and that fellow pilots were able to fly a number of sorties from the Cairo to Suez road during the next several days.

Meanwhile, for Flt Lts Brisk and Larcombe, the British instructors at Bilbeis, the situation had become life threatening:

"Events moved swiftly after the first British raid. The British instructors were ordered to go home to their flats in Heliopolis and stay there. As our wives and families had already left for England about a month before, the six of us decided to stay together in one flat. At ten minutes to six the following morning our door was broken down by a mob of soldiers and we were forced at gunpoint into the street in our pyjamas and were lined up against a wall with the evident intention of being shot. Fortunately, a higher ranking Egyptian officer came on the scene at that moment and ordered the soldiers to take us instead to the police station. While this was going on, the flat was searched and every book and document we possessed was stolen. After a series of abusive questioning and having been in and out of gaol several times, we were at last told we must get out of the country within ten days."

With help from the Swiss Legation and the manager of SABENA, the Belgian airline, they were able to get seats on a specially chartered Air Jordan aircraft, and were evacuated safely.

During the night RAF Canberra and Valiant bombers from Malta and Cyprus again bombed Cairo West, Fayid, Luxor and Kasfareet.

PLAN OF ATTACK
Malta Bomber Wing/Cyprus Bomber Wing, 1/2 November 1956

RAID 6 – Target: CAIRO WEST

From Cyprus
4 Canberra B6s of 139 Squadron (Markers)
2 Canberra B2s of 10 Squadron
2 Canberra B2s of 15 Squadron
2 Canberra B2s of 44 Squadron
1 Canberra B6 of 139 Squadron

From Malta
6 Valiant B1s of 138 Squadron
4 Canberra B6s of 12 Squadron
3 Canberra B6s of 109 Squadron

RAID 7 – Target: LUXOR

From Cyprus
4 Canberra B6s of 139 Squadron (Markers)
8 Canberra B2s of 27 Squadron
6 Canberra B2s of 10 Squadron

Four Canberras of 139 Squadron dropped their markers over Cairo West, the target for six Valiants of 138 Squadron led by Wg Cdr Oakley (WZ400), with WZ402 flown by Sqn Ldr A.G. Steele of 49 Squadron, who had been sent to Malta for briefing duties and filled a vacancy on the operation when the detailed crew reported sick. Of the night's operation, Sqn Ldr Collins, a Valiant captain of 138 Squadron, wrote:

> "Thanks to the very considerable effort of our ground crews, all eight aircraft were serviceable. Six aircraft, once again led by the Squadron Commander [Wg Cdr Oakley], had another go at Cairo West and this time there was no recall."

Wg Cdr Oakley added:

> "It was our job to put the airfield out of commission. By the time we were over Egypt we had a brilliant starlit sky. Here and there in the Nile Delta we could see an odd light or two. Our bombs accurately straddled the runway."

Canberras from Cyprus and Malta also targeted Cairo West, and Sqn Ldr Bill Donley of 12 Squadron, who had been flying WH965, reported:

WH729, a Canberra B2 of 27 Squadron, seen at Nicosia. (*Andy Thomas*)

"There was a tremendous concentration of bombs on Cairo West during our run. In view of what had happened to one runway intersection, bombing instructions were switched to another intersection. We met only one heavy flak gun, near Mena. It fired intermittently, but the shells fell hundreds of feet beneath us."

Following the attack on Luxor an hour later, led by Wg Cdr Helmore of 27 Squadron in WH732, the Canberras were apparently credited with the destruction of four of the estimated 20 to 28 Il-28s that had fled there from their northern bases. One aircraft of 27 Squadron had been unable to release two of its bombs due to premature release of tail fins prior to take-off. Four Canberras of 139 Squadron released their markers over Luxor before joining in the bombing, as Sqn Ldr Peter Mallorie (WT370) recalled:

"On that occasion the marker aircraft carried a mixed load of TIs and 1,000lb bombs which were proximity fused. Having dive-bombed with TIs in the last light, we were supposed then to see the raid through and add our contribution of straight and level attacks with thousand-pounders. By that time the gyros were completely toppled, the navigators confused and the bombsights useless. So we made dive-bombing attacks on the parked Beagles [Il-28s] which were there."

18 Squadron sent four Canberras to Fayid to drop markers for the Valiants, Wg Cdr Burnett (XD815) leading the 148 Squadron quartet to the airfield, the attack being joined by Canberras from Cyprus and Malta. On returning to Malta from this raid, Flg Off M.J. Hawkins' Canberra (WJ982) of 109 Squadron suffered an engine failure although the pilot was able to land safely on one. Kasfareet was also on the receiving end of a combined Valiant/Canberra attack, Wg Cdr Trent (WZ397) leading a pair of Valiants from 214 Squadron, with Sqn Ldr H.A. Smith (WZ405) in command of the pair from 207 Squadron. Again 18 Squadron sent marker aircraft. The attacking force was made up of eight Canberra B6s from 9 and 101 Squadrons from Malta, Wg Cdr B.L. Duigan from

AHQ leading the latter quartet in WH945. Large fires were seen in the target area and hits were also reported on the runway intersection. One Valiant, WP219 of 207 Squadron flown by Flt Lt E.A.J. Crooks AFC, sustained a cracked canopy but the cause was unknown since anti-aircraft fire was light. Canberra WH961 of 9 Squadron, captained by Flg Off T. Hillard, diverted to El Adem on the way back to Malta due to shortage of fuel.

The Air Traffic Control problem posed by bomber operations from Malta was one of handling large numbers of aircraft at two airfields – Luqa and Hal Far – situated close together, as explained by Sqn Ldr H.C. Scott:

"Basically the recovery of aircraft during *Musketeer* was divided into three phases: marshalling, holding and let-down. The marshalling phase began at a point 75 miles from Malta on the direct track from the target area and ended overhead at Luqa. The holding phase began at the initial 'overhead Luqa' and consisted of two loop holding patterns: one tracking 315° was taken by aircraft landing at Luqa, the other, tracking 240°, by aircraft bound for Hal Far. Both these patterns extended to an entry point 20 miles from the 'overhead', through a gate, and returning to final 'overhead' for Luqa or Hal Far. The let-down phase from final 'overhead Luqa' at 20,000 feet (Hal Far, 25,000 feet) was a standard Bomber Command jet let-down. To achieve smooth control the marshalling and holding phases were handled by a Bomber Command controller based at Luqa, the aircraft being handed over to the local control staff at Luqa and Hal Far at the 'final overhead' position.

To make stream landings at three-minute intervals, with safety, requires aircraft to position overhead with great accuracy using Gee or a similar navigational aid. No such aids were available at Malta. Consequently, to give the necessary positive control it was essential that the ground radar should be of such calibre that aircraft could be seen at the earliest possible moment after leaving the overhead position. One aspect of the operations which must be stressed is that the staff at Luqa handled the whole of the Transport Command airlift during the period of the bomber operations without let or hindrance to either, and continued to control civil traffic with little or no inconvenience to operators."

All returning Valiants and Canberras landed safely, a testimony to the skills of the aircrews and controllers alike.

Meanwhile, events in Eastern Europe had also taken a turn for the worst, following the announcement by President Nagy of Hungary that his country had withdrawn from the Soviet-dominated Warsaw Pact. His government even asked the United Nations to recognise Hungary as a neutral country in the Cold War between East and West, and to be seen in much the same light as neighbouring Yugoslavia. This proved too much for Bulganin and Khrushchev, and within hours Soviet and other Warsaw Pact troops were preparing to crush the Hungarian revolt. Whether the Soviet government was taking advantage of the world's preoccupation with events in the Middle East, or had intended to move against Hungary anyway, remains a matter of debate. It is also possible that the crisis in Eastern Europe was seen by some in the British, French and Israeli governments as a useful distraction for their own attack on Egypt.

Chapter Eleven

FIRST ALLIED AIR CASUALTIES
2 November 1956

"The effect of even a couple of MiGs, flown perhaps by Russians, flying over Nicosia with a load of rockets. . ."

General Sir Charles Keightley, Allied Commander-in-Chief

What an enterprising MiG pilot might have seen! Line-up of F-84Fs at Akrotiri (36 can been seen) together with three RAF Venoms. (*SHAA via Albert Grandolini*)

By daylight on 2 November Anglo-French air raids had destroyed in excess of 100 EAF aircraft and seriously disrupted many air bases. When possible, Egyptian pilots continued to fly aircraft out of the country or to remote road strips to escape destruction, although British and French pilots reported only brief sightings in the air of MiGs during the first two days of intensive strikes against the airfields. However, the threat of air attack against Cyprus remained, but now possibly from the direction of Syria. Since the EAF had effectively been put out of action, as had the main Egyptian airfields, a close eye was therefore kept by PR Canberras and French RF-84Fs on Syrian airfields, from where it was feared that Egyptian or even Russian aircraft might strike at Cyprus. One PR crew returned having sighted four Il-28s at Damascus, and another reported seeing four swept-wing fighters, believed to have been MiGs. These were undoubtedly Egyptian aircraft. Another unrelated report mentioned that four, and possibly six, EAF jet bombers had arrived at Jedda in Saudi Arabia, one of which bore the letter G painted six feet high on its starboard nose.

At this stage, Allied HQ Cyprus decided that Phase I of the operation – the neutralisation of the Egyptian Air Force – had been achieved, and accordingly Phase II was set in motion at 0800. Phase II, as planned, was to be an air offensive coupled with psychological warfare to bring about the collapse of the will to resist of the Egyptian people, and consequently the downfall of President Nasser. However, it was generally realised that this would not now occur, and that only military targets, and not Egyptian minds, were to be attacked.

Due to the lack of aerial opposition, the decision was taken to carry out a precision low-level, high-speed, daylight attack against the Cairo Radio Station at Abu Za'bal (a suburb of Cairo). The broadcasts emanating from this station were proving to be a nuisance, hence its elimination was ordered. A force of 18 Canberra bombers departed Nicosia at 0700 (Raid 10), led by Wg Cdr Peter Helmore in WH732 at the head of four aircraft from 27 Squadron, followed by four each from 44 and 61 Squadrons, and three each from 10 and 15 Squadrons, the latter led by Sqn Ldr Scott in WD980. An escort for the bombers was provided by a dozen F-84Fs, while two Canberras from 18 Squadron dropped markers ahead of the main force, although bomber crews complained that:

"The target marking was inaccurate, the TIs were not easily seen and the marker's instructions were difficult to follow. The results were that the [Radio Station] buildings were not hit. The high bombing speed and low height [between 3,000 and 4,000 feet] gave a sighting angle too large to be used."

Wg Cdr Helmore reported:

"We saw no other aircraft apart from the excellent top cover which the French fighters gave us, and didn't encounter any opposition. We didn't go anywhere near the city [Cairo]. I flew low over the target. There was some inaccurate light flak beneath us but it did not interfere with the mission. The attack achieved a high degree of success. We took some pictures of the results of that raid and they showed it was satisfactory."

Sqn Ldr Alan Thompson in WK132 of 15 Squadron similarly considered that his attack had been reasonably successful:

"We approached at about 1,500 feet or so at 300 plus knots and shot up to 3,000 feet to drop bombs at a low speed. The bomb sighting angle was certainly in excess of 70° and [Flt Lt] Harry Bullen, my navigator, about 16½ stone and suitably rotund, had some difficulty in getting down low enough to sight properly. Additionally, flying at relatively high speed and low level over the Cairo suburbs made visual map reading extremely difficult. We missed flying over the target the first time and, against briefing, turned round for another go. I think we were fairly close the second time and happy enough with the accuracy to offload the bombs. I believe Cairo Radio did go off the air."

Subsequent reconnaissance photographs revealed a lack of substantial damage

Wg Cdr Peter Helmore (right), CO of 27 Squadron, who led the raid against the Cairo Radio Station on 2 November 1956. (*Authors' collection*)

to the radio station, although one antenna had been knocked down. Air Marshal Barnett wrote:

> "This attack met no opposition and, although the bombing was not as accurate as it might have been, the radio station was put off the air."

While Air Marshal Sir Harry Broadhurst remarked later:

> "We didn't get it all wrong – for example, the Canberras blew off the wall of Cairo Prison and released most of the inmates, who may well have caused the authorities in Egypt a few problems."

In fact, nearly one hundred prisoners and warders were killed. The radio station was off the air for a few hours only, but when the Venom and F-84F pilots at Akrotiri offered to destroy it with rockets, permission was not granted owing to the proximity of the station to civilian property. Already the Canberra attack had raised an outcry.

AKROTIRI STRIKE WING

The Venom fighter-bombers of 6, 8 and 249 Squadrons, together with the F-84Fs of EC1/3 and EC3/3, were again very active, the first strikes leaving Akrotiri at 0515. Of the intense activity, the Brombergers wrote:

> "Akrotiri base, shared by French and British, was the scene of fabulous activity. Every two minutes four aircraft took off in pairs, wing to wing, coming back in to land an hour and a quarter later. As they touched down,

8 Squadron Venom coming in to land at Akrotiri. (*Sqn Ldr R.K.J. Hadlow*)

others took off. It needs no great effort of imagination to appreciate the effect of such a continuous bludgeoning. The Egyptian aircrews and ground staff, already stunned by the thunderous crash of the first attack, had not time to leave their shelters and reach the runways before another wave of fighter-bombers was upon them."

6 Squadron flew six ground attack operations during the day, but due to aircraft unserviceability were unable to complete as many sorties as planned. Cannons only were used on the first three strikes, which were directed against Shallufa, Kabrit and Abu Sueir, and although only one MiG was destroyed, a further six were damaged, while hangars, buildings and soft-skinned vehicles were also strafed. The first section of Venoms encountered heavy anti-aircraft fire from Ismailia, but it was inaccurate. On attacking Kabrit, the pilots reported a lack of anti-aircraft fire although light machine-gun fire was noticed, but no ground fire was experienced at either Shallufa or Abu Sueir. The third section, led by Sqn Ldr Ellis (Venom T), observed a number of Mystères – which they assumed to have been Israeli aircraft – strafing a convoy ten miles east of Ismailia, although they may have been French Mystères of EC2. They were not the only unusual aircraft encountered on this flight, as Flt Lt Harrison (Venom Z) recalled:

"On the way to my targets of Kabrit and Shallufa we passed directly over the American Sixth Fleet who were manoeuvring about 30 miles off the Egyptian coast. At about the top of the climb, or shortly after, on the way back, my No2 [Flg Off] Brian Hurn called me reporting two MiGs coming in on a high quarter attack. We broke hard into them and, being very light at this stage, went round quickly and were soon in a firing position. I was beginning to range on the leader and would have started to fire within seconds. They were surprised by our rate of turn and at this stage rolled over and pulled through. Only at this time did I recognise them as American fighters – I believe Cougars [apparently Sidewinder-equipped F9F-8s of VA-46 from the USS *Randolph*]. I recall that, as a result of this incident, the Royal Navy Admiral in command sent a rather rude signal saying that if they were not with us, they should bugger off!"

Sqn Ldr Maitland (WR504/Z) led one 249 Squadron strike against Fayid and Abu Sueir, strafing a number of MiGs seen on the airfield. Fayid was also the target for Flt Lt Slade's section (the leader flying WR506/W), where a Meteor F8 and a Vampire were claimed, the latter by Flg Off Moyes (WR398/H). A later strike, led by Flt Lt Dallison (Venom A), flew to Kabrit where Flg Off Williams (having taken over WR504/Z) damaged a MiG. Flg Off Lecky-Thompson (WR527/C) also claimed a MiG damaged but then had to abort and return to Akrotiri. Meanwhile, Flg Off Gronert (WR533/F) claimed two MiGs and a Proctor:

> "We were enjoying things now. There was no resistance from the ground, they had all been silenced during the first day. We were starting to diversify our targets now. The first sortie [against Kabrit and Abu Sueir] was similar to the first day, but our second one was an armed recce between Deversoir, Geneifa and Fayid [where Flg Off Gronert possibly destroyed a tank and a bowser]."

Flg Off Moyes' section, led by Flt Lt Slade (WR420/T), flew to Abu Sueir, where Moyes strafed a number of MiGs and claimed two destroyed although his aircraft (WR489/D) was again hit; a bullet penetrated an aileron and entered the engine:

> "Being a No4 was a vulnerable position. They [the Egyptian gunners] heard No1, saw No2, aimed at No3, and fired at No4! And No4 always used more fuel than any other position."

All told, the section claimed two MiGs destroyed and three damaged, and strafed four hangars which, it was believed, contained more MiGs. Of the morning's attacks by 249 Squadron, Flg Off George Garner wrote:

> "Twenty more sorties were made against the same targets as yesterday's operations. Once again considerable damage was done to Egyptian aircraft and installations without loss to ourselves. No enemy air opposition was encountered and anti-aircraft fire was reported to be light and inaccurate."

8 Squadron sent sections of aircraft, including one quartet led by Sqn Ldr Blyth in WR485/C and another led by Flt Lt Harcourt-Smith (WR480), to attack Abu Sueir, Fayid and Kabrit. Flg Off von Berg (WR376/Y) was with the section that flew a dawn strike against Kabrit, where he claimed a MiG destroyed and another as damaged. Many aircraft were claimed destroyed on the ground, as noted by the Squadron's diarist, Flg Off Brian Carroll:

> "No opposition was met from the Egyptian Air Force, who seem to rely on moving their aircraft around on the ground to avoid defeat! As most of their aircraft were dispersed on these airfields, it was found that 20mm cannon was the most effective weapon. In all [during the two days] 43 aircraft were claimed as destroyed by the Squadron, plus six probably destroyed, and many others damaged."

By mid-morning, Anglo-French air commanders, having concurred that the

Venom FB4 'B' of 8 Squadron landing at Akrotiri after a mission over Egypt on 2 November 1956; s/n obscured by Suez stripes but believed to have been WR505. (*Andy Thomas*)

Egyptian Air Force had been effectively destroyed, ordered strikes to be switched away from the airfields and, instead, directed against the Egyptian Army's main tank and transport depot at Huckstep Camp near Almaza, where reconnaissance photographs showed over 1,000 vehicles tightly parked. The morning's strikes claimed a further 44 EAF aircraft believed to have been destroyed or disabled, which increased the overall total to at least 170, the majority of claims against MiGs.

SUMMARY OF SORTIES FLOWN BY VENOMS and F-84Fs by 0930

ETA Target	Target	Aircraft	Claims
0600	Abu Sueir	4 Venom	No aircraft seen intact
0605	Fayid	4 Venom	4 MiGs destroyed, one damaged, Vampire damaged
0600	Kabrit	4 Venom	MiG destroyed, 3 damaged
0605	Kasfareet	4 Venom	No results observed
0615	Fayid	7 F-84F	No attack due to smoke haze
0620	Abu Sueir		2 MiGs damaged, hangar afire
0625	Kasfareet	4 Venom	No aircraft seen intact
0630	Kabrit		MiG destroyed, Fury destroyed, 2 MiGs damaged
0635	Shallufa		4 vehicles destroyed, 2 damaged
0640	Kabrit	4 F-84F	U/i aircraft destroyed, one damaged
	Kasfareet	4 F-84F	Hangars afire
0700	Abu Sueir	4 F-84F	2 MiGs damaged
0705	Fayid		Meteor damaged
0700	Kasfareet	4 F-84F	Hangars attacked
0705	Kabrit		U/i aircraft afire

ETA Target	Target	Aircraft	Claims
0735	Kabrit	4 Venom	MiG damaged
0740	Abu Sueir		2 MiGs damaged
0750	Kabrit	4 Venom	3 MiGs destroyed, 2 damaged, Proctor probably destroyed
0755	Abu Sueir		Barracks left in flames, 11 intact MiGs seen near small hangar
0830	Kabrit	4 Venom	Fury destroyed, one damaged, MiG damaged
0835	Abu Sueir		4 MiGs destroyed, 4 damaged
0840	Kabrit	4 Venom	2 MiGs damaged
0845	Abu Sueir		No results observed
0853	Cairo	12 F-84F	Escort to Canberras attacking Cairo Radio Station

With Huckstep Camp now the priority target, 6 Squadron was given the task of carrying out a surprise strike against the depot. The Venoms arrived over the target area at 1025, led by Flt Lt Harrison (Venom T):

"Prior to the flight we were given a long and detailed briefing by the intelligence people and were shown photographs taken by the French RF-84Fs. They were keen to have as many tanks destroyed or damaged as possible because they did not want them being deployed. We carried eight rockets in two banks, but only the first four could be aimed accurately because there was a delay before the second bank fired. In order to be really effective one needed to carry out two attacks so that each bank of four rockets could be well aimed. The intelligence people were sure that Huckstep Camp was only lightly defended and convinced me that we should carry out two attacks. I therefore briefed for this, planning to come in a second time from a different direction."

One aircraft went unserviceable on start-up so only seven of the Venoms departed. They found the target easily and carried out their first attack as planned, with a slow-speed dive in order to achieve accurate sighting. Harrison continued:

"There was some anti-aircraft fire but it was relatively light. My own attack was a good one on a line of about six tanks and I believe that the whole section carried out effective attacks. We broke off at low level and re-formed as planned and I then led the section in from a different direction as quickly as we could – a matter of only a few minutes. As soon as we pulled up on the second run 'all hell let loose'. The camp was very well defended and they were now all firing. For the first time we were seeing radar-ranged predicted shells. Needless to say, our second attack was hurried a little more and I doubt whether the accuracy was quite up to the standard of the first run. However, equipment was packed in tight and it would not have missed.

243

Huckstep Camp photographed by an RF-84F of ER4/33, showing rows of apparently undamaged tanks in the foreground and burnt-out vehicles to the left. (*SHAA via Albert Grandolini*)

> On the low-level departure I experienced a near squeak with a shell missing the cockpit, so near that I heard it before seeing it explode in the sand just ahead of me. I recall my intense relief when I called for my section to check in and heard them all respond although, I believe, three of them had been hit. The most serious damage was to Flg Off Joe Daniels' aircraft [WR473/U] which had damage to a wing and was losing fuel. He was desperately short on arrival at Akrotiri and was landed first. The damage was found to have been caused by part of a truck [in fact, part of its axle] being embedded in the wing!"

WR408 returned with a hole in its rudder. During the attack several tanks were claimed damaged, a small building in the tank compound was seen to explode and a number of SSVs were left in flames. A dozen rocket-armed F-84s arrived as the 6 Squadron Venoms completed their attacks. 249 Squadron also despatched three flights each of four rocket-armed aircraft to Huckstep, led by Sqn Ldr Maitland (WR497/B). Another section was led by Flt Lt Syme in

Sqn Ldr Jock Maitland of 249 Squadron flanked by his Flight Commanders, Flt Lt Doug Dallison (left) and Flt Lt Leo Dodds. (*Bob Byrne*)

WR499/V, whose aircraft suffered flak damage during the attack, causing a hydraulic failure although he, too, was able to land safely at Akrotiri on return from the strike. WR506/W also sustained minor damage when debris or shrapnel struck its port wing leading edge. Meanwhile, several sections from 8 Squadron similarly attacked Huckstep. One of the sections was due to be led by Flt Lt Scarlett but his aircraft went unserviceable when about to take off and he ordered the remainder of his section to join that already airborne, hence Flt Lt

Harcourt-Smith (WR532/R) found himself leading seven aircraft to attack Huckstep:

> "It was heavily defended and subjected us to more flak than any other target. It was the first time I had come across tracer being fired at me – exciting! We also re-attacked this target which was unwise and was probably an indication of over-confidence after the turkey shoot attacks on the airfields."

A member of the second section, Flg Off Hadlow, fired eight of his rockets into the assemblage of vehicles but received shrapnel damage to the armoured windscreen of his aircraft, WR405/B, although he was not aware of this until his return to Akrotiri:

> "The flight started somewhat eventfully as my leader [Flt Lt Scarlett] had to abort his take-off due to an overheating engine. I ended up as No7 out of seven, instead of No2 in the formation. This was to prove relevant later on! We attacked from the south in order to initially confuse the AA gunners. Diving on the long, neatly parked lines of tanks we started with 20mm cannon to keep the gunners' heads down, and then released our eight R/Ps at the armour. Then it was low-level jinking away from the target area and, as No7, the gunners were getting the range! I still have vivid memories of bursts of flak ahead and above me as I sped away. One shell was close enough to cause a large chip out of my windscreen."

Flt Lt Tanner similarly led his section to Huckstep, Flg Off Bryn Jones (WR509) participating. The 8 Squadron report continued:

> "The Station Commander [Grp Capt Macdonald] flew on one of these sorties. In all [over the two days of intensive operations when 68 sorties were flown] 226 rockets were released and 21,000 rounds of 20mm HE ammunition were fired. Eight of our aircraft were damaged by flak of small-arms fire, fortunately none seriously."

Sqn Ldr Blyth added:

> "We did over yards containing tanks and vehicles and other equipment. Used 20mm cannon and rockets. The rockets were for primary targets, with 20mm for primary and secondary."

The Egyptian fighter airfields were not entirely neglected, however, a section from 249 Squadron visiting Abu Sueir and Kabrit again just after midday; three MiGs were destroyed at the former and two more at the latter, where a Harvard was attacked just as it had become airborne which Flg Off Brian Carroll apparently claimed destroyed. Two flights of F-84Fs also visited the main airfields during the mid-afternoon and claimed two MiGs damaged at Abu Sueir, three Vampires and a Meteor damaged at Fayid, plus several vehicles left in flames. F-84Fs also carried out a strike against the radar station at Abu Sultan, where the main installations were claimed destroyed and a hangar was damaged.

8 Squadron despatched a section for a dusk strike against Abu Sueir, Flg Off

Another view of Huckstep Camp taken by ER4/33 showing burning vehicles. (*SHAA via Albert Grandolini*)

von Berg (WR501) amongst those who strafed the airfield. Meanwhile, Sqn Ldr Blyth took off at the head of another section, on this occasion flying WR485/C, and carried out an armed reconnaissance over al-Qantara, Ismailia and Deversoir, returning 45 minutes after sunset. 249 Squadron also despatched two sections shortly before dusk, one to attack the military barracks at Almaza, F-84Fs strafing targets on the same airfield. Another 249 Squadron quartet flew to Shallufa and included Flg Off Lecky-Thompson (WR527/C):

> "Had a very aggressive AA group trying to get us. I remember being the closest and so I immediately dropped down as low as I could (below 50 feet above ground level) and went under the flak straight at them until at about 500 yards I opened up with four 20mm cannons and thankfully silenced them. I then realised how frightened I had been!"

The last two strikes flown by 6 Squadron during the day were against the airfields at Kabrit (the section led by Sqn Ldr Ellis in Venom Z) and Abu Sueir, where five MiGs, a Harvard and a Fiat trainer were added to the tally, and further damage was inflicted on already damaged aircraft owing to the lack of alternative suitable targets. A dozen F-84Fs were active over the airfields at the same time, one flight strafing vehicles and gun sites at Almaza, the other flight striking at Fayid and Abu Sueir where three Vampires and two Meteors were claimed damaged. The Akrotiri-based fighter-bombers flew 167 sorties during the day, again for no loss.

SUMMARY OF SORTIES FLOWN BY VENOMS and F-84Fs, 0930-1730

ETA Target	Target	Aircraft	Claims
1010	Abu Sueir	4 Venom	Hangars strafed
1015	Kabrit		Hangars strafed
1025	Huckstep	8 Venom	Vehicles attacked
1115	Huckstep	6 F-84F	Vehicles attacked

SUMMARY OF SORTIES FLOWN BY VENOMS and F-84Fs, 0930-1730 (contiued)

ETA Target	Target	Aircraft	Claims
	Huckstep	6 F-84F	Vehicles attacked
1145	Huckstep	8 Venom	Vehicles attacked
1200	Huckstep	4 Venom	Vehicles attacked
1215	Abu Sultan	8 F-84F	Radar station installations destroyed
1300	Huckstep	8 Venom	Vehicles attacked
1405	Kabrit	4 Venom	2 MiGs destroyed, Harvard destroyed
1410	Abu Sueir		3 MiGs destroyed
1435	Huckstep	4 Venom	Vehicles attacked
1540	Abu Sueir	4 F-84F	2 MiGs damaged
1545	Fayid		3 Vampires damaged, Meteor damaged
1540	Kabrit	4 F-84F	No aircraft seen intact
1545	Kasfareet		No aircraft seen intact
1600	Almaza	4 F-84F	Barracks attacked
1620	Almaza	4 Venom	Buildings attacked
1625	Almaza	4 F-84F	Vehicles damaged
1645	Fayid	6 F-84F	3 Vampires damaged
1650	Abu Sueir		2 Meteors strafed
1700	Kabrit	4 Venom	Appeared deserted
1705	Abu Sueir		Fiat destroyed, 5 MiGs damaged, Harvard damaged
1700	Shallufa	4 Venom	Many vehicles damaged

Line-up of F-84Fs at Akrotiri; nearest aircraft is 1-PP of EC1/3; next is 1-NL (s/n 29102) of EC1/1, then 1-NM (s/n 28943) also of EC1/1. (*SHAA via Albert Grandolini*)

Although none of the Vampires or F-84Fs had been lost during the two days of intensive operations, several had suffered minor damage from flak and debris. Ground personnel of all squadrons worked round the clock to keep the aircraft serviced, as recalled by 249 Squadron's Cpl Bob Byrne:

"When the conflict began the squadrons were operating dawn and dusk strikes in their ground attack role. Several aircraft were damaged, mostly by debris from the low-level attacks. Hence work had to be carried out on the dispersal with arc lights, to change engines, fuel tanks that had been pierced, plus other structural reports on the airframes by the best means we had. In the rush to get aircraft back in service there were inevitable accidents. One night we were ground testing a new engine fitted to an aircraft while the armourers were loading up the ammunition bays, which were immediately above the air intakes. Unfortunately, due to the haste, we did not fit the engine debris guards and a whole ammunition belt got sucked into the engine air intake and wrecked the new engine. As I recall, there were no inquests – we just got on with installing the replacement and having the aircraft ready for dawn, come what may."

Canberra PR7s of 13 Squadron again flew eight reconnaissance sorties, while ER4/33's RF-84Fs recorded a further 12 sorties. All aircraft returned safely although there were momentary scares, as graphically described by Lt Bertin-Maghit of ER4/33:

"On the way to Egypt we saw the Sixth Fleet, a magnificent formation of concentric circles of warships. At 36,000 feet a flash of silver passed in front of us, climbing with full afterburner, so we had a plan-view. It was a Panther [sic – Cougar] of the US Navy with the fine white star . . . A drop of fearful sweat . . . then we turned keenly our heads towards the shore and told ourselves there was nothing to be afraid of.

There is the objective, 495 knots on the dial, that's OK. Some small white clouds [AA fire], as expected . . . it's time to check . . . a glance behind, a trail of a dozen white clouds accompanies the RF [RF-84] . . . puff! There's another one . . . this is rather unhealthy; the hand pushes forward the throttle . . . the foot also . . . quick, the cameras, the tape-recorder. I see that the airstrip is intact the whole length. There, on the right, on the 'daisy' (the flower-shaped turning taxiway) is one MiG-15. There, another close to the taxi-way . . . next there is the rapid disengagement, the turn towards the dual-lane highway . . . finally the return, the sea . . . a quick glance behind, the coast stretches away, I climb . . . the island of Cyprus looks good in this light, ready to greet me."

The last sortie of the day for the French reconnaissance jets was undertaken by Cdt Lapiche, his task to search for Il-28s which had taken refuge in Syria, "but night falls and our chief returns empty-handed; he has seen nothing," recorded Bertin-Maghit.

Patrolling pairs of Hunters from Cyprus were again kept busy throughout the day, intercepting a variety of intruders into Cypriot airspace including three US Navy AJ-2 Savage twin-engine tanker aircraft from one of the carriers, two returning French F-84Fs (apparently off course), four Venoms, two Shackletons from Malta, and two unannounced French aircraft – an Armée de l'Air Noratlas and an 'airbridge' Constellation. Another interception almost resulted in tragedy, as recalled by 34 Squadron's CO, Sqn Ldr Kingsford, who wrote:

"Two aircraft of the Squadron were vectored on to an unidentified target at 40,000 feet, well over 100 miles from Cyprus in the direction of the Canal. The interception was successful and it was established the target consisted of four aircraft, but a stern chase had to be carried out before positive identification was possible . . . it was thought that MiGs might be in the area. No2 of the Hunter section had a faster aircraft than his leader and had closed to within about 3,000 feet of one of the targets before he realised that the targets were in fact F-86Ds [sic – FJ-3 Furies] from the American Sixth Fleet! Up to that time he thought he might be on to the real thing. It is noteworthy the Americans, although flying in battle formation, did not see the Hunter until he was at very close range."

SUMMARY OF GROUND ATTACK CLAIMS AGAINST AIRCRAFT
OF THE EGYPTIAN AIR FORCE by Venoms and F-84Fs, 2 November 1956

Missions: Venoms 19   F-84Fs 12
Sorties: Venoms 88 (3 aborts)   F-84Fs 79

	Destroyed	Probables	Damaged
Claims for MiG-15s			
by Venoms:	21	0	23
by F-84Fs:	2	2	4
Claims for other types:			
by Venoms:	4	1	2
by F-84Fs:	1	1	3
	28	4	32

CARRIER STRIKE FORCE

Aircraft from the Anglo-French Task Force were in action before dawn when two rocket-armed Corsairs, flown by Second Maître Hamard and Ens deV(R) Deret, were launched from *La Fayette* at 0345, the pilots briefed to search for Egyptian warships. Off the port of Rosetta (Rashid) what was believed to have been an MTB was sighted, attacked and was reported to have sunk. On receiving the news of the attacks, *Arromanches* sent off two Avengers armed with rockets and depth charges, and although two destroyers were sighted off Alexandria, they turned out to be American vessels. At debriefing it transpired that the 'MTB' attacked by Hamard and Deret was in fact the French submarine S606 *La Creole* which escaped damage, having dived following the explosion of the first rocket in the water nearby. The two pilots were severely reprimanded for having not carried out an identification pass before making their attacks, their action being put down to excessive zeal.

Three further sections of rocket-armed Corsairs were despatched on offensive reconnaissances during the early morning, but no other naval shipping was observed by the French pilots. The patrouille led by Maître Berger (15F-1) was intercepted by a twin-boom jet fighter from above, whereupon Berger ordered drop tanks to be released as the Corsairs prepared to turn to face the threat, but the attacker was a Sea Venom from one of the British carriers and not an Egyptian Vampire as feared. The Royal Navy pilot apparently identified the French fighters in good time and broke away.

The pattern of attacks on various airfields by Fleet Air Arm aircraft was continued until midday.

First strike launched at 0520:

	Designated Target/Duty
HMS Eagle	
897 Squadron 6 Sea Hawks ⎱	
899 Squadron 3 Sea Hawks ⎰	Cairo West
892 Squadron 4 Sea Venoms	Cairo West/Bilbeis
893 Squadron 2 Sea Venoms	CAP HMS Eagle
HMS Albion	
800 Squadron 4 Sea Hawks ⎱	
802 Squadron 3 Sea Hawks ⎰	Dekheila
809 Squadron 4 Sea Venoms	Inchas
809 Squadron 1 Sea Venom	CAP HMS Albion
HMS Bulwark	
804 Squadron 4 Sea Hawks	Almaza
810 Squadron 8 Sea Hawks	Inchas
895 Squadron 4 Sea Hawks	CAP HMS Bulwark

The Sea Hawks of 897 and 899 Squadrons, led by Lt Cdrs Rawbone (WV907/190) and Clark (XE382/490) respectively, visited Cairo West airfield, where it was noticed that 'resistance had stiffened markedly'. A large camouflaged hangar was destroyed and another damaged, Lt Cdr Rawbone noting that his bomb scored a direct hit, while aircraft in their dispersals and on the perimeter tracks were strafed. Lt Mills (XE379/197) of 897 Squadron wrote:

> "We set off in the dark to Cairo West, much further south than the day before. Cairo West was joint military/civilian but was the main Il-28 bomber base. The danger of a mass attack on the fleet or worse, on the landing force, was obvious but, when we got there, the birds had flown. A few aircraft were on the hardstandings including some civil airliners which we left strictly alone. There was flak here, but this time we had flak suppression Sea Venoms who made the first attack to keep the gunners' heads down."

The four Sea Venoms of 892 Squadron then flew to Bilbeis, where three Harvards and a Fury were strafed and claimed destroyed, and two more Harvards and two Chipmunks damaged. Albion's Sea Hawks flew to Dekheila, where a Beechcraft Expediter of 4 Squadron EAF was seen to burst into flames when strafed, and a second of the same type was damaged. Two aircraft reported as 'Walrus-type' amphibians* were seen on the airfield, but there was

---

* These were probably redundant Supermarine Sea Otters, a number of which had been sold to Egypt in the early 1950s.

no sign of any MiGs. Light anti-aircraft fire was heavy and accurate, the pilots reporting intense flak from a destroyer in Alexandria Harbour and one Sea Hawk – XE455/100 of 800 Squadron – sustained slight damage to its port intake. Meanwhile, 809 Squadron's four Sea Venoms, led by Lt Cdr Shilcock (with Lt Hackett, in XG669/224), failed to sight any aircraft on the ground at Inchas airfield so fired at the control tower and hangars. Sub Lt Yates (with Sub Lt Dwarika, in XG673/227) fired at the already burning control tower, causing further damage, as the Sea Venom roared across the airfield. The observer remembered the excitement of the low-level strikes:

> "You could feel and see the ground-to-air fire searching us out, which made us feel uncomfortable.'

Sea Hawks of 810 Squadron, flying in the wake of the Sea Venoms, did however locate a number of transport aircraft on the airfield, which were duly strafed. Lt Cdr Lamb (flying XE396/167 of 804 Squadron) claimed a C-46 damaged, and another pilot a Dakota, while the 804 Squadron section strafed an array of aircraft at Almaza and claimed damage to a MiG and a Fury. Of the strike, 804 Squadron's diarist wrote:

> "Today they [Egyptian anti-aircraft gunners] were waiting for us and we encountered much accurate anti-aircraft fire from Cairo International as we turned in for the attack and even more actually from Almaza. However, no aircraft sustained damage, probably due to our high-speed attack and low-level retreat. Sub Lt Chris Hall [an 804 Squadron pilot] 'bottomed' No 6 wire and snapped off the hook from the shaft assembly. The aircraft [WM933/463, an 895 Squadron machine] went over the port bow with full power on but no flying speed. It hit the sea, the rear fuselage and tail unit surfacing briefly and then vanished without further trace of pilot or aircraft."

Bulwark put up a CAP to cover the returning Sea Hawks, and when these landed at 0635, sent off a further CAP of four Sea Hawks to protect the next launch of the next strike at 0740, five Sea Hawks of 895 Squadron – the sections led by Lt Cdr Morris-Jones (WM928/460) and Lt Anson (XE409/161) – flying to Bilbeis in company with three from 810 Squadron. As a result of the strike, seven Harvards were claimed damaged of which two were probably destroyed; two Chipmunks were also damaged. At the same time three Sea Hawks from *Albion*'s 802 Squadron carried out a strike against Helwan, where hangars were strafed although no aircraft were seen nor anti-aircraft fire experienced. As the returning Sea Hawks overflew Almaza, the pilots observed two Il-28s on the south-west apron but were unable to attack these since their ammunition had been expended. On their return to *Albion*, the presence of the two apparently undamaged Ilyushins was reported, prompting a further strike by two Sea Hawks of 802 Squadron, accompanied by two Sea Venoms from 809 Squadron. On reaching the airfield, the pilots observed a number of MiGs and Vampires dispersed around the airfield and claimed three of the former and two of the latter damaged, also damaging one of the two Il-28s. Lt Cdr Eveleigh, who led the strike, claimed a MiG and a Vampire damaged. Flak was moderately accurate and Sub Lt Clarke's aircraft (WM977/136) had most of its canopy blown away by a burst which exploded just above him, as his Commanding Officer remembered:

Sea Hawk FGA6s of 804 Squadron: XE409/161; XE396 and XE365/171, and Wyverns of 830 Squadron including VZ79?. (*Andy Thomas*)

"Nobby Clarke [from Trinidad], who was flying No2 on my wing, had his cockpit hood shattered by a black burst of 4.5 AA which burst just above us as we were making the run-in at about 8,000 feet. My own aircraft was rocked by the explosion but sustained no major damage. Nobby dived down to low level. In fact, we all thought he was going in. He levelled off but was not able to communicate so I detached No4 to escort him back to the ship, remaining at low level. They made it quite safely whilst the rest of the Squadron carried on with the mission."

On landing, however, Clarke found there was a hole in his helmet and on investigating discovered that a piece of shrapnel had penetrated to within an inch or so of his scalp. Almost immediately on the return of *Albion's* strike, *Bulwark* launched eight Sea Hawks of 804 and 895 Squadrons (the 895 Squadron section led by Lt Anson in XE405/232*) to carry out a repeat strafe of Almaza, where half a dozen Dakotas of 3 Squadron EAF were seen. The Sea Hawks made one firing pass and destroyed one of the transports, inflicting damage on the remaining five.

Eagle's squadrons had, in the meantime, also been busily engaged, five Wyverns of 830 Squadron having been sent at 0720 to attack Dekheila once again. There, one hit with a 1,000lb bomb was claimed on a large hangar north of the actual airfield, plus four near misses; the hangar was believed to have been destroyed. Six bomb-carrying Sea Hawks of 897 Squadron returned to Cairo West at 0930, again led by Lt Cdr Rawbone (XE439/200) where bombs were seen to explode in the east dispersal and around the main runway inter-section, while another hit a hangar, the roof of which partially collapsed. *Eagle's* other Sea Hawk unit, 899 Squadron, sent six aircraft to join in the strike against

---

* XE405 may be incorrect although recorded in Lt Anson's logbook as such.

Lt Ted Anson of 895 Squadron. (*Vice Adm Sir Edward Anson*)

Almaza, where a number of aircraft were seen. The pilots returned having added two MiGs destroyed to their tally, plus a third damaged, and also claimed damage to one Meteor, two Furies, a Vampire and three transports.

Bilbeis was again the target of five Sea Venoms from 892 and 893 Squadrons (led by Lt Cdr Henley in WW285/091) from *Eagle*, these departing at 1035, and were followed 20 minutes later by three Sea Hawks from *Bulwark*. The Sea Venom pilots claimed three Harvards destroyed, three damaged, and two Chipmunks damaged, while the Sea Hawk pilots reported the destruction of one Harvard, with a second damaged. The Sea Venom leader had been ordered to pay a visit to Inchas on the way back where, by chance, a MiG was observed, strafed and claimed destroyed.

Even though the carrier pilots had gained the impression that the Egyptians were placing unserviceable or previously damaged aircraft on the airfields, to lure strike aircraft into low-level attacks where they would be more vulnerable to anti-aircraft and small arms fire, one further strike was carried out against Almaza when *Albion* launched eight Sea Hawks (800/802 Squadrons) and two 809 Squadron Sea Venoms at 1100. As a result of the strafe, two Furies, a Vampire, a MiG and an Il-28 were claimed damaged, and a previously damaged Meteor was destroyed. Light flak was reported to be fairly accurate, although none of the strike aircraft was hit. 809 Squadron's diarist recorded:

"We encountered slight opposition in the form of light ack-ack flak, but there was no opposition in the air. The nearest we got to seeing an Egyptian aircraft, in the air, was when Lt [Ron] Davidson saw a MiG-15 on 'finals', but didn't have enough fuel to make a pass at it."

Sea Hawk pilots of 802 Squadron also observed Egyptian aircraft – presumably MiGs – in the air:

"It was noticeable that the intensity of the flak had increased, though it was still inaccurate, and although we saw a few aircraft about, no one was attacked by them."

The four Sea Hawks of 800 Squadron were led by Lt Cdr Tibby in XE435/104:

"We hit a MiG and an Il-28. Medium flak was encountered but it was not accurate – they were firing at the aircraft so that the shells were exploding behind us. We were too quick. The general method of attack was to come in from altitude to do a fairly lengthy diving manoeuvre, to finish up with a steep dive. Having conducted your firing, you continued almost to ground level then literally dodged out at high speed amongst the sand dunes."

Pilots of 800 Squadron pose in front of Sea Hawk XE438/105 aboard HMS *Albion*; rear, from left to right: Lt Don Richardson, Lt Jack Worth, Lt Geoff Ellis, Sub Lt Bob Northard, Lt Cdr Des Russell (CO), Sub Lt Rupert Sinnott (AEO), Lt Cdr Maurice Tibby (SP), Sub Lt Brian Day, Sub Lt Dave Mears; kneeling: Sub Lt Tony Rowed, Lt Pat Reed, Lt John Stuart-Jervis. (*Cdr Maurice Tibby*)

At midday, with the apparent demise of the EAF, the main target for the carrier strike aircraft was changed to Huckstep Camp, the Egyptian Army's transport depot. First off were six bomb-carrying Wyverns of 830 Squadron from *Eagle*, followed an hour later by eight Sea Hawks of 897 Squadron, while *Bulwark* launched ten Sea Hawks to the same target – eight of 895 Squadron led by Lt Cdr Morris-Jones in XE335/234, and two of 810 Squadron including Lt Hoddinott in XE394/165. Two camera-equipped Sea Hawks from *Albion*'s 802 Squadron flew independently to Huckstep to photograph the results of the attack. 897 Squadron's diarist noted:

> "The western part of the vehicle park was obscured by smoke and flames caused by 830 Squadron when they had attacked an hour previously. The tanks were attacked with rockets but results were not observed."

Of the attack on Huckstep, 895 Squadron's diarist recorded:

> "The RAF had just bombed and started fires amongst Army lorries but there appeared to be large numbers of lorries and tanks parked nose to tail, side by side, still undamaged."

The first and third sections attacked with both rockets and 20mm cannon:

> "After the attack the lorries were setting each other on fire and the tanks blowing each other up. The pall of smoke could be seen from the coast 140 miles away."

255

A pair of 895 Squadron Sea Hawks was despatched from *Bulwark* at 1305 to carry out a photographic run over Almaza; the leader, Lt Anson (in XE396/167 of 804 Squadron), another veteran of the Korean War, recalled:

"The sortie was in fact a series of vertical line overlap pictures over Almaza airfield as well as a series of oblique photographs of Huckstep Camp. The reason for the vertical pictures was twofold. Firstly, we needed to assess the damage done by previous strikes so that subsequent sorties could be targeted more specifically. Secondly, because the Royal Air Force would not believe us when we told them that they had not bombed the runways at Almaza, but had instead bombed the civil airport at Cairo International."

Albion sent a strike to Huckstep at 1305, eight Sea Hawks of 800 and 802 Squadron making up the force, where two successful rocket attacks were carried out and the pilots reported several flamers among the tanks and lorries targeted. Lt Cdr Eveleigh, flying WN109/139 of 802 Squadron, reported six SSVs left in flames following the attack, while Lt Worth of 800 Squadron in XE411/108 reported that his flight rocketed a group of 86 tanks. Lt Cdr Lamb (XE335/234) led seven more Sea Hawks of 810 Squadron from *Bulwark* at 1410 to strike at Huckstep, including Lt Hoddinott in XE463 on his second strike of the day against this target. Forty-five minutes later, four Wyverns from *Eagle* struck at the same target. These were joined at 1515 by eight Sea Hawks from 800 and 802 Squadrons. As a result of these attacks, at least a dozen of the Egyptian Army's British-built Centurion tanks were reported damaged or destroyed. Lt Cdr Tibby of 800 Squadron (in XE438/105) noted:

"This time we were firing rockets. On that particular sortie, we claimed two tanks destroyed, with two probably destroyed, despite medium flak."

One of the Sea Hawks was flown by Lt Brian Ellis, who was the Mirror Control Officer aboard *Albion* and had managed to "borrow a Sea Hawk for an hour or so". Lt Ellis had flown Sea Furies with 802 Squadron during the Korean War, when he had successfully participated in combats with Communist MiG-15s.

A final carrier strike was carried out against Huckstep Camp at dusk, eight Sea Hawks of 899 Squadron from *Eagle*, led by Lt Cdr Clark in XE404/496, being joined by eight more from *Bulwark*'s 810 Squadron. Much damage was believed inflicted on tanks, lorries and stores dumps and many fires were started. Of the successful series of attacks on Huckstep, Admiral Power wrote later:

"Wyvern and Sea Hawk sorties had been employed with marked success against the Egyptian Transport Depot at Huckstep Camp. Not one bomb or rocket aimed at this massed target fell outside the target area."

Airfield attacks were not completely ignored during this period, a dozen bomb-carrying Corsairs of 15F Flotille from *La Fayette* flying the Aeronavale's first such strike at 1220; the pilots were briefed to attack Dekheila in three sections each of four aircraft. The patrouille led by Lt deV Degermann was armed with 500lb delayed-action bombs and went in at low level with cannons blazing to keep the gunners' heads down. Two hangars were seen to receive direct hits and

Vehicles on fire at Huckstep; photograph taken by Sea Hawk of 895 Squadron flown by Lt Cdr John Morris-Jones. (*Cdr John Morris-Jones*)

other bombs were seen to fall on the east–west runway. This strike was followed by that of Lt deV de Saint-Quentin's patrouille, and then by the final quartet led by Lt deV Campredon which had overflown the Aboukir peninsula before attacking from the north-east. All runways were considered to have been rendered unserviceable as a result of this and the earlier strikes by the Wyverns.

One Corsair was lost during the day when Lt deV Nève's aircraft crashed over the side of *La Fayette* as he misjudged his landing on returning from an armed

Corsair 15F-11 of 15F Flotille crashes over the side when landing on *La Fayette*. Lt Nève was able to extricate himself and was picked up by the planeguard HUP-2. (*via Joss Leclercq*)

257

HUP-2 Pedro 23S-7 of 23S Escadrille hovering above *Arromanches*'s deck. (*via Joss Leclercq*)

patrol. He opened up the throttle in an attempt to go around again but gained too much speed and the aircraft (15F-11) rolled on to its back into the sea, shedding a wing-tip as it went. The pilot was fortunately able to extricate himself and was soon picked up by the carrier's planeguard, an HUP-2 Pedro helicopter (23S-4) flown by Maître Rignault.

Three Sea Hawks flown by 895 Squadron, accompanied by four from 804 Squadron, visited Almaza at 1415, when seven Dakotas and a Vampire were claimed destroyed by the 804 Squadron section; an eighth transport aircraft was damaged by Lt Anson's trio from 895 Squadron. *Eagle* launched four Sea Hawks of 899 Squadron at 1350 and the section flew to Bilbeis where three Harvards and a Chipmunk were claimed destroyed. An hour later *Eagle* despatched eight Sea Venoms (of which six were from 893 Squadron led by Lt Cdr Henley in WW285/091) to attack Almaza, where a Vampire and a MiG were destroyed, as were a Spitfire and a transport aircraft, while a second Spitfire was damaged. During the attack, Lt Cdr Willcox's 893 Squadron aircraft, WW281/095, received a flak burst under the forward fuselage, as he recalled:

"On reaching the airfield we carried out the first attack, each pilot selecting his own target from the many aircraft which were widely dispersed on the ground. We then reformed a short distance away and carried out a second attack, more or less from the same direction. By this time there was plenty of anti-aircraft fire, which I assumed to be of the light 40mm Bofors type. Following this second attack [against a C-46] I broke away in a starboard climbing turn and had reached about 500 feet when there occurred a rather loud noise and a very large hole appeared in the bottom of the cockpit.

Following a brief period of intense inactivity I was able to ascertain that the aircraft was still capable of normal flight, though with the loss of all hydraulic pressure. The normally power-assisted controls reverted to manual and I found that the emergency pump handle had been neatly severed at its

Lt Cdr John Willcox's flak-damaged Sea Venom WW281/095 of 893 Squadron being lifted off the deck after its wheels-up landing on HMS *Eagle*. (*Andy Thomas*)

base. It then became apparent that my most able observer, Flg Off Bob Olding [one of the two RAF navigators attached to the Squadron], had suffered severe injury. I well remember that he injected himself with a pain-killing morphine capsule during the short flight back to the ship. I had by this time decided to land without wheels or flaps since the possibility of asymmetric operation of either would have resulted in further complication. We fortunately had a green light from the arrester hook, which usually drops with hydraulic failure, so after waiting for all other aircraft to land on, we made our first approach.

Bob, who had remained conscious throughout, was able to call the air-speed as he usually did. I was however unable to slow the aircraft sufficiently in order not to place too great a strain on the arrester hook. My second approach was slower, though the angle of attack had increased sufficiently to obscure my forward view. I closed the throttle and let the nose fall, the hook caught the first wire; a slight bump, an expensive grinding noise, rapid deceleration, and we were down. The engine was still running perfectly and I went through the shut down procedure, by which time we were surrounded by rescue personnel who rushed Bob off to the sick bay."

Lt Neave added his own tribute:

"Bob received multiple shrapnel wounds to his legs. They lost hydraulic power so were forced to do a wheels-up, flapless landing without the benefit of power controls. Needless to say, [John Willcox] made a superb job of a difficult situation."

Lt Cdr Henley commented:

"Apparently Bob, despite his wounds, continued to call out the airspeeds during the approach in the usual way, but passed out on landing. The damage and injuries might have been much worse but for the fact that the hit was in the gun bay and the 20mm cannon absorbed a lot of the shock."

After treatment in *Eagle's* sick bay, Flg Off Olding was flown in a Skyraider of 849 Squadron's A Flight to Cyprus. Sadly, his wounds became infected, gangrene set in and it was necessary for his leg to be amputated above the knee in order to save his life.*

Shortly before dusk *Bulwark* launched three sections each of three Sea Hawks, to strike at Bilbeis. The 804 Squadron section claimed four Harvards destroyed and one damaged, while those from 895 Squadron (led by Lt Cdr Morris-Jones in XE394/165) claimed a Harvard and two damaged; the trio from 810 Squadron reported a MiG trainer destroyed and four Harvards damaged. That evening, the carriers received a signal from the Commander-in-Chief:

"My warmest congratulations to all officers and ratings of the carrier group on the splendid results of your operations over the last 24 hours. The results show a skill in planning and a courage and determination in execution at all levels which are worthy of the highest praise. The high technical efficiency of aircraft also shows the very brilliant work which has been done by maintenance crews. I wish you all good luck in our future operations. Well done indeed."

A summary of the day's operations revealed that the British carriers had flown a total of 314 sorties, 74 of which had been directed against Huckstep Camp where much damage had been inflicted on the estimated 1,000 vehicles parked there. In addition, *Arromanches'* Avengers flew eight anti-submarine and maritime patrol sorties, and *La Fayette's* Corsairs a further 20.

SUMMARY OF GROUND ATTACK CLAIMS AGAINST AIRCRAFT OF THE EGYPTIAN AIR FORCE by the Fleet Air Arm, 2 November 1956

	Destroyed	Probables	Damaged
Claims for MiG-15s:			
HMS *Eagle's* squadrons	4	0	1
HMS *Albion's* squadrons	0	0	3
HMS *Bulwark's* squadrons	1	0	1
	5	0	5
Claims for other types:			
HMS *Eagle's* squadrons	14	0	16
HMS *Albion's* squadrons	2	0	7
HMS *Bulwark's* squadrons	7	2	20
	23	2	43

---

* For his performance on this operation, Flg Off Bob Olding was awarded the Navy's Distinguished Service Cross, and was later fitted with an artificial leg, allowing him to continue his flying career, serving with a Javelin squadron. He eventually retired from the RAF as a Group Captain in 1984.

Lt John Ford's Sea Hawk WM995/138 of 802 Squadron returns to *Albion* with a flak-damaged drop tank. (*Andy Thomas*)

Canberra B2 WH718 of 44 Squadron at Nicosia about to receive its bomb load. (*Authors' collection*)

A number of Sea Hawks and Sea Venoms had suffered minor damage during the two days of intensive ground attacks. The experience of 802 Squadron was typical: Lt Paddy McKeown returned from one sortie with a hole in the tail unit of his Sea Hawk, Lt Ken Kemp from another with a damaged drop tank, while Lt John Ford's WV995/138 also suffered flak damage to a drop tank, and Sub Lt Ron McLean's aircraft took a hit in its port wing, but after an hour or two in the carrier's hangar all four aircraft were back on line.

RAF bombers from both Malta and Cyprus kept up the round-the-clock assault on Egyptian targets, when a total of 48 Canberras and six Valiants participated in attacks against Luxor air base and Huckstep Camp during the hours of darkness. Bad weather in the central Mediterranean prevented further planned raids by the Malta Bomber Wing.

PLAN OF ATTACK
Malta Bomber Wing/Cyprus Bomber Wing, 2/3 November 1956

RAID 11 – Target: LUXOR

From Cyprus
4 Canberra B6s of 139 Squadron (Markers)
5 Canberra B2s of 15 Squadron
4 Canberra B2s of 61 Squadron
3 Canberra B2s of 10 Squadron
3 Canberra B2s of 44 Squadron
3 Canberra B2s of 27 Squadron   One returned early

RAID 12 – Target: HUCKSTEP CAMP

From Cyprus
4 Canberra B6s of 139 Squadron (Markers)
4 Canberra B6s of 139 Squadron
4 Canberra B2s of 18 Squadron

From Malta
7 Valiant B1s of 138 Squadron   One returned early
7 Canberra B6s of 9 Squadron

RAID 13 – Target: HUCKSTEP CAMP

From Cyprus
4 Canberra B2s of 18 Squadron (Markers)
4 Canberra B2s of 18 Squadron

From Malta
Operation cancelled owing to bad weather

Luxor was again the target for Canberras from Cyprus, when a total of 22 set out from Nicosia although one of 27 Squadron's aircraft, WJ723 flown by Flg Off B.B. Haywood, had to return early due to its undercarriage failing to retract. The quartet from 61 Squadron led by Sqn Ldr Hartley* (WJ642) departed from Nicosia at 1350. All returned safely by 1740, although WH860 of 27 Squadron, captained by Flg Off J.I. Miller, had sustained slight flak damage, a shell splinter making a three-inch hole through the starboard tailplane. Seven Valiants of 138 Squadron had set out from Malta to bomb Huckstep but the undercarriage of Wg Cdr Oakley's WZ400 failed to retract, and he was obliged to return to Luqa. The remaining six duly arrived over the target area, where

---

* Sqn Ldr Hartley, together with his crew, was killed in a flying accident on 8 March 1957, when Canberra WH915 crashed in Hertfordshire; this was the aircraft involved in the 'nose-wheel' incident at Nicosia.

Sqn Ldr Collins, captain of WZ401, discovered that his bombs would not release; he recalled:

"This time the attack was to be launched on Huckstep barracks, east of Cairo. There was a large concentration of armour there, and, according to intelligence reports, army conscripts were also assembling there. The bomber stream began to take off at 1700. This time the Canal Zone was blacked out and the only lights visible were from cars and the occasional flash of ineffectual anti-aircraft fire. Once again, the proximity markers, flares and target indicators went down accurately and on time. The Canberra marker leader on this raid did a good job at low level, encouraging and advising each bomb aimer where to aim his bombs."

The Valiants from Malta were accompanied by seven Canberras of 9 Squadron, which also raided Huckstep, where flares and markers were dropped by four Canberras of 139 Squadron from Cyprus. 9 Squadron's Commanding Officer, Sqn Ldr George Bastard, emphasised the extremely accurate bombing was 'due to perfect placing of the target markers'. Eight Canberras, drawn equally from 18 and 139 Squadron, also participated in the attack on Huckstep. Poor weather at Malta prevented a further force of bombers from being despatched, as intended, an hour later, leaving eight Canberras of 18 Squadron from Cyprus to strike again at Huckstep.

The continual aerial bombardment and prospect of impending invasion was undoubtedly and inevitably beginning to have a severe effect on the morale of Egypt's leaders, as can be judged from the diary kept by Wg Cdr al-Bughdadi, who was called to attend a special meeting presided over by President Nasser:

"During the course of the debate [Colonel] Salah Salim [editor of al-Sh'ab and a former minister] arrived. He started by saying: 'We must prevent further calamities and destruction in this country.' He proposed that Gamal [Nasser] address the nation and declare that for the benefit of the people and in order to prevent further disaster and destruction he [Nasser] was about to request a ceasefire and a surrender. But I could not put up with these words of his and I answered him: 'My opinion, Salah, is that it is more honourable for me to commit suicide, before doing such a thing [surrender].' Here Gamal interjected: 'Far better for us all to commit suicide here, before taking such a step.' He asked Zakariya [Muhi al-Din, Minister of the Interior and future Prime Minister] to bring some vials with phosphatecyanide so that there would be enough for us all should the need arise. He stressed: 'I am serious about what I've said.' Here Salah said that he was withdrawing his proposal."

Colonel Salah Salim was dismissed from his posts after the Suez War; he died in 1962 aged 42.

Chapter Twelve

ALLIED AIR LOSSES MOUNT

3 November 1956

"We are not at war with Egypt . . . this is just a police action."

Prime Minister Eden

Air activity over northern Egypt and Sinai at this time was described by Egyptian witnesses as fantastic, but it was almost all flown by British, French or Israeli aircraft. Military targets near Port Said and the Suez Canal were bombed in preparation for the ground assault. However, it was becoming increasingly obvious to the British and French that it would be difficult to justify to world opinion the maintenance of an air offensive, whether on military or civil targets, until the assault forces were available to land. As a result, orders were issued to the Task Force commanders to implement the airborne assault for the morning of 5 November.

With an appreciation of the lack of Egyptian air opposition, further daylight bombing attacks were undertaken by the Cyprus Wing at about 0800, when eight Canberras of 15 Squadron led by Sqn Ldr Scott in WD980 bombed on markers released over the Almaza Barracks (Raid 14) by two Canberras of 139 Squadron, followed 20 minutes later by further attacks by a dozen Canberras, drawn equally from 10 and 44 Squadrons, with an escort provided by Hunters. One of the marker aircraft, WT371 flown by Flt Lt Slater, sustained damage to the main spar and integral tank (believed to have been inflicted by a .303 bullet), although Slater was able to fly back to Cyprus safely.

Later that morning another force of Canberras (Raid 15) – seven of 61 Squadron, six of 27 Squadron led by Wg Cdr Helmore in WH732, three each from 18 and 139 Squadrons, and a lone bomber from 44 Squadron – set out from Nicosia to attack the Nfisha railway marshalling yards near Ismailia. This force was also escorted by Hunters, the target having been marked by two 139 Squadron Canberras. Nearby gun emplacements were strafed by a section of 8 Squadron Venoms led by Flt Lt Harcourt-Smith (WR501), who recalled:

"We were on an anti-flak mission, our purpose to silence the guns to enable the Canberras to bomb unhindered from 30,000 feet – not that the Egyptian flak could reach that height."

The 61 Squadron formation was led by Sqn Ldr Hartley in WJ642, another of

Canberra B2 WH907 of 61 Squadron over Egypt. (*M. Freestone via Andy Thomas*)

the Squadron's aircraft (WJ740) flown by Grp Capt John Woodroffe DSO DFC* from Air HQ with Air Marshal Barnett occupying the navigator's seat. One aircraft, the jinxed WH918 flown by the luckless Flg Off Price, returned early with a blown bombsight fuse. The remaining Canberras carried out shallow dive bombing attacks and a total of 39 bombs were seen to explode in the main yard and others hit the tracks leading to the yard. Fuel and oil storage tanks were also hit and set on fire and the raid was described as having been 'particularly successful', although this was not the impression harboured by Flt Lt Harcourt-Smith, who commented: "I recall hearing that it had been a large effort for little return."

Despite heavy damage to airfields and the loss of more than 150 aircraft, the EAF continued to fight back as best it could. However, Anglo-French air attacks continually disrupted EAF repair and counter-attack efforts. The need to disperse surviving combat aircraft, sometimes to locations with minimal support facilities, also hampered the EAF's efforts.

AKROTIRI STRIKE WING

In the meantime the air strikes continued, although operations were switched from airfield attacks to armed reconnaissances over specified areas. 6 Squadron flew four missions in all, each of four aircraft; the returning pilots complained that targets were becoming increasingly difficult to find. At Kabrit, the first section claimed the only intact MiG observed by the Squadron throughout the day, and the second section, led by Sqn Ldr Ellis (Venom T), found two Meteor F8s at Fayid, apparently ready to fly, which were strafed and set on fire, as were an attendant petrol bowser and two armoured vehicles. The next section, which also flew to Fayid, observed a staff car drawn up by the smouldering wreckage

---

* Grp Capt Woodroffe was killed in 1957 while flying as a passenger in a USAF B-47. At the time he was commanding a detachment of Vulcan bombers visiting the United States for the annual Strategic Air Forces Competition.

Rockets and ammunition for the F-84Fs at Akrotiri. (*SHAA via Albert Grandolini*)

of the two Meteors destroyed earlier. The occupants of the car dashed for cover as the Venoms swooped in at low level and strafed, leaving it in flames. One of the sorties was flown by the Squadron's commander-designate, Sqn Ldr George Elliott, who had previously been kept busy at Wing Operations. Flt Lt Harrison (WR404/X) noted:

> "It became our policy to take some of the less experienced pilots, particularly on the reconnaissance missions, and these included Sqn Ldr Elliott. On one such flight I took Flg Off 'Bonce' Richardson as my No2. He was a keen lad and had been pestering me since Day One for a trip. We found two APCs (Armoured Personnel Carriers) going at speed across the desert. I took one and asked Richardson to take the other, selecting two rockets for the attack. I hit mine, and was quite surprised and delighted to see that the other had also been destroyed. I think I even bought him a beer that evening!"

A section of F-84Fs followed 6 Squadron's Venoms to Fayid where the pilots reported seeing the remains of the two Meteors. Two Vampires were also seen, attacked by rockets and cannon and were claimed destroyed. During a dawn armed reconnaissance by F-84Fs in the al-Qantara/Ismailia/Abu Sueir area, one of the French fighter-bombers was damaged by ground fire although the pilot was able to return to Cyprus safely. Pilots of 8 Squadron were similarly briefed on the military targets they were to attack, which included sorties against airfields attacked previously. Having set out at 0510, four rocket-armed Venoms led by Flt Lt Cater* carried out a low-level reconnaissance between al-Qantara and Ismailia, as recalled by Flg Off Bryn Jones (WR485/C):

> "Doug Cater led us down the east side of the road to Ismailia, then we turned

---

* Flt Lt Doug Cater had previously flown Harvard anti-terrorist operations in Kenya, and had joined 249 Squadron to complete his tour.

round at the lakes and came up along the west side of the road, looking for suitable targets. We flew as low as possible, perhaps ten feet above the sand dunes, to avoid the flak. I was flying No2 to Ted Sheehan – we were parallel – when we ran into lots of flak. Every time there was a near burst over the cockpit one tended to duck and drop a bit lower! Suddenly I saw a flash beside me, and a ball of flames with the silhouette of a Venom turning over and over. I called Doug over the R/T as I could not see him and he climbed to 500 feet, thereby placing himself in grave danger, until I was able to catch up. Quite a brave thing to do."

It was not known if Flt Lt Sheehan's aircraft, WR505, had inadvertently struck the ground or had been hit by ground fire. Ted Sheehan, from Enfield, Middlesex, was killed. He had been married for only seven weeks and had recently arrived on the Squadron having ferried a Venom to Cyprus from RAF Valley, as Flt Lt Harcourt-Smith remembered:

"It was normal for squadrons in peacetime not to have the full complement of pilots: pilot to aircraft ratio was low. Ted Sheehan, with Venom experience in Germany (I was with him on 123 Wing at Wunsdorf from 1952 to 1954) was sent to Akrotiri as a war reinforcement pilot. He had no experience of ultra-low flying over the featureless terrain of the desert."

Sqn Ldr Blyth led a second armed reconnaissance in WR532, departing Akrotiri at 0750 and headed for the Deversoir/Kabrit area. The Venoms struck at Fayid, using rockets and 20mm cannon, but no aircraft targets were to be seen. Sqn Ldr Blyth noted:

"We were fired upon by ground fire. One particular 'johnny' was constant throughout from Ismailia but we were forbidden to take it out. We were instructed to certain targets. I had a go at a radar station, which was naughty."

Flt Lt Scarlett's section also attacked Kabrit where Flg Off Hadlow (WR405/B) saw his rockets score a direct hit on a hangar. The quartet of Venoms then flew along the Kabrit to Ismailia road, where two bowsers were strafed:

"Back to Kabrit for R/P attacks on hangars and installations. This followed by a low-level armed recce between Kabrit and Ismailia looking for the interestingly named targets of opportunity. All we found were two petrol tankers which were despatched. The abiding memories here were the tanker drivers baling out of their cabs when they realised they were the targets, and who could blame them? Also, nearly flying into the ground striving for target acquisition at low level."

During the course of one of these strikes, WR446/S suffered damage to the leading edge of one wing although the pilot was able to fly back to Akrotiri. Flt Lt Syme (WR533/F) of 249 Squadron led an armed reconnaissance to the Deversoir/Geneifa area where he rocketed and strafed a fuel bowser, a tank transporter and two lorries. Meanwhile, Flg Off Lecky-Thompson (WR507/S) noted that one of his rockets hit a tank transporter before he and Flt Lt Waterhouse strafed three bowsers and three trucks.

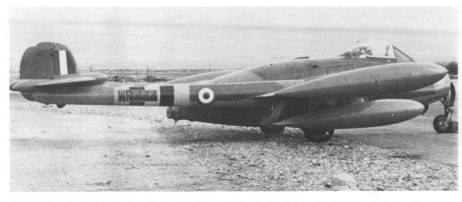

Venom FB4 WR444/E of 249 Squadron at Akrotiri (*Bruce Robertson via Andy Thomas*)

By midday, the Venoms had logged 32 sorties during the course of which visits were made to the airfields at Abu Sueir, Deversoir, Fayid, Kabrit and Kasfareet:

	SUMMARY OF SORTIES FLOWN BY VENOMS and F-84Fs by midday		
ETA Target	**Target**	**Aircraft**	**Claims**
0600	al-Qantara Abu Sueir Ismailia	4 Venom	Armed recce: slight AA fire at Ismailia; no intact aircraft seen at Abu Sueir
0600	Deversoir Fayid Abu Sueir Kabrit Geneifa	4 Venom	Armed recce: MiG destroyed at Kabrit; no other aircraft appeared intact
0615	al-Qantara Ismailia Abu Sueir	4 F-84F	Armed recce: rocket and cannon attack on military vehicles
0630	Kabrit Kasfareet	4 Venom	Armed recce: 6 bowsers, a 10-ton lorry and 5 trailers destroyed
0745	al-Qantara Ismailia	4 F-84F	Armed recce: rocket and cannon attack on military vehicles
0830	Fayid	4 F-84F	Armed recce: rocket and cannon attack, 2 Vampires destroyed
0900	al-Qantara Ismailia	4 Venom	Armed recce: rail traffic attacked and locomotive stopped
0930	Kabrit Fayid	4 Venom	2 Meteors destroyed, Vampire damaged, bowser destroyed
1000	Fayid Deversoir	4 Venom	Armed recce: runways attacked at Deversoir; light flak Port Said
1000	al-Qantara Ismailia Abu Sueir	4 F-84F	Armed recce: attacked train between al-Ballah and al-Firdan; 3 vehicles probably damaged near Nfisha

1030	al-Qantara Ismailia Abu Sueir	4 F-84F	Armed recce: car and 2 lorries damaged; AA site probably damaged
1123	Nfisha	4 Venom	Flak suppression in support of Canberra raid
1130	Fayid	4 Venom	Hangars rocketed
1130	al-Qantara Ismailia Abu Sueir	4 F-84F	Intense flak from Abu Sueir

Although the F-84F pilots claimed two Vampires destroyed on the ground at Fayid during the morning, it would appear that these were previously damaged aircraft and the claims were not credited. After lunch, sections of Venoms of 249 Squadron continued to hunt for military vehicles in the Canal Zone, the strafing of airfields now considered to be of secondary importance. Flg Off Williams (WR507/S) was in the section that later flew to Shallufa, where a mobile power unit was strafed, while Flg Off Gronert (WR492/U), in Flt Lt Dallison's section, noted:

"We carried out only one sortie today. Army intelligence had reported a build up of armour at Almaza so we were to go and sort it out. We employed our usual system of the long approach to attack and shortly after breaking cloud at 20,000 feet we found that we were being fired at by what appeared to be radar-controlled anti-aircraft guns. We pressed on down to the target only to find that any armoured vehicles which might have been there had since disappeared. We fired our rockets into the barracks and flew at below the level of the house tops with guns still firing at us. They didn't hit us but they must have given a lot of work to the local builders!"

Akrotiri's Station Commander, Grp Capt Macdonald, flew one of the 15 sorties carried out by 249 Squadron during the day. The final mission of the day was flown by a section from 249 Squadron, the Venoms following hard on the tails of four F-84Fs to strike at Abu Sueir. While the French pilots strafed vehicles and buildings, the 249 Squadron section destroyed two MiGs and damaged two others. The Venoms had notched up a further 16 sorties during the afternoon, four fewer than the F-84s, flying mainly armed reconnaissances to the Fayid area:

SUMMARY OF SORTIES FLOWN BY VENOMS and F-84Fs, 1230-1700

ETA Target	Target	Aircraft	Claims
1230	Fayid	4 Venom	Armed recce: bridge at al-Firdan destroyed
1230	Ismailia Ismailia	4 F-84F	Armed recce: Army camp near rocketed and strafed

ETA Target	Target	Aircraft	Claims
1315	al-Qantara Ismailia Abu Sueir	4 F-84F	Armed recce: hangar damaged at Abu Sueir
1400	Fayid	4 Venom	Armed recce: 3 bowsers damaged
1425	al-Qantara Ismailia Abu Sueir	4 F-84F	Armed recce: convoy attacked - car and four lorries afire
1515	Fayid	4 Venom	Armed recce: no report
1615	al-Qantara Ismailia Abu Sueir	4 F-84F	Armed recce: attacked three AA batteries – one probably destroyed, one damaged
1615	al-Qantara Ismailia Abu Sueir	4 F-84F	Armed recce: attacked buildings at Abu Sueir; probably destroyed 3 vehicles including jeep
1630	Fayid Abu Sueir	4 Venom	Armed recce: 3-ton vehicle destroyed, Sherman tank damaged; 2 MiGs destroyed, 2 damaged

F-84Fs in flight; note variation in stripes on 1-NA (s/n 28903) of EC1/1 and 3-HK (s/n 29030) of EC1/3. (*Joss Leclercq collection*)

Canberra PR7s of 13 Squadron flew seven reconnaissance sorties, while ER4/33's RF-84Fs recorded a further 17 sorties. All aircraft returned safely. One of the Canberra sorties was a reconnaissance of Syrian airfields. An RF-84F (RF327) was despatched from Cyprus to reconnoitre the coastline for the Army in preparation for the imminent landings. The pilot, Lt Martin, reported seeing a vessel on fire at Port Said. Another of the French pilots, Lt Bertin-Maghit, wrote:

"Today, here things are happening fast . . . the English are full of admiration for our work and ask us to undertake almost all the missions."

Bertin-Maghit returned from one mission early when his JATO [Jet Assisted Take-Off] rocket gear – to help heavily laden fighter-bombers to get airborne from short runways quickly – punctured one of his drop-tanks which he thought had set his aircraft on fire. Fortunately this was not the case and he was able to land safely after jettisoning his auxiliary fuel tanks.

Cyprus's defensive fighters had a quieter day, one pair of Hunters intercepting another pair and a French DC-3, while four Venoms were sent to investigate an approaching aircraft which turned out to a French DC-6, part of the air bridge. A second DC-6 was intercepted after dark by a 39 Squadron Meteor NF13.

SUMMARY OF GROUND ATTACK CLAIMS AGAINST AIRCRAFT
OF THE EGYPTIAN AIR FORCE by Venoms and F-84Fs, 3 November 1956

Missions: Venoms 12   F-84Fs: 11
Sorties: Venoms 48 (1 abort) F-84Fs: 44

	Destroyed	Probables	Damaged
Claims for MiG-15s			
Venoms:	3	0	2
F-84Fs:	0	0	0
Claims for other types			
Venoms:	11	0	2
F-84Fs:	0	0	0
	14	0	4

CARRIER STRIKE FORCE

With *Albion* having withdrawn northwards to refuel, the two remaining Royal Navy carriers maintained the series of air strikes, assisted by the two French carriers. Pairs of Avengers from 9F Flotille were out during the morning on anti-submarine patrols, each of about four hours' duration, before being relieved by the next patrouille. The aircraft flown by Ens deV Mienville picked up a blip on its radar and Second Maître Malaise was sent to investigate. As the Avenger swooped low over the sea, a submarine periscope was observed. Permission for an attack was requested from *Arromanches* but this was refused when it was established that no hostile submarine was known to be in the area. The frustrated Avenger crews flew back to the carrier where they learned later that their quarry had been the USS *Cutlass*. Appropriate signals were sent to the commander of the US Sixth Fleet.

The destruction of Gamil Bridge, to the west of Gamil airfield – the area designated for the British paratroop drop and carrying the only road connecting Port Said to the Delta – was now given priority status. The directive called for its destruction as soon after first light as possible. 897 Squadron's commander, Lt Cdr Rawbone, recalled:

"We were confident that the Egyptian Air Force had been put out of action and, whilst monitoring the airfields closely, the carriers moved to destroy Egyptian Army equipment and lines of communication. Gamil Bridge was targeted and lines of communication, between the Israeli front line with the Egyptians and the Canal and Egyptian rear bases, were attacked. Soft-skinned vehicles were added to the target list but other than Almaza, which was heavily defended, most targets were so lightly defended that one had an uneasy, almost guilty, feeling."

Eagle's first strike was scheduled to be flown by eight Sea Hawks of 897

Squadron against Huckstep Camp but, on the strength of an intelligence report received at 0300, the target was changed to Almaza as it was thought that the Egyptians might attempt to get some aircraft, including MiG-15s, airborne at first light. The Sea Hawks departed at 0530 and arrived over the airfield before sunrise, led by Lt Cdr Rawbone (WV907/190). Little activity was observed although a Dakota and an Il-28 were destroyed, as Lt Mills remembered:

> "We launched again before dawn to attack Almaza, an airfield north of Cairo where large numbers of MiGs had been photographed the day before by Canberras from Cyprus. This time they were waiting for us and the flak was more intense and accurate, with the result that a few aircraft sustained minor damage including mine, but miraculously nobody was shot down. After three attacks we had destroyed another batch of aircraft on the ground and I claimed an Il-28, as I saw it disintegrate."

Eight Sea Hawks of 810 Squadron from *Bulwark*, led by Lt Cdr Lamb (XE396/167), were also sent to Almaza at about the same time, and these claimed damage to a Meteor, a C-46 and a Harvard. One of the Sea Hawks, XE409/161, was flown by Lt Hoddinott. With the return of strike aircraft, the carriers each launched a further four Sea Hawks to fly an armed reconnaissance along the Ismailia to Tel al-Kebir road, where those of 899 Squadron (led by Lt Cdr Clark in XE404/496) destroyed a tank with rockets and 20mm cannon. The section from *Bulwark* also encountered a tank, which was left damaged before the same pilots attacked and damaged a Bren-gun carrier. 899 Squadron despatched a further section at 0720 and these attacked the railway goods yard at Ismailia with rockets, where at least one wagon was hit. Six more Sea Hawks from *Bulwark* took off at 0740 for the same area, where the sections led by Lt Cdr Morris-Jones (WM918/111) and Lt Anson of 895 Squadron (WV796) encountered heavy tanks and claimed one destroyed and two damaged. Two more sections from the same carrier followed two hours later; two medium tanks were damaged during this operation, as were two 37mm AA guns. In between these launches, 810 Squadron's Lt Cdr Lamb (flying XE394/165 of 804 Squadron) took off with Lt Hoddinott (XE335/234) to carry out a photo-reconnaissance of Almaza and the Alexandria area, where they were greeted by heavy flak, although neither was hit.

Since air superiority had been gained over the battle zone, French Corsairs were released to attack airfields and other targets inland. Thus, a dozen Corsairs of 15F Flotille from *La Fayette*, under the command of Lt deV Degermann, together with eight more from Lt deV Cremer's 14F Flotille aboard *Arromanches*, were ranged for take-off at 0655 to attack Almaza. At the moment of launch from *Arromanches* however, Cremer's aircraft (14F-6) developed engine problems and his Senior Pilot, Lt deV Lancrenon, took over as leader of the section, while Ens deV Doniol (14F-7) assumed command of the second section from 14F Flotille. On reaching Almaza, the Corsairs of 15F Flotille attacked first, diving from about 12,000 feet to deliver their 1,000lb bombs, closely followed by the seven aircraft from 14F Flotille. Ens deV Caron, one of the first to attack, saw two Egyptian Meteors speeding down the runway and called over the radio that he was about to pursue them but was ordered to concentrate on the bombing. The Meteors became airborne although they did not attempt to interfere with the attack on their airfield, and were last seen heading southwards.

Lt deV Lancrenon of 14F Flotille was shot down by AA fire when attacking Almaza on 3 November 1956; he did not survive. (*via Joss Leclercq*)

Having completed its attack, Lt deV Lancrenon's aircraft (14F-10) was seen to turn away from the target but it failed to return to the carrier. None of the pilots had witnessed its demise and the fate of the missing pilot was not known. Another Corsair (14F-15) returned to *La Fayette* with a bomb hung up under its wing. Despite attempts to release it over the sea, Second Maître Trochon was eventually obliged to carry out a landing, luckily without the bomb falling off. Due to a faltering engine, Second Maître Pons pondered the possibility of ditching his 15F Flotille Corsair but was eventually able to reach *La Fayette* safely, much to the relief of the young French pilot. Cairo Radio reported later that the missing aircraft had been shot down by anti-aircraft fire and had crashed on the outskirts of Cairo. Lt deV Lancrenon, father of four young children, was reported to have been killed, and the wreckage of the Corsair was put on display in a Cairo square. There remains some mystery regarding Lancrenon's death, since an Italian naval attaché later advised French Admiral Nomy that the pilot had been captured alive but had been stoned by incensed civilians and had died of his injuries in an Egyptian gaol.

Gamil Bridge was the target for the six Wyverns of 830 Squadron which departed *Eagle* at 0720, and although the pilots of these were able to claim only near misses, they reported that the foundations of the bridge had been damaged. One of the bombs intended for the bridge hit and damaged a nearby radar station. However, Lt Dennis McCarthy's aircraft (WN330/379) was hit when in its bombing dive:

> "I got rid of the bombs as quickly as I could and levelled out, heading out to sea. I lost about 200 knots coming out of the dive – it was like hitting a brick wall."

Smoke began to fill the cockpit and McCarthy felt a wave of heat down his legs. He flew out to sea for about three miles before successfully ejecting. Whilst floating in his dinghy with the remainder of the Flight circling above, he was

Lt Dennis McCarthy of 830 Squadron (second from left) on arrival aboard HMS *Eagle* immediately after his rescue from the sea by a Whirlwind flown by Lt Cdr Pete Bailey (third from right). (*Authors' collection*)

shelled by shore batteries, although these were soon dealt with by Sea Hawks. Sections of aircraft were despatched to provide protection over the downed pilot until, some 75 minutes later at 1030, rescue arrived in the form of Whirlwind XG581/973 from *Eagle*, flown by Lt Cdr Pete Bailey, who had created a record by flying 100 miles to make the recovery. A damp and bedraggled but happy McCarthy was soon reunited with his colleagues aboard *Eagle*.

The bridge was attacked again at 1000 by five Sea Hawks of 897 Squadron, again led by Lt Cdr Rawbone (XE367/197), armed with 500lb bombs, three of which were seen to explode on the western end of the structure, causing a segment of the road to collapse. Lt Mills (XE379) wrote:

> "The next trip was to Gamil Bridge. It is a few miles west of the town and was the easiest route to bring in reinforcements. It therefore had to be destroyed before the landing to isolate the garrison. I am ashamed to say that we made a low-level bombing attack on the bridge and I missed."

The Wyverns were back at 1030, six aircraft bombing from low level, one bomb scoring a direct hit although the others missed. Attacks continued during the afternoon; four Wyverns bombed at 1515 and the pilots reported one hit. Then eight Sea Hawks of 899 Squadron struck at dusk. Following their attack, Lt Cdr Clark (XE383/491) was able to report "one third of the bridge, from the west end, destroyed". He recalled:

"After two days of strikes on airfields, I found that I had a Squadron with nothing to do. I had heard that a lot of effort was being put into trying to destroy Gamil Bridge so that the paratroops could go in. To take an interest, I sat in on the briefing of another squadron (Wyverns, I think). They were told that Gamil Bridge was a swing bridge and they were to dive-bomb with 500lb or 1,000lb bombs. Looking to the rather poor photograph provided with a powerful magnifying glass, I could see that it was not a swing bridge but a massive causeway built of stone blocks similar to the pyramids, with a road and railway on top. I could just make out some tunnels under the structure and decided there must be sluice gates operated by a winch mounted on the rail track. Dive-bombing had been going on for sometime and without any joy. I suggested to the Command that they were wasting their time (popular boy!) and requested permission to attempt to put some 500lb bombs (20-seconds' delay, tailed fused) either into or up against these tunnels.

This was agreed and I took eight aircraft, each with two bombs. I led the first flight of four in at very low level from inshore. They were in tight formation. Sighting was by guesswork. I merely said '3–2–1–now' and we then pulled up quite sharpish. I saw some of the bombs bounce and they flew way out to sea. Twenty seconds seemed a very long time, but right on time a large section of the causeway took off, leaving a bloody great gap. I went ashore later and inspected the damage. I was impressed, but what impressed me most of all was just how poor our intelligence had been. After all, we built the ruddy thing!"

Sections of Sea Hawks from *Eagle* continued to search for targets along the Ismailia to Tel al-Kebir road during the late morning. During one such armed reconnaissance, four aircraft of 897 Squadron forced a convoy of lorries to disperse before encountering a tank, which was hit by a rocket. Another convoy of lorries was forced to scatter into the desert as the Sea Hawks swept by at low level. Lt Cdr Rawbone, who led the section in XE371/199, noted:

"Armed recce with rockets. Eight transports damaged or destroyed."

Two sections from 899 Squadron followed in their wake and these met four tanks lumbering along the road, two of which were left damaged. The attacks along the road continued into the afternoon and eight Sea Hawks from 897 Squadron destroyed three lorries during the first of these, although:

"Strike activity restricted due to numbers of refugees on the road, some of whom were mounted in military vehicles."

A later armed reconnaissance by four Sea Hawks from 899 Squadron resulted in the destruction of five lorries, with a further six damaged. An armoured vehicle was also reported damaged but a tank apparently escaped when attacked by rockets. *Bulwark* despatched two strikes against military vehicles during the afternoon, when several jeeps and lorries were rocketed and strafed, two troop carriers being left in flames. One section was led by 810 Squadron's Lt Cdr Lamb (in XE393/164, an 804 Squadron aircraft). A further three vehicles were set on fire at 1330 by another section of Sea Hawks. French rocket-armed Corsairs –

four each from *La Fayette* and *Arromanches* led by Lt deV Cremer of 14F Flotille – similarly hunted for targets along the Ismailia to Bilbeis road where a total of 11 lorries were claimed destroyed. After their return, mechanics found some of the aircraft had flown so low that earth and debris had entered the air scoop on the leading edge of the wing. Of these attacks, Lt Cdr Rawbone of 897 Squadron noted:

> "On one occasion, 897 Squadron attacked a column of tanks, armoured vehicles and soft-skinned vehicles retreating from the Canal towards Cairo. The Egyptians manning the column appeared to be a mixed bag of soldiers, some uniformed, some in Arab dress. We attacked the column and destroyed several transport; there was obvious panic and so little return fire that we wondered whether the Egyptians were able or capable of resistance. On return to the carrier we conveyed our unease to Admiral Power, who immediately stopped further action against such targets."

Meanwhile, *Eagle*'s Sea Venoms had also been active, four from each squadron having raided Almaza at midday, when two Furies were claimed destroyed and a third damaged. A Dakota was also strafed and damaged by the 892 Squadron section. Four Sea Hawks from *Bulwark* had visited the airfield shortly before when the pilots reported damage to two Spitfires seen. *Bulwark* sent a further strike against Almaza at 1410, eight Sea Hawks from 895 Squadron, the sections led by Lt Anson (WV796) and Lt Palmer, strafing a variety of probably already damaged aircraft and claimed damage to two Chipmunks, a Meteor, a Fury and a Harvard. Towards the end of the day, Sea Venoms from *Eagle* were launched for a dusk strike and the trio from 892 Squadron claimed damage to a MiG, a Meteor and a Dakota at Almaza, while the 893 Squadron quartet, led by Lt Cdr Henley in WW223/098, visited Cairo West where two Lancasters seen there were strafed. Of the continuing strikes against the near devastated and mainly abandoned airfields, Lt Neave, who piloted WW265/094 on this occasion, remembered:

> "My general recollection is that there was very little flak at high level and that, although it was quite intense over the target, it was not distracting. By the time we got to most targets, most of the aircraft on the ground were burnt out and we were left with gun emplacements, hangars and buildings to attack."

The Sea Venom attack was followed by another by eight Sea Hawks of 804 Squadron from *Bulwark*, whose pilots destroyed a MiG and damaged a Vampire, also strafing two AA positions. At 1600 Lt Cdr Morris-Jones (XE395/166) took off at the head of a section of Sea Hawks from 895 Squadron tasked to carry out a seaward reconnaissance in the Alexandria area. Only one merchant vessel, of about 4,000 tons, was sighted. Lt Cdr Morris-Jones recalled:

> "I was the only fully trained photographic pilot in the Fleet. So, if vital photos were needed, I was asked to take them.'

	Destroyed	Probables	Damaged
Claims for MiG-15s:			
HMS *Eagle*'s squadrons	0	0	1
HMS *Bulwark*'s squadrons	1	0	0
	1	0	1
Claims for other types:			
HMS *Eagle*'s squadrons	3	0	7
HMS *Bulwark*'s squadrons	0	0	11
	3	0	18

La Fayette's Corsairs flew 26 sorties during the day, 18 of these in a strike against Almaza airfield although no EAF aircraft were claimed during the attack.

The RAF's nocturnal bombers had the night off, although two Valiant/Canberra strikes (Raids 16 and 17) by the Malta Bomber Wing had been planned, one against the Egyptian coastal town of al-Agami and the other against Huckstep Camp, but both were abandoned due to the continuing bad weather at Malta and over the Mediterranean. However, one Allied aircraft did venture over Egypt – a leaflet-dropping Hastings. Two Noratlases and two Hastings had been detailed for leaflet dropping but the operation was cancelled at the last moment when it was learned of the cancellation of bomber operations, but not before the two Hastings had departed from Tymbou. A Meteor night fighter was scrambled after them and succeeded in recalling one but the other was not located. The crew of the 511 Squadron aircraft duly dropped half a million

Canberra T4 WT479 of RAF Upwood Station Flight at Nicosia, used as a high speed courier aircraft. (*M. Freestone via Andy Thomas*)

leaflets over Port Said and Cairo, urging the Egyptian population to accept Allied proposals and, by implication, to overthrow President Nasser. No opposition was encountered and the aircraft returned safely.

Shortly after 0400 on the morning of 4 November, a Canberra touched down at Nicosia airfield following the long flight from London. On board was Mr Anthony Head, Minister of Defence, and General Sir Gerald Templar, Chief of the Imperial General Staff. They brought with them confirmation of America's stand against the Anglo-French venture. As it was therefore inevitable that pressure would soon be applied on Britain and France to cease hostilities, plans for the landings were implemented with all haste.

At just about the time the Canberra touched down at Akrotiri, Soviet tanks suddenly rolled into the Hungarian capital of Budapest. President Nagy was deposed and a new communist government under János Kádár was proclaimed. This made a number of seemingly conciliatory promises to the people but the bulk of the Hungarian population was not convinced. Fighting had already started and now spread widely. Like the Egyptians, the Hungarians were not prepared to take the invasion and occupation of their country lying down. Both were hopelessly outmatched on the battlefield but, unlike the Egyptians, the Hungarians faced a far more ruthless foe. Their revolution was crushed, though savage fighting was to last almost two weeks and a subsequent general strike even longer. In Egypt events unfolded in an entirely different manner.

Chapter Thirteen

PREPARING FOR THE AIRBORNE ASSAULT
4 November 1956

"The British Lion has tried to roar, but everyone can see that it has got no teeth, and now the Egyptians are going to cut its tail off."

Soviet Secretary-General Khrushchev to
Egyptian Ambassador Mohamed al-Kouni

Heavy British and French air strikes paved the way for the ground assault. Allied jets maintained their interdiction of airfields and the EAF lost a number of aircraft during the day to these raids.

AKROTIRI STRIKE WING

6 Squadron flew three operations during the morning, but only 11 sorties because one aircraft was unable to raise its undercarriage after take-off. The first section flew to Abu Sueir where, at 0635, a MiG and two fuel bowsers were destroyed, and followed this with the destruction of a Vampire trainer at Fayid. Four Venoms of 249 Squadron followed shortly after, when Flg Off Moyes (WR507/S) destroyed four MiGs by cannon fire, and another was claimed by Flt Lt Slade (WR420/T) and his section. Two fuel bowsers, trucks and hangars were also strafed. However, only one MiG appears to have been credited to the Squadron on this occasion.

The second 6 Squadron section was tasked with attacking radar installations near Gamil airfield, where two scanners were destroyed at 0805 and a third damaged, while huts and light anti-aircraft emplacements were strafed. Four flights of F-84Fs also concentrated their attacks on the radar installations around Gamil during the morning, when they used rockets to demolish scanners and associated buildings. Meanwhile, Sqn Ldr Blyth (WR480) of 8 Squadron led a rocket strike against gun emplacements at al-Raswa shortly after 0830, during which Flg Off Hadlow (WR432/R) lost his starboard tip tank, although he was not aware until he landed back at Akrotiri:

> "The R/P and cannon strike was straightforward. However, on climbing away I discovered that my starboard wing tip fuel tank was missing. This reduced my fuel available and I only just made it back to Akrotiri. Had we been operating further south I should have required the Air-Sea Rescue services south of base! On inspection of the tip tank area, it was found that

a small piece of shrapnel had entered the bottom of the wing and triggered the tip tank release mechanism; a freak occurrence."

Other sections from 8 Squadron flew armed reconnaissances in the Canal Zone area, where military vehicles were attacked, one section led by Flt Lt Harcourt-Smith in WR488. Another section included Flg Off von Berg (WR501) on an armed recce over the Canal:

"They tried to conceal their equipment from us and the [three] soft-skinned vehicles I destroyed were parked under palm trees by the Sweetwater Canal. I remember a distinctly South African voice on our common natter frequency say, 'I can see a tank, a bloody great tank, and its got a bloody great gun on it!' I hit them with squash-head rockets which we were supposed to use on tanks, but as they restricted our performance for the return to Cyprus we had to get rid of them at the end of our time over the target area."

Flg Off Nick von Berg in the cockpit of his 8 Squadron Venom FB4 at Akrotiri. (*Andy Thomas*)

6 Squadron despatched another section at 1115, the pilots briefed to fly a long-range operation to destroy vehicles and tanks in an army camp a few miles south-east of the Giza Pyramids, topped up their fuel tanks at the end of the runway before take-off, but the mission was not particularly successful. On arrival over the target area at 1209 – which had 25 minutes earlier been visited by a section of F-84Fs – the section leader was unable to fire his rockets and his No2 failed to locate the tanks which had tents erected around them. The other pair misjudged their pull-up point and failed to release their rockets, so instead strafed a number of SSVs, meeting light but accurate anti-aircraft fire.

SUMMARY OF SORTIES FLOWN BY VENOMS and F-84Fs by midday			
ETA Target	Target	Aircraft	Claims
0635	Abu Sueir Fayid Deversoir	4 Venom	MiG destroyed, 2 bowsers destroyed at Abu Sueir; Vampire destroyed at Fayid
0650	Abu Sueir Fayid	4 Venom	5 MiGs destroyed at Abu Sueir; 2 bowsers destroyed, vehicle destroyed

ETA Target	Target	Aircraft	Claims
0650	Gamil	4 F-84F	Destroyed radar scanners north and south-east of Gamil with rockets
0655	Gamil	4 F-84F	Destroyed radar scanners north and south of Gamil with rockets
0705	Kabrit Kasfareet	4 Venom	MiG destroyed at Kasfareet, 2 bowsers destroyed, hangar damaged
0805	al-Raswa	4 Venom	2 radar scanners destroyed
0835	al-Raswa	4 Venom	Rocket attack on AA site
0845	al-Raswa	4 Venom	20mm attack on AA site
0850	Gamil	4 F-84F	Destroyed radar scanner south-east of Gamil with rockets
0900	Gamil	4 F-84F	Damaged radar scanners near Gamil
1121	Port Said	3 F-84F	Attacked tented camp and vehicle park: tank, 2 radar vehicles and AA battery destroyed; 9 vehicles damaged
1145	Giza	4 F-84F	Attacked 100 vehicles south-east of the Pyramids
1200	Giza	4 Venom	Attacked 50 vehicles south-east of the Pyramids
1209	Giza	4 Venom	Attacked 100 vehicles south-east of the Pyramids

Huckstep Camp was on the receiving end of further attacks by both RAF and French fighter-bombers during the afternoon. The section from 249 Squadron led by Flt Lt Syme (WR531/R) claimed damage to a tank and three or four trucks before three of his guns stopped. 6 Squadron also put up a section at this time and the four Venoms attacked armoured vehicles, probably including tanks, which were covered by tarpaulin. F-84Fs had been there shortly before the arrival of the Venoms, and the target area was covered with smoke, some flames being visible. It was therefore not possible for the Venom pilots to make any definite claims. Light but accurate anti-aircraft fire from the northerly limit of the depot hit Venom WR443/Y in the starboard wing and port tip tank.

The day's final sorties were armed reconnaissances by both Venoms and F-84Fs over the Port Said area where military vehicles were strafed, including half-tracks and a small convoy of jeeps. The Venoms were led by Sqn Ldr Maitland (WR499/V) of 249 Squadron. Anti-aircraft guns at Port Said were also attacked. Flg Off Williams (WR497/B) attacked a three-ton truck during the sortie. The other two Venoms, WR531/R and WR375, both sustained minor damage, the latter returning with a small hole in the cockpit canopy. Neither pilot was hurt.

281

In flight profile of F-84F (1-NK, s/n 28914) of EC1/1 its s/n partly obliterated by the application of Suez stripes. (*Jacques Lebourg via Albert Grandolini*)

SUMMARY OF SORTIES FLOWN BY VENOMS and F-84Fs, 1200–1730

ETA Target	Target	Aircraft	Claims
1320	Huckstep	4 Venom	20 SSVs destroyed, 5 cars severely damaged
1330	Huckstep	3 F-84F	Rocket and strafing attack on vehicles
1410	Huckstep	4 Venom	Rocket and strafing attack on vehicles
1430	Port Said	4 Venom	Armed recce: SSV attacked and Ismailia left in flames, second damaged
1521	Huckstep	4 F-84F	Rocket and strafing attack on vehicles
1600	Huckstep	4 F-84F	Rocket and strafing attack on vehicles
1630	Port Said	4 F-84F	Armed recce: rocket and Ismailia strafing attacks on military vehicles
1640	Fayid Kabrit	4 Venom	Armed recce: no attacks made
1645	Port Said Ismailia Abu Sueir	3 F-84F	Armed recce: half-track destroyed, 3 jeeps damaged
1645	Port Said Ismailia Abu Sueir	4 Venom	Armed recce: half-track destroyed, 3 jeeps damaged; installations near Ismailia rocketed

Of the intensive campaign against ground targets, 6 Squadron's Flt Lt Harrison recorded:

"All Squadron pilots took part in the daily operations and morale was justifiably high among both air and ground crews when the results came in. A special word of praise must be said for the keenness of the maintenance staff. As soon as an aircraft landed it was inspected for damage caused by enemy flak or from debris thrown up by rockets. Then work began on the servicing, with such enthusiasm that it was difficult to persuade the airmen to take adequate sleep and meals. On a few occasions in the early days, airmen who had been sent away to sleep were found to have crept back to work after a hasty snack in the airmen's mess."

SUMMARY OF GROUND ATTACK CLAIMS AGAINST AIRCRAFT OF THE EGYPTIAN AIR FORCE by the Akrotiri Strike Wing, 4 November 1956

Missions: Venoms 13 F-84Fs 10
Sorties: Venoms 48 (3 aborts) F-84Fs 40 (3 aborts)

	Destroyed	Probables	Damaged
Claims for MiG-15s:			
by Venoms:	2	0	0
by F-84Fs:	0	0	0
Claims for other types:			
by Venoms:	1	0	0
by F-84Fs	0	0	0
	3	0	0

Canberra PR7s of 13 Squadron flew a further seven reconnaissance sorties, including one by WH801 piloted by Grp Capt Macdonald, Station Commander at Akrotiri, and another (WT540 flown by Sqn Ldr Field) in which Wg Cdr Button was on board as an observer; ER4/33's RF-84Fs recorded nine sorties. One of these was flown by Lt Bertin-Maghit in RF335 who had been briefed to photograph Huckstep at 1145. His subsequent pictures revealed probable damage to 90 of the 120 tanks seen, with about one third of the 500 lorries present also damaged. In addition, a dozen gun carriers showed signs of damage, while ten hangars and two ammunition depots had been destroyed. All aircraft returned safely from these sorties.

CARRIER STRIKE FORCE
During the early morning hours *Albion* returned to station, having refuelled, while *Eagle* and the two French carriers withdrew for replenishment. The break from continuous operations gave *Eagle*'s crew the opportunity to carry out repairs to the carrier's starboard catapult, while aircraft losses were made good. 830 Squadron's Lt George Barras and Sub Lt Peter McKern were flown in Skyraiders to the RAF base at El Adem (Libya), where they collected two replacement Wyverns, as was Lt Cdr William Ferguson of 892 Squadron who returned in replacement Sea Venom WW277/447. All three carriers returned to their stations that night refuelled, restocked and ready for action.

Sea Hawk WN118/137 of 802 Squadron, Flt Lt Black's usual aircraft. (*Air Vice-Marshal G.P. Black*)

The first strike of the day was launched by *Bulwark* at 0512, when eight rocket-armed Sea Hawks of 895 Squadron led by Lt Cdr Morris-Jones (XE396/167) attacked six-inch gun emplacements at Port Fuad. On the way to the target two low-flying swept-wing fighters had been seen, which were believed to have been American FJ-3 Furies, but there was no contact. Fifteen minutes later *Bulwark* launched a further eight Sea Hawks, flown by 804 Squadron pilots, which flew to Almaza, where three hangars were hit and set on fire. Within minutes, a further nine Sea Hawks from *Albion* arrived, the pilots from 800 and 802 Squadrons observing a burning hangar from *Bulwark*'s strikes. Hangars south-east of the airfield were targeted, where the north hangar received a direct hit and burst into flames, while the middle hangar of another three also burst into flames from a direct hit. Lt Cdr Eveleigh (WN109/139) reported damage to two hangars and the control tower, while Lt Cdr Tibby (XE435/104) of 800 Squadron recalled:

> "This time we had 500lb bombs and gained two hits on a hangar. As a general rule we operated in Flights of four, and each target was allocated to a Flight. Normally we retained the same four if at all possible; we tried to keep the same team together because we had worked up as a team. My normal Flight comprised Lt Don Richardson, Sub Lt Brian Day and Sub Lt Tony Rowed."

During the return flight, the Sea Hawks of 802 Squadron overflew Cairo International, partly obscured by smoke, where four civil aircraft were seen, but not attacked. Within the hour, a further section of 802 Squadron Sea Hawks, accompanied by three Sea Venoms of 809 Squadron (including Sub Lts Yates and Dwarika in XG677/221), revisited Cairo International where a damaged Meteor observed on the airfield was strafed; an overshot Vampire was seen on its nose at the end of Runway 23. The pilots reported sighting a number of transport-type aircraft parked on the south side of the airfield although these were not attacked. Two Sea Hawks from 802 Squadron flew photo-reconnaissance sorties to Almaza and Cairo International at 0930, protected by two others flying top cover, the section led by Lt Cdr Eveleigh (WM996/135). At the former airfield the hangars were still burning from the earlier attacks, while at the latter only civil aircraft were to be seen.

At 0700 two sections of 809 Squadron Sea Venoms were launched from *Albion* to investigate reports that Egyptian Navy MTBs had possibly penetrated the destroyer screen, as recalled by Lt Wigg (flying XG663/227, with Lt Bowman):

"I was on readiness in my aircraft, on the booster, when the order to launch came through. We were given a course to steer and told to investigate unidentified surface vessels. The day was gin clear, with just a few fog banks dotted about. Eddie Bowman found the blips on his radar scope after only a few minutes and shortly after that we had visual contact. There were three of them, long slim shapes, moving at fairly slow speed in the general direction of the Fleet. They were spread out in a wide line abreast formation, a good three quarters of a mile apart. We were armed with cannon only, which meant getting close to the target for full effect. On the first run in along the length of my target, I could make out a very brave gunner standing fully exposed behind a mounted cannon, puffs of smoke coming out of his gun, and then the boat took evasive action, turning so as to expose her flank, so giving us, in effect, a smaller target to shoot at. Both I and my wingman got some shots home and the boat disappeared in a cloud of spray from the under and over shots. When I looked back she was turning in a crazy arc with smoke trailing behind her."

Lt Cdr Shilcock was leading the second section, flying XG670/220 with Lt Hackett as his observer. Lt Wigg continued:

"I could hear him [Lt Cdr Shilcock] on the radio talking to his No2. His target was also on fire and heading for one of the fog banks we had noted earlier. We saw it disappear into the fog with its mast sticking out the top – that's how shallow the fog banks were. And then the fog bank seemed to erupt, black smoke billowing out of it."

The Sea Venoms were soon joined by two Sea Hawks from *Bulwark*, two of 804 Squadron flown by Lt Cdr Kettle and Lt Hamilton, two from 810 Squadron, armed with rockets, and two from 895 Squadron. Lt Hoddinott, flying one of the 810 Squadron aircraft, XE393/164, recalled:

"On arrival at the identified position, three E boats were sighted. I fired 60lb SAP rockets at one but missed. This was followed by strafing with cannon fire which hit the target. At the point of impact, my guns jammed and I returned to *Bulwark*. Later reconnaissance confirmed that the boat had been disabled."

WV972/462 of 895 Squadron was flown by Lt Anson:

"We were warned of three MTBs and there was a mad scramble to get the first aircraft on the flight deck. On arrival there was low fog and one MTB

Lt Graham Hoddinott of 810 Squadron; stills from his gun camera show the Egyptian MTB attacked on 4 November 1956. (*Lt Cdr G.B. Hoddinott*)

had already been attacked and had blown up (probably the victim of 809 Squadron's attack). I could see the wake of another but due to the fog could not see the actual boat, so attacked with the fixed cross of the gunsight just ahead of the wake. A pilot of 810 Squadron was flying above and could see the MTB, so called fall of shot, so to speak. My guns jammed at the bottom of the firing run and, as I fiddled with the on/off switch, I entered the fog. When I pulled out over the sea below the fog bank, I realised I was alongside the MTB, which was on fire, and later blew up. The third MTB had been damaged and other aircraft were on their way to finish it off, but the Captain of *Bulwark* ordered that it should be allowed to pick up survivors and return to its base, to serve as a warning to others not to venture out to sea."

During this action, the American carrier USS *Coral Sea* passed through *Bulwark*'s screen and operated its own aircraft within the screen, before retiring to the north-west. The Egyptians claimed later that the MTBs had attacked an enemy destroyer near Lake Burullos, and had left it sinking, before the British fighters had forced them to break away; and that the destroyer's logbook, several bodies and debris had been washed up on the coast.

Lt Cdr Morris-Jones was requested to obtain photographs of Port Said and he departed at 0830 in XE396/167, with an escort provided by three other Sea Hawks of 895 Squadron. Both vertical and obliques were secured from 10,000 feet, the Canal apparently devoid of any shipping. Half an hour earlier, at 0800, two sections of Sea Hawks – four each from 800 and 802 Squadrons – were launched by *Albion*, their pilots tasked to bomb the gun battery at Port Said, which had been rocketed an hour earlier by eight Sea Hawks from *Bulwark*. All aircraft returned safely. *Albion*'s pilots claimed that the west battery had been destroyed, and the east battery damaged, although Lt Cdr Tibby, leading the 800 Squadron section, noted that he had missed the target on this occasion. *Bulwark* launched further strikes against the Port Said guns at 0740 (four aircraft), 0950 (four aircraft), 1055 (eight aircraft), noon (seven aircraft) and 1305 (eight aircraft), 1410 (four aircraft), 1515 (four aircraft) and 1620 (four aircraft), two of the strikes led by 810 Squadron's Lt Cdr Lamb and two by Lt Anson of 895 Squadron; *Albion* despatched Sea Hawks at 1115 (eight aircraft) and 1220 (six aircraft) although these were not successful, while five Sea Hawks which struck at 1500 claimed a radar aerial damaged and two huts left burning. By the end of the day the two six-inch main battery guns, plus two twin-barrelled six-pounders – one on each breakwater – and various light anti-aircraft guns had been rendered inoperable, as had their radars. All Sea Hawks returned safely from these operations.

Albion launched eight Sea Hawks at 1325, the pilots briefed to strike at military vehicles and a tented camp near Almaza seen by an earlier section. Heavy flak was encountered during the strafing attack and two of the four Sea Hawks of the 800 Squadron sustained damage: XE455/100 flown by Lt Don Richardson returned with a 20mm shell hole through the starboard intake duct which had torn the lower and upper wing surfaces (the second time in three days that XE455 had suffered damage), while Lt John Stuart-Jervis's XE454/101 suffered a small hole through one wing. A third aircraft of this section, XE438/105, believed flown by Sub Lt Brian Day (Lt Richardson's usual No2), had been overstressed and its stub planes were wrinkled beyond the acceptable limits. The remaining Sea Hawk, XE411/108, flown by the flight leader,

Lt Worth, did not escape damage:

> "As we departed at low level and high speed, a flock of birds, startled by
> the flak, suddenly appeared in front of us out of a copse of trees. I got the
> full impact which also removed the nose cones of both drop tanks, producing
> a superb air brake!"

As *Albion*'s aircraft returned to the carrier, they were passed by a section of
three rocket-armed Sea Hawks from *Bulwark* heading for Cairo West, where
the pilots found four apparently undamaged aircraft – a Vampire, a Meteor and
two C-46s – which were attacked and claimed destroyed.

Mid-afternoon saw 802 Squadron despatch two of its camera-equipped Sea
Hawks, with two others flying top cover, to photograph Alexandria Harbour,
where three destroyers were seen berthed. Three 40mm anti-aircraft guns were
observed and these opened fire with determined and accurate bursts though
none of the aircraft was hit. On their return, the pilots reported nets and blockships in place at the harbour entrance.

**SUMMARY OF GROUND ATTACK CLAIMS AGAINST AIRCRAFT OF
THE EGYPTIAN AIR FORCE by the Fleet Air Arm, 4 November 1956**

	Destroyed	Probables	Damaged
Claims for MiG-15s:			
HMS *Albion*'s squadrons	0	0	0
HMS *Bulwark*'s squadrons	0	0	0
	0	0	0
Claims for other types:			
HMS *Albion*'s squadrons	1	0	0
HMS *Bulwark*'s squadrons	4	0	0
	5	0	0

As the Anglo-French invasion fleet from Malta and Algeria approached the
Egyptian coastline in preparation for the landings on the morrow, HMS *Tyne*
departed Limassol Harbour (Cyprus) at 1300 with the Task Force Commanders
embarked, the cruiser having been designated as the HQ ship for the operation.
The two helicopter carriers *Theseus* and *Ocean*, in which were embarked large
numbers of assault troops including 45 Royal Marine Commando, had departed
Malta during the forenoon of the previous day. Activity aboard both carriers
was intense. Even at the eleventh hour helicopter training continued, 845
Squadron having been loaned two pilots by the Joint Helicopter Unit aboard
Ocean – Capt J.F.B. Shaw of the RASC and Flt Lt James Stuart – who found
it necessary to undertake familiarisation flights in the Whirlwind HAS22s with
which 845 Squadron was equipped, while pilots carried out small-arms training
in preparation for the assault. Capt Shaw, an Army officer, had previously flown
Auster AOP aircraft on anti-terrorist operations in Malaya, followed by a spell
with an AOP Flight during the Korean War.

As the Task Force approached the Egyptian coast to take up station, so the

US Sixth Fleet withdrew to the north-west. In the meantime, however, the softening-up process of Egyptian defences continued unabated during the evening.

PLAN OF ATTACK
Malta Bomber Wing/Cyprus Bomber Wing, 4/5 November 1956

RAID 18 – Target: al-AGAMI

From Cyprus
4 Canberra B2s of 18 Squadron (Markers)

From Malta
5 Valiant B1s of 207 Squadron   One returned early
2 Valiant B1s of 214 Squadron
5 Canberra B2s of 12 Squadron
4 Canberra B6s of 109 Squadron

RAID 19 – Target: HUCKSTEP CAMP

From Cyprus
4 Canberra B6s of 139 Squadron (Markers)

From Malta
5 Valiant B1s of 148 Squadron
1 Valiant B1 of 214 Squadron
7 Canberra B6s of 101 Squadron
2 Canberra B6s of 9 Squadron
2 Canberra B6s of 109 Squadron
1 Canberra B6 of 12 Squadron

At 1645, seven Valiants from Malta – five from 207 Squadron led by Sqn Ldr F.C.D. Wright DFC in XD813 (although one of the latter, WP219 flown by Flg Off H.C. Richford DFC, had to return early with undercarriage problems), together with two from 214 Squadron and nine Canberras (five from 12 Squadron and four from 109 Squadron) struck at the coastal gun emplacements at al-Agami, just west of Alexandria. There they met intense anti-aircraft fire, having been preceded by four 18 Squadron marker Canberras from Cyprus, although none of the attacking aircraft was damaged. The purpose of the attack against al-Agami was to lead the Egyptians to believe that the Anglo-French amphibious landing would be near Alexandria. However, it was not a success. Although the Target Indicators were dropped on land they bounced into the sea and were soon extinguished, thus preventing the majority of aircraft from bombing.

An hour later, a further dozen Canberras (seven from 101 Squadron, two each from 9 and 109 Squadrons, and one from 12 Squadron) together with five Valiants of 148 Squadron and one from 214 Squadron raided Huckstep Camp, the target having been marked by four 139 Squadron Canberras from Cyprus. Sqn Ldr Woods of 148 Squadron (XD815) recalled:

"Target Huckstep Barracks, halfway between Ismailia and Cairo, where Egyptian Army tanks and other vehicles were stored, as well as oil and

Back from Egypt. Sqn Ldr B. Moorcroft, navigator CO of 101 Squadron, holds a press conference at AHQ Malta; on his right is Flg Off B.S. Bull (his pilot) and on his left Flt Lt T.D.W. Manley, navigator/plotter. (*Air Clues*)

ammunition dumps. Some bombs fitted with proximity fuses to detonate a few feet above the ground for greater destructive power against vehicles. XD815 returned with eight bombs which had not released – greater fuel consumption noticed on return flight although no danger of running out."

The Canberra formation was led to Egypt by the navigator CO of 101 Squadron, Sqn Ldr Moorcroft, who reported:

"Cairo, some miles away from our target, was fully blacked out and all the lights we could see came from Alexandria, the only unblacked-out place in the whole area, as far as we could see. Bombing was accurate. On our way back we ran into some pretty bad thunderstorms – it was rather a long trip, about 2,000 miles."

His pilot, Flg Off B.S. Bull AFM, flying WH948, added:

"We met some light flak. There was a gigantic explosion in the target area and, in its light, I could see the contrails of what I took to be a Valiant four-jet bomber far above us."

On the return flight to Malta, Flg Off J. Hart discovered his aircraft (WJ864 of 101 Squadron) to be short of oxygen, so he diverted to El Adem to replenish supplies before continuing to Malta. There were no further bombing attacks from Malta during the night, nor would there be any on the following nights. Political pressure effectively curtailed the bombing campaign, although a number of sorties were still to be flown by the Cyprus-based Canberras. Of the night's operation, Sqn Ldr Scott, Senior Controller at Luqa, wrote:

"The final night operational recovery is worth special mention. If all the emergencies reported during the marshalling phase had persisted, the recovery might well have proved an extremely difficult task. However, in the event, aircraft with no brake pressure found sources of supply during the let-down, and three green lights on Canberras were obtained in record time by overworked navigators using hand pumps. To add to all these incidents the first aircraft to land at Luqa burst its nosewheel tyre on landing; the pilot drove the aircraft under power clear of the edge of the runway. The third aircraft also burst a tyre – a main wheel this time – but was able to taxi clear in time for the next aircraft to land. Eventually, thanks to a truly inter-Service combined effort, all the aircraft were safely gathered in."

Chapter Fourteen

FIREWORKS OVER GAMIL – THE AIRBORNE INVASION
5 November 1956

"If enemy air opposition had been effective and had disrupted our plans, there is no doubt that communications would have been hopelessly inadequate."

Air Marshal Denis Barnett, Air Task Force Commander

For the airborne invasion of the Port Said area, 668 men of the 3rd Battalion Parachute Regiment and the 16th Parachute Brigade Tactical Group, commanded by Brigadier Mervyn Butler DSO MC, had been assembled at Nicosia, together with 492 French paratroops of the 2e Regiment Parachutistes Coloniaux at Tymbou, under the overall command of Général Jean Gilles, tasked to drop near the Interior Basin south of Port Said. The codename chosen for the airborne invasion was *Operation Telescope*. Venoms and F-84Fs from Akrotiri were to provide continuous air cover for the paratroopers throughout the day, as were fighters from the carriers. Although all appeared to be going according to plan, in reality there was much confusion and lack of communication. In his subsequent report of proceedings, Admiral Power, commander of the Carrier Task Force, wrote:

"The directive for D+5 ordered priority support for *Operation Telescope* [the airborne assault]. The name and nature of this operation were unknown to me. An aircraft had been sent to Akrotiri to collect important correspondence, however, and it was thought that this might give a clue as to what *Telescope* was. The correspondence arrived in *Albion* after dark [on the evening of the 4th]. By means of non-committal briefing on the Inter-Carrier Briefing wave, the Captain of *Albion* [Capt R.M. Smeeton MBE] was instructed to discover whether any light could be shed on *Telescope*: on opening the envelopes he discovered four copies of the operation order. *Albion* was instructed to deliver copies to *Eagle* and *Bulwark* by helicopter. It was not possible to get a copy to the French Carrier Task Unit, who were briefed on the Inter-Daily Orders' circuit."

Thus belatedly informed, Admiral Power immediately set in motion the necessary arrangements to implement *Operation Telescope*, which called for, as far as the carriers were concerned, all possible direct support to the landings and for subsequent operations to ensure the maintenance of air supremacy. British aircraft were to support the landing at Gamil and French aircraft the landing south of Port Said. Continuous air alert sorties were to be flown throughout the day and a staggered operating cycle was to be employed, whereby a Cabrank of at least a dozen aircraft were to be instantly available to the Forward Air Controllers (FAC) at Gamil, and six Corsairs were to be similarly constantly on call to assist the French paratroops. During the night the Carrier Task Force sailed east to a position some 40 to 50 miles north of Port Said.

The actual paratroop assaults were to be led respectively by Lt Colonel Paul Crook of the 3rd Battalion and Colonel Pierre Château-Jobert of the French paras. The aircraft available to transport the British force to Gamil airfield, on the outskirts of Port Said, were the Hastings and Valettas of the Transport Air Task Force, neither type ideally suited for the task, whereas the French Noratlas was specifically designed for paratrooping duties and could carry 35 fully armed men, as against 30 for the Hastings and 20 for the Valetta. Of the moment Ray Bellm, a journalist with the *Cyprus Mail*, wrote:

Hastings C2 WJ328 of 70 Squadron at Nicosia. (*Andy Thomas*)

"Around the tarmac ghostly shapes moved in the darkness. Alongside each plane I picked out the forms of crash-helmeted, parachute-lugging troopers receiving the last equipment check. NCOs passed down the ranks, feeling the harness of their chutes and the quick-release gear. Under the bellies of the four-engined Hastings were slung jeeps and artillery-holding canisters. The crews [wearing flak jackets] joked among themselves, confident of the success of the mission. Had not their jet-flying comrades swept the EAF from the skies and crippled it on the ground? Aircraft engines roared suddenly into life and a great cloud of sand was blown into the night sky, framing the parade as it taxied in line astern towards the take-off runway. In two hours the human loads would kick up the sand of Suez. I waved my salute."

First off at 0500 were 18 Valettas – a dozen from 30 and 84 Squadrons following six from 114 Squadron (including VW811 flown by an 84 Squadron crew with Grp Capt Avion Case, OC Nicosia, on board as an observer) – these setting course for Gamil in three flights of six, the first pair flying at 600 feet followed by the others of the formation at intervals of 15 seconds. They were followed by nine Hastings (three each from 70, 99 and 511 Squadrons), five carrying underslung loads of heavy equipment. The slow and vulnerable transports were escorted by Hunters from both 1 and 34 Squadrons, which flew a defensive sweep ahead of the air armada. Grp Capt Brian Macnamara DSO, the Transport Air Task Force commander and former Battle of Britain pilot, flew as co-pilot in the leading Valetta, VW817 captained by Sqn Ldr Delany, the Commanding Officer:

> "We made an impressive stream taking off at five a.m. and flew to Damietta, the point where we formed up in the darkness. Then we flew along the coast until we got to the airfield."

Meanwhile, Venoms from Akrotiri strafed targets on and close to the airfield, including guns sited on the Mole at Port Said. 249 Squadron flew eight flak suppression sorties before the arrival of the transports, one section led by Sqn Ldr Maitland who recalled:

> "When strafing Egyptian vehicles I buzzed them first to allow the occupants to escape. I had no argument with the Egyptians."

The remarkable lack of personal bitterness often seen on the British side during the Suez War was also reflected on the Egyptian side.* Flg Off Lecky-Thompson (WR533/F) remembered:

> "The locals had got used to us only firing if they had abandoned their vehicles, so they were very stubborn and only when we took off the front wheels of the transports did they stop and run. I also remember going for tanks at very low level – 20 feet or so – so that we could go at the tracks from very close range. These early dawn (and dusk) strikes showed where the ricochet damage was flying: it was like a peacock array of feathers, the flashes curving up and away, whilst those that went horizontally had gone to earth before we got to the target; thus the safest escape route was to dip a wing and go down the side of the target, rather than pull up."

During this sortie Lecky-Thompson claimed the destruction by cannon fire of an armoured troop carrier, two three-ton lorries and a Land Rover, plus damage to a tank, a scout car and another Land Rover. Flt Lt Dallison's section also flew to the Port Said area, as did that led by Flt Lt Slade (WR420/T) who noted that a number of vehicles were destroyed including a tank and two bowsers; the sections included Flg Off Moyes (WR504/Z) and Flg Off Gronert (WR497/B), who recalled:

> "We took off before dawn and arrived in the target area at first light. There

---

* In 1971, during the height of the War of Attrition between Egyptian and Israeli forces along the Suez Canal, one of the authors, David Nicolle, was introduced to a young Egyptian teacher who promptly shook his hand and said: "Hello, my father commanded a tank in 1956. He was killed by an English aircraft. How do you do, would you like some tea?"

were a couple of smallish guns there, which were taken out without any trouble, and we did a sweep along the beach. I had not had the opportunity to fire my rockets due to the fact that there were no targets in the vicinity, so I brought them home with me. When we arrived back at base the ground crew found that my aircraft had been hit by small-arms fire, and they gave me a piece of shrapnel taken from near my right foot. They also found that the electric cable to my rockets had been severed by a bullet, so I could not have fired the rockets even if I had wanted to. [Flg Off] Bill Barker, my No2, told me later that he had noticed an Egyptian soldier firing what appeared to be a Bren gun from the hip, on the shore near Port Said. I would have been very cross had he shot me down."

The 249 Squadron sections did not escape unscathed. Apart from WR497/B two further Venoms returned to Akrotiri with minor damage from the morning sorties: WR507/S with a hole in its engine cowling, and WR412 with a damaged aileron. Meanwhile, Sqn Ldr Ellis similarly led a 6 Squadron section to Gamil. However, no military targets of significance could be seen, so airfield buildings were rocketed and strafed, including the control tower into which Sqn Ldr Ellis (Venom T) fired a salvo of rockets and set the building on fire. *Eagle* despatched a section of 897 Squadron Sea Hawks to carry out a reconnaissance of Gamil and Port Said, where the pilots reported RAF Venoms in action over the harbour area and were approached by two F-84Fs over Port Said. Due to their similarity to MiG-15s, the presence of the French fighters caused more than a little distraction. No movement of military vehicles was observed on the roads, although up to 100 stationary SSVs were seen.

Valetta C1 VW202/C of 84 Squadron over the Med en route to Egypt, 6 November 1956. (*Chris Thomas via Andy Thomas*)

As the transports approached Gamil, some two hours after their departure from Nicosia, two Canberras of 139 Squadron released marker flares over the Gamil DZ. Overhead the Hunters circled, ready to repel any interference by the EAF; however, no hostile aircraft were seen. The first troop-carrier to arrive over Gamil was Sqn Ldr Delany's 114 Squadron Valetta, which disgorged its human load without incident at 0715, followed by the others. Grp Capt Macnamara continued:

"It [the DZ] had been well marked by Canberras for us and we were able to do the drop, which was completely uneventful, without difficulty. There appeared to be some obstructions such as oil barrels on the airfield. There was no real opposition. Occasional shells could be seen dropping in the water. I don't know who they were directed at but they came nowhere near us. Towards the end there was a little light flak seen by some of the planes. I did not see any activity on the ground but there were flames and smoke coming from the control tower. The drop appeared to be compact and well concentrated."

One of the Valettas of 30 Squadron was flown by Polish-born Flt Lt Roman Andrusikiewicz DFC AFC, who reported:

"It was quite easy. We dropped the paratroops at 700 feet and as far as I knew all landed well. I didn't see any opposition, nor any sign of resistance on the ground. There were 20 men on my plane, fully equipped and armed with, among other weapons, mortars and bazookas."

Flt Lt A.J. Bell, a Hastings pilot of 99 Squadron, added:

"I thought it was an exceptionally good drop. That from my plane was made at 700 feet. There did not appear to be much, if any, opposition. Our fighters had really worked the airfield over, picking their targets. I think they clobbered them sufficiently to make them keep their heads down. We saw 60 to 70 soldiers running hard along the beach. They were going in the opposite direction – hard."

A section of Sea Venoms from 892 Squadron patrolled the DZ, as recalled by Lt Cdr Ferguson:

"The sight as the troop carriers came in over the Dropping Zone was very impressive. Our job was flak suppression during the landings over Gamil airfield. We attacked several strongpoints and then gave a few quick bursts at some soldiers coming towards the airfield. They made off smartly in the opposite direction."

Sections of Sea Hawks from the carriers were ready to attack ground targets, as Lt Cdr Eveleigh (WM996/135) of 802 Squadron recalled:

"We supported the paras as they dropped on Gamil airfield. I remember well their call-sign which was 'Bellyache'. We talked to their leader as they dropped, and he called us in to suppress the mortar fire which was coming from the cemetery on the airfield boundary. We took out the mortars and watched as the paras landed and spread out."

The Hunters circled above as the drop got under way. Leading the formation was Sqn Ldr Alistair Wilson, who told a reporter on his return to Cyprus:

"In our line of business we don't have time to notice much. But I was terribly impressed to see the shadows of the parachutes, thrown by the early morning

---

Hunter F5 WP130/S of 34 Squadron at Nicosia. (*Bruce Robertson via Andy Thomas*)

sun, gradually diminishing in size on the DZ as the paratroopers dropped lower and lower, until they landed smack in the middle of the airfield."

The Hunter pilots were keen to meet the anticipated aerial opposition to the armada, as recalled by Flt Lt Freddie Davis of 34 Squadron:

"All felt disappointed that there was no chance to try our Hunters against the MiGs, but relieved that the war was being contained as there had been a threat of a general conflagration throughout the Middle East. Also our relations with Israel, the US and Russia were not clear."

The main anti-aircraft defences had been subdued by the Venoms, although some light bursts of fire were experienced and five of the transports (four Hastings and one Valetta) suffered minor damage from shrapnel and machine-gun fire. TG621, flown by 70 Squadron's Commanding Officer, Sqn Ldr W.K. Greer AFC, received a .303 bullet in No1 engine plus shrapnel damage to the underside of the port mainplane and bullet damage to a tail spar, while Flg Off A.E.W. Waigh's TG612 sustained bullet holes in its starboard wing. A Hastings of 511 Squadron was slightly damaged, as was another from 99 Squadron, while a Valetta of 30 Squadron also suffered minor damage. One of those who 'dropped' over Gamil was Lt Sandy Cavenagh of 3 Para:

"At 600 feet, straight and level, the Valetta flew into the eye of the rising sun. Our ears strained for the pregnant revving of engines which precedes the green light. Against the overwhelming glare of the sun he [the pilot] was picking up the smoke flare which marked the dropping point. A low-flying Canberra bomber had dropped this a few minutes earlier. I was half expecting the Valetta to be hit by anti-aircraft fire. I had watched a number of aircraft trundling over Dropping Zones shedding their loads of parachutists."

As Cavenagh jumped, he was wounded in the right eye by a piece of shrapnel from a nearby flak burst but landed safely and was able to carry out his duties. The 99 Squadron Hastings (WD497) flown by Flt Lt J.A. King DSO DFC suffered engine problems en route and had fallen behind the main stream but, nevertheless, by skilful handling of the overheating engines King was able to successfully drop his load of 14 paratroopers, a jeep, its trailer and six containers, over the DZ (an action recognised later by the award of the AFC).

There occurred one fatality during the drop when a paratrooper landed in a minefield; two others almost drowned when they drifted out to sea and a fourth was seriously injured when he landed on top of the burning control tower. Others were wounded or injured including journalist Peter Woods of the *Daily Mirror*, who jarred both ankles on landing, and a paratrooper who broke both legs on landing after his parachute canopy had been shattered by shrapnel.

The British force was accompanied by Cdr François Collet of the French Navy, who was to call for and co-ordinate French aircraft for ground strafing duties; also by Flt Lt Stan Roe and an RAF sergeant, who were to arrange DZ markings for the second drop. Lt Colonel Crook's paratroopers initially encountered stiff opposition, including six Russian-built SU100 self-propelled guns, but after some three hours it began to slacken. The airfield was secured by 0900 and was ready to receive aircraft by midday, although a Whirlwind from *Albion* arrived within half an hour, laden with beer and cigarettes – a gift from the ship's company. Others, from all three carriers, then commenced a shuttle service between Gamil and the ships, evacuating casualties. Lt Cdr Summerlee, OC *Eagle*'s SAR Flight, recalled:

"I had been flying a Whirlwind [XJ399/974] from *Eagle* to Gamil airfield. We had been asked initially to take in medical supplies to the forces landing at that spot. Fighting was still in progress on the perimeter when I landed with my crew of L/Airman Ben Hazel and N/Airman Roger Mitchell. We landed on the protected side of the Air Traffic Control building. As the crew were off loading supplies, there was a bang on the side of the helicopter. I thought we had been hit! Not so, a Red Beret was offering a cup of tea! There were several injured men in the sheltered area and I suggested that we took the most seriously injured back to the ship. So the CASEVAC operation began – back to the *Eagle* with injured soldiers."

Akrotiri's Venoms chalked up 20 sorties during the morning in support of the air drop. Apart from the flak suppression operations over Gamil airfield during the early morning, sections of Venoms flew armed recces in the vicinity of Port Said. Following the dawn strike against Gamil, 6 Squadron flew an additional 15 sorties during the remainder of the day, mainly in support of the paratroops. One section destroyed a three-ton truck near the Canal, while the next section caught a convoy of lorries and claimed 16 destroyed. A later section also encountered a number of military vehicles, six of which were set on fire. Two of the Venoms were slightly damaged by debris and ricochets during the day's strikes: WR410/N (hole in nose section and port wing tip tank) while WR379 was also hit in port tip tank. Meanwhile, Sqn Ldr Blyth (WR509) of 8 Squadron led a strike against Shallufa, followed by an armed reconnaissance of the Ismailia/al-Qantara area in company with Flt Lt Harcourt-Smith (WR528/G). They overflew a lagoon in which several fishing boats were observed:

"Suddenly I saw a lot of stuff coming from the Boss's aircraft. He was shooting at the boats. I followed suit. Perhaps we shouldn't have shot at them. We knew it was strictly forbidden to fire at civilians. It may have been a sign of frustration. For the last few days the campaign had seemed to be without any real purpose. There was virtually no opposition, but we were still waiting for a D-Day style landing. I recall wondering why we didn't just drop a few paras with their jeeps and tell them to drive down the Canal with a Union Jack. Simple thoughts of a humble Flight Lieutenant!"

A section of Venoms visited the airfields at Kabrit, Shallufa and Kasfareet around 1245 but the pilots failed to sight any new targets, although at least 30 lorries were strafed on the Ismailia to al-Qantara road. However, a section of F-84Fs sent to Abu Sueir, Fayid and Deversoir did locate apparently undamaged

Flt Lt David Harcourt-Smith, B Flt Commander 8 Squadron. (*ACM Sir David Harcourt-Smith*)

aircraft on all three airfields. Subsequently, a MiG was claimed probably destroyed at Abu Sueir, another was damaged at Fayid, while an unidentified aircraft and a vehicle were strafed at Deversoir.

Flt Lt Harcourt-Smith (WR480) of 8 Squadron led an evening strike against Huckstep Camp, the flight landing back at Akrotiri in the dark. Two of the Squadron's Venoms experienced problems during these sorties: WR484 suffered damage to its rocket-firing mechanism, while WR528/G burst both tyres on landing at Akrotiri. 249 Squadron similarly undertook a further 15 sorties between midday and dusk; one of these was led by Flt Lt Syme (WR504/Z), who noted:

"Armed recce of French Dropping Zone. Nothing there. Recced road south of Port Said. No2 hacked a jeep."

Flg Off Williams (WR492/U) recorded:

"R/P and 20mm attacks on gun installations at Port Said. Five HAA and LAA positions silenced. The underside of the Venom was damaged by shrapnel which penetrated the lower engine cowl, piercing one of the burner cans. This produced a certain amount of heat and consequent fire hazard, all of which I was blissfully unaware of."

The Venom was repaired overnight. However, WR533/F was more seriously damaged, having taken a hit in its rear fuselage which holed the rear spar.

Although much of the Egyptian Army was destroyed by the low-level attacks by Venoms and F-84Fs, some units managed to escape the carnage, including vehicles of the Egyptian 4th Armoured Division which were hidden in camouflaged positions in the Sharkia area and, although attacked by the RAF, were not damaged. Another section from 8 Squadron, led by Flt Lt Tanner and including Flg Off Bryn Jones (WR488), attacked gun emplacements on the West Mole at Port Said. Venoms of the Akrotiri Strike Wing flew a total of 68 sorties (of which two were aborted) during the day. Hunters flew a further 11 sorties as escort to the transports.

Earlier in the day, just before 0630, a force of 16 Canberras from Nicosia – two markers of 139 Squadron, two bombers from the same unit, plus six each from 44 and 61 Squadrons – raided Huckstep Camp to ensure that no reinforcements from the vehicle depot could be sent to the aid of the defenders of Port Said. One of the 61 Squadron bombers (WH724) was flown by Wg Cdr P. Dobson DSO DFC AFC, Deputy Commander of the Cyprus Bomber Wing. Two hours later a second wave of Canberras (six each from 10, 15 and 27 Squadrons, plus one from 61 Squadron) guided by two markers from 18 Squadron repeated the attack. Both raids were considered successful and were carried out without interference or obvious resistance. Throughout the day, reconnaissance jets from Cyprus continually overflew the battlegrounds and airfields and at least one Canberra ventured into Syrian skies. The Canberras from 13 Squadron recorded five sorties, which included WJ858 (a T4) piloted by Sqn Ldr John Field with Air Marshal H.L. Patch CB CBE, Commander-in-Chief RAFMEAF, in the navigator's seat, which carried out a visual reconnaissance of the Canal Zone; the French RF-84Fs flew a further 11 sorties.

CARRIER STRIKE FORCE

Aboard the *Arromanches*, Avenger crews had received orders which allowed them to attack small surface vessels such as MTBs. During an early morning patrol, the radar-equipped Avenger flown by Lt deV Lemaire (9F-11) picked up a possible target and his wingman, Second Maître Fourgaut, was ordered to investigate. Three vessels identified as Egyptian MTBs were observed and Fourgaut prepared to attack but, as he closed range, he realised that his opponents were in fact frigates, which all opened fire at his lone aircraft. Nevertheless, he held his line of attack and fired a salvo of rockets at the nearest vessel, observing strikes on its stern before he released two anti-submarine bombs from low level. As he pulled away, pursued by numerous black puffs of bursting AA, he rendezvoused with Lemaire's aircraft, only to hear a warning from the controller that two fighters were closing in from astern. Immediately the two Avengers started a series of 'scissors' manoeuvres at sea level to reduce their chances of being hit, before the pilots realised that their 'attackers' were in fact US Navy jets. Both Avengers reached *Arromanches* safely and Fourgaut was later awarded the Croix de Guerre for his attack on the frigate.

Meanwhile, Sea Hawks and Sea Venoms, joined by the Wyverns of 830 Squadron, operated continuous air patrols over Gamil and Port Said:

0545	*Bulwark*:	7 Sea Hawks Cabrank 895 Squadron	
0705	*Eagle*:	5 Wyverns 830 Squadron	5 x 1,000lb bombs and R/P attack on Coast Guard Barracks, also AA gun attacked by R/P
0720	*Albion*:	6 Sea Venoms 809 Squadron	Dug-in tank possibly damaged.
0810	*Eagle*:	8 Sea Hawks 897 Squadron	Tank destroyed, one damaged truck destroyed, one armoured vehicle damaged
0825	*Bulwark*:	6 Sea Hawks	Coast Guard Barracks damaged; 804 Squadron vehicles strafed
0835	*Albion*:	6 Sea Hawks 800/802 Squadrons	Bren Gun Carrier in flames; 4 trucks destroyed and 6 damaged, all on seafront
0915	*Eagle*:	4 Sea Venoms 892 Squadron	Light AA gun silenced; MTB damaged by R/P
0930	*Bulwark*:	6 Sea Hawks 810 Squadron	MTB hit and left listing; MTB badly damaged
0945	*Albion*:	6 Sea Venoms 809 Squadron	3 medium tanks reported in Slaughterhouse; not located; mortar positions attacked
1020	*Eagle*:	5 Wyverns 830 Squadron	3 x 1,000lb bombs and R/P attack on cemetery
1055	*Albion*:	5 Sea Hawks 800/802 Squadrons	Sports stadium containing infantry strafed; jeep destroyed on seafront
1140	*Bulwark*:	4 Sea Hawks 895 Squadron	Infantry and mortar positions strafed

Soon after 0730, the flight of 809 Squadron Sea Venoms led by Lt Cdr Shilcock (with Lt Hackett, in XG670/220) was called down by the FACs to carry out a strike, as recalled by Sub Lt Dwarika, Sub Lt Yates's observer in XG620/226:

> "Another exciting occasion was trying to destroy a tank dug into the ground outside a hospital, without hitting the hospital; that was a tricky operation."

One particular obstacle which interfered with the British advance eastwards was the Coast Guard Barracks on the beach road, since this had been turned into a strongpoint by the Egyptians. Rocket attack had proved ineffective, so the bomb-armed Wyverns of 830 Squadron were given the task of destroying the building. The first strike knocked out several nearby gun emplacements, although a number of hits were registered on the barracks. A second strike of Wyverns was called in to destroy guns and mortars sited in the local cemetery,

Lt Cdr Ron Shilcock, CO of 809 Squadron, making a deck landing in Sea Venom XG669/224. The hook is just about to catch an arrester line. (*Lt Cdr R.A. Shilcock*)

while two MTBs moored alongside a jetty near the cemetery were attacked by Sea Venoms and Sea Hawks. One of the craft caught fire and settled on its side. Of the morning's intensive flying activities over the DZ, Lt Cdr Rawbone of 897 Squadron recalled:

> "I can remember one amusing incident when my Flight was supporting paras in a fierce battle in a cemetery in Port Said. I was being guided by a Forward Air Controller (FAC) on to an Egyptian strongpoint in the cemetery when I was urgently ordered to stop firing. There followed some explicit expletives from the FAC amid words to the effect of 'you will never believe this . . .' Evidently a civilian funeral procession had arrived in the middle of a furious battle causing alarm and despondency to both sides! There was a respectful lull before battle recommenced. Such was war in Egypt!"

At about 1000, six Sea Hawks flying Cabrank (four of 810 Squadron and two of 895 Squadron) were called down to engage two MTBs seen near Port Said. 810 Squadron's leader, Lt Cdr Lamb (XE389/162), claimed one destroyed, and a second was damaged. Quite why the Egyptian Navy was operating its MTBs in these dangerous waters – with Sea Hawks hovering constantly overhead like their feathered namesakes, ready to pounce on any movement below – is unclear. Perhaps they were endeavouring to disperse these, the most effective warships Egypt possessed, into nearby Lake Manzala where the MTBs could have hidden amongst the numerous islands to carry out a naval guerilla war against the invaders.

Lt Cdr Morris-Jones (XE378/168), leading six Sea Hawks of 895 Squadron on Cabrank, was asked by forward troops if he could provide covering fire on Egyptian forces dug in at the cemetery for a period of ten minutes prior to a mortar bombardment, after which the paratroops hoped to advance. The plan worked admirably and it was learnt afterwards that the paratroopers had felt sufficient confidence in the accuracy of the Sea Hawks' attacks to advance even during the strafe.

Although the carrier fighters shared Cabrank duties with Akrotiri's Venoms and F-84s over the DZ, particular attention was also paid to Almaza airfield, where photographic-reconnaissance reports indicated movement of aircraft on the airfield and analysis of the photographs revealed what appeared to be six new MiGs in a pen in a hutted grove, south of the airfield. First off at 0500 to carry out a strike against Almaza were eight Sea Venoms of 892 and 893 Squadrons from *Eagle*. However, the Strike Leader, Lt Cdr Henley of 893 Squadron (WW205/090), remembered details differently:

"The strike on Almaza was again a first light affair with four pairs of Sea Venoms in quick succession. Study of recent recce photographs the previous evening revealed no aircraft on the airfield but numerous aircraft-sized packing cases in the trees around and about, so we turned our attention to them with R/P and 20mm. No idea what we achieved but the Egyptians were very sensitive about Almaza, which seemed to have more 30mm flak than all the rest put together."

The 892 Squadron section fared better and claimed destroyed an aircraft, believed to have been a MiG, concealed under a net east of the dispersal, and a second MiG south of the airfield beyond the overshoot area, where others seen parked were damaged. A further unidentified aircraft was damaged on the perimeter track at the north end of the north-south runway and huts south of the airfield were set afire, as were oil tanks to the west.

Almaza was visited again just before 0700 when eight Sea Hawks of 899 Squadron, led by Lt Cdr Clark (XE387/494), attacked shortly before three more from *Albion*'s 800 Squadron arrived; their leader, Lt Cdr Tibby (XE435/104), noted:

"Another strike at Almaza firing rockets – quite successful, left hangar and aircraft burning. Other aircraft also attacking, so we were all timed and therefore others may have also hit the hangar and aircraft. As a result of the combined attacks, Almaza was looking quite a mess by this time."

Eagle's Sea Hawks claimed damage to four hangars, two at the east dispersal and two at the west disperal, while *Albion*'s trio reported sighting about 20 miscellaneous aircraft parked outside the south-west hangars, possibly including a few MiGs and Il-28s. These were strafed and four claimed destroyed with a further six damaged. This attack was followed closely by another performed by four Sea Venoms of 893 Squadron from *Eagle* and four Sea Hawks of 804 Squadron and one from 895 Squadron from *Bulwark*; the Sea Venoms rocketed hangars and a heavy anti-aircraft battery north-west of the airfield, and also strafed an SSV. The Sea Hawks claimed a Fury destroyed and two damaged, plus a Harvard probably destroyed and a second damaged. Next to arrive over Almaza, by then partly obscured by smoke, were a pair of 899 Squadron Sea Hawks, followed by four more of 810 Squadron from *Bulwark* (plus one from 895 Squadron), led by Lt Cdr Lamb (WV796). *Eagle*'s pair reported damage inflicted on a MiG and two Vampires, but believed these were already damaged by earlier strikes, while *Bulwark*'s quartet claimed damage to a Fury. Next on the scene at about 0830 were four Sea Hawks from 897 Squadron, which bombed the hangars once again, followed closely by six more of 895 Squadron from

Bulwark led by Lt Cdr Morris-Jones (XE463/232) and Lt Anson (WM928/460); the pilots returned to report rocket strikes on hangars and a Spitfire damaged by cannon fire. A final strike against the airfield was carried out at midday by five more Sea Hawks from *Bulwark*. Hangars were again rocketed and a light anti-aircraft post strafed.

Cairo West was also visited twice during the morning, six Sea Hawks of 804 and 810 Squadrons from *Bulwark* carrying out an attack at about 0700, when two Vampires were claimed damaged and a building set on fire. Lt Hoddinott (XE396/167) participated in this strike. A second attack was mounted at 1100 by eight Sea Hawks of 899 Squadron, but Lt Cdr Clark (XE447/496) was able only to report:

"Target appeared deserted except for destroyed aircraft. Bombs dropped in fuel area, no fires seen."

A strike of four Sea Hawks from *Bulwark* (probably 804 Squadron) was despatched to Abu Sueir at 1035, but no aircraft were seen, rockets being fired into the hangar instead, which was left burning. On the return flight, a Bren Gun Carrier seen on the Port Said road was duly strafed.

Before the midday all-clear at Gamil, a French Dakota from Cyprus landed unexpectedly, its pilot having skilfully weaved the transport aircraft between oil drums and other obstacles. Colonel Becq de Fouquières emerged from the aircraft as it drew to a halt. He had been despatched by GHQ to obtain first-hand information as to whether troops could be landed at Gamil. The pilot, Colonel René Laure, offered to take casualties back to Cyprus with him, an offer gratefully accepted on behalf of several of the more seriously wounded. Then, at 1315, a further small drop of 58 paratroopers, plus additional supplies,

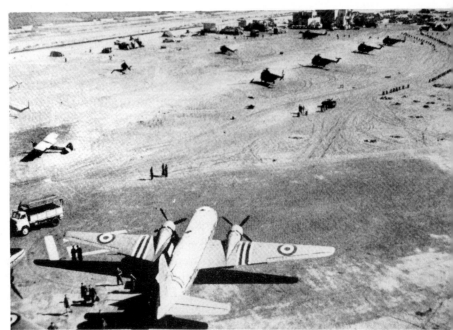

Unidentified Valetta seen at Gamil airfield with Whirlwinds and Sycamores of the JHU, together with an Auster of 1913 Flight. (*Authors' collection*)

was carried out by two Valettas and five Hastings (including TG577 and TG665 of 70 Squadron) from Cyprus, the transports again escorted by Hunters; two Canberras of 139 Squadron marked the DZ.

Cabrank sorties by the carrier fighters continued unabated throughout the afternoon.

1205	*Albion*:	6 Sea Venoms 809 Squadron	The Infectious Diseases Hospital and a building to the north damaged by R/P attack
1210	*Bulwark*:	3 Sea Hawks 895 Squadron	TAC/R Tel al-Kebir/Ismailia/ Port Said; pillbox strafed
1230	*Eagle*:	8 Sea Hawks 897 Squadron	Vehicles and tanks attacked with R/P and 20mm; AA gun at end of East Breakwater rocketed
	Eagle:	4 Sea Venoms 893 Squadron	Detailed as CAP but ordered to attack building with R/P
1245	*Bulwark*:	6 Sea Hawks 810 Squadron	Cabrank – Port Said
1305	*Albion*:	6 Sea Hawks 800/802 Squadrons	Coast Guard Barracks attacked by R/P; one truck and 2 LAA guns damaged
1335	*Eagle*:	4 Sea Venoms 893 Squadron	CAP directed to MTBs – left blazing and awash, R/P attack
1345	*Bulwark*:	8 Sea Hawks 895 Squadron	The Governorate building hit with 16 R/Ps
1355	*Eagle*:	8 Sea Hawks 899 Squadron	Attacked Coast Guard Barracks with R/P, 3 vehicles destroyed
1410	*Albion*:	6 Sea Venoms 809 Squadron	Truck destroyed; recce along the coast, no sign of enemy troops
1440	*Eagle*:	6 Wyverns 830 Squadron	Bomb attack on Coast Guard Barracks
1515	*Albion*:	7 Sea Hawks 800/802 Squadrons	Proposed strike on Slaughterhouse called off; 20 military trucks blown up were believed to be carrying ammunition
1605	*Bulwark*:	1 Sea Hawk 804 Squadron	Both catapults u/s after one Sea Hawk launched
1620	*Albion*:	2 Sea Hawks 802 Squadron 6 Sea Venoms 809 Squadron	Buildings south of the Slaughterhouse damaged by R/P and strafing
1635	*Eagle*:	4 Sea Venoms 892 Squadron	No target – temporary truce
1723	*Bulwark*:	7 Sea Hawks 804 Squadron	Bombs jettisoned on run in to Port Said, aircraft orbited until dark

The attack by 809 Squadron against the Infectious Diseases Hospital in Port Said just after midday was led by Lt Wigg (XG673/227, with Lt Bowman):

"The job involved knocking out a heavy machine-gun nest which was pinning the paras down from a high vantage point near the top of what looked like Port Said's tallest building. It was in fact a hospital. Our controller told us to take the position out anyway. By flying at the building from below the offending floor and then firing on the 'up', we were able to put some shells in the right place without spraying the whole building. A further tweak back on the stick put us over the top. It took a second run to silence the machine-guns, or to convince the gunners to take their business elsewhere."

The afternoon Wyvern attack on the Coast Guard Barracks was very successful, as revealed by the official report:

"Bombs on western two blocks at target. West block probably destroyed; next block badly damaged by bomb and R/P. 20mm on third block, slight damage. Ground explosion from west of building due to 20mm fire. Strike attacked Port Fuad battery with 20mm. This target appeared deserted."

However, the Strike Leader, Lt Cdr Cowling (WN328/374), was shot down:

"I was unlucky to be hit. We (Sub Lt Scott and myself) were attacking the Coast Guard Barracks which was full of troops pinning down the Royal Marines who were trying to break out of Gamil airfield where they had been dropped a short time before. Rockets and dive-bombing were ineffective so I decided to go in very low and lob a 500 pounder in the window. It worked, but I was hit by small calibre stuff. I was not aware of it until I was pulling away. Funny noises – like impellor blades disappearing out of the jet pipe! The engine went into the 'Red' and I decided to get as much height as possible and get away from the land. In the event I got up to 1,200 feet and had to throttle right back as all indications were that the engine was about to break up. I called Scottie in close to see where I had been hit and to take a picture of me ejecting (with his lateral camera) and also at this time started screaming 'Mayday'. The carrier acknowledged. So did [Lt Cdr] Jim Summerlee, who was the rescue helicopter pilot. He got a bearing on my voice transmission and set course. I had to continue closing the throttle and finally reached a point where a stall was imminent. I gave Scottie, who was alongside, a five to nought countdown for camera purposes and at 1,000 feet I pulled down the face-blind which actuates the explosive under the seat. Scottie unfortunately pushed the button prematurely and got a picture of me with my hands still on the blind, sitting in the cockpit. I ejected about five to six miles off the coast of Port Said. Everything worked perfectly."*

---

* Lt Cdr (later Cdr) Cowling added: "This was a unique ejection in as much as the escape velocity had been increased on Wyvern aircraft because of previous unsuccessful ejections. I believe I am the only aviator to have been ejected at something like 124 feet per second; the Wyvern was the only aircraft modified in this way and I was the last person to eject from one."

Lt Cdr Bill Cowling about to eject from his flak-damaged Wyvern WN328/374 on 5 November 1956. He was plucked from the sea by a Whirlwind from HMS *Eagle*. (*Cdr W.H. Cowling*)

Lt Cdr Summerlee, who had been ferrying supplies to Gamil airfield aboard Whirlwind XJ399/974 was returning to the carrier with wounded soldiers, when:

"I heard Smokey [Cowling] reporting a failing engine, having been hit with something. It became obvious that he would pass over me on my way back to *Eagle*. He decided to eject when we had made contact. I watched him fly past over my right shoulder ahead and eject, and descend smoothly by 'chute. He dropped his bonedome from about 100 feet and then gradually descended on to it – perfect, as per the book. We slowed down and at the appropriate moment handed the strop and hauled my dripping pal out of the drink. The cabin space was filled with injured soldiers (possibly including Egyptians). On the way again, a wet message was passed up to the cockpit from the cabin: 'What's this then, standing room only?' Smokey had to stand for the remainder of the journey amid the injured soldiery. That evening Smokey and I celebrated his safe return with lots of champagne. We were old pals and had served together on Firebrands with 813 Squadron."

Meanwhile, *Eagle*'s other Whirlwind, XG581/973, was also busily occupied during the day: Lt Cdr Pete Bailey – with N/Airman Webster and a medical orderly on board – flew supplies to Gamil and returned with three French casualties from south of Port Said. A second sortie did not prove quite so straightforward. On this occasion accompanied by L/Airman Gammer and a medical orderly, Lt Cdr Bailey delivered further supplies including fresh water to Gamil. By then the numbers of wounded were accumulating so he agreed to evacuate nine casualties (five French and four British). He later related his experiences to his friend Lt Cdr Dick Needham, then AEO of 890 Squadron at Yeovilton, who recalled:

"[Peter] was heavily overloaded in the Whirlwind with nine Army personnel, plus his own crew, and a full fuel load. I believe all the soldiers were

307

wounded; he was initially tasked to evacuate the British contingent – the French were last-minute 'extras'. He could only get airborne by doing a lengthy running take-off across sand dunes and just managed to hold the aircraft at sea level on his way back to the carrier. When he arrived, he couldn't get enough height to lift to the Flight Deck and had to spend some time [about an hour] reducing his fuel load before being able to get high enough to land on [by which time darkness had fallen]."

While the helicopters were thus engaged, protection for the vulnerable machines was provided by Sea Venoms, one sortie being undertaken by Lt Cdr Willcox in WW261/094 of 893 Squadron, with Sub Lt Peter Wilkins as his observer. Meanwhile,

Lt Cdr Pete Bailey of *Eagle*'s SAR Flight was responsible for a number of rescues. (*Mrs Nancy Bailey*)

The Governorate Building in the centre of Port Said under attack by Sea Hawks of 895 Squadron on 5 November 1956. (*Cdr J. Morris-Jones*)

eight Sea Hawks of 895 Squadron led by Lt Cdr Morris-Jones (XE395/166) were called down to carry out a rocket strike against a substantial building known as the Governorate in the centre of Port Said, as recalled by 895 Squadron's Lt Anson (flying XE375/239 of 810 Squadron):

"I was leading a group of six Sea Hawks each armed with six 60lb rockets. Apparently General Stockwell [Lt-General Sir Hugh Stockwell, Land Force Task Commander] decided that the Governorate was being used as the Egyptian Headquarters. Accordingly we were requested to hit the Governorate. Because it was a target of such magnitude, in the centre of town, we queried it and obtained definite confirmation. We hit it with 35 rockets. One rocket just missed the left-hand end but, as luck would have it, the rocket proceeded down the street and hit an anti-aircraft gun which had been placed at the intersection of two streets!"

Fleet Air Arm fighters had flown a further 473 sorties during the day, of which 399 were in the close support role. 809 Squadron's Sea Venoms had put up five Cabrank missions during the day, four of these being led by Lt Cdr Shilcock/Lt Hackett in XG670/220, while the crew of Sub Lts Yates/Dwarika also flew four sorties, each one in a different Sea Venom.

SUMMARY OF GROUND ATTACK CLAIMS AGAINST AIRCRAFT OF THE EGYPTIAN AIR FORCE by the Fleet Air Arm, 5 November 1956

	Destroyed	Probables	Damaged
Claims for MiG-15s:			
HMS *Eagle*'s squadrons	2	0	5
HMS *Albion*'s squadrons	0	0	0
HMS *Bulwark*'s squadrons	0	0	0
	2	0	5
Claims for other types:			
HMS *Eagle*'s squadrons	0	0	3
HMS *Albion*'s squadrons	4	0	6
HMS *Bulwark*'s squadrons	1	1	7
	5	1	16

THE FRENCH AIRBORNE ASSAULT

At the same time as the British paratroopers dropped over Gamil during the morning, 22 paratroop-laden Noratlases of ET1/61 and ET3/61 headed further south, escorted by a dozen F-84Fs from Akrotiri. The French drop was made near the al-Raswa bridges, the DZ having been targeted by two Canberras from 18 Squadron. The capture of the bridges would open the road to Suez, and the paratroopers were met by heavy automatic fire but no artillery or tanks. One French paratrooper was killed the moment he touched the ground, and another, trapped by his parachute at the tail of the aircraft, released himself from his harness as the Noratlas flew low over an empty shore, as close as possible to the shallow water. The hanging man was seen to fall into the sea, then to wave his rifle in a farewell gesture. However, next day a French patrol found his rifle

Dawn 5 November 1956: French paratroopers boarding Noratlas 61-QJ for the airborne assault. (*SHAA via Albert Grandolini*)

on the shore and his machine-gunned body two miles inland. He had apparently been captured and killed.

Meanwhile, the French Air Liaison Officer, Lt Andrieux, called for air support from the F-84Fs circling overhead, which were soon joined by five 14F Flotille Corsairs from *Arromanches*, led by Ens deV Doniol (14F-12). Colonel Château-Jobert's paratroops moved in and forced the Egyptians to retire from the western bridge as the fighter-bombers passed up and down, strafing and rocketing. However, they could not prevent the eastern pontoon bridge being destroyed by the retreating troops. A patrouille of Corsairs from 15F Flotille led by Maître Berger (15F-21) took over from *Arromanches*'s aircraft, and one of these strafed French troops crossing an exposed area, fortunately without hitting any of them. Second Maître Cousyn (15F-19) reported that his rocket attack on a building housing Egyptian soldiers had blown the roof completely off, after which other Corsairs strafed the fleeing survivors. The paratroop detachment at the waterworks was attacked by SU100 armoured vehicles and an air strike was called in to relieve the situation. The F-84Fs also set alight two oil tanks, the smoke from which hung over Port Said for several days. 809 Squadron's Lt Wigg remembered:

> "All the while we were Cabranking, they [the French Corsairs and F-84Fs] were doing likewise on the east side of the Canal, and on the same [radio] frequency – they all shouted at once! They were having a high old time with the oil storage depot by the sound of it. In the end our ground controller told them to belt up, in French! They were taken aback for a few seconds – and then started up again!"

Up above the attacking Corsairs, a circling Noratlas flown by Colonel Lamy carried Général Gilles' airborne HQ, equipped with all-frequency radio, with which he was able to report to Général Beaufre (the French Task Force Commander) at sea aboard HMS *Tyne*, and to GHQ in Cyprus. He was also in

Second Maître Berger (left) and Enseign deV Doniol with crewman aboard *La Fayette*. (*via Joss Leclercq*)

touch with the fighter pilots and sector commanders. Now and again the flying radio station was rocked by close AA bursts with caused Général Gilles, a veteran of France's struggle in Indo-China, to comment: "It's not a command post one is likely to grow old and grey in, but it has its uses for all that."

Loading supplies, including medical, aboard a Noratlas at Tymbou. (*SHAA via Albert Grandolini*)

A further drop of French paratroopers, 522-strong and led by Lt Colonel Fossey-François, was made on a DZ in the Port Fuad area at 1315, again with close support provided by F-84Fs. The intensity of French air operations can be gauged by the number of sorties flown by the Corsairs:

0410-0645	*La Fayette*:	4 Corsairs	Locomotive damaged
0456-0700	*Arromanches*:	4 Corsairs	Buildings set afire
0655-0729	*La Fayette*:	5 Corsairs	2 buildings in Port Said attacked with rockets
0750-0910	*Arromanches*:	5 Corsairs	Troops and non-armoured vehicles attacked
0930-1142	*La Fayette*:	5 Corsairs	2 trucks destroyed; 2 hangars, 2 houses and 50 enemy troops attacked
1117-1302	*La Fayette*:	4 Corsairs	3 trucks attacked; 30 enemy troops strafed
1320-1540	*La Fayette*:	8 Corsairs	12 military trucks set afire Port Fuad; 2 houses containing enemy troops attacked; quayside at Port Said strafed
1320-1540	*La Fayette*:	6 Corsairs	4 x 500lb bombs on buildings sheltering enemy troops; supply depot bombed; 20 enemy troops strafed

One section of four Corsairs from *Arromanches* was ordered to land on *La Fayette* on returning from a strike. The afternoon having become becalmed, *Arromanches* could not sail faster than 24½ knots, while the minimum required for a Corsair to land was 27 knots. The final patrouille from 14F Flotille, led by Ens deV Doniol, was obliged to land in the dark, and although none of the six pilots was qualified for night deck landings, all nevertheless hooked safely.

F-84Fs continued to support the ground forces during the afternoon, flying armed reconnaissances over a wide area and strafing targets of opportunity during the course of a further 24 sorties. One of the French fighter-bombers failed to return from a sortie led by Lt Villain to the al-Qantara/al-Ballah area, although the pilot, Sergent Choblet, was able to eject safely when his aircraft was hit by flak. He landed in the middle of a pack of jackals which, although aggressive, fortunately did not harm him. After trekking across the desert for some considerable time, when lack of water was his major concern, he eventually reached a small oasis, from where some friendly Bedouin took him to a nearby Israeli Army unit.

By mid-afternoon the defenders of Port Said had clearly had enough. At 1500, details of ceasefire negotiations at Port Said between the Egyptian Army commander of the Port Said/al-Qantara district and Colonel Château-Jobert were referred to Brigadier Butler aboard HMS *Tyne*. Butler himself arrived at Port Said by helicopter at 1630 to complete the surrender terms and conditions, which gave the local Egyptian commander until 2130 to gain acceptance, but these were rejected by Cairo and fighting resumed at 2215. While the 'peace parley' was in progress, Sea Venoms of 893 Squadron provided CAP, which included WW277 crewed by Lt Cdr Willcox and Flg Off Watson. With the end of another day of intensive flying, Lt Cdr Summerlee recalled an amusing incident:

"It was the habit to withdraw the Fleet to the north away from the more active area at night to avoid possible counter-attack. On one night we thundered along trying to evade two following blips clearly visible on the radar. As dawn broke we were able to identify our 'followers': they were two flocks of migrating Arctic terns trying to land on this bloody evasive island!"

On the political stage the Soviets began making dire threats to the Allied governments and Marshal Bulganin, the Soviet premier, sent warning notes to Britain, France and Israel:

"The Soviet government considers it necessary to draw your attention to the aggressive war being waged by Britain and France against Egypt, which has the most dangerous consequences for the cause of peace . . . In what position would Britain have found herself if she herself had been attacked by more powerful states possessing every kind of modern destructive weapon? And there are countries now which need not have sent a navy or air force to the coasts of Britain, but could have used other means, such as rockets . . . We are fully determined to crush the aggressors and restore peace in the Middle East through the use of force. We hope at this critical moment you will display due prudence and draw the corresponding conclusions from this."

This ominous warning – indeed, threat – followed another delivered by the Labour Party's Aneurin Bevan to the British government:

"If the Government wants to reimpose the law of the jungle, they must remember that Britain and France are not the most powerful animals in it. There are much more dangerous creatures prowling around."

Despite the initial shock of the Soviet warning, the threat of a nuclear missile attack on Britain was not taken seriously by the British government since any such attack against a NATO member, even if the Russians had the capability, would attract immediate response in kind. However, continued international pressure did have the desired effect, and the Soviet threats undoubtedly influenced American attitudes. Marshal Bulganin's note to President Eisenhower included a suggestion of US-Soviet armed co-operation:

"The USA has a strong navy in the zone of the Mediterranean, and a powerful air force. The joint and immediate use of these means by the USA and the Soviet Union, backed by a United Nations decision, would be a sure guarantee of ending the aggression against the Egyptian people and the people of the Arab East . . . If this war is not stopped, it contains the danger of turning into a Third World War."

The Americans rejected any idea of using force to stop the fighting in Egypt. Indeed, in response to the Soviet threat of missile attack against Britain, France and Israel, the Americans made their position crystal clear when they issued their own warning to the Soviets via the NATO Supreme Allied Commander, General Alfred Gruenther, who publicly announced that the Soviet Union would be 'destroyed' if it attacked the West, adding:

> "Whether or not such rockets exist, they will not destroy the capacity of NATO to retaliate. No nation is going to press the button if it means national suicide – that is just what it would mean."

As far as Nasser was concerned, however, the aggressive attitude of the Soviets was nothing more than a bluff, since the message he received from Moscow, via the Syrian President Shukri al-Quwatli on the latter's return from a visit to the Russian capital, was that "Russia would not risk getting involved in a Third World War for the sake of the Suez Canal" and that Egypt was advised to make peace as soon as possible, while Russia would give her moral support although there would be no direct Soviet military involvement.

It has been suggested that MI5 had tapped the Egyptian Embassy's cypher machine in London and thereby, once the code had been broken, had access to Egyptian-Russian traffic before and during the Suez crisis including, allegedly, one report 'in which the Russians outlined their intentions to mobilise aircraft in preparation for a confrontation with Britain'. It was also alleged that this report 'did as much as anything to prompt Eden into withdrawal' from Egypt. However, the deciding factor for the British government was the United States' ultimatum in the face of Britain's growing economic crisis. An appeal was made to Washington for backing for an IMF loan of £300 million (one billion US dollars) within 24 hours to halt the run on the pound sterling. An affirmative response was accompanied by the demand for a complete ceasefire, which was to be followed by a prompt withdrawal from Egyptian soil. For several days the United Nations had been working under heavy pressure from the American and Russian governments to secure a ceasefire, and Dag Hammarskjöld, the United Nations Secretary-General, approved a plan which called for international peacekeeping forces to rapidly deploy to Egypt. The UN demanded that British, French, Israeli and Egyptian forces cease hostilities forthwith. Britain had no alternative but to agree and a ceasefire was ordered for midnight the following day.

Notwithstanding this, the Egyptian populace was encouraged to continue the resistance by military broadcasting vans which roamed the streets, announcing that Russian help was on its way and that London and Paris had been bombarded by Soviet missiles. In the wake of this spiteful propaganda, arms were handed out in Port Said to willing Egyptians, young and old alike. The National Liberation militia enrolled boys as young as 12 and 13 and armed them with Russian automatics, many of whom were subsequently killed in the fighting; others were more fortunate:

> "Out of one house the Tommies drove two little woolly-haired boys in shorts and relieved them of rifles that were still warm. They stared at their 12-year-old enemies with astonished admiration. Since something had to be done, a chevroned arm came down with one slap for each urchin. One of them reeled, the other fell down, trembling with fear."

The youngsters were allowed to return to their families. Others were not so lucky. By the end of the day the British revealed that four paratroopers had been killed, with 20 wounded and 15 missing; the French had suffered five dead and ten wounded, but during the night reported that their troops had occupied Port Fuad. Egyptian casualties were undoubtedly much higher. However, it was clear that Port Said could not be captured by the paratroopers alone and that the commandos would have to make the anticipated landing in the morning, despite the impending ceasefire.

Chapter Fifteen

ENTER THE COMMANDOS – THE SEABORNE INVASION
6 November 1956

"War is really a pretty simple thing. It only becomes complicated when the politicians take a hand."

Lt Colonel H.E.N. Bredin, 3/Parachute Regiment

AKROTIRI STRIKE WING

Akrotiri was awakened at 0215 by a loudspeaker van announcing that all the pilots of the three Venom squadrons were to report immediately to the Wing Operations briefing room. On assembling there, the pilots were informed that they were to suppress a number of troublesome guns in concrete emplacements, most on the West Mole breakwater running north from Port Said. Thus, before first light, a total of 31 Venoms from all three squadrons climbed into the stormy darkness above Akrotiri; 32 had been ranged for take-off but Flg Off Lecky-Thompson's 249 Squadron aircraft went unserviceable. Once airborne, the Venoms formed up in sections for the series of attacks which were to be co-ordinated by Sqn Ldr Ellis of 6 Squadron, who was to call down each section in turn, tactics necessary because of the danger of mistiming and confusion with so many aircraft contesting the same small area of sky. However, on take-off Sqn Ldr Ellis discovered that the radio of his aircraft (Venom H) was unserviceable and Sqn Ldr Maitland of 249 Squadron took over the role of Master Bomber, Ellis following at a distance as a freelance. Flg Off Hadlow of 8 Squadron remembered:

"By now the weather was breaking, with rain and thunderstorms. Take-off, with wave after wave of aircraft taking off into the pitch darkness in the rain, with lightning flashes here and there, was exciting and demanding – and somewhat Wagnerian, to say the least. However, there was no time to dwell on such fanciful thoughts with too much else to do, and with a job to be done. The strike had to be on time as the landing force would be close behind."

Over the sea, the leading 249 Squadron section was intercepted by an unidentified aircraft, as Sqn Ldr Maitland recalled:

"In the very early morning, the flight I was leading was shadowed by a jet of some sort. It was too dark to identify but if it was hostile, as presumably

316

it was, that was the only Egyptian aircraft any of us saw airborne during the entire campaign."

A Venom of 6 Squadron flown by Flg Off Nigel Budd, which had joined up in the darkness with a 249 Squadron flight, tried to intercept what was undoubtedly a MiG-15, but the Egyptian aircraft easily escaped, passing close to Flt Lt Martin's aircraft. The British pilots claimed that the MiG had Russian markings rather than the green and white roundel of the EAF. However, a handful of EAF MiGs continued to operate from a road in the Delta area,* and the interceptor was probably one of these and was probably the same aircraft which strafed the British base on Gamil airfield at dawn, although this was reported to have been an Egyptian aircraft:

> "Dawn brought a series of aggravations to the men of 3 Para. First they were strafed by a MiG, the only hostile plane to be seen that day; the men on the ground had watched it approach, confident that it was either British or French until a stream of green and white tracer bounced along the runway and they saw its Egyptian markings."

Heavy cloud over the target area made any chance of a co-ordinated attack difficult; the Venoms instead struck in sections and fired their rockets into an area covered by smoke and dust caused by the initial strike. Flt Lt Harrison (Venom D) of 6 Squadron wrote:

> "When [Sqn Ldr Ellis's aircraft] went unserviceable on start, my section, which was planned to follow, went off first and, in fact, led the attack. All our aircraft had fired their rockets before there was any control at all. Mine were fired in quite dark conditions and I remember well being too low over the target when the rockets hit and being very worried about debris damage. There was much confusion and quite a few pairs became separated due to the extreme turbulence, heavy rain and much lightning. I believe that further back quite a number were unable to join up and were sent in on their own."

Flt Lt Harcourt-Smith (WR480), who led 8 Squadron in the absence of Sqn Ldr Blyth (as it was his morning off duty), recalled:

> "Major problems with radio communications as 30-plus aircraft from various parts of the airfield taxied out in pitch darkness and pouring rain to line up for take-off in a designated sequence. We then climbed up to altitude in pairs in line astern through some very heavy and rough weather. The most important point made at the pre-flight briefing concerned the order not to fire any weapons after a specified time, H-Hour, and so avoid killing any of our own forces who were then committed to the landing. At H-Hour I was at 10,000 feet in a dive on the Mole which I could see quite clearly. I was therefore faced with the choice of firing my rockets (designed to be fired from 800

---

* The Egyptian authorities have not released information about the road-strip in the Nile Delta, but in later years four such emergency airstrips were constructed on the main Cairo to Alexandria highway at Quwaysina, Minskat Sabri, Tukh and Qaha. They played a vital role in the 1967 June War and the October War of 1973.

Trio of Venom FB4s of 249 Squadron wearing their Suez stripes – WR431/R nearest the camera, WR499/V in centre. (*Tony Gronert via Andy Thomas*)

yards from the target) in the certain knowledge that they would never reach the target but fall into the Med, or I could take them back to Akrotiri. After the shambles of the departure from Akrotiri and the very unpleasant climb through such filthy weather, I opted for the former. A silent protest and release of tension! In the event it was my last and somewhat useless act in this brief, unusual and not very successful piece of British history."

Flg Off Hadlow (WR446/S) did manage to launch eight of his rockets at the target, believing his aim to have been fairly accurate:

"We attacked out of the west just as it was getting light, a difficult time of the day for judging a dive attack, and with the dark sky behind us so we would not be too visible against the lightening eastern sky."

However, some of the following pilots were unable to see the designated target so attacked others, as Flt Lt Syme of 249 Squadron (WR443/Y) noted:

"Abortive strike against Mole at Port Said. Recce on road to Ismailia. Rocketed trucks in Army camp. Flak and tracer."

Sea Hawks and Sea Venoms were also operating over the area, 8 Squadron's Flg Off Carroll commenting:

"By this time the weather had broken, and the cloud, darkness, and the presence of many carrier aircraft ensured an exciting trip for all concerned."

Meanwhile, Sqn Ldr Ellis had been circling above, watching the operation, and reported:

"A long sea wall near the town was positioned with AA guns which although

318

they had been bombed the previous day were still active. My aircraft shot them up and dropped rockets to make sure the landing area was free from Egyptian activity. As I flew over Port Said I saw people gathering in the streets. Some were on rooftops wearing pyjamas. I did not see any Russian MiGs but one of my pilots saw a MiG from about 300 yards away. It made off."

He added that in his opinion only 50 per cent of the rockets hit the breakwater, although in the event the subsequent landings went ahead unhindered by the West Mole guns. Meanwhile, the strike leader, Sqn Ldr Maitland, observed:

"While over the area west of the place where the British troops were fighting, I saw several dumps and buildings on fire. One was very big, sending a long column of smoke into the sky."

THE SEABORNE INVASION

The main seaborne assault at Port Said was launched at 0545 by 40 and 42 Commandos, preceded by a bombardment from the covering destroyers on the area of the beach where the Marines were to land, since it was thought to be mined. As soon as the bombardment had finished, Sea Hawks swept down to strafe the beaches as the Marines went ashore, as witnessed by Douglas Clark:

"I was taken completely by surprise at the speed of these jet fighters. In the short time it took us to travel the last hundred yards, each fighter did two runs. Although I was happy to see them, I began to feel that we and they were drawing much too close to each other during their second run, and I was very thankful to see the last one climb almost vertically away as we grounded . . . If the planes had been frightening, at least I'd had the comfort of knowing that they were friendly."

A number of wooden huts on the beach apparently contained ammunition and these caught fire, resulting in continual explosions throughout the morning until the fires burned themselves out. As soon as the beaches had been secured, a squadron of 6th Royal Tank Regiment Centurions arrived aboard landing craft, while further along the coast at Port Fuad, the 1e Regiment Étranger Parachutistes (Foreign Legion Parachute Regiment) and three French Navy commando units (each about 80-strong) landed to assist the French paratroopers.

The first helicopter to land at Port Said, about an hour after the seaborne landing, was piloted by Lt Cdr Ron Crayton, Senior Pilot of 845 Squadron (with Capt Shaw of the JFU as co-pilot), and had taken off from *Ocean* with an advance party of five Marines of 45 Commando under Lt Colonel Norman Tailyour, their task to reconnoitre a suitable landing area for the main helicopter force. Apparently momentarily confused by the clouds of black smoke rising from the burning fuel tanks (hit by the F-84Fs the previous afternoon), Crayton landed the Whirlwind (WV205/W) on a football field and not in the beachhead as intended; he recalled:

"I had barely taken off again when I saw scores of armed civilians make for the stadium. I knew our lads wouldn't stand a chance against such odds,

Whirlwind HAS22 WV222/P of 845 Squadron. (*Andy Thomas*)

despite the fact that I saw the Marine sergeant mow the chaps down; but they wouldn't hold for long. I landed again and picked our boys up, putting them down a little nearer the main landing site, in a safer zone. As I took off from the stadium we were shot at, but luckily the shots whizzed pass [although he did suffer a minor wound to one hand]. The aircraft managed to return safely [to *Ocean*] with a few punctures in the fuel tank and main fuselage [in fact, it was hit 22 times in the fuselage and once in each rotor blade]. Although it was reported unserviceable, by sunset it was serviceable again and ready for action."

The main body of 45 Commando followed in the Whirlwinds and Sycamores of JHU and 845 Squadron and landed on a patch of waste ground beside the De Lesseps statue without incident. Between five and seven men could be carried in the Whirlwind, but only three in the Sycamore:

"The men flying in the Sycamores sat on the floor of the helicopter, the one in the middle with six mortar bombs in his lap holding on to the other two, who were compelled to sit at the door edge with their legs over the side, whilst each hugged a three-foot-long 106mm shell. In the Whirlwinds the passengers were able to get into the body of the machine but there were no seats, doors or windows and precious few handholds. Communication between the pilot and his passengers was effected by shouts or by one of the Marines tugging at the pilot's legs."

One naval officer wrote:

"Immediately beside us helicopters were landing in coveys of half a dozen. Each scarcely touched the ground before the commandos jumped clear and she was airborne again. I was impressed by this."

The first real opposition encountered was at the Arsenal Basin; there the

---

Customs Shed and the old Navy House had been set on fire by air strikes, and Marines of 40 Commando and Egyptian sailors were engaged in a firefight. Meanwhile, 45 Commando met opposition at the back of a block of buildings known as the Governorate and called in air strikes, one section of Wyverns being ordered down 1000, even though queried by the strike leader, which resulted in 18 casualties to 45 Commando HQ; amongst those wounded was Lt Colonel Tailyour, hit in the arm, and his signaller, Marine Michael Fowler, who died from his injuries, together with seven men of B Troop.

During the morning, Grp Capt W.V. Crawford-Compton DSO DFC and a few of his staff from 215 Wing were airlifted from *Ocean* to Gamil, there to establish the airfield to receive transport. The Wing was to be prepared, to begin with, to handle up to 15 transport aircraft a day in the resupply and casualty evacuation roles, and to operate the Venoms of 249 Squadron, one flight of Meteor FR9s from 208 Squadron (then at Malta), the helicopters of the JHU and the Auster AOP6s of 1913 Flight. The Wing's deputy commander, Wg Cdr M.H. Le Bas DSO AFC, wrote later:

"Action stations [aboard *Ocean*] had been in force since before first light and all the carrier's AA guns were closed up. Except for one false alarm when an F-84F was mistaken for a Badger [Le Bas presumably meant Beagle, the NATO codename for the Il-28], no incidents occurred. For some of us a slight air of unreality pervaded the operation. We had been preparing for it since August. Was this the real thing at last? Were those Marines with their feet dangling over the side of the Sycamore helicopters. Are we really going into battle? Were those real bombs and shells bursting on the Port Said waterfront? It wasn't long, however, before the first wounded were brought back aboard and we realised that this was indeed the real thing.

On arrival at Gamil airfield contact was made immediately with the local commander. The airfield had been well secured by the paratroopers although some quite heavy fighting was still going on in the outskirts of Port Said near the cemetery. Very occasionally a salvo of shells would explode about 200 yards out to sea and the first reaction was to blame the Royal Navy. It was soon explained however that it was an Egyptian multi-barrelled rocket launcher which had been firing intermittently from the town. The runway was found to be serviceable and the control tower, although damaged, usable."*

Among the first aircraft to arrive at Gamil was a Skyraider from *Albion*, reacting to a signal from the paratroopers that the local water supply was contaminated and that fresh water be delivered urgently. C Flight of 849 Squadron aboard *Albion* was asked to help, as recalled by Lt Jan Stuart, an observer:

"The first reaction was to fit long-range tanks [to the Skyraider], fill them with water and take it ashore, but although the tanks were new the ship's MO would not pass the water as fit for human (or paratrooper) consumption.

---

* Grp Capt (later Air Vice-Marshal) Bill Crawford-Compton, a New Zealander, was one of the RAF's top-scoring fighter pilots of the Second World War. Wg Cdr Mike Le Bas (later Air Vice-Marshal) was also a notable fighter pilot, having served at Malta during the siege of 1942.

Senior crew of C Flight/849 Squadron aboard HMS *Albion*; second left Lt(O) Jan Stuart; Lt Cdr Noddy Fuller (CO) centre; Lt Cdr L.C. Waters (Senior O) right, with maintainers. (*Lt Cdr Jan Stuart*)

The ship's Welfare Committee then rose to the occasion by offering to send canned beer ashore. We found that by packing beer crates in every available space, including up the radar tunnel, and by leaving out one observer, the capacity of the AD4W [Skyraider] was 1,000 cans.

At 1015, Noddy [Lt Cdr Fuller] and I had a free take-off in WV178 and took 1,000 cans to Gamil. The paras were not slow in unpacking and getting to grips with it. By coincidence, Noddy's brother was a captain in the Para Brigade and we decided to look him up, but alas, he had been shot in the goolies by one of his own sentries and was lying in the hospital ship *Empire Fowey*. As *quid pro quo* for the beer, the paras took us off in a comman-deered Egyptian Cadillac and we visited said brother and were each donated with a trophy in the shape of captured Siminov carbines."

There was a sequel to this 'act of mercy', as Lt Stuart remembered:

"A few days later, the paras were shouting for more beer but there was no way *Albion* was going to run herself dry, so a deal was struck with the NAAFI at RAF Akrotiri in Cyprus and the whole of C Flight, to wit four Skyraiders, set off to fetch beer. To allow maximum capacity three aircraft carried pilot only, and I was the lone observer with Noddy in WV102. We were airborne, free take-off at 1200 and arrived Akrotiri 1310. To give good radar range, we flew there at 9,000 feet and planned to do the same on the way back. Full to the flaps with canned beer, the four aircraft took off from Akrotiri at 1405 and climbed away to the south with something like 5,000 cans of beer between them. About 20 minutes later, when passing through

Skyraider WV178/424 of C Flight/849 Squadron launching off HMS *Albion*. (*Andy Thomas*)

8,000 feet on the way up, there was a radio message from the NAAFI manager at Akrotiri to warn us that the beer cans were pressurised and on no account should we fly above 5,000 feet! So we split the difference and came back at 6,500 feet – and never lost a drop."

The first two Valettas duly arrived at Gamil at 1330, conveying personnel and equipment from Cyprus. The first to land was VW850 of 114 Squadron with Grp Capt Case (OC RAF Nicosia) as captain. Just before dusk a badly wounded paratroop sergeant arrived at Gamil. The medical staff explained that he would be unlikely to survive the night unless he could be evacuated to Cyprus. As it was too late for a helicopter to take him to a carrier, Cyprus was asked to send a Valetta to Gamil without delay, where a flarepath would be provided. The aircraft arrived at 0200, complete with a nursing sister; the paratrooper survived.

Meanwhile, all helicopters had been kept busy until dusk evacuating casualties to the carriers offshore, allowing Capt I.W.T. Beloe, *Ocean*'s Captain, to comment:

"Not only did it give the medical staff the best possible chance of dealing with wounds, but it was also extremely good for the morale of the troops. When they found they were in bed within an hour or so of being wounded, they appreciated what care was being taken of them."

As if to prove the point, one Marine of 45 Commando who was wounded almost as soon as he had landed, found himself back on board the carrier some 20 minutes after having departed. But not all went according to plan. One unexpected arrival at Gamil aboard a Whirlwind of JHU was Lt General Campbell Hardy, Commandant-General of the Royal Marines. Also arriving by helicopter was Brigadier Butler, flown to Gamil by Lt Cdr Bailey in *Eagle*'s XJ399/974; on his departure from the airfield, Bailey evacuated five wounded soldiers. Brigadier Butler was followed a little later by General Stockwell, Admiral Durnford-Slater and Air Marshal Barnett aboard a naval launch from their HQ ship, HMS *Tyne*. Shortly after passing the Casino Palace Hotel at Port Said, the launch came under fire, luckily without casualties to the distinguished passengers embarked, as remembered by Grp Capt Denis Smallwood DSO DFC (Group Capt Plans, Air Task Force):

> "We were passing the statue of De Lesseps at the north end of the Mole when the bridge of the launch was struck by a ricochet. We all flung ourselves to the deck and looking through the canvas awnings could just see British tanks firing down the Mole."

At 1315, when Whirlwind XJ400/X of 845 Squadron was transferring two wounded French paratroopers from *Eagle* to *Theseus*, it ran out of fuel when only half a mile from its destination. Lt John Morgan, the pilot, informed *Theseus* and another Whirlwind, flown by Lt Michael Cooper, was despatched immediately for the scene. Just as Morgan's machine touched the surface of the water, he opened the door of the compartment and got both casualties to jump into the sea – Caporal Rey Louis with a shoulder wound and Caporal Paul Valandro with a leg injury. Following on the tail of Cooper's helicopter was another flown by Lt Peter Spelling, with Lt John Armstrong as crewman, who recalled:

> "We were following fairly close behind and saw this accident happen. We dropped our dinghy, which inflated on the way down. One casualty quickly got into it."

Lt Cooper added:

> "I hovered over the casualty as low as possible. The winch was lowered and the casualty in the dinghy was picked up."

The other French paratrooper and Lt Morgan were both picked up by Lt Spelling, who reported later:

> "It is interesting to note that for the first time two men have been pulled up by winch without any strop at all. The whole operation lasted four minutes."

Later, a Sycamore of the JHU was seriously damaged following loss of power on take-off and it crashed back on the deck, without injury to the crew, however. In all some 37 casualties, including two Egyptians, were evacuated by helicopter to the carriers. However, many other casualties, mainly French, were collected by helicopter from the French zone and transported to Gamil, from where they were flown to Cyprus for treatment. In addition, a doctor was flown ashore, while 1,000 gallons of fresh water, medical stores, wireless batteries, beer and cigarettes were also airlifted to the troops. During the course of the hectic day, apart from 450 commandos, the helicopters had landed 23 tons of stores and equipment.

Following the dawn strike on the guns at Port Said, Akrotiri's Venoms were required to fly only a few operational sorties throughout the remainder of the day. 6 Squadron despatched two sections each of four aircraft, one reconnoitring the road to al-Qantara where the pilots strafed a suspected ammunition dump, which erupted following the attack. The other section, which included Grp Capt Macdonald, strafed two vehicles on the way to Abu Sueir, where three fire engines and two fuel bowsers were destroyed. Heavy cloud was reported between Cyprus and Egypt. 8 Squadron similarly sent two sections on armed recces of the roads in the Canal Zone and returning pilots claimed a number of vehicles destroyed, while 249 Squadron also sent a flight to the area: Flg Off Gronert (WR492/U) and Flg Off Barker carried out an armed reconnaissance between Tel al-Kebir and Ismailia:

"We had orders to attack any target that could be considered military. In the event we found plenty of targets, each of us taking turns at attacking them while the other gave cover. I had some spectacular ciné film of that sortie, particularly the attack on a tank where the rockets were seen to hit and the cupola was tossed spinning into the air. On the way back we saw a lot of aerial activity on our track and wondered what it was. As it turned out, it was the US Sixth Fleet being awkward. We had very frosty relations with the Sixth Fleet, which was positioned to the north of the Suez Canal. Aircraft from their carriers had been operating in the area of the eastern Mediterranean in considerable numbers. We had decided amongst ourselves that we were not going to let them interfere with us and, if necessary, we would take any action considered necessary to maintain our security.

I instructed Bill to carry on [back to base] as his fuel state was at the stage where you wonder how good a glider pilot you are. I climbed above all this and kept watch over everything going on and when they [the American fighters] started to interfere, I made as to attack even though the situation was that while I was comparatively flush with fuel, I had no ammunition. While they did threaten, they did not actually interfere, so we left them behind and landed without further incident."

The F-84Fs also flew armed reconnaissance sorties during the day. Sections ranged over the airfields to ensure that any surviving Egyptian aircraft were not able to interfere with the landings. During the course of one intrusion, hangars at Deversoir were rocketed. Other sections strafed and rocketed rail and road traffic in the al-Qantara/Ismailia area, the final sortie of the day being flown to Fayid, Kabrit and Kasfareet. No undamaged aircraft were seen on the airfields. By the end of the day the F-84Fs had logged 33 sorties, the Venoms an additional 50; an aircraft of 6 Squadron, WR413, was hit in the starboard wing-tip during one sortie. Meanwhile, the Hunters of 1 and 34 Squadrons had conducted fighter sweeps at 30,000 feet over the Nile Delta. One Hunter patrol reached as far south as Cairo, the pilots keen to engage in combat, but no hostile aircraft were encountered. However, one section did see a single Egyptian fighter but were unable to intercept as it was flying at speed in the opposite direction.

Earlier in the day, Canberra WT371 of 139 Squadron – the aircraft which had suffered minor battle damage during the attack on Almaza Barracks on 3 November – crashed near Nicosia with the loss of the crew. It was due to be flown back to the United Kingdom by a 9 Squadron crew who had earlier ferried out a replacement Canberra. A few minutes after take-off the pilot, Flg Off Ian Collins, radioed to report a suspected fire in the starboard engine. After requesting priority for landing and completing one circuit, a normal approach was made but, when slightly short of the runway, the aircraft veered to starboard and

Sea Hawk XE399/167 of 804 Squadron about to attack target in the Nile Valley, south of Cairo (*Authors' collection*)

commenced a steep climbing turn before rolling on to its back and diving into the ground. Killed with Flg Off Collins were Flg Off Ken Banyard and Flt Sgt Morris Rhodes.

CARRIER STRIKE FORCE

Cabrank duty was the order of the day and was carried out by all squadrons. British and French, throughout the daylight hours, relays of Sea Hawks, Sea Venoms and Corsairs patrolling over the battle zones waiting to be called into action by the FACs. *Bulwark*'s catapults were not serviceable until 0900, however. During the early morning, before 1000, a total of 74 sorties were flown.

0400	*La Fayette*	4 Corsairs	R/P attack on 2 mortar sites, and strafing attack on line of trees showing enemy fire
0415	*Arromanches*	4 Corsairs	Attack on small wood sheltering enemy element
0530	*Eagle*	6 Sea Hawks 897 Squadron	Attacked with R/P slit trenches and possible dug-in gun positions at Golf Course Camp, Port Said. Results not observed
	Albion	7 Sea Hawks 800/802 Squadrons	Building and beach hut bombed and strafed
0550	*La Fayette*	4 Corsairs	Petrol dump set afire; munitions dump blown up; 10 trucks destroyed or damaged
0615	*Albion*	2 Sea Hawks 802 Squadron 6 Sea Venoms 809 Squadron	Strafed Golf Course Camp, seafront and Shell oil tanks, but tanks in Golf Course Camp not found

0630	*Eagle*	6 Sea Hawks 899 Squadron	To attack tanks in wood; tanks not seen but dropped bombs on wood
0720	*Eagle*	4 Sea Hawks 899 Squadron	Attacked machine gun position east of Canal firing at helicopter; dropped bombs on suspected self-propelled gun; one aircraft recce road to al-Qantara; jeep destroyed
0735	*Eagle*	4 Sea Venoms 892 Squadron	Gun position or tank attacked with R/P; also attacked by Sea Hawks
0753	*Arromanches*	4 Corsairs	Armoured car/recoilless gun attacked
0800	*Albion*	8 Sea Hawks 800/802 Squadrons	R/P attack on building
0905	*Albion*	1 Sea Hawk 802 Squadron 6 Sea Venoms 809 Squadron	One truck destroyed and a medium tank damaged; 16 medium tanks 6 trucks seen to be under fire by artillery from the east
0910	*Bulwark*	6 Sea Hawks 895 Squadron 6 Sea Hawks 810 Squadron	Strike on Almaza; R/P attack on aircraft park Cabrank – Port Said
0920	*Arromanches*	4 Corsairs	Cabrank – protection of downed pilot by strafing armoured car, 6 trucks and enemy troops
0930	*Eagle*	6 Wyverns 830 Squadron	Attacked troops with R/P and 20mm, also two guns and a tower; leader identified target and thought it own troops; after several checks, leader was ordered to carry out strike
		6 Sea Hawks 899 Squadron	Attacked Cairo West; six bombs on north-south runway; one on north-west/south-east runway

Lt Worth (XE435/104) was the leader of 800 Squadron's strike at about 0830:

> "We were in the process of conducting an R/P strike on an Egyptian strong-point, situated in a corner of a building overlooking a square near the sea front, which was holding up the assault. Stuart-Jervis, who was my No2, suddenly called up that he was ejecting due to engine failure, cause unknown."

Lt Stuart-Jervis reported later that he heard explosions coming from the engine of his Sea Hawk (XE400/107) and both fire warning lights came on. He headed out to sea and successfully ejected from the fighter, which crashed in flames. Within minutes of landing in the sea, Stuart-Jervis was picked up by a launch from HMS *Meon* and, shortly after, one of *Albion*'s helicopters arrived and flew him back to the carrier. He was unaffected by the experience and flew again next day.* The lost Sea Hawk was promptly replaced by a replacement, WV827, from the FAA depot at El Adem, the Squadron having already received two reconditioned Sea Hawks (WV832 and WV829) from the depot, which replaced XE455 and XE438 damaged in action two days earlier.

Bulwark's catapults were working again by 0900 and six Sea Hawks were launched for Cabrank duties over Port Said, while Lt Cdr Morris-Jones (XE461/170) and Lt Anson (XE392/163) led a further six from 895 Squadron to Almaza, where rockets were fired into the aircraft park; the strike leader, however, was carrying two 500lb bombs and reported dive-bombing a C-46. The Sea Hawks of 897 Squadron were also active over the battle area, as Lt Mills (XE388) noted:

> "I flew the first detail which was to protect the landing ships and craft as they deployed for the assault and this passed without incident ... there was an urgent call for fire from the leading craft, and [Lt Cdr] Pete Newman [of 899 Squadron] put a rocket through one of the windows of the Customs House to destroy a gun concealed there that was hitting the first wave. This was a prime example of the weeks of training paying off."

The carriers continued to launch sections of fighter-bombers throughout the morning.

1010	Bulwark	5 Sea Hawks 804 Squadron	Recce of Gulf of Suez; no MTBs seen; ship in Canal entrance
		6 Sea Hawks 810 Squadron	Cabrank – Port Said
	Albion	8 Sea Hawks 800/802 Squadrons	Cabrank – Port Said; no targets given
1025	La Fayette	6 Corsairs	Cabrank – no call for support
1035	Eagle	4 Sea Venoms 893 Squadron	Cabrank – no targets given
		4 Sea Hawks 897 Squadron	Cabrank and road recce – jeep destroyed
		4 Sea Hawks 897 Squadron	Photo recce Port Tewfik
1110	Albion	2 Sea Hawks 802 Squadron	4 medium tanks seen on main road along north side of Arsenal
		5 Sea Venoms 809 Squadron	Basin; identification uncertain
1140	Eagle	4 Sea Venoms 892 Squadron	Armed recce in al-Qantara area; attacked 8 AFVs but results not observed
		4 Sea Hawks 899 Squadron	Cover for rescue of crashed pilot; 2 vehicles destroyed on road running north-east from al-Qantara

* In September 1995, 68-year-old Lt Cdr John Stuart-Jervis MBE RN retired, former Naval Attaché at St Croix, US Virgin Islands, was killed when the air balloon in which he was flying was shot down by a military helicopter over the Belarus Republic (formerly part of the Soviet Union). Apparently the balloon, which was taking part in the annual Gordon Bennett Trophy Balloon Race, had strayed near the Osovtsy military air base. Both occupants were killed.

The 897 Squadron section of Sea Hawks which departed from *Eagle* at 1035 found no suitable targets but, while cruising around waiting to be called down, the leader was informed to be on guard since the MiG attack on Gamil airfield earlier that morning. Within the next minute or so, a swept-wing fighter passed close to the Sea Hawks, and although it was identified by Lt Jock Hare as a Mystère, it nevertheless caused 'the greatest excitement'. The Squadron lost one of its aircraft shortly before midday, which resulted in a daring rescue operation. Lt Cdr Rawbone (XE362/194), who led the section, recalled:

> "My flight (four aircraft) was detailed for Cabrank duty. On crossing the coast we split into two pairs, each pair being detailed by a FAC in the Port Said area, and Don Mills and his No2 were deployed further south towards al-Qantara. At the end of our sorties we were to re-form and return to *Eagle*."

Lt Mills wrote:

> "I was briefed to make a reconnaissance down the Canal to see what was there as the Army ashore was ready to break out of the perimeter and drive to Suez. Off I went with my No2, [Lt] Gerry Maynard, at about 5,000 feet keeping our eyes peeled for any movement. We went all the way to Suez on the west bank of the Canal and could not see any activity that would cause trouble for the advancing troops. We turned back and flew up the east bank and this time saw a squadron of tanks in the desert, outside a village called al-Qantara between Port Fuad and Ismailia. We attacked them with three-inch R/P and registered some hits and I circled round with Gerry behind me to make another attack. I had a problem because my gyro gunsight had given up the ghost and so I had no proper aiming point in the cockpit. Even so, I got off a rocket and hit the tank which exploded.
>
> Something hit the aircraft [XE377/195] and immediately my tank fire-warning light came on. I pulled up out of the dive and climbed to several thousand feet and prayed. The SOP for a tank warning was to bale out immediately, as the aircraft could explode at any second, and there was indeed a nasty burning smell. I made a conscious decision to stick with the aircraft for a few seconds, as ejecting on top of some tanks I had just been attacking didn't seem like a good idea."

Lt Donald Mills of 897 Squadron whose Sea Hawk was shot down near al-Qantara on 6 November 1956; he was rescued by a Whirlwind from *Eagle* flown by Lt Cdr Pete Bailey. (*Mrs Drucie Mills*)

Lt Cdr Rawbone continued:

> "At the due time I flew to rendezvous with Don Mills, a manoeuvre easily effected because I could see a long stream of black smoke coming from Don's aircraft. I could hear Don discussing a possible fire with his No2. I confirmed that he was on fire and advised him to eject over the desert as soon as possible."

Other Sea Hawks were in the area, including that flown by Lt Paddy McKeown, Senior Pilot of 802 Squadron:

> "It so happened that I and my No2, Sub Lt [P.R.] Miller, had just crossed the coast inbound to some target, when I overheard on the radio the inter-change between Mills and his CO who informed Mills he was on fire and to bale out, which he smartly did. I saw him descend in his parachute and we headed for him to give cover, while informing the ship what we were up to and calling for a chopper etc."

Lt Cdr Rawbone also contacted the carrier:

> "I called *Eagle*, reported Don's position and asked for aircraft to cover the downed pilot. My Flight, now down to three aircraft, was running short of fuel but we orbited Don until relief aircraft arrived. We did see an approaching Army vehicle coming from the east towards Don (probably Israeli) and we strafed ahead of it as a warning shot not to close further. We then had to leave."

As soon as *Eagle* received the news of Mills's plight a Whirlwind (XJ399/974) of the SAR Flight was launched with Lt Cdr Bailey at the controls, and crewed by L/Airman Gammer and N/Airman Webster. Sea Hawks and Sea Venoms were despatched from the carriers as cover. Mills continued:

> "I called a 'Mayday' on the emergency frequency, gave my position, jettisoned my hood and ejected. The seat functioned perfectly and, before I really knew what was happening, my parachute had deployed and I was floating gently in a clear blue sky. I could see the tanks, still not far away, and they were heading in my direction. The ground then came up much more quickly than I had anticipated and I landed with a thud, not helped because I was trying to bring my pistol out in case somebody popped out from behind a sand dune. I was dazed by the impact, but soon came to my senses, released my harness and considered my next move. Gerry was circling overhead, but I knew he would have to leave soon or run out of fuel! In the event, he just made it back to the ship."

Lt McKeown added:

> "Mills was safely down. A lone jeep approached, undoubtedly Israeli, but I was not certain, so I gave it a quick burst of 20mm cannon fire across the bows, as you might say. The occupants sensibly held their distance. At first, RESCAP was provided only by me and my No2, but things being very quiet

at that time, every spare aircraft having nothing to do got in on the act, and soon Mills had RESCAPS in layers up to 20,000 feet! I handed over at low-level to a flight of French Navy Corsairs (better endurance) and Miller and I returned to *Albion*."

Meanwhile, Mills gathered his thoughts:

"There I was, some 40 miles behind enemy lines clutching my pistol and I could hear the noise of tank engines in the distance. I have never felt so utterly alone in all my life. It is curious that my overriding emotion was not fear but sadness that I would not see my family again and I thought of Drucie and baby Helen far away in Montreal, but at least they would have the support of loved ones. It seemed to me that my only chance was to move away from my parachute as soon as possible and try and avoid capture until nightfall and then head north towards our lines. Whatever happened I resolved not to be captured as I had no confidence at all that the Egyptians would apply the Geneva Convention. As I started to walk, my life really did flash before my eyes but, at the same time, training made me check my assets. At least I had water, some food in the survival kit, money if I needed it, which seemed unlikely, and, in spite of a backache from landing, I was in one piece. It never occurred to me that help was already on the way. I had been walking for some time when I heard aircraft noise and then four Corsairs from *La Fayette* appeared. Two of them flew off to the south-west and then I saw them dive at the ground in the direction of the approaching tanks. Palls of black smoke rose into the desert air and I slowly realised that I was not to be abandoned."

One of the protecting Corsairs from 14F Flotille was fired at by the battered Egyptian convoy as it passed within range, Ens deV Kieffer responding by leading a rocket and strafing attack on the remaining vehicles. Following the final pass, a group of camel-mounted soldiers were seen approaching from the east. Unaware of their intention, Kieffer carried out a very low-level pass, with flaps down and cockpit hood open, following which he fired a warning burst and waved them away from the downed pilot. The warning was heeded, and Kieffer flew back to where Mills was located:

"The Corsair leader motioned to me to return to my parachute which I then did. A few minutes later, a division of Sea Hawks arrived and they attacked something in the desert to the east. Much later, I learnt that they had stopped an Israeli column by firing in front of them. The Israelis had seen what had happened and were on their way to pick me up. If they had succeeded I would probably have had a hero's welcome in Tel Aviv! After about an hour the Corsairs waved goodbye as, even with their long endurance due to their piston engines, they had to go home but, by this time, there were three divisions stacked above me and anything that moved within fifteen miles was attacked. I was lucky because there was a lull in the proceedings whilst everybody waited for the order to move south, so I had four carriers to look after me!

Eventually I heard the swish of helicopter blades in the distance, followed by the friendly face of Pete Bailey, grinning at me from his chopper. He

Corsair 14F-9 (s/n 123690) of 14F Flotille aboard *La Fayette*. (*via Joss Leclercq*)

touched down [at 1225], I climbed in and away we went, accompanied by his escort and mine until we reached the coast, refuelled and continued on to *Eagle* [arriving at 1330]. I was taken to the sick-bay and given a check by the PMO. I was cheered up by a signal from the *La Fayette* from [Lt Cdr] Keith Leppard which said in effect, 'Trust you to be the first ashore – you owe the 14eme a crate of champagne', a sentiment with which I fully agreed. The 14eme Flotille were of course the Corsairs. For years afterwards, people walked up to me in a carrier or air station mess and said, 'You were quite safe you know, I was looking after you.' "

While most of the activity centered on the rescue of Lt Mills, 897 Squadron's Lt Middleton led a section of four Sea Hawks to carry out a photographic reconnaissance of Port Tewfik. Many oil tankers and cargo ships were observed anchored at Suez, with more of the latter under way northwards in the Little Bitter Lake. Several small warships and patrol boats were also seen at Suez, and another patrol boat was spotted steaming up the Canal from Suez. As the section overflew Kabrit airfield, two aircraft were observed on the ground, and another two, assumed to be Israeli, were seen flying north on the east side of the Canal.

During the afternoon the Sea Hawks, Sea Venoms and Corsairs continued to provide cover for the Marines and paratroops fighting in and around Port Said, some pilots flying three or four sorties.

| 1200 | *La Fayette* | 4 Corsairs | 7 military trucks damaged south of Port Said; several military vehicles which appeared u/s strafed near al-Qantara |
| 1205 | *Albion* | 8 Sea Hawks 800/802 Squadrons | 2 briefed as RESCAP then Cabrank; Bren Gun Carrier destroyed and 2 damaged; several trucks damaged |

1215	*Bulwark*	4 Sea Hawks 810 Squadron 2 Sea Hawks 895 Squadron	Cabrank – Port Said; R/P and strafing attack on 6 Bren Gun Carriers at al-Ballah; diverted to RESCAP over al-Qantara
1245	*Eagle*	4 Sea Venoms 893 Squadron 8 Sea Hawks 897 Squadron	Strike on Almaza Armed recce of Army camp at al-Qantara, R/P attack; 2 guns and a tank also attacked
1255	*Bulwark*	2 Sea Hawks 895 Squadron	Photo recce Port Said/Port Suez; diverted to RESCAP over al-Qantara
1315	*Albion*	2 Sea Hawks 802 Squadron 6 Sea Venoms 809 Squadron	Several 5-ton trucks marked with white star inside white circle seen 6 miles north-east of al-Qantara; presumed Israeli
1350	*Eagle*	4 Sea Venoms 892 Squadron 8 Sea Hawks 899 Squadron	Attack on MTB base at Ras Ada Biya, south of Suez Cabrank al-Qantara; damaged AFV destroyed by R/P
1420	*Albion*	2 Sea Hawks 800 Squadron 4 Sea Hawks 802 Squadron	Truck destroyed during armed recce as far south as Ismailia; no sign of enemy except for MG posts, none of which appeared to be manned
1430	*Bulwark*	2 Sea Hawks 804 Squadron 4 Sea Hawks 804 Squadron 6 Sea Hawks 810 Squadron	Photo recce – Port Tewfik to al-Qantara road Armed recce – Cairo to Suez road; attacked MTB, and 4 trucks set afire Cabrank – Port Said
1455	*Eagle*	6 Sea Hawks 897 Squadron	Armed recce MTB base at Ras Ada Biya, south of Suez; wharf and pier rocketed
1525	*Albion*	6 Sea Venoms 809 Squadron	Armed recce Suez Canal to Ismailia; trucks and Bren Carrier attacked
1600	*Eagle*	4 Sea Venoms 893 Squadron	Armed recce of Almaza and Cairo International
1630	*Albion*	3 Sea Hawks 800 Squadron 4 Sea Hawks 802 Squadron	Strike on Navy House by R/P; damaged, then strafed Armed recce from Port Said to Edku; no sign of enemy movement
1635	*Eagle*	6 Sea Hawks 899 Squadron	Attacked Navy House, Port Said; on fire when strike arrived; all R/P on target

Some aircrew of 809 Squadron aboard HMS *Eagle*, from left to right: Midspm Ed Weiss, Lt(O) Carter, Lt(P) Ron Davidson, Sub Lt(O) Charlie Dwarika, Sub Lt(P) Ince-Jones, Lt Cdr(P) Ron Shilcock, Lt(O) John Hackett, Lt(P) Mahany, Sub Lt(O) Hughes, Sub Lt(P) Tony Yates. (*Lt Cdr R.A. Shilcock*)

Lt Cdr Shilcock (with Lt Hackett, in XG670/220) led the armed reconnaissance by six Sea Venoms of 809 Squadron during the mid-afternoon, when six trucks at al-Kirsh Camp were strafed, as were half a dozen Bren Gun Carriers. Before returning to the carrier, a railway wagon and six three-ton trucks were observed and these received similar treatment. The Sea Venom (XG669/224) crewed by Sub Lts Yates and Dwarika participated in this mission, the pair's third sortie of the day and 16th (and final) sortie of the brief campaign.

During the attack on Almaza by four Sea Venoms of 893 Squadron, a Harvard, a Meteor and two Furies were claimed destroyed, although the pilots believed these aircraft had been damaged by previous strikes. At dusk, another section from the same squadron was sent to Cairo International and Almaza; as no transport aircraft were seen at the latter, the full load of rockets was fired into hangars and MiG assembly sheds. Another quartet of Sea Venoms from 892 Squadron were despatched to attack the MTB base at Ras Ada Biya, south of Suez, where two MTBs were observed alongside the jetty. Following an R/P attack, both patrol boats were left in flames. Another MTB was also attacked by a quartet of Sea Hawks from *Bulwark* and the pilots reported that it 'blew up'. When six Sea Hawks of 897 Squadron arrived over the MTB base an hour later, no MTBs could be seen, so it was assumed that the three Egyptian craft had sunk. Rather than return with the weapon loads, the Sea Hawks fired a total of 24 rockets at the wharf and pier which set the latter on fire and destroyed two buildings.

With the onset of darkness, and with the ceasefire to come into force at midnight, air operations effectively ended with the strike on the Navy House at Port Said by Sea Hawks of 800 and 899 Squadrons. As one historian wrote:

"When the Fleet Air Arm planes attacked last light, their performance was an impressive and terrifying sight. Plane after plane dived on to the now isolated Navy House and fired rockets into it; shortly afterwards all Egyptian resistance inside ceased and the following morning about 20 men came out of the blazing building to surrender; they left behind them 30 dead."

One of the last carrier sorties of the day was flown by Lt Worth of 800 Squadron in WV832, who carried out a shipping reconnaissance between 1525 and 1640, during which he sighted the French submarine *La Creole* and a Shackleton of 37 Squadron from Malta. Reconnaissance jets from Cyprus were also very busy throughout the day and flew a total of 18 sorties, eight of which were undertaken by 13 Squadron Canberras, the remainder by the RF-84Fs. Lt Bertin-Maghit of ER4/33 again experienced problems with his JATO pack, jettisoning it over a Royal Navy vessel in Limassol harbour although "happily no damage was done". During this period both PR Canberras and RF-84s had overflown Syria on a daily basis to monitor activity at SAF bases. On a number of occasions, Syrian Meteor F8s had been scrambled to intercept but had achieved little success.

Among the Syrian pilots active at this time was Lt Hafiz al-Asad, who had been based at al-Mezze but when the war broke out was posted to Nayrab base near Aleppo. Air defence was rudimentary, such early warning as existed being provided by police look-outs around the country who phoned in if they spotted an unfamiliar aircraft, although usually by the time the observer could reach a telephone the intruder was long gone. Major Moukabri, a SAF controller, explained that by taking the calls as they came in, he was able to co-ordinate the bearings obtained by each observer and deduce the track of the aircraft and its approximate speed. The Meteors were launched to climb to an intercept point on the extrapolated track line.

Once the shooting war had started, the Syrians expected British and French reconnaissance aircraft to violate their airspace, which they did on an ever-increasing scale as the fighting in Egypt progressed, the Allies anxious to verify reports that Russian MiGs were being delivered to secret airstrips in the desert. These reports, emanating from the US Embassy in Damascus, spoke of Russian arms arriving at the Syrian port of Latakia, while 'not more than 123 MiGs' had arrived in Syria, no doubt causing panic at GHQ Cyprus. Thus, Canberras were over Syria at first light and, shortly after 0800, the police frontier post at Abu Kamal on the Euphrates called to say that a Canberra had been sighted flying in from Iraq. Lt al-Asad was sent off in his Meteor to engage and had the satisfaction of firing his 20mm cannons at it before it flew off towards Cyprus. By this time the Syrian fighter pilots were practically living in their cockpits. The Canberra crew, who had been sent to photograph Syrian airfields but found them covered in cloud, reported on their return to Cyprus that they had been chased by Meteors in unidentified markings". Air HQ insisted that a second Canberra be despatched forthwith to secure the photographs, Flt Lt Bernie Hunter, the Canberra Flight Commander, taking it upon himself to fly the sortie:

"So I briefed my crew. [Flg Off] Roy Erquhart-Pullen was my navigator and the rear view position was occupied by [Flt Lt] Sam Small, another Canberra pilot, who had come out to reinforce the Squadron during the Suez period. So we went off [at 1230 in WH799] to photograph Rayak (in the Lebanon rather than Syria), Aleppo and al-Raschid. Navigation was extremely good: under cloud cover then towards 12,000 feet, down to 11,000 feet then 10,000 feet slowly in order to get overlaps. We were heading towards Damascus, when to our horror – blue sky! Normally a pilot's dream, but under operating conditions we were, to say the least, in a very unenviable position. My first reaction was to climb on full power to get back into cloud cover, as it would have been absolutely fatal if we tried to go over Damascus airfield at that height and speed. At about the same time Sam Small warned of a pair of Meteors coming in from port or starboard, I can't remember which. I had to turn into their attack. I think it was port, I can't remember. So there were three factors in this particular problem, none of which was helpful to the others as no matter where the Meteors were coming from, I had to turn towards them. It went on like this for a few minutes, which seemed like several hours, and during the first attack almost certainly we did not get hit; then Sam said almost immediately after the first attack, with us still climbing, another pair [probably the same pair] were coming in, so we turned again. I turned hard towards them and that's when the starboard engine was hit."

Major Moukabri, the Syrian air controller, stated later that the Meteor pilot performing the interception initially could not see the Canberra until he was told to look down. The Canberra was below him and was subsequently shot down in an astern attack. Flt Lt Hunter continued:

"I had been calling Roy, who was in the prone position to take photographs, to come back to the rumble seat (so-called spare seat located alongside the pilot). He got the message, I think, but did not come back. Eventually it got to the stage where I was rapidly losing control of the situation: one engine out, still burning. I told Sam to get out, to eject, and from the rear navigation position he ejected quite safely. We were still under attack and I started the desperate business of trying to get hold of Roy. I never did contact Roy on the R/T and, as far as I know, he must have gone back to the rear navigation position to try to eject. Since the ejection seat had gone, I assume he tried to bale out. I am not sure, but I think I heard a big thud on the aircraft, which could have been Roy's body hitting the tail plane. I suspect it was. I then ejected and it seemed only seconds before I hit the ground and broke my left ankle. The sequence of events was very quick so I couldn't possibly estimate how low I was, but can remember thinking at the time: if I don't get out now I won't get out.

I didn't know whether I got out over the Lebanon or not [the Canberra apparently crashed in the Beka'a Valley in Lebanon]; my mind was revolving round the fact that if I'm in Syria they're not going to be very friendly. But Lebanon was largely a Christian country although Arabs lived there. A crowd got together almost immediately they saw the parachute. We were not armed since I failed to see much use for a pistol with six bullets, and that became our saviour in fact, as I was surrounded by people, mainly young kids and old men who automatically assumed I was an Israeli as I was wearing normal flight kit – overalls. The crowd grew very quickly; they got sticks and started to hit me – I received a number of injuries on my hands as I tried to protect my face, but soon, thank the Lord, I heard somebody speaking English and shouting at the youngsters to keep away. It turned out he was

Unlike EAF Meteors, those in Syrian Air Force service were fully camouflaged and carried their s/n in small Arabic figures on the tail fin. These particular F8s are numbered, from the closest, 412, 411 and probably 407. It was a SAF Meteor F8 which shot down an RAF PR Canberra on 6 November 1956. (*Authors' collection*)

a Christian teacher at the local school. I said to him, tell these people I am not an Israeli, I am RAF. He eventually got his way and simmered things down. To this day I'd like to thank him; without his help, I might not be here. I was handed over to the military at the Border Post and interrogated by a Syrian. I convinced him I was doing weather recce over the Lebanon and had got lost. That was all that happened for some little time, until I saw Sam brought in. Said to him, 'Weather recce, got lost', all I was able to say. Heat of situation removed."

Both Hunter and Small were eventually taken to a hospital in Beirut, where they were advised that they would remain as prisoners of war. However, following a visit by the British Deputy Air Attaché, they were able to escape and with help from Embassy staff found themselves secreted aboard a small passenger vessel bound for Cyprus.

Later that afternoon, some 40 minutes before sunset, Lt al-Asad of the Syrian Air Force was again ordered to scramble in his Meteor although on this occasion he was unable to locate the intruder, which may have been an American U-2, since one of the CIA's spyplanes penetrated Syrian airspace also searching for signs of the elusive Russian jets. With darkness falling, an unserviceable radio and lacking night flying aids, al-Asad was barely able to see the runway at Nayrab. He landed downwind and overshot, his brakes proving to be ineffective. The Meteor crashed through a wall, narrowly missing a tented camp of Palestinian refugees, shedding its undercarriage en route. The unfortunate al-Asad, who admitted that he had known his brakes to have been defective before he had taken off, was reprimanded and given a suspended jail sentence.

As a result of the downing of Flt Lt Hunter's Canberra, subsequent reconnaissance flights over Syria by Canberras were escorted by Hunters from 1 and 34 Squadrons on withdrawing from the target areas, while French RF-84Fs were sent out in pairs.

During the day reports were received at GHQ of unidentified jets flying at 40,000 feet from the direction of Turkey on their way to Egypt. The pro-Western Turkish Air Force was placed on full alert, while Hunters from Cyprus were scrambled during the afternoon to identify an aircraft reported 50 miles north of Cape Andreas. The Hunters climbed to 60,000 feet where they spotted the aircraft 10,000 feet higher. It was the U-2 spyplane heading towards the Turkish coast. There was at least one further major scare during the hours of darkness when a large unidentified jet aircraft was detected by radar, flying over Cyprus at 54,000 feet. It approached from the east and turned back over Famagusta. The inference was that this was a Soviet aircraft with a performance superior to the MiG-15 or Il-28, but the identity of the intruder has not been established: 'The purpose of this visit is obscure but it could not have been for visual or photographic reconnaissance', concluded an official report.

With the fear of a Soviet strike from the East against the Anglo-French remaining a possibility, combined with the unyielding pressure exerted from the West by the Americans and wholesale condemnation of the military action from most other nations, Prime Minister Eden reluctantly agreed to a ceasefire. The French declared that they could not continue the fight on their own, but the ground fighting continued until the last moment – a minute before midnight – by which time British forces had advanced as far as al-Cap, a small village a few miles short of their objective, al-Qantara.

Chapter Sixteen

CONCLUSIONS AND IMPRESSIONS

"Broadly speaking it can be said that the combined forces of Naval, RAF and FAF ground attack aircraft was completely successful in achieving its aim."

Air Marshal Denis Barnett, Air Task Force Commander

For the Egyptian Air Force the conflict had been a disaster. Five days and nights of intense air strikes by the massive air armada had destroyed most of its aircraft and caused serious damage to airfields and support facilities. However, despite the heavy Anglo-French air bombardment, the EAF had suffered fewer than 200 casualties, of whom about 25 were fatal, including five pilots (killed in action against the Israelis), during the Sinai-Suez War – proportionally much less than the Egyptian Army had suffered.

Although the fighting had all but ceased, the psychological war continued unabated, albeit with a marked lack of success. Radio Cyprus put out the following broadcast to the Egyptian people on the first day of the ceasefire:

"This is the Allied High Command. Listen to the truth.

It is now two days since Port Said and Port Fuad are safe in Allied hands. We have been most interested to hear what Nasser has been saying about our losses. We have nothing to hide and we will tell you exactly what our losses have been since the air operations began on 1st November at dawn. On that day we attacked five airfields, at Almaza, Inchas, Abu Sueir, Kabrit, Cairo West and elsewhere. We lost no aircraft, although, as we told you before [in an earlier broadcast], one was slightly damaged. But it flew again next day against Luxor. Yet Nasser claimed that nine had been shot down. The truth was – not one.

Next day our aircraft flew again, to Kasfareet, Fayid and other places, including Abu Za'bal. We lost one aircraft that day; it had flown from a carrier, it made a bad landing and fell into the sea. What did Nasser claim that day? Two shot down over Port Said, two over Alexandria, nine over Cairo. Who has seen their wreckage? Nobody, for we lost no aircraft that day, except for the one that fell into the sea. Nobody knew about that one except us; you wouldn't have known if we didn't tell you now; there is no need for us to tell you now, but we tell the truth.

On the morning of the 4th November we lost one aircraft, although we had many in the sky. So up to then our total loss was two, one that was shot

---

339

down and the one that fell in the sea. By that time Nasser's claims had risen still further. We have lost count of his claims. But up to now in a week's fighting we have lost five aircraft altogether – five. As for the aircraft of the Egyptian Air Force, they are nearly all destroyed. We have counted from the air the total wreckage of 200 and many more damaged, and as we said the other night, we calculate that they cost you at least £80,000,000 – something like £4 for every person in Egypt. You cannot afford a man like Nasser. What could you not have done with all that money to spend on the things for peace?

At sea we have not lost a single ship. The Allied Forces destroyed a destroyer, a frigate and three E-boats, besides damage to another. Nasser has been saying too that we have bombed towns and villages. Nasser is a liar. We warned you over and over again to give you a chance to avoid areas where we were to bomb. We have tried hard to avoid doing damage to any but military targets. A number of houses in Port Said were damaged; that was because the soldiers fought in the streets for a few hours and had to be dealt with. But never before in the history of air fighting has any air force taken so much trouble to avoid hurting civilian people or damaging houses. We are telling the truth, O Egyptians. We British and French think it a shame to tell lies. We tell the truth.

Believe him if you like. Believe this man who told you that his air force would dominate the skies. Believe the man who has spent the money which could have been spent to your benefit on 270 aircraft which are now nothing but twisted metal. Believe the man whose lies are choking Egypt like weeds, who promised you greatness and is bringing you ruin. Believe him if you like. But you know in your hearts that we, the voices of the Allies, are not lying. Listen to the Truth!"

President Nasser retorted by calling the Allied claims nonsense and denied that his air force had been destroyed. He claimed that dummy aircraft had been placed on the airfields and that it was these that had been destroyed.

Despite the ceasefire, Allied aircraft continued to violate Egypt's airspace, mainly Canberra PR7s and RF-84Fs keeping an eye on the situation although, at 0800 on 7 November, Lt Cdr Shilcock (in XG670, with Lt Hackett) led four Sea Venoms of 809 Squadron to carry out an armed reconnaissance over Egypt, as noted by the Squadron diarist:

"Carried out recce Port Said to five miles along the coast to the west, nothing to report. Thence to al-Sahiya and Abu Sueir. Runways appear serviceable; two unserviceable MiGs positively identified. Possibly about 30 others on the airfield. Avoided Ismailia due to flak but nothing seen on northern outskirts of town. Nothing seen on Ismailia or al-Firdan airfields. No troops or equipment noticed at al-Kirsh camp. Numerous single vehicles seen parked on Treaty Road between al-Ballah airfield and al-Qantara. British troops including about 20 tanks observed to have proceeded as far south as al-Cap Station. Moderate flak over north Ismailia accurate, bursting up to 6,000 feet."

Three days later, on the morning of 10 November, an Egyptian military spokesman announced:

Dekheila photographed by an RF-84F of ER4/33 on the morning of 7 November 1956. The main runway appears to have been repaired and four apparently undamaged aircraft can be seen on the original print. (*SHAA via Albert Grandolini*)

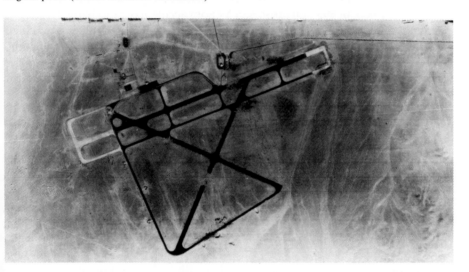

Inchas was also photographed by an RF-84F of ER4/33, flown by Cne Rieuneau, on the morning of 7 November 1956. The runways have yet to be repaired. (*SHAA via Albert Grandolini*)

"Two enemy aircraft on a reconnaissance flight over our positions in Ismailia were shot down by our armed forces last night."

The Anglo-French air forces suffered no losses on that date, nor did, as far as is known, the IDF/AF. That same day, EOKA terrorists on Cyprus managed to infiltrate Nicosia air base and plant a time bomb on Hunter WP180/F of 1 Squadron, which was damaged beyond repair. Elsewhere, a special CAP was provided by Sea Hawks of 810 Squadron when they met and escorted General Edison Burns's UN Dakota to Israeli territorial limits.

Meantime, unaware of how the Soviet-supported Egyptian forces would react to the ceasefire, Air Marshal Barnett and his staff made contingency plans should the EAF – which they believed was about to be strengthened by between

50 and 80 MiGs reported to have been seen in Syria* – now take the offensive. Photographs taken by PR aircraft revealed that the runways at Abu Sueir, Fayid and Almaza had been repaired and were capable of receiving the MiGs. It was intended that should hostilities recommence, *Operation Musketeer* would be resumed. It was assumed that (a) any such Egyptian offensive would start before the arrival of UN troops, (b) the MiGs would arrive from Syria at the last possible moment, (c) any Russian aircraft provided would be flown by Russian or volunteer pilots, and (d) the Egyptian offensive would be aimed at Port Said and airfields in Cyprus. All Allied units were kept at readiness.

The airlifting of the advanced element of UN police force had in fact already begun and 51 Danish soldiers were on their way to Naples aboard C-124 Globemasters of the USAF. Similar aircraft were to pick up Norwegian soldiers in Oslo and also convey them to Naples, while a force of troops from 17 countries was in the process of being ferried to Egypt by Swissair DC-6Bs.

Meanwhile, at sea on 14 November, Sub Lt J.M. Widdington's 810 Squadron Sea Hawk (XE375/239) was lost when the arrester hook pulled out on landing back on *Bulwark*. The aircraft struck another Sea Hawk and went over the side but fortunately the pilot was rescued by the planeguard Dragonfly "wet, and with a headache, but otherwise all right". A further incident occurred shortly afterwards, when an 893 Squadron Sea Venom accidentally discharged about 30 rounds of 20mm into the hangar of *Eagle*. At least one maintainer was killed and the resultant fire caused considerable damage, both to aircraft and the hangar. Aboard the *Arromanches*, one of 14F Flotille's Corsairs came to grief when Second Maître Karmann's aircraft hooked 'off-centre' when landing, but caused only minor damage and no casualties.

However, the Armée de l'Air lost the services of one of its RF-84Fs on 18 November when RF326, the aircraft of Lt Bertin-Maghit, caught fire at Akrotiri as it was being readied for flight. During the latter half of November, a Hunter of 34 Squadron came to grief on taking off from Akrotiri when its engine cut. It pancaked back on to the airfield although the pilot, Flt Lt J.B. Fitzpatrick, was unhurt.

At this time *Theseus* was on her way back to Malta with wounded on board, but was short of certain medical supplies for treating casualties. An urgent message was put through to Malta and on the morning of 16 November a Shackleton of 37 Squadron appeared, made two runs alongside the carrier and released two yellow-painted canisters, filled with 50lb of serum and medicines, over sea markers which had been laid for the purpose. Already airborne were two Whirlwinds of 845 Squadron and, as the containers hit the sea, they swept down and had them on the ship within two minutes. During the first run the Shackleton had to fly at 120 feet through a blinding rainstorm, as recalled by the pilot, Flt Lt Richard Buckwell:

> "Our instructions were to deliver medical supplies at first light. We linked
> up with the carrier when she was 385 miles east of Malta. Dropping

---

* It seems that the MiGs seen in Syria were Soviet MiG-19s from bases in the Caucasus region. They had overflown Turkey via the 'back door' route south of Lake Van, a desolate, mountainous area devoid of radar coverage and, according to one contemporary report, were "ready to go into action against Israel if she did not withdraw from Egyptian territory".

Second Maître Karmann's Corsair aboard *Arromanches* following a landing mishap. (*via Joss Leclercq*)

instructions were passed to us by radio although at the time we could not see the ship because of the huge raincloud in the area."

Despite the political setback, the Allies had accomplished one of their goals: the fighting had shattered Egypt's armed forces, although reports were received on 21 November of the first two replacement MiG-15s arriving at Abu Sueir, flown by Russian pilots. The Allied air campaign against Egypt had been the most intense aerial bombardment anywhere in the world since the Korean War. The raids had caused extensive damage to runways and facilities at many EAF bases in Egypt and, before they withdrew from Sinai, Israeli forces systematically destroyed Egyptian air bases, Egyptian Army positions along with roads, railways and other elements of infrastructure.

Initial British estimates of the number of EAF aircraft damaged or destroyed by air attack in the conflict were 229 destroyed, 24 probably destroyed and 239 damaged, which included 104 MiG-15/17s, 11 Meteors, 30 Vampires, 26 Il-28s, plus 63 trainers and support aircraft. This estimate appears to be high given the fact that many EAF aircraft had flown out of Egypt to safety during the fighting, while PR analysis revealed only 105 aircraft destroyed, including 62 MiG-15s, although this figure apparently excluded trainer aircraft. President Nasser refuted claims that his air force had been destroyed. He said that most of the aircraft claimed destroyed during the Anglo-French attacks were dummies. While some dummy aircraft had been deployed on the airfields, the great majority of machines identified as destroyed in air reconnaissance photographs were clearly genuine.

SUMMARY OF GROUND ATTACK CLAIMS
AGAINST AIRCRAFT OF THE EGYPTIAN AIR FORCE
by Venoms of the Akrotiri Strike Wing, 1–6 November 1956

Date	Missions	Sorties	Aborts	MiG-15s			Other types		
				Des'd	Prob	Dam'd	Des'd	Prob	Dam'd
1/11	19	106	2	48	7	28	11	4	9
2/11	19	92	3	21	0	23	4	1	2
3/11	12	46	1	3	0	2	11	0	2
4/11	12	45	3	2	0	0	1	0	0
5/11	17	66	2	0	0	0	0	0	0
6/11	15	41	9	0	0	0	0	0	0
	94	396	20	74	7	53	27	5	13

Total RAF claims: 101:12:66 aircraft on the ground

	Destroyed	Probables	Damaged
6 Squadron	28	0	21
8 Squadron	43	6	30
249 Squadron	30	6	15

	No of sorties flown	20mm rounds fired	Rockets launched
6 Squadron	128	34,920	491
8 Squadron	134	32,720	490
249 Squadron	134	25,947	430

Venoms lost/damaged

6 Squadron	one Cat 3, plus nine minor damage
8 Squadron	one Cat 1, plus seven minor damage
249 Squadron	one Cat 3, plus ten minor damage

SUMMARY OF GROUND ATTACKS by F-84Fs of the Armée de l'Air, 1–6 November 1956

Date	Sorties	Aborts	Rockets launched	12.7mm fired
1/11	75	5	528	14,000
2/11	68	4	184	35,000
3/11	39	3	156	16,000
4/11	38	2	276	11,000
5/11	48	0	176	22,000
6/11	34	2	146	9,000
	302	16	1,466	107,000

Total Armée de l'Air claims: 19:12:11 aircraft on the ground, of which 14:10:8 were for MiGs; the F-84Fs also claimed destroyed: two radars, three tanks, 24 lorries, seven wagons, one locomotive, one half-track; and damaged: seven hangars, four gun batteries, one tank, four half-tracks, eight lorries, three wagons, one casemate. In return, one F-84F was lost, eight damaged by ground fire, and one damaged by rocket debris.

In addition, RAF Valiants and Canberras from Malta and Cyprus flew a total of 18 bombing strikes on 13 targets and dropped a total of 1,962 bombs. Nicosia's Canberras alone logged 266 operational sorties. The RF-84Fs flew a total of 84 reconnaissance sorties, more than the Canberra PR7s of 13 Squadron achieved; in addition, 86 transport sorties were flown, almost 60 of these by Hastings and Valettas during the airborne assault.

SUMMARY OF GROUND ATTACK CLAIMS AGAINST AIRCRAFT OF THE EGYPTIAN AIR FORCE by the Fleet Air Arm, 1–6 November 1956

Date	MiG-15s			Other types		
	Destroyed	Probably Destroyed	Damaged	Destroyed	Probably Destroyed	Damaged
1/11	22	5	9	58	4	76
2/11	5	0	5	23	2	43
3/11	1	0	1	3	0	18
4/11	0	0	0	5	0	0
5/11	2	0	5	5	1	16
6/11	0	0	0	4	0	0
	30	5	20	98	7	153

Total FAA claims: 128:12:173

	Destroyed	Probables	Damaged
HMS *Eagle*'s squadrons:	59	6	48
HMS *Albion*'s squadrons:	36	0	60
HMS *Bulwark*'s squadrons:	33	6	65

800, 804 and 897 Squadron each lost a Sea Hawk, while 830 Squadron lost two Wyverns, and 845 Squadron a Whirlwind.

A total of 1,130 operational strike sorties was flown by the Fleet Air Arm, excluding CAP, anti-submarine and helicopter sorties. *Eagle*'s squadrons flew 621 sorties (including 169 by 897 Squadron alone), dropped 72 1,000lb bombs, 157 500lb bombs, launched 1,448 three-inch rockets and fired 88,000 rounds of 20mm. *Albion*'s squadrons flew 415 sorties, plus a further 130 by her two Whirlwind helicopters which included planeguard duties and evacuation of casualties. *Bulwark*'s figures are not known but would have matched the totals achieved by the other two carriers.

The Aeronavale Corsairs of 14F and 15F Flotille flew a total of 132 operational sorties, while 9F Flotille's Avengers recorded a further 51. Although only one Corsair was lost in action, another was lost in an accident, and a third damaged. The Corsairs dropped 36 1,000lb and 30 500lb bombs, fired almost 500 rockets and 16,650 rounds of 20mm.

The Anglo-French Air Task Force suffered a total of seven fatalities during the six-day war:

Sub Lt C.J. Hall, 804 Squadron, killed in accident 2/11/56
Flt Lt E.A. Sheehan, 8 Squadron, killed in action 3/11/56
Lt deV A. Lancrenon, 14F Flotille, killed in action 3/11/56
Flg Off G.R. Erquhart-Pullen 13 Squadron, killed in action 6/11/56

The Duke of Edinburgh, accompanied by Admiral Manley Power, congratulates FAA squadron commanders, from left to right: Lt Cdr C.V. Howard (830 Sqn), Lt Cdr B.J. Williams (849 Sqn), Lt Cdr M.W. Henley (893 Sqn), Lt Cdr A.B.B. Clark (899 Sqn), Lt Cdr A.R. Rawbone (897 Sqn), Lt Cdr M.H.J. Petrie (892 Sqn), Lt Cdr P.M. Lamb (810 Sqn), Lt Cdr J. Morris-Jones (895 Sqn). (*Lt Cdr P.M. Lamb*)

Flg Off L.I. Collins, 9 Squadron, killed in accident 6/11/56
Flg Off K.W. Banyard, 9 Squadron, killed in accident 6/11/56
Flt Sgt M.A. Rhodes, 9 Squadron, killed in accident 6/11/56

All told, the British forces lost 23 killed (nine Royal Marine Commandos including two officers; one Army officer and seven soldiers, plus the RN and RAF personnel as listed), while the French lost ten killed, including six paratroopers and the Aeronavale officer. The Allies also suffered 129 wounded, of whom 96 were British. Estimates for the number of Egyptians killed varied although Mohamed Heikal recorded the figure for both the Sinai and Suez operations as 921 killed. Israeli fatalities were believed to be in the region of 200.

IMPRESSIONS AND REFLECTIONS

With the abrupt end of the fighting in Egypt came not only the anticipated political recriminations, but also praise for the fighting man. British Prime Minister Eden was quick to defend his position when criticised by Foreign Secretary Harold Macmillan, who declared that the Suez operation had been a tactical defeat. Eden retorted:

> "I do not think that the events of Suez can be reckoned as a tactical defeat. It is much too early to pronounce on an operation of this kind. This much is certain: the Soviet-Egyptian Air Force has been destroyed. The Israelis have eliminated one third of the Egyptian Army and its equipment. The extent of Soviet penetration into the Middle East has been exposed, with the result that the United States at last seems to be taking the action for which we pleaded in vain throughout 1956."

However, it is interesting to note that Eden resigned two days after receiving the memo, on the grounds of deteriorating health, and that it was Macmillan who succeeded him as Prime Minister. Shortly before Eden's resignation, former Prime Minister Churchill – who remarked of the Suez operation, "I am not sure I should have dared to start, but I am sure I should not have dared to stop" – had written to President Eisenhower, expressing his regrets at the whole sorry episode, adding however:

> "Whatever the arguments adduced here and in the United States for or against Anthony's action in Egypt, it will now be an act of folly, on which our whole civilisation may founder, to let events in the Middle East come between us."

To which the American President replied:

> "Starting almost at the instant that Nasser took his high-handed action with respect to the Canal, I tried earnestly to keep Anthony [Prime Minister Eden] informed of public opinion in this country and of the course that we would feel compelled to follow if there was any attempt to solve by force the problem presented to the free world through Nasser's action . . . I argued that to invade Egypt merely because that country had chosen to nationalise a company would be interpreted by the world as power politics and would raise a storm of resentment that, within the Arab states, would result in a long and dreary guerilla warfare.
>
> I tried to make it clear that we share the opinion of the British [and] others that . . . we would have to concert our actions in making certain that he [Nasser] did not grow to be a danger to our welfare. But for the reasons I have given above, I urged that the nationalisation of the Canal Company was not the vehicle to choose for bringing about correction in this matter. Sometime in the early part of October, all communications between ourselves on the one hand and the British and French on the other suddenly ceased ... so far as Britain and France were concerned, we felt that they had deliberately excluded us from their thinking . . . The first news we had of the attack and of British-French plans was gained from the newspapers and we had no recourse except to assert our readiness to support the United Nations."

The President continued, revealing a more benevolent attitude towards the British than had his openly hostile Secretary of State, Foster Dulles:

> "I still believe that we must keep several facts clearly before us, the first one being that the Soviets are the real enemy and all else must be viewed against the background of that truth. The second is that nothing would please this country more, in fact could help us more, than to see British prestige and strength renewed and rejuvenated in the Mid-East. We want those countries to trust and lean towards the Western world, not Russia. A third fact is that we want to help Britain right now, particularly in its difficult fuel and financial situation, daily growing more serious . . . I hope that this one may be washed off the slate as soon as possible . . . I shall never be happy until our old-time closeness has been restored."

347

If the sentiment expressed was genuine, and American interests had been made clear sooner rather than later, perhaps the outcome of the conflict would have had a more satisfactory conclusion for Britain and France in particular, and for Western interests in general, although possibly not for Egypt and her allies. Mohamed Heikal, with a hint of cynicism as one would expect, wrote:

"Suez had many losers, and two clear victors: President Nasser and the Americans. Britain's attempt to re-establish itself in the area it regarded as peculiarly its own had resulted in disaster, as had France's attempt to sneak in by the back door. So the Americans could see no rivals . . . Of the three principal forces which interacted on one another, one, Britain, has ceased to have any major role to play. But the other two, America and Arab nationalism, are left confronting each other."

Pressure by the United Nations, and America in particular, had obliged Britain and France to halt the assault on Egypt before most of their political and military objectives had been achieved. British MP Julian Amery speculated:

"Britain and France were in possession of one end of the Canal, and within 48 hours could have the whole of it. There might have been a tank battle outside Cairo, but with the Soviet instructors departed this seems unlikely. Nasser would probably have left Cairo. I believe [he] would have withdrawn to the Sudan and probably the Soviet Union. A shadow Egyptian government was waiting in the wings in Cairo. Its leaders proposed to come out to parley with us once Nasser had gone. They would have offered to negotiate a new treaty over the Canal. I had personally been in touch with a number of Egyptian personalities including the former Prime Minister, Nahhas Pasha [Mustafa al-Nahhas], who were only too anxious to achieve such a solution both on its merits and to get rid of the increasingly pro-socialist government of Nasser."

Apparently the Soviets believed that they had played a vital part in ending the fighting in Egypt. Soviet Secretary-General (and future Premier) Khrushchev recalled:

"In our notes to the three governments who led the aggression against Egypt, we said:

'You have attacked Egypt, knowing that it does not have much of an army, and that it does not have many weapons. But there are other countries which are entirely capable of coming to Egypt's defence.'

We were clearly hinting that the Soviet Union was such a country, and that we were ready to intervene if necessary. We warned that we couldn't remain neutral because, if the conflict in the Near East spread, it would threaten our own national interests. They took us very seriously . . . twenty-two hours after the delivery of our note the aggression was halted. We only had to issue our warning once."

The threat of involvement by units of the Soviet Air Force was considered a serious possibility by the men fighting the war, as recollected by Flg Off Tony Gronert of 249 Squadron (later Captain, British Airways):

> "It was rumoured that the Russians, who were very friendly with the Egyptians at the time, would be drawn into the conflict especially as there were unofficial reports that several of their pilots, with the Egyptians, had been killed."

As has been seen, there is no evidence of Russian or any non-Arab subject flying with the EAF, although undoubtedly Sudanese nationals did so.

General Sir Charles Keightley GCB GBE DSO, Commander-in-Chief Allied Forces, wrote in his Despatch:

> "I should like to record my admiration and gratitude to the sailors, soldiers and airmen who achieved all the military objectives given to them. The skill and gallantry required, particularly of parachutists, commandos and pilots, was equal to that demanded in any operation of war and it is they more than anyone else who deserve praise."

However, Général Andre Beaufre, French Task Force Commander, commented cynically:

> "The Suez adventure was the work of nations whose prestige was reduced. In 1900 a British gunboat had the whole weight of the Empire behind it. In 1956 a major Franco-British expedition could not have similar authority."

The Air Task Force Commander, Air Marshal Denis Barnett (later Air Chief Marshal Sir Denis GCB CBE DFC) reflected on the vulnerability of Cyprus to retaliatory air attack:

> "It has always surprised me that the Russians who had come with the MiGs that had been supplied to Egypt could bear to see them being defeated, without themselves volunteering to come and have a go at us."

On the question of airfield defence, Grp Capt T.O. Prickett, Chief of Staff Task Force (later Air Chief Marshal Sir Thomas KCB DSO DFC), commented:

> "The air defence of the airfields in Cyprus . . . was not the responsibility of the Air Task Force. It was the responsibility of the AOC Levant. This is another illustration of the absolute balls-up that was going on in the command set-up. I'm quite sure that the AOC Levant was not at all happy about it."

Not only was the AOC Levant – Air Vice-Marshal W.J. Crisham CB CBE – unhappy about his role but he was critical of the RAF's equipment:

> "It should be noted that although the EAF, equipped with a fair number of high-performance fighters, was completely neutralised by a force containing a high percentage of fighters of inferior performance, no firm conclusion can be drawn from this because of the imponderable factor of the morale and general willingness to fight of EAF.

(1) The Venom has many shortcomings; it is no longer good enough to use obsolete fighters in this role.

(2) The need for a fighter reconnaissance capability was demonstrated but so also was our lack of an aircraft for this role. On the other hand, the RF-84F operated by the FAF [French Air Force] was in every respect excellent in the FR role.

(3) If it is ever again necessary to use the Canberra PR7 on tasks appropriate to FR, its limitations should be appreciated from the outset.

(4) Throughout *Musketeer*, the FAF operated with great elan and were most effective allies. The RF-84F and Noratlas aircraft appeared to be superior to our own equipment.

Further praise for the performance of the F-84Fs and RF-84Fs and the French pilots came from the detachment commander, Colonel Gauthier:

"Of the 52 French pilots involved in the Suez operation, only three had seen combat during World War Two, though 11 others had flown operationally in Indo-China. For more than 75 per cent of the French pilots, the Suez operation was their first active combat mission. Fifty-two pilots proved to be sufficient number for this campaign, but the fact that some of them had to fly three missions on a single day proved excessive, particularly as these missions could take one and a half hours each. Some pilots were clearly showing fatigue by the fifth day of operations. Twelve per cent of the pilots also suffered from dysentery, one seriously.

The F-84F proved to be fast at low altitude with excellent visibility and was robust. It performed very well and was trusted by the pilots. It was also remarkably resistant to the effects of dust. Its firepower was suitable for tactical strikes. The five-inch rockets were highly effective but their use and sighting made the aircraft vulnerable to ground fire.

It is not possible to end this report without underlining the excellent relations which existed between the personnel of the RAF and that of [the French detachment], and in particular I must mention the spirit of co-operation and cordiality which always marked the attitude of Grp Capt Macdonald, Commander of the Air Base at Akrotiri, towards myself."

Despite Air Vice-Marshal Crisham's criticism of the Venom, 249 Squadron's Flt Lt Charlie Slade (later Grp Capt) was full of praise for the nimble aircraft:

"The Venom was a fine aircraft with twice the thrust of the Vampire and could maintain Mach 0.8 above 50,000 feet. Squadron practice interceptions started at 48,000 feet and we were often up to 52,000 feet before 'combat' started."

But he was critical of the lack of organisation:

"The RAF effort was badly organised and handled. Nothing of the ground attack skill gained in 1941 to 1945 seemed to have been formally retained. For example, no one could remember the sighting picture for the 25lb rocket.

Co-ordination of RAF and Naval air operations was non-existent: no common frequencies for rescue; no post-strike photographs available for follow-on missions. There was no indoctrination of the forces involved, many of whom were National Servicemen, who could see quite plainly that [Prime Minister] Eden was lying when he denied co-operation with the Israelis. Two wings of French F-84Fs and Mystères had been refuelled in Squadron dispersals at Akrotiri en route to Israel in the week before operations commenced."

A more balanced view was taken by Air Commodore David Lee (later Air Chief Marshal Sir David GBE CB), Secretary to the Chiefs of Staff Committee, in his appraisal of the air campaign:

"It was a success in that it achieved the object of eliminating the Egyptian Air Force, but the campaign then came to an end in an astonishing and most unsatisfactory way. However, the air forces . . . had done their stuff, and done it very well. But there is a great danger here in saying that this was a splendidly successful campaign. You really must apply it to the conditions under which it was fought. Knowing there was virtually no opposition and that we had an overwhelming force, and there are certain aspects of it that make one feel that it wasn't quite as successful as one would like to feel.

It is quite clear that the object of the bombing was not to destroy the airfields . . . but to shock the Egyptian Air Force by doing a great deal of widespread damage over their main airfields in the hope that they would be really discouraged and put off and present excellent targets for the fighter-bombers which were due to follow up immediately afterwards.

The Middle East Air Force had Venoms and Meteors; the latter, 208 Squadron, were the fighter-reconnaissance version, the FR9; they did not have the range to do any worthwhile photographic or reconnaissance work over Egypt and they were banished to Malta. All the fighter-reconnaissance work was done by the RF-84s of the French Air Force which had better performance, and did the job extremely well. The Venoms were all right, but were getting long in the tooth, and were being superseded at home by the generation of swept-wing fighters of which the Hunter was the most successful. The Venoms' 20mm guns were not as good as the 30mm of the Hunters, but nevertheless the Venoms did their stuff extremely well."

One of those Venom pilots, Flg Off Dave Williams of 249 Squadron (later Sqn Ldr), recalled:

"Fleeting impressions of the operation – taking off heavily loaded into an early dawn. The first sight of the Egyptian coastline. Hunting for targets. Sweeping low over the tenement buildings of Port Said looking for gun emplacements. Flak that puffed so innocently lethal alongside you. Pouring 20mm cannon into ground targets and seeing the devastating effect. Always aware of your fuel state for the relatively long flight home to Cyprus. Excited debriefings then a cold beer in the Mess. Fighter pilots at last!"

On a lighter note, Flg Off Gronert added:

351

"Following the cessation of hostilities, our section of four [Flt Lt Doug Dallison, Flt Lt Mike Waterhouse, Flg Off Bill Barker being the others] managed to arrange a visit to Gamil airfield. We flew over in a Valetta and spent a couple of nights there. We met the people we would have been working with had things gone ahead as planned [249 Squadron was to have been temporarily based at Gamil had the capture of the Canal taken place]. Half the Squadron equipment had been on the high seas when the operations ceased, along with some of the groundcrews. The Group Captain in charge of the airfield [Grp Capt Crawford-Compton] and the Wing Commander Flying, Wg Cdr Le Bas, had been seconded from 2nd TAF in Germany. I don't know how good they would have been operationally, but the two days there were spent either drunk or getting towards that state! We had a good look round Port Said and apart from one or two areas, it looked very much as it always looked."

8 Squadron's Flg Off Dick Hadlow (later Sqn Ldr) offered:

"I suppose we all felt a mixture of anti-climax and anger at not being allowed to finish the job we had been tasked to do. We had by then effectively won, so being forced to stop was a pointless gesture and one that caused no end of problems in the years to follow. Many of us probably thought, as I did, 'Well, I could have done better', but you do your job as best you may at the time. It certainly brought home the difference between training and the real thing. It was rewarding and satisfying to have taken part. The ground crews worked so hard to keep us in the air, working long hours and in the open most of the time, in all weathers. The serviceability was excellent despite the best efforts of the Egyptians and the occasional pilot!"

Lt Cdr Ray Rawbone of 897 Squadron (later Rear Admiral CB AFC) added a tribute to the performance of the Fleet Air Arm:

"As a Fleet Air Arm squadron commander I was very proud of the effectiveness of the carrier-borne aircraft. Contrary to public opinion the British and French naval aircraft took out and neutralised the Egyptian Air Force within two days and from then onwards provided the bulk of the air support for our ground forces. The RAF helped but in a secondary role. Many of our pilots were inexperienced in war but they responded quickly and the rapid improvement in weapon accuracy was impressive.

Bearing in mind the time spent in Egypt prior to 'Suez' our intelligence information was generally poor. We were led to expect much stronger resistance, especially from aircraft superior to our own. This inevitably affected our early movements and initial attacks. Moreover, the political overtones, including Mr Gaitskill's [Leader of the British Labour Party] denouncement of the whole operation, came as an unwelcome surprise to those taking part in the battle. Having committed us to war those in the field were also amazed at the emerging divisions at home (forerunner to Vietnam, perhaps). Political reaction afterwards did little to dispel military uneasiness, almost as though the politicians wished to sweep the whole incident under the carpet. Overall Suez was a successful operation. Unfortunately politicians had much to learn."

But he was somewhat scathing of the RAF's bombing strategy, and accuracy:

"Canberras flying at extreme range were forced to bomb from high altitude without precision weapon guidance and were not effective. I always felt that it was a great pity that this was not made clear to our politicians, many of whom remained blissfully unaware of the limitations of the equipment provided to our Air Forces."

In his memoirs, Lt Don Mills, also of 897 Squadron (later Cdr OBE), wrote:

"Looking back on Suez, there is no doubt that it was a watershed and affected many events in later years. The political furore that came after has totally obscured the fact that, in military terms, it was a well planned and executed operation. We destroyed a numerically superior air force and carried out an amphibious landing on a defended coast with no civilian casualties [sic] and very little loss of life on either side. We had fought the cleanest war ever, although people often think that Suez was a complete walkover, but they didn't see the flak at Almaza which our seniors told us was as heavy as anything in WWII. We felt let down, almost betrayed, by the politicians, the nation, and in some cases like me, by our families. We had been brought up in a time when the British armed forces were the heroes of the nation, but there was no heroes' welcome for us."

On the other hand, Lt Jack Worth of 800 Squadron (later Captain RN) was critical of those in command of the overall operation:

"Command and Control – this was appalling, being conducted from London and Paris simultaneously with contradictory results. This was compounded on the UK side by trying to use Cyprus as a local Command and Control centre, especially for air operations. They were so out of touch that on one occasion they sent an RAF Venom flight to attack Port Fuad installations which had been captured by the French airborne troops the previous day. I had to tell the Flight Leader to clear off back to Cyprus as he was jamming the airwaves; unbelievably, he was using old WWII Pathfinder direction techniques to conduct his attack."

Lt Cdr Bill Henley (later Lt Cdr DSC) of 893 Squadron wrote:

"Looking back after all this time and with the knowledge of all the political goings-on of which we knew nothing at the time, I still think participants in the carrier operations can be proud of their efforts. Admiral Power, a big man in every meaning of the word, inspired great confidence and *esprit de corps* which in turn led to efficiency. This was very marked on the day the paras went in and the word got round that they needed our assistance. The whole ship seemed to leap into action even more so when helicopters brought out some casualties. Off watch sailors were almost queuing up to help with the stretchers and walking cases, and the aircraft maintenance crews and flight deck parties excelled themselves."

809 Squadron's Senior Observer, Lt John Hackett (later Lt Cdr), reflected:

"Historically and politically it may have been a disaster, but to those of us who were engaged in it on the ground or in the air it was a job to be done with whatever resources we had available. There is nothing like a war situation to 'stiffen the sinews, summon up the blood', and when all the dust has settled, what one remembers above all else is the comradeship and friendship of everyone concerned. For me personally Suez was a rewarding experience which I recall vividly and with emotion."

International political pressure, especially the emphatic and convincing threats from the United States and the Soviet Union, forced British, French and Israeli forces to withdraw from Egyptian soil. Indeed, the Soviet Tass News Agency warned:

"The Peoples of the USSR are unanimous in the condemnation of those guilty in the aggressive war against the Egyptian people and fully support the resolute measures of the Soviet Government aimed at cutting short aggression in Egypt. The USSR is fully determined to give effect to the statements contained [in Bulganin's letters to Eden, Mollet and Ben-Gurion] unless an end is put to aggression against Egypt. In leading Soviet circles it has been stated that if Britain, France and Israel, contrary to the decisions of the UN, do not withdraw all their forces from the territory of Egypt . . . the appropriate authorities of the USSR will not hinder the departure of Soviet citizen volunteers who wish to take part in the struggle of the Egyptian people for their independence."

This rhetoric encouraged President Nasser's political adviser, Wg Cdr 'Ali Sabri, to declare:

"Should the British and French fail to withdraw, the world will face a major crisis, and nobody can prophesy the consequences of a delay in the withdrawal. We shall willingly accept aid from anybody."

Despite the success of the British, French and Israeli attacks they did not, however, bring about the fall of the Egyptian government and similarly failed to establish international control over the Suez Canal. United Nations intervention cast Britain and France in the role of colonial aggressors. Shortly after the ceasefire, a United Nations team led by American engineers began the task of removing sunken ships and war debris from the Suez Canal which resumed the flow of shipping and eventually brought much-needed revenue to Egypt. Continued United Nations actions, aggressively supported by President Eisenhower and Soviet leaders, forced the British and French to withdraw from Egypt by 22 December 1956. With the rundown of Allied forces, personnel of the RAF's 8 Squadron returned to Khormaksar, Aden, on 17 December, departing Akrotiri aboard Hastings of Transport Command; their Venom FB4s were left behind, the Squadron taking over 73 Squadron's old Mark Is at Aden, the latter unit having disbanded as a FGA squadron to re-equip with Canberras.

Cyprus remained on alert, however, its air defence fighters constantly ready to investigate unidentified intruders. These had recently been reinforced by a flight of Fighter Command's latest Hunter F6s of 92 Squadron, the detachment led by Flt Lt Don Arnott, a Korean War veteran. One such sortie almost ended in tragedy for the crew of a 39 Squadron Meteor NF13 scrambled from Nicosia. The intruder was soon picked up on the aircraft's radar and the pilot was directed to intercept. As the Meteor closed in there was an 'almighty bang' and the crew thought their aircraft had hit a ship but it had, in fact, hit the sea! On returning to Nicosia, the Meteor's starboard jet pipe was found to be missing and the turbine exposed, while the ventral fuel tank had been ripped off. The intruder turned out to be an Israeli Dakota on a 'training' flight.

For Israel its military victory in Sinai bore some fruit; President Eisenhower guaranteed the right of passage for shipping bound for Israel and the presence of United Nations Forces minimised the threat of attack by Arab guerilla forces.

Nonetheless, Israeli forces were also compelled to pull out of Sinai, but Israel delayed its departure until March 1957 when units of the United Nations Emergency Force were in place to patrol Gaza, Sharm al-Sheikh and monitor activities along the Sinai frontier.

Chapter Seventeen

AFTERMATH

"America and Russia, oddly associated in the UN, stifled the invasion of Egypt at birth. Britain, accustomed to losing all the battles but the last, on this occasion lost the last one too."

Merry and Serge Bromberger

Few events had such a dramatic impact on Egypt's relations with the Arab states and with the world in general as the brief Suez War of 1956. In military terms Egypt lost this war but politically Egypt, and particularly President Nasser, emerged from the conflict as the victor. Israel had been forced by the United Nations and international political pressure to withdraw from the Sinai, while Britain and France had been compelled to retreat from Egypt in humiliation despite having overwhelmed the Egyptian armed forces. Mohamed Heikal wrote:

"In the end the Suez affair became a personal business, a duel between two men. It could only end in total victory for one and total defeat for the other. Nasser won and he never felt one speck of pity for Eden."

While Egypt's armed forces had again been defeated in battle and the Sinai seized by Israeli forces, the Sinai-Suez War strengthened President Nasser's position in Egypt and the Arab world, where Nasser was seen as having fought against three invaders and of scoring a diplomatic victory. Following the end of the war, and with the Anglo-French invasion forces gone, he consolidated Egyptian control over the strategic waterway and nationalised most British and French property and companies. The Egyptians also began repairing damaged facilities and rebuilding its armed forces, while the 40-odd aircraft which had been flown out of the country to safety now returned. A number of aircraft had also survived the onslaught against Egyptian air bases, including at least one Meteor F4, but the bulk of the Air Force's inventory and considerable Army equipment had been destroyed during the assault.

The United States failed to follow up on the goodwill achieved by its tough stand against Britain and France during and after the crisis and, as a result, the Soviet Union strengthened its position as Egypt's international patron and major arms supplier and promptly responded to requests for assistance. Thus, in March 1957, three Romanian ships arrived with 15 crated MiG-17s, ten disassembled Il-28s and other military equipment, although the cost of such support was to

An EAF MiG-15, probably one of those which escaped to Syria or Saudi Arabia, under the watchful eye of a UN soldier following its return to Egypt. (*Authors' collection*)

be the 'permanent' presence in Egypt of hundreds of Soviet and East European military officers and technicians. This massive resupply programme provided the Egyptian Armed Forces with late-model Soviet-built weaponry and allowed the EAF to standardise on fewer types of aircraft and streamline its maintenance and training. As a result the EAF faced fewer problems converting from British to Soviet equipment than might have been the case if the EAF had to operate mixed equipment for several years. Along with this military aid, the Soviet Union agreed to increase its funding for the Aswan Dam project and other pressing Egyptian infrastructure improvement projects. Egypt was allowed to pay for this assistance with raw materials such as cotton, and was also given long-term, low-interest loans.

With the stationing of United Nations forces in the Sinai effectively separating Egyptian from Israeli, the opportunity for conflict was thereby greatly reduced. This enabled Egypt to concentrate on domestic matters and the task of rebuilding its military. Thousands of officers and enlisted men were recruited and current staff retrained to support the government's ambitious Air Force expansion plan. The Air Force was reorganised along Soviet lines and many aircrew and ground personnel were sent to the Soviet Union and Warsaw Pact countries for training. Close co-ordination between Egypt, the Soviet Union and its allies was demonstrated on 14 May 1957 when Plt Off Abd al-Moneim al-Shennawy landed his Czechoslovak Air Force MiG-15 at Schwechat airport outside Vienna (Austria). When the Egyptian pilot demanded that he be allowed to fly back to Czechoslovakia, he generated considerable press attention.

EAF morale soared as new jets poured in to Egypt; by June 1957, 100 MiG fighters and 40 Il-28 jet bombers had arrived. On 23 July 1957 the EAF staged a massive airshow over Cairo which served notice that the country had rebuilt its airpower. Air Vice-Marshal Muhammed Sidqi Mahmud, head of the EAF, delivered a fiery speech as 21 MiG-15s, 18 MiG-17s and a dozen Il-28s flew

A squadron line-up of MiGs early in 1957. The nearest three aircraft are MiG-17s, the furthest five being MiG-15s; they are likely to have been machines which escaped to Syria or Saudi Arabia during the course of the Anglo-French assault. Note damaged hangars on the left. (*EAF*)

overhead. To celebrate the EAF's 25th birthday on 19 December 1957 an impressive static display of aircraft was highlighted at Almaza, while flights of MiG-17s and Il-28s buzzed over Cairo. Other celebrations were held to spotlight the EAF and promote its history to boost recruitment and national pride.

Egypt now entered a period of great political and social change. The old élite of the monarchist days was superseded by a new class of merchants, bankers, government bureaucrats and military officers. Liberal political factions lobbied for radical change while other groups called for a return to Islamic principles. President Nasser embraced a strong Arab nationalist political position and domestically was implementing his doctrine of Arab socialism through government domination of economic enterprises and activities. Increasingly Nasser voiced an anti-Western and anti-imperialist line in foreign affairs while adopting socialist and authoritarian policies within Egypt. Slowly he increased his control over all aspects of Egyptian government and he did not tolerate groups or individuals who challenged his authority.

The political and social tensions of the time had an impact on the Armed Forces. The Suez War was not only a watershed in the relationship between Arab states and their former colonial masters, but it also confirmed Egypt's leadership role in the Arab world and Nasser's hold over his people was never greater. However, the failings associated with one-man rule soon became apparent. Wg Cdr Labib reflected on how the results of the war reinforced a particular form of Egyptian government, a form of government he called "the opportunistic élite":

"Nasser's success in taking control of the situation and then making effective decisions on his own at critical moments enhanced this form of one-man rule. For example, the correct decision to withdraw the Egyptian Army from Sinai and to instruct Egyptian pilots to avoid combat [with Anglo-French aircraft], plus his diplomatic success despite a clear military defeat, were just some of the things which led the President to develop an exaggerated sense of his own abilities. The result of his success in seizing control of the decision-making process during the invasion led to a new form of government. Nasser used this success of decision-making by a single man as a justification for its continuation in subsequent years.

A normal consequence of such a system of government was the appearance of individuals who could be called 'favourites'. These people circled around the man with power in order to gain greater status as his surrogates. For his part, the man in power looked upon them as his élite who would help him in the success of his policies. The consequences of this situation clearly had an impact on the Armed Forces; above all on the Air Force. Training was seriously affected and became a means of showing off, competing for power and even personal gain from whatever sources became available. One could even say that a deterioration in the fighting capabilities of the Armed Forces was a clear result of the domination and leadership of this closed and privileged élite."

But not every Egyptian loved Nasser. An EAF intelligence officer, Major Issam al-Din Mahmud Khalil, discovered that members of the Royal Family and other individuals who had lost out in the 1952 Revolution were plotting an anti-Nasser revolt. Khalil was contracted by Murtada al-Maraghi, Farouk's one-time Minister of the Interior, and Hussein Khairy, a relative of the King, and offered a large sum of money to help organise a *coup d'etat*. He played along with the plotters and assisted the Egyptian police in arresting the conspirators.

Following the Suez War the Soviet bloc sent a significant amount of aid to Syria to strengthen her defences. Towards the end of 1956 Syria had ordered 60 MiG-17s and in December of the same year a group of SAF pilots (about 20) had gone to the Soviet Union for conversion training, while a further 18 went to Poland including Lt Colonel Musafaz al-Asasa, commander of the SAF's fighter units, who had earlier received training in both Italy and Britain. The first batch of 12 MiG-17s arrived in Syria in January 1957. Egyptian pilots flew some of these over Damascus on Syrian National Day in April 1957 because of a shortage of Syrians qualified to fly the new jets. All 60 MiG-17s had been delivered by late 1957. When the SAF pilots returned from training in Russia and Eastern Europe they manned the new fighter squadrons and began flying operational air defence missions over Syria. Jet training was resumed in Syria itself in 1957 when a fighter conversion course was established at Hama, under the direction of Soviet instructors.

By the end of 1957 the SAF had two operational MiG-17 squadrons defending the capital from their base at al-Mezze near Damascus. Two additional MiG-17 squadrons were being established and advanced training at Hama on night and blind interception techniques was intensified to prepare for the delivery of the MiG-17PF night fighters, which replaced the Meteor NF13s in 1958. Some 30 pilots a year passed through initial instruction at an Air College outside Aleppo where support personnel were also trained at the SAF's Aeronautical Technical Institute. Other pilot candidates continued to be sent to the USSR and Eastern bloc countries for training.

In an attempt to expand Egypt's (and his own) power and influence, President

Nasser took the bold step of forming a political union with Syria and Yemen. The confederation with Syria was known as the United Arab Republic (UAR). For the Syrian Ba'ath party this move was an attempt to consolidate their power and head off a looming *coup d'état* by the military. The Iman of Yemen used the union to deflect British and Saudi efforts to challenge his government. The political union between Egypt and Syria was announced in February 1958 and Yemen joined into a loose confederation with Egypt named the United Arab States a month later. Consequently President Nasser's prestige soared within Egypt and the Arab world. While a lofty goal, political unification and military co-operation was elusive.

Plans were drawn up for a united military command and the Egyptian, Syrian and Yemen armed forces began to co-ordinate their activities. Egyptian military and political missions were sent to Yemen to cement relations. The military leaders of Egypt and Syria met to plan unification plans and the aircraft of the three countries were repainted with a common UARAF national insignia. Yemen fielded a very small and inexperienced air arm; the Syrians had a well organised Air Force but one which had been badly impacted by the series of coups the country had experienced. The Egyptian and Syrian air arms faced similar challenges and the same Israeli adversary. President Nasser hoped that closer co-operation among Egyptian, Syrian and Yemeni armed forces would increase Egyptian prestige and put pressure on Israel. Since the Jewish state now faced a common foe on two fronts, in Sinai and on the Golan Heights, UAR leaders hoped to pressure Israel into a defensive situation. While the confederation with Yemen gave Egypt a vital bridgehead at the southern end of the Red Sea, it would also soon bring Egypt into that country's savage and prolonged civil war.

Neither Jordan nor Iraq, both countries maintaining strong ties with Britain, would consider joining the UAR, their refusal to do so inflaming the more militant members of the union into seeking recompense. Thus, on 14 July 1958, King Feisal III and Crown Prince Abdul Illah of Iraq, together with the Iraqi Minister of Defence and a former Prime Minister of Jordan, were assassinated in Baghdad during a *coup d'état* by elements of the Iraqi military, supporters of the pro-Soviet UAR. The bloody incident had repercussions for a small group of RAF ground personnel, seconded to the RIrAF at Habbaniya, some of whom had witnessed the killings, and the subsequent decapitation of the young King, a cousin of Jordan's King Hussein. Among those detained by Iraqi military forces was LAC David Bickel, an aircraft mechanic on attachment from Cyprus, where he had served with 114 Squadron. Despite protests from Britain and the United Nations, the RAF detainees were not released until 20 September, when they were flown to Nicosia aboard a Red Cross aircraft, and from there back to the UK. David Bickel died in 1969, but his mother remembered:

> "David took a photo of King Feisal's head on a spike over the city gate, which caused the Arabs to confiscate his camera. These young chaps were kept in a compound surrounded by wire, with hardly anything to eat although we were able to send food parcels via the Red Cross, who were responsible for sending him home by air transport two months after his 21st birthday. We waited for David to come home to a celebration of about 150 people."

On the same date (14 July), a coup had also been intended in Jordan, although

LAC David Bickel, one of the RAF airmen interned at Habbaniya in 1958. (*Authors' collection*)

this had been thwarted. In response to Jordanian pleas for help, British paratroopers from Cyprus were dropped at Amman three days later in a show of support for King Hussein, Israeli fighters buzzing the RAF transport aircraft en route since the formalities of obtaining Israeli permission had not been completed. The British troops remained in Amman until 29 October, the final detachment departing via Aqaba four days later. Lebanon's President Chamoun also felt threatened by the unrest and US Marines were hurriedly sent to Beirut in reponse to his request for help.

A second attempt on King Hussein's life was made on 10 November 1958, when he departed from Amman in a RJAF Dove to fly to Lausanne, via Cyprus, Athens and Rome. With the King as co-pilot was Wg Cdr Dalgleish, and on board were four passengers. The flight plan took them over Syria and Lebanon, countries with which Hussein had fallen out in recent times. While flying over Syria, the Dove was contacted by the controller at Damascus and ordered to land at Damascus airport. Refusing to do so, Hussein headed the Dove back towards Amman but as the aircraft approached the Jordanian border, two SAF MiG-17s commenced a series of attacks (although it is not clear if they actually opened fire), Dalgleish taking over the controls. Turning sharply into each successive attack, he was able to keep the Dove in the air and out of trouble, as the King recalled in his memoirs:

"We had to turn inside their circle at the precise moment they began to get us lined up in their sights . . . The scrape with the Syrian MiGs was the narrowest escape from death I have ever had."

Britain continued to court both Jordan and Iraq, supplying refurbished ex-RAF Hunter F6 jet fighters for their respective air forces in 1958, as she did in a small way for the Lebanese Air Force. In addition, Iraqi pilots received their conversion to the Hunter at RAF Chivenor, home of the RAF's Hunter OCU in England.

One of the UAR's long-term military goals was the expansion and modernisation of its air force with the Soviet Union providing material and training. Fundamental to this upgrading was a thorough reorganisation of the Egyptian, Syrian and Yemeni air arms along Soviet lines. Air regiments and Soviet-style ranks became the norm and important changes were made in training techniques and in the chain of command. Egyptian military plans called for the UARAF to significantly increase the size of its fighter and bomber elements and maintain a large transport element. While the fighter force was primarily a defensive force, it could also be used to escort Il-28 bombers on strikes against Israeli targets. It was Egypt's jet bomber force which had most worried British, French and Israeli planners in 1956 and the formation of the UARAF meant that Israel had to be prepared to counter a co-ordinated air attack from both Egypt and Syria. While on paper the UARAF was an imposing threat, the force had limited experience, a lack of technical expertise and suffered from poor training. Soviet training focused on how to fly safely, maintain aircraft and follow commands. Senior officers and ground controllers gave orders, leaving the pilot little initiative. Training limitations and the rigid nature of Soviet techniques had a dampening impact on Arab armed forces, the result of which was later revealed in future conflicts.

As the armed forces of the three countries began to co-ordinate their activities, Egyptian officers received most of the top command and advisory positions. Long-serving Syrian and Yemeni officers were upset at having been moved aside, and with the overbearing attitude of some of their Egyptian counterparts.

								UARAF				
	Fighter Jet/Prop	Bomber Jet/Prop	Transport Jet/Prop	Other	Total Personnel
Egypt	178 15	70 3	48	10 70	4,375
Syria	50 16	0 0	10	18 106	1,259
Yemen	30	0 0	3	12	400

The new UARAF had a long-term plan to expand the 30 front-line squadrons but in 1958 many of these new units were just ideas. Two years later the UARAF had only expanded slightly but was much more capable of sustained operations. By mid-1960 the Syrian element of the UARAF included a dozen Il-28 bombers, 15 Il-14 transports and some 60 MiG-17 fighters; Yemen had only added a small number of new aircraft while Egypt's air arm had expanded to 70 Il-28s, 200 MiG-17s, 50 transports and a small number of Mi-1 helicopters.

The formation of the UAR increased the responsibilities of the Egyptian armed forces and gave officers and enlisted men experience on Israel's northern border and in Yemen. Due to United Nations peacekeeping forces, the Egyptian-Israeli border and the Gaza Strip remained relatively quiet following the Israeli withdrawal in 1957, but this was not the case on the Golan Heights. Israel and Syria each had substantial fortifications along the border and both sides aggressively patrolled the area with tanks and infantry. In the late 1950s Israel constructed a canal to divert a portion of the water of the Jordan River to irrigate the Negev Desert. Syria and Jordan objected strongly to this project which affected their own water resources and future irrigation plans. Tension along these borders increased and in 1958 Syrian and Israeli forces traded artillery fire while both sides staged commando raids. Israeli and UARAF jets flew regular patrols in the area and occasionally crossed the border to maintain pressure and gather intelligence information.

Israel learned a powerful lesson from the events which followed the 1956 war: United Nations pressure had forced Britain, France and Israel to pull out of Egypt and eliminated the benefits of the Allied military victory. Israeli political

A survivor of Suez: this Meteor F4, s/n 1410, was photographed at Almaza in 1958, when it carried the new UARAF markings. (*Authors' collection*)

and military leaders vowed that this would not happen again. In the event of a future war they could not count on external assistance like that provided by Britain, and especially France, in the 1956 conflict. The formation of the United Arab Republic and United Arab States highlighted the fact that Israel was surrounded and outnumbered. To overcome disadvantages in geography and manpower, Israeli military leaders developed an offensive military doctrine which called for tanks and aircraft to spearhead a pre-emptive strike.

In support of this new doctrine, during the late 1950s Israel substantially expanded its tank inventory and strengthened its air force. Second World War-era Mustangs, Mosquitos and B-17s were rapidly replaced by modern jet fighters from France. In addition to more Ouragan and Mystère IVA jets which had proved themselves in the 1956 conflict, Israel purchased small numbers of Sud-Aviation SO-4050 Vautour (Vulture) fighter-bomber aircraft which performed attack, reconnaissance and night fighter missions. The Vautour had a very long range, up to 1,550 miles, which suited Israel's intention of being able to penetrate Egyptian airspace to a considerable depth. In addition, its capability as a light bomber enabled it to carry a variety of weapons, from heavy freefall bombs to air-to-air and air-to-ground missiles. In fact, it was even able to deliver an atomic bomb with considerable accuracy. As such, the Vautour combined all the characteristics demanded by Israel for a multi-purpose offensive aircraft, of which 24 had arrived by early 1957.

The rapid resupply of the Egyptian element of the UARAF maintained rough numerical parity between the air arms of the two countries. When Syrian aircraft were added, the IDF/AF was outnumbered and given equal pilot quality; UARAF MiG-17 fighters outperformed Israel's Ouragan and Mystère jets. The UARAF's biggest advantage was its force of 80 Il-28 bombers, which were a serious threat to Israeli cities and military targets. However, Israel held the edge in training and tactics. Israel continued to invest heavily in air power and by early 1959 the IAF received the first of 24 Super-Mystère B2 fighters from France. The first European fighter capable of sustained supersonic flight, the Super-Mystère was considerably faster than the MiG-17 and could perform both fighter and attack missions.

363

On the Egyptian front, UARAF jets violated the border and flew aggressive patrols to support Syria and keep Israel on a state of alert. UARAF aircraft flew over Israel on the night of 14 December 1958 and dropped flares on several villages near the border. A week later Israeli Mystères intercepted Egyptian jets flying near al-Arish and shot down a MiG-17 which crashed at Bir Larfan, 40 miles inside Egyptian territory. The victor was Rav-Seren Nevo, who had shot down two EAF MiGs during the Sinai War. A Jordanian civil Dakota had narrowly avoided becoming a victim of the Mystères a few months earlier when it strayed over the Negev, as did a Lebanese Dragon Rapide which violated Israeli airspace a few months later, although this aircraft was forced to land in Israel. Also fortunate to avoid being shot down by a pair of Mystères (flown by Serens Yoseph Tsuk and Ya'acov Yariv) was a Lebanese Air Force SM79P transport intercepted near Haifa; the ancient trimotor was forced to land at the nearby Israeli air base. Three days earlier a Mystère from the same squadron had similarly forced an unannounced UN Dakota to land at Lod.

During this period, a Super-Mystère was scrambled after a high-flying aircraft had been reported over Israel although the pilot, Rav-Seren Joe Alon,* was unable to make an interception of what turned out to be an American U-2 spyplane. Tensions in the region remained strained and in January 1960, following an Israeli raid on the Syrian border village of Tawafik, both sides massed troops and armour along the Syrian border although nothing more serious than isolated skirmishing resulted. Another MiG-17 fell to IDF/AF fighters in April 1961, when a Super-Mystère flown by Tzur Ben-Barak shot down the Egyptian aircraft near Nitzana; the pilot was seen to eject.

On 28 September 1961 Syria withdrew from the United Arab Republic following a *coup d'état* which toppled the government. While political and military unification appeared to be a good concept, the union never really came about. The reasons were many and complex, but basically they reflected the simple fact that the three countries involved, though all Arab, differed socially, culturally, politically and in their religious make-up. Many Syrians complained of Egyptian high-handedness, even arrogance, while some Egyptians cited Syrian unreliability. In November 1961 Yemen withdrew from the federation with Egypt. The dissolution of the UAR left a legacy of mistrust which was to have an effect for many years to come. The break-up also had a regional impact as all the countries now pursued their own political and military agendas.

Following the 1952 coup, the military pervaded all aspects of Egyptian life. As part of his move to change to a more socialist structure, in the early 1960s President Nasser reorganised the Egyptian military. The officer corps was split into two groups: professional soldiers and separate civil bureaucracy which performed political and administrative roles. The separation of political/administrative and military roles was not, however, carried out completely and many uniformed officers continued to be involved in the political process. General Amr, a close friend of President Nasser, was very active in the political arena. Amr had been Viceroy of Syria and UARAF Deputy Supreme Commander during the political and military union of the three countries. This gave him effective control of the United Arab Republic's armed forces and considerable political power.

---

* In 1973, Israeli Air Attaché Yossef 'Joe' Alon was assassinated by Arab agents in Washington.

During the late 1950s and early 1960s Egypt pursued an ambitious defence industry development programme. In the late 1950s Colonel Mahmud Khalil gathered together a team under the direction of the famous German designer Willi Messerschmitt. Their first project was production of the Hispano Ha-200 jet trainer which had been developed with Spanish assistance. This project began in 1959 and Factory 72 at Helwan was re-tooled to build the new jet. Four Spanish-produced Ha-200 jets in UARAF markings flew over Cairo in July 1960 to announce the project. By the late 1960s, 63 Ha-200 al-Kahiras trainers had been built in Egypt. However, after several years of service the trainers were retired after the engines of the jets proved to be unreliable.

During this period, Egypt was committed to an ambitious project to develop and produce a supersonic fighter aircraft. Again with Spanish assistance, Professor Willi Messerschmitt and his design team conceived a lightweight supersonic fighter. When Spain ended its support for this project in 1960, the entire Messerschmitt team was moved to Egypt to continue its work. The Austrian jet engine expert Dr Ferdinand Brandner went to Egypt to develop a new turbo-jet for the small fighter, since the British Orpheus engine originally planned for the Ha-300 was not powerful enough to enable the new jet fighter to reach supersonic speeds. Test facilities, workshops for the new fighter and engine were built at Helwan. Brandner's jet engine ran for the first time in July 1963 while the Ha-300 prototype made its first flight on 7 March 1964. India supported the E-300 engine development programme, in order to acquire a new powerplant for its HF-24 Marut jet fighter.

Two Egyptian pilots were sent to India in 1964 where they attended the Indian Air Force test pilot school to prepare for the HA-300 flight development. Major Zohair Shalaby was a pilot of exceptional ability and Major Sahby al-Tawail was both a pilot and engineer. Both of these officers completed their courses successfully. Grp Capt Kapil Bhargara of the IAF flew more than one hundred flight hours with test versions of the E-300 engine. However, engine development problems and the 1967 June War prompted Egypt to cancel this fighter development programme.

Although the Soviets and their Eastern European allies provided the Arabs with MiGs, jet bombers and many other weapons, they had refused to supply missiles. However, Egypt was determined not to fall behind Israel in weaponry and military power. In the late 1950s Egypt embarked on a missile development programme. A design team of foreign and Egyptian technicians based at the ultra-secret Factory 333 at Helwan developed several different missile designs, and when it was discovered that Israel had successfully test-fired a surface-to-surface rocket in 1961, both sides intensified their efforts to win this missile race. Israel had received considerable assistance from France and was in the lead. However, fear of the threat from the German-Egyptian team reportedly prompted Israel's secret service to launch a campaign of terrorism against Factory 333 and its personnel. Dr Emil Kleinwachter was machine-gunned in his car, Dr Hassan Kalmil died when his plane crashed, and a bomb blast at Helwan killed five workers. Within weeks three other personnel died in unexplained accidents and a woman secretary was blinded by a mail bomb. These attacks prompted most of the foreign members of the Egyptian missile development team to flee the country. Egyptian scientists continued their development work and constructed three types of missiles: the small Kahir, the larger Zafir and the two-stage Ared. All of these missiles were test-fired but they suffered difficulties with their guidance systems. Despite years of effort and a substantial investment, none of the missiles ever entered operational service. In the 1960s Egypt was finally allowed to purchase Grog and Scud missiles from the Soviet Union to counter Israeli missiles. These weapons were armed with both conventional high-explosive and chemical warheads. Israeli missiles were thought to be armed with nuclear and conventional armament.

For almost a decade following the end of the political union, Egypt's air arm retained the title of United Arab Republic Air Force. Egypt continued to expand its air force to match the growth and modernisation of Israel's air arm. Due to a limited base of experienced personnel, the UARAF was forced into the classic trap of sacrificing quality for quantity. However, the massive investments of the late 1950s and early 1960s in training, facilities and equipment bore fruit. A new generation of Air Force personnel educated in the Soviet Union, Eastern Europe and new Egyptian schools such as the Air Force Technical Training Institute and Bilbeis Air Academy entered service in the 1960s. For new pilots the accident rate in training, which had reached high levels in the early 1950s, had been reduced to the same level experienced by the Soviet Air Force at that time. Egyptian pilot candidates, aircrew and technicians received training from Polish, East German, Czech, Indian and Russian instructors.

An aggressive flying schedule honed the skills of Egyptian aviators and technicians. However, the training given by Soviet and East European instructors did not properly prepare Egyptian aviators for the war they would face in the future. Maj-General Adel Nasr, who served as the EAF Director of Operations in the 1980s, commented on Soviet training:

"When the Russians came they emphasised training to make us staff and general officers. They didn't teach us tactics but they succeeded in teaching us to think in a proper and organised manner . . . When I was in the Soviet Union I had many relations with the training department because of my job. I was discussing with them how to train our troops. I discovered that they gave us a course in elementary training but they didn't teach tactics. They had their own tactics but they wouldn't be good for us because they depended upon massing and the use of large numbers that were not available to us."

Maj-General Nobil Shoarky, a former Chief-of-Staff of the EAF who trained with both Russians and Americans, said:

"In the 1960s we sent young men to take their courses in the Soviet Union. When they came back they had unbelievable safety measures. They were afraid of the aircraft. They were told, 'If you do this you will spin and die, and if you do that you will crash.' When we took back these pilots from the Russians and they returned to Egypt, we gave them a refresher course to get rid of that conservativeness. We were developing concepts while the Russians were here. We developed low-speed manoeuvres for the MiG-21 and we didn't give these tactics to the Russians. The Pakistani instructors asked us not to tell the Russians because they would give it to the Indians who flew MiG-21s."

By then, however, both Israel and the Arab states were on the path leading towards the next major conflict: the 1967 June War – but that is another story.

Appendix I

MACCHI CV205V IN REAF SERVICE

15 Macchi MC205Vs reached Egypt before the end of hostilities in January 1949; four were despatched from Italy (by sea) on 16 September 1948, three on 6 October, four on 26 October and four on 24 November, and were alocated REAF serials 1201–1215.

REAF Serial	Regia Aeronautica Military Serial	Temporary Civil Reg*	Type
1201	9305	–	C205V
1202	91804	–	C202
1203	9666	–	C202
1204	6573	–	C202
1205	7944	–	C202
1206	91834	–	C202
1207	92173	–	C205V
1208	9358	SU-XXE	C205V
1209	9309	SU-XXF	C205V
1210	9363	SU-XXG	C205V
1211	9515	SU-XXH	C202
1212	8382	SU-XXI	C202
1213	7897	SU-XXL	C202
1214	91812	SU-XXM	C202
1215	8103	SU-XXN	C202

* Temporary Egyptian civil registrations were used only for Certificate of Airworthiness test flights; the C202s were refurbished and re-conditioned to C205V standard.

A Status Report dated 25 January 1949, following the end of hostilities, revealed that 1204, 1208 and 1215 had been written off (probably lost in action), and that six others had been seriously damaged (and probably crash-landed), as noted:

	To be replaced	To be repaired
1202	fuselage bulkheads, engine, propeller	radiator, wings, undercarriage fairings
1207	wings, propeller	fuselage, radiator, undercarriage
1210	radiator	wings, undercarriage
1211	engine, tail, rudder, wings	fin
1212	radiator, propeller, windscreen	port wing
1213	wings, tail, radiator	undercarriage fairings, wheels

The nine remaining aircraft of the first order reached Egypt by early 1949, and were:

REAF Serial	Regia Aeronautica Military Serial	Temporary Civil Reg	Type
1216	8352	SU-XXO	C202
1217	8087	SU-XXP	C202
1218	6608	SU-XXQ	C202
1219	92182	SU-XXR	C205V
1220	92179	SU-XXS	C205V

1221	9342	SU-XXT	C205V
1222	6576	SU-XXU	C202
1223	9555	SU-XXZ	C202
1224	9065	SU-XXV	C202

A second batch of 18 aircraft was delivered before the end of 1949; these were:

REAF Serial	Regia Aeronautica Military Serial	Temporary Civil Reg	Type
1225	9362	–	C205V
1226	7811	–	C202
1227	91806	–	C202
1228	9397	–	C202
1229	9695	–	C202
1230	9436	–	C202
1231	92175	–	C205V
1232	8089	–	C202
1233	6602	–	C202
1234	9704	–	C202
1235	9669	–	C202
1236	9714	–	C202
1237	92202	–	C205V
1238	9503	–	C202
1239	9694	–	C202
1240	6567	–	C202
1241	9681	–	C202
1242	9750	–	C202

When, in December 1950, an Aer Macchi team visited REAF bases to provide short-term assistance, at least 26 Macchis were inspected. Amongst these, distributed between Helwan, Almaza, al-Arish and al-Ballah, were war veterans 1201, 1207, 1213 and 1214, all still fully operational.

REAF Halifax prior to delivery, wearing REAF markings and s/n 1160 in Arabic together with temporary British civil registration G-ALVK. Such sales were so sensitive that the crescent and stars were sometimes omitted from the centre of the roundel to make the aircraft's identity less obvious. (*A.J. Jackson collection*)

The nine Halifax A9s supplied to Egypt were:

REAF serial number

G-ALOF (ex-RT846)/REAF 1155;   G-ALVI (ex-RT793)/REAF 1156;
G-ALOR (ex-RT888)/REAF 1157;   G-ALON (ex-RT787)/REAF 1158;
G-ALVJ (ex-RT852)/REAF 1159;   G-ALVK (ex-RT901)/REAF 1160;
G-ALVM (ex-RT938)/REAF 1161;   G-ALVL (ex-RT907)/REAF 1162;
G-ALVH (ex-RT788)/REAF 1163.

The last of the nine Halifax A9s to arrive in Egypt, G-ALVM, was the final production machine, RT938, which had been accepted by the RAF in November 1946.

The nine ex-RAF Lancasters on order were:

PA476/REAF 1801;   PA441/REAF 1802;   SW308/REAF 1803;
TW894/REAF 1804;   PA435/REAF 1805;   PA391/REAF 1806;
TW890/REAF 1807;   SW313/REAF 1808;   TW656/REAF 1809.

REAF Lancaster, s/n 1808, in England prior to delivery. As with all the Lancasters and Halifaxes sold to Egypt, it was unarmed. (*A.J. Jackson collection*)

The 19 Spitfire F22s were:

PK541/REAF 680;	PK435/REAF 681;	PK484/REAF 682;	PK512/REAF 683;
PK598/REAF 685;	PK374/REAF 686;	PK502/REAF 687;	PK517/REAF 688;
PK562/REAF 689;	PK600/REAF 690;	PK390/REAF 691;	PK509/REAF 692;
PK327/REAF 693;	PK524/REAF 694;	PK319/REAF 695;	PK314/REAF 696;
PK323/REAF 697;	PK516/REAF 698;	PK356/REAF 699.	

The sole Spitfire T9 trainer was G-ALJM, which became 684.

Reconditioned Spitfire F22 s/n 681 of the REAF in England prior to delivery, 1950. Note the long-range fuel tank beneath the fuselage. All Spitfires in Egyptian service had serial numbers in the 600 range but the Mk22s were unusual in the size and positioning of their numbers. (*Peter Arnold collection*)

370

Appendix III
AIRSPEED CONSULS IN IDF/AF SERVICE

The UK registrations and former RAF serial numbers of the Consuls supplied to Israel in 1949 and 1950 were:

G-AHMC (ex-HN583)	
G-AHMB (ex-LX281)	became 4X-ACO
G-AHXP (ex-HN840)	became 4X-ACV
G-AJAX (ex-LX599)	
G-AIUT (ex-LX666)	
G-AICZ (ex-PK253)	
G-AIOL (ex-PK257)	became 4X-ACR
G-AIOR (ex-PK289)	became 4X-ACP
G-AIIN (ex-PK292)	
G-AIUV (ex-HN191)	
G-AJGF (ex-HN199)	
G-AIUW (ex-PH503)	became 4X-ACQ

Later, two additional Consuls were purchased (G-AIKY and G-AJLN). Also on the strength of the IDF/AF by the mid-1950s were four Airspeed Oxfords (formerly G-AMFJ, G-AMFK, G-AMFL, and G-AMHE).

Flying School Consul on its nose following a minor accident. (*IAF Magazine collection*)

Appendix IV

AIRCRAFT BELIEVED TO HAVE PARTICIPATED IN THE SUEZ WAR

ROYAL AIR FORCE

24 Valiant B1s of the Malta Bomber Wing were:
138 Squadron: WP215, WP220, WZ363, WZ384, WZ389, WZ400, WZ401, WZ402
148 Squadron: XD814, XD815, XD816, XD817, XD819
207 Squadron: WP219, WZ403, WZ404, WZ405, XD812, XD813
214 Squadron: WZ377, WZ379, WZ393, WZ395, WZ397

Canberra B2s included:
10 Squadron: WH646, WH665, WH667, WH668, WH672, WH853, WJ975, WJ518
15 Squadron: WD951, WD961, WD980, WF916 (returned to UK), WH724, WJ976, WK107, WK132, XA536 (replacement)
18 Squadron: WH919, WJ648, WJ719, WJ728, WJ733, WJ751, WJ752, WJ753
27 Squadron: WH729, WH732, WH742, WH860, WJ578, WJ604, WJ723, WK112
44 Squadron: WH178, WH717, WH718, WH959, WH967
61 Squadron: WH724, WH740, WH907, WH908, WH910, WH915, WH918, WJ636, WJ642, WJ647

Canberra B6s included:
9 Squadron: WH961, WH969, WH972, WH973, WH974, WH977, WH981, WH995, WT205
12 Squadron: WH951, WH954, WH956 (returned to UK 27/10), WH960, WH963, WH965, WH968 (replacement), WH970, WH971
101 Squadron: WH945, WH948, WJ756, WJ758, WJ760, WJ761, WJ762, WJ764
109 Squadron: WH977, WJ771, WJ772, WJ781, WJ782, WJ783, WT210, WT303
139 Squadron: WJ767, WJ768, WJ773, WJ774, WJ776, WJ778, WT302, WT306, WT369, WT370, WT371, WT372

Canberra PR7s (of 13 Squadron) **included:**
WE137, WH775, WH799, WH801, WJ821, WT548

Canberra T4s included:
WJ858 (13 Squadron), WT479 (61 Squadron)

Hunter F5s included:
1 Squadron: WP180/F, WP188/X
34 Squadron: WP124, WP130/S, WP132/T, WP136/N, WP142/W, WP185/E

Venom FB4s included:
6 Squadron: WR379, WR382/C, WR400/R, WR408, WR409, WR410/N, WR413, WR436, WR440, WR472, WR473/U, WR474, WR476, WR477, WR479, WR481.
8 Squadron: WR376, WR399/T, WR405/B, WR428, WR432/R, WR445, WR446/S, WR480, WR484, WR485/C, WR487/A, WR488, WR501, WR505/B, WR509, WR528, WR532, WR548/F.
249 Squadron: WR375, WR398/H, WR412, WR420/T, WR439, WR443/Y, WR444/E, WR487, WR489/D, WR492/U, WR497/B, WR499/V, WR502, WR504/Z, WR506/W, WR507/S, WR527/C, WR529, WR531/R, WR533/F.

Valetta C1/C2s included:
30 Squadron: VX576/JNC
84 Squadron: VW196, VW202/C, VX562
114 Squadron: VW150, VW161, VW811, VW817, VW844, VW850, WJ496

Hastings C1s/C2s included:
70 Squadron: TG535, TG577, TG612, TG621, TG665, WJ328
99 Squadron: WD497
511 Squadron: TG510, TG531, TG551, TG604/GAC, WD495/GAN, WJ329/JAM
NB: 99 and 511 Squadrons apparently pooled their aircraft.

FLEET AIR ARM

Sea Hawk FB3s included:
802 Squadron: WM911, WM922/132 (lost 24/10/56), WM938/131, WM963/136,
      WM971/133 (lost 5/10/56), WM977, WM979, WM995, WM996/135,
      WN109/139, WN118/137, WV995/138
895 Squadron: WM928/460, WM923/457, WM926/461, WM937, WM962/465,
      WM972/462

Sea Hawk FGA4s included:
810 Squadron: WM914, WV918/230, WM985, WV796/235, WV860/239, XE333/233,
      XE335/234, XE370/231, XE375/239, XE385, XE395, XE403/238,
      XE405/232 (lost 2/10/56), XE408/237, XE409, XE451, XE463/232

Sea Hawk FGA6s included:
800 Squadron: XE391/109, XE400/107, XE411/108, XE435/104, XE436/103, XE437/102,
      XE438/105, XE454/101, XE455/100
804 Squadron: XE365/171, XE378/168, XE383/166, XE389/162, XE392/163, XE393/164,
      XE394/165, XE396/167, XE407/160, XE409/161, XE461/170
897 Squadron: WV907/190, XE340, XE362/194, XE367/197, XE371/199 XE377/195,
      XE379, XE381/192, XE388, XE439/200, XE441/198, XE448/191
899 Squadron: WM928/461, WM944/458, WN111/466, XE364/485, XE382, XE383,
      XE387, XE392/490, XE399/468, XE401/492, XE402/486, XE404, XE447,
      XE457

Sea Venom FAW21s included:
809 Squadron: XG620/226, XG665, XG669/224, XG670/220, XG673/227, XG677/225,
      XG679/220 (lost 1/10/56)
892 Squadron: WW154/448, WW190, WW277/447, WW286/452
893 Squadron: WW149, WW193/096, WW196, WW205/090, WW206, WW208, WW209,
      WW212, WW218/092, WW223/098, WW261, WW265/094, WW270,
      WW281/095, WW282, WW285/091, WW287
NB: 892 and 893 Squadrons apparently shared their aircraft

JHU:

Sycamore HR14	Whirlwind HAR3
XG500/1	XJ764/7
XG502/2	XJ765/8
XG507/3	XK968/9
XG515/4	XK969/10
XG523/5	XK970/11
XG548/6	XK986/12

Whirlwind HAS22s
845 Squadron: WV199/T; WV203/V; WV204/Q; WV205/W; WV220/Y; WV222/P,
      WV223/U; WV224/S XJ400/X; XG587/Z

Wyverns included

830 Squadron   VZ758/376, WN325/373, WN328/374, WN330/379, WP337/378,
          WP338/377

Skyraider AEW1 (849 Squadron) **included:**
          WJ954/417 (A Flt), WT947/422 (C Flt), WV178/424 (C Flt),
          WV181/414 (A Flt)

Dragonfly HR3 (HMS *Bulwark*):
          WG720/984, WG750/985, WP502/983

ARMÉE DE L'AIR

F-84Fs included:

1/1 Corse	52-8903/1-NA, 52-3068/1-NF, 52-8914/1-NK 52-9102/1-NL, 52-8943/1-NM, 52-9340/1-NN 52-9358/1-N?, 52-9111/1-N?
2/1 Morvan	
3/1 Argonne	52-9110/1-PX, 52-7300/1-P?
1/3 Navarre	52-9030/3-HK, 52-8946/3-HN, 52-9370/3-HR
2/3 Champagne	52-8899/3-I?, 52-9520/3-IS, 52-8947/3-IV
3/3 Ardennes	52-8953/3-VH, 52-9075/3-VS, 52-8842/3-VW
Other F-84Fs	included 52-8885, 52-8955, 52-9040, 52-7205

RF-84Fs (of ER4/33) **included:**
          52-7300/33-CC, 51-1709/33-CF, 52-7395/33-CO, 52-7327/33-CP,
          52-7325/33-DD, 52-7329/33-DH, 52-7321/33-DG

SELECT BIBLIOGRAPHY and SOURCES

Reference to the activities of British units involved in the Suez operations can be found at the Public Record Office in Air 27 records for RAF squadrons and ADM 205 records for the Fleet Air Arm. Information on the activities of the Armée de l'Air units was made available via the offices of the Armée de l'Air Service Historique.

Published sources (figures in brackets indicate chapters from which quotes have been used):

ADVENTURES IN THE SKIES: Oded Abarbanel
AIM SURE; a history of XV Squadron (9)
AIRBORNE TO SUEZ: Sandy Cavenagh (14)
A KING BETRAYED: Adel Sabit
ALONE IN THE SKY: Daniel Shapira
AL QUWAT AL-JAWIYAH: Air Brigadier Jabr Ali Jabr
AN ILLUSTRATED GUIDE TO THE IAF: Bill Gunston
AN UNKNOWN MISSION: Meir Mardoir
BLOWN OUT FLAME: In memory of Israel Lahav
BOOK OF HAGGANA: Ben-Zion Dinor (Ed.)
BRITAIN AND THE SUEZ CRISIS: David Carlton
BY DAY, BY NIGHT: Yoash Tsiddon-Chatto
CHEL HA'AVIR: Ze'ev Schiff
CHEL HA'MODYIN: Oded Granot
CLEAR TO TAKE-OFF: Yoseph Offer
CUTTING THE LION'S TAIL: Mohamed Heikal (6,8)
DIARY OF THE SINAI CAMPAIGN: Moshe Dayan (6,7)
DIVIDED WE STAND: W. Scott Lucas
DRAGON LADY: Michael R. Beschloss
EL AL: STAR IN THE SKY: Marvin G Goldman
ENGLISH ELECTRIC CANBERRA: Ken Delve (9)
FIGHTERS OVER ISRAEL: Lon Nordeen (7)
FLYING UNDER TWO FLAGS: Gordon Levett
FROM THE WAR OF INDEPENDENCE TO OPERATION KADESH: Maj Itshak Steigman
G-SUIT: Merav Halperin & Aharon Lapidot
HEYMAN, THE MAN & THE PERIOD: Zvi Dreznin
HISTOIRE DE L'AFFAIRE DE SUEZ: Général Robineau (8)
ISRAEL, ARMY & DEFENCE: Ze'ev Schiff & Eitan Haber
ISRAEL'S BEST DEFENCE: Eliezer Cohen (7)
ISRAELI AIR FORCE AIRCRAFT: Danny Shalom
IT IS UPON THE NAVY: Cdr Donald Mills OBE RN (8,10,11,12,15,16)
KHRUSHCHEV REMEMBERS: Nikita Khrushchev (5)
LASKOV, A BIOGRAPHY: Mordechai Naor
MEMOIRS OF SIR ANTHONY EDEN, Vol 2: FULL CIRCLE (8)
NASSER: Anthony Nutting
NASSER: A POLITICAL STUDY: Robert Stephens
NASSER: THE CAIRO DOCUMENTS: Mohamed Heikal
NO MARGIN FOR ERROR: Ehud Yonay
ON EAGLE'S WINGS: Ezer Weizman (6,7)
ONE HUNDRED HOURS TO SUEZ: Robert Henriques (7)
OPEN SKIES: Aharon Lapidot
PROCUREMENT IN THE US: Doron Almog
RABBI WITH WINGS: Chai Goldstein

REVOLT ON THE NILE: Anwar al-Sadat
SPITFIRES OVER ISRAEL: Brian Cull, Shlomo Aloni & David Nicolle
SUDDENLY IN THE MIDST OF LIVING: Devora Omer
SUEZ: Keith Kyle
SUEZ 1956: Paul Gaujac
SUEZ 1956: OPERATION MUSKETEER: Robert Jackson
SUEZ: THE SEVEN DAY WAR: A.J. Barker (15)
SUEZ: THE DOUBLE WAR: Roy Fullick and Geoffrey Powell (15)
SUEZ TOUCHDOWN: Douglas Clark (15)
THE ARMED PROPHET: Michael Bar-Zohar
THE BOSS: Robert St John
THE FAILURE OF THE EDEN GOVERNMENT: Richard Lamb
THE HISTORY OF THE ISRAELI PARATROOPERS: Uri Milstein
THE HISTORY OF THE WAR OF INDEPENDENCE: IDF Historical Branch
THE ISRAEL AIR FORCE ALBUM: IDF MoD
THE ISRAEL AIR FORCE STORY: Murray Rubinstein & Richard Goldman
THE ISRAELI AIR FORCE STORY: Robert Jackson
THE LION'S LAST ROAR: Chester Cooper (16)
THE MILITARY INDUSTRY IN ISRAEL: Yoseph Avron
THE MOSQUITO LOG: Alex McKee (7)
THE PLEDGE: Leonard Slater
THE SECRETS OF SUEZ: Merry & Serge Bromberger (6,11,14,17)
THE SOUTH IN THE WAR OF INDEPENDENCE: Yad Tabenkin
THE STORY OF THE ISRAELI AIR FORCE: Avigdor Shachan
THE STRUGGLE FOR SYRIA: Patrick Seale
THE SUEZ AFFAIR: Hugh Thomas
THE SUEZ EXPEDITION: Andre Beaufre (8,16)
THE SUEZ-SINAI CRISIS OF 1956: Selwyn Ilan Troen and Moshe Shemash (11,16)
THE THIRD ARM: A HISTORY OF THE EGYPTIAN AIR FORCE: Ali Muhammad
Labib (7,8,9)
THE WAR OF INDEPENDENCE, BEN-GURION'S DIARY: G. Rivlin & Dr E.
Orren (Eds.)
THE WAY OF AN EAGLE: Shmuel Bavli
THE WESTERN GALILEE IN THE WAR OF INDEPENDENCE: David Coren
THE WHITE HOUSE YEARS, WAGING PEACE: Dwight D. Eisenhower (16)
THE YOUTH OF THE TEL AVIV SQUADRON: Adam Shatkai
THEY TOOK OFF UNDER COVER: Binyamin Kagan
TIME OF MY LIFE: Wim Van Leer
UNEASY LIES THE HEAD: King Hussein of Jordan (5,7,17)
UP HIGH: Mordechai Naor
WARRIORS AT SUEZ: Donald Neff
WATERY MAZE: Bernard Fergusson (15)
WINGS IN THE SUN: Air Chief Marshal Sir David Lee (9)
WINGS OF VICTORY: Avigdor Shachan
WOMAN PILOT: Jackie Moggridge

SUEZ 1956 – AIR ASPECTS, Proceedings of the RAF Historical Society (8,9,10,15,16)
AIR CLUES (10,11,13,15)

Various copies of magazines including RAF FLYING REVIEW, AIR INTER-
NATIONAL, AIR PICTORIAL; French publications AIR FAN; LE FANA DE
L'AVIATION, LE PIEGE, MACH 2.2; Israeli publications BIAF, BA'AVIR, IDF/AF
Magazine, MA'ARACHOT, ROMACH.

Various copies of newspapers of the period including the DAILY EXPRESS, DAILY
TELEGRAPH, TIMES OF MALTA, CYPRUS MAIL, plus the JERUSALEM POST,
EGYPTIAN GAZETTE, and Israeli publications HA'ARETZ, MA'ARIV and
YEDIOT ACHARONOT.

INDEX

Personnel

Nachman, Ovadiah IDF/AF 130
Nevo, Ya'acov IDF/AF 53, 116, 123, 131, 133, 134, 364

Orbach, Moshe Politician 52
Orly, David IDF/AF 46
Ostrof, Arye IDF/AF 59

Paz, Eldad IDF/AF 136
Peled, Binyamin IDF/AF 43, 50, 53, 64, 65, 92, 149, 150, 152
Peled, Moshe IDF/AF 41
Peres, Shimon MoD 65
Peri, Yehuda IDF/AF 61
Portigali, Avraham IDF/AF 46

Rafaeli, Ya'acov IDF/AF 139
Raizner, Eliezer IDF/AF 47
Ratner, David IDF/AF 53
Remez, Aharon IDF/AF 34, 37, 49
Roof, Meir IDF/AF 40, 43

Schirer, Adam IDF/AF 55
Schlessinger, Uri IDF/AF 131
Shadmi, Ohad IDF/AF 122
Shalmon, Ya'acov IDF/AF 60
Shamir, Shlomo Chel Ha'Avir 41, 44
Shapira, Dani IDF/AF 34, 46, 53, 149, 151
Sharet, Moshe Prime Minister 52
Sharon, Ran IDF/AF 48, 122, 132, 133, 138
Sharon, Ze'ev IDF/AF 100
Shatil, Oded IDF/AF 47
Shavit, Aharon IDF/AF 128
Shefer, Meir IDF/AF 105
Shefer, Shmuel IDF/AF 105, 146
Shemer, Amram IDF/AF 141
Shimhoni, Assaf IDF 153
Sirotkin, Paltiel IDF/AF 148
Somekh, Yehezkiel IDF/AF 105, 125, 150

Tadmor, Moshe IDF/AF 34, 105, 139
Tavor, Ze'ev IDF/AF 116, 117, 142
Tolkowsky, Dan IDF/AF 51, 65, 92
Tse'elon, Aryeh IDF/AF 100, 116, 119, 137, 138
Tsiddon, Yoash IDF/AF 44, 61, 94, 105, 113, 125, 142, 147
Tsuk, Yoseph IDF/AF 123, 131, 133, 364

Weizman, Ezer IDF/AF 35, 40, 43, 54, 56, 65, 102, 106, 114, 127, 146, 152

Yaffe, Uri IDF/AF 92
Yalon, Yitzhak IDF/AF 48
Yarom, Uri IDF/AF 109, 121
Yariv, Ya'acov IDF/AF 364
Yavneh, Itshak IDF/AF 43, 92, 105, 116, 149
Yodfat, Avraham IDF/AF 55
Yoeli, Aharon IDF/AF 53, 56, 60-62, 116, 137
Yoffe, Avraham IDF/AF 33, 40, 130

Zelinger, Itschak IDF/AF 55

Egyptian

Abbas Halim, Prince Royal Family 8
Abdullah, Tameen Fahmy Civilian 199

Afifi, Plt Off Mahmud Wael EAF 129
Ahmad, Sqn Ldr Ahmad Massud EAF 70
Ahmad Fuad, Prince Royal Family 25, 26
al-Bughdadi, Wg Cdr Abd al-Latif EAF 8, 24, 27, 28, 71, 118, 263
al-Gazawy, Sqn Ldr Farouke EAF 135, 226, 233
al-Hinnawi, Sqn Ldr Mustafa Shalabi REAF/EAF 16, 143, 223, 224
al-Kouni, Mohamed Ambassador 279
al-Maraghi, Murtada Minister 359
al-Masri, Gen Aziz Egyptian Army 24
al-Messiry, Sqn Ldr Mohammed Nabil EAF 218
al-Nahhas, Mustafa Prime Minister 348
al-Raouf, Sqn Ldr Abd al-Monein Abd REAF 24, 27, 74
al-Sadat, Col Anwar Egyptian Army 24, 26
al-Sharawy, General REAF 6, 27
al-Shennawy, Plt Off Abd al-Moneim EAF 357
al-Tawil, Plt Off Abdel Moneim EAF 77, 134, 199
al-Tawail, Maj Sahby EAF 365
al-Wahab Mugahid, Cpl Abd EAF 70
Amr, Gen Abd al-Hakim CinC 24, 71, 110, 112, 114, 364
Aqaba, Grp Capt REAF 24
Aqif, Air Commodore Hassan REAF 25
Attia, Air Marshal Ali Air Attaché 95

Bahig, Plt Off REAF 16
Bakir, Sqn Ldr Omar REAF 17

Farag, Air Commodore Muhammad EAF 77
Farouk, King Monarch 2, 5, 7, 9, 11, 13, 24-27, 71, 359
Fawzi, Dr Mahmoud Foreign Minister 82

Gazerine, Air Commodore Ibrahim REAF 22, 71

Hatem, Dr Abdel-Kader Information Service 97
Heidar, al-Ferik Muhammad 23
Heikal, Mohamed Nasser aide 109, 181, 346, 348, 356
Helmi, Flt Lt Baghat Hassan EAF 79, 129
Hilmi, Sqn Ldr Mustafa EAF 125

Ibrahim, Wg Cdr Hassan REAF 24, 27
Ismail, Sqn Ldr Mustafa Mahmud Helmi EAF 114
Iwais, Plt Off Hafiz Mohammed EAF 134

Kalmil, Dr Hassan Scientist 365
Khairy, Hussein Royal aide 359
Khalil, Maj Issam al-Din Mahmud EAF 359, 365

Labib, Wg Cdr Ali Muhammad EAF Ops Officer 85, 120, 125, 130, 196, 232, 358
Lufti, Flt Lt EAF 93

Mahmud, Air Commodore Hassan REAF 27, 71
Mansour, Plt Off REAF 16
Messiry, Ibrahim Sa'ad REAF MoD 5
Mikaati, Air Vice-Marshal Abd al-Moneim REAF 14, 22, 27, 69
Muhi al-Din, Zakariya Minister 263
Mubarak, Hosni EAF 77

Narriman, Queen Royal Family 26
Nass, Plt Off Adel EAF 130
Nasser, Col Gamal President 2, 15, 24, 26, 32, 63, 68, 69, 71, 73, 74, 78, 81-83, 91, 95-98, 100-102, 109-111, 118, 123, 124, 127, 140, 157, 186, 187, 197, 232, 233, 238, 263, 278, 314, 339, 340, 343, 347, 348, 354, 356, 358-360, 364
Nasr, Maj-Gen Adel EAF 366
Neguib, Gen Mohammed President 25-27, 71, 73
Niyazy, Sqn Ldr EAF 92

Rahim, Sqn Ldr Kamal al-Din Ahmad Abu'l EAF 114
Ramadan, Mohamed EAF 43

Sabit, Adel Royal Family 2, 26
Sabri, Wg Cdr 'Ali Political adviser 24, 26, 354
Salim, Wg Cdr Gamal al-Din Mustafa REAF 24, 26, 27
Salim, Col Salah Minister 24, 263
Shalaby, Maj Zohair EAF 365
Sharmi, Plt Off 'Ali EAF 140, 185
Sherif, Sqn Ldr Sa'ad al-Din EAF 114
Shoarky, Maj-Gen Nobil EAF 77, 366
Sidqi Mahmud, Air Vice-Marshal Muhammed EAF 71, 118, 357

Tamzan, Lt Cdr Hassan Rusdi Egyptian Navy 126, 127
Tawfiq, Wg Cdr H.M. REAF 6

Zaher, Sqn Ldr F. EAF 76
Zaki, Flt Lt Tahseen REAF/EAF 139, 185
Zaky, Flg Off REAF 16

Syrian

al-Asad, Lt Hafiz SAF 88, 335, 337
al-Asasa, Lt Col Musafaz SAF 359
al-Assali, Sabri Prime Minister 127
al-Quwatli, Shukri President 314

Moukabri, Maj SAF 335, 336

Jordanian

Abdullah, King Monarch 2, 18

Hussein, King Monarch, 18, 19, 31, 83, 89, 90, 100, 124, 360, 361

Nair, Emir Royal Family 19
Nuwar, Maj-Gen Ali Abu Royal Jordanian Army 166

Talal, Emir Royal Family 19

Air Units

Royal Jordanian AF 30, 31, 83, 89, 93, 112, 361
Lebanon AF 29, 88, 364
Syrian AF 23, 28, 32, 72, 79, 88, 93, 94, 226, 335, 337, 359, 361
Syrian AF College 359
Syrian AF Technical Institute 359
United Arab Republic AF 360-366
Pan-Arab Air Force 7
Sherifan Royal AF 30
Czech AF Academy 33
Burma AF 58, 59
Indian AF 365
70th Recon Wg, USAF 181
306th Bomb Wg, USAF 181
VA-46, USN 240
VP-24, USN 181, 231
Pan-Am (USA) 223
TWA (USA) 186
Aer Macchi (Italy) 5, 29, 78, 79
Air Jordan 233
Arab Airways (Jordan) 40
CGT (Lebanon) 41
SABENA (Belgium) 233
Syrian Airways 57
Air Orient 224
Swissair 342

Naval/Merchant Shipping – British

HMS *Albion* (aircraft carrier) 167, 168, 170, 173, 175, 176, 213, 214, 217, 218, 222-224, 226, 228, 229, 231, 251-256, 260, 271, 283-285, 287, 288, 292, 301, 303, 305, 309, 321, 322, 326-328, 331-333, 345
HMS *Ark Royal* (aircraft carrier) 168, 170
HMS *Bulwark* (aircraft carrier) 165, 167-169, 175, 176, 213, 214, 217, 220, 222, 224, 228, 229, 231, 251-256, 260, 272, 275-277, 284, 285, 287, 288, 292, 301, 303-305, 309, 326-328, 333, 334, 345, 374
HMS *Crane* (destroyer) 151
HMS *Daring* (destroyer) 171
HMS *Decoy* (destroyer) 229
HMS *Eagle* (aircraft carrier) 167-169, 173, 175-177, 213, 214, 219, 222-226, 228, 229, 231, 251, 253-256, 258, 260, 271, 273-277, 283, 292, 295, 298, 301, 303, 305, 307, 309, 323, 324, 326-330, 332, 333, 342, 345
HMS *Loch Killisport* (frigate) 225
HMS *Meon* (HQ vessel) 327
HMS *Newfoundland* (cruiser) 147
HMS *Ocean* (helicopter carrier) 167, 175, 176, 288, 319-321, 323
RNA *Olna* (fleet tanker) 178
HMS *Theseus* (assault carrier) 167, 175, 176, 179, 288, 324, 342
HMS *Tyne* (cruiser) 288, 310, 312, 324
HMNZS *Royalist* (destroyer) 179
Empire Fowey (hospital ship) 322
Queen Mary (liner) 69

French

Arromanches (aircraft carrier) 167, 173-176, 185, 213, 226, 231, 250, 260, 271, 272, 276, 300, 310, 312, 326, 327, 342
Dixmude (helicopter carrier) 173
Georges-Leygues (cruiser) 142
La Fayette (aircraft carrier) 167, 173-176, 213, 226, 231, 250, 256, 257, 260, 272, 273, 276, 277, 312, 326, 328, 331, 332
Jean Bart (battleship) 167
Kersaint (destroyer) 126
S606 La Creole (submarine) 250, 335

Israeli

Eilat (destroyer) 126, 127
Haifa (destroyer) 127
Yaffo (destroyer) 126
Bar Giora (merchant vessel) 54, 55
Bat Galim (merchant vessel) 56
Rimon (M/V) 132

Egyptian

Akka (blockship) 220, 222, 224, 226
al-Nasr (destroyer) 185, 213
al-Zafr (destroyer) 185
Domiat (frigate) 147, 151
Ibrahim al-Awal (destroyer) 125-127
Mahroussa (Royal Yacht) 26
Star of Aswan (freighter) 80
Tarek (frigate) 213

American

US Sixth Fleet 96, 142, 176, 180, 181, 185-187, 191, 213, 229-231, 240, 249, 250, 271, 289, 325
USS *Coral Sea* (aircraft carrier) 176, 287
USS *Cutlass* (submarine) 271
USS *Randolph* (aircraft carrier) 176, 240
USS *Salem* (cruiser) 176

Others

Stalingrad (Soviet freighter) 83

Military Units/ Organisations/Operations – Israeli

Golani Brigade 44
7th Brigade 44, 139, 148
9th Brigade 147, 148
27th Brigade 146
37th Brigade 148
202 Brigade 117, 121
13th Regiment 44

Egyptian

Free Officers' Movement 2, 24-27, 71, 74
Wafd Party 9
Moslem Brotherhood 27, 74
1st Armoured Brigade 130, 137
2nd Infantry Brigade 119, 122
4th Armoured Brigade 130, 146, 300
5th Infantry Brigade 141
5th Infantry Battalion 122
6th Infantry Battalion 122
Palestinian Brigade 140

Others

40 RM Commando (British) 319, 321
42 RM Commando (British) 319
45 RM Commando (British) 288, 319-321, 323
3/Parachute Regt (British) 292, 293, 297, 316, 317
16th Parachute Brigade (British) 292
6th Royal Tank Regt (British) 319
1e Regiment Etranger Para (French) 319
2e Regiment Para Coloniaux (French) 292
Pan-Arab Army 7
Anglo/Iranian Oil Co 18
MI5 314
CIA 28, 78, 181, 232, 337
EOKA (Cyprus) 109, 110, 341
FLN (Algeria) 64
CU du CM de Suez (Suez Canal Co) 96, 97, 101, 347

Treaties/Pacts

Anglo-Egypt Treaty 19, 73, 95
Anglo-Iraq Treaty 30
Anglo-Jordan Treaty 30, 64, 100, 103, 167
Baghdad Pact 67, 78, 81-83
Warsaw Pact 88, 236, 357
Treaty of Sèvres 102, 167
NATO 3, 70, 181, 232, 313, 314, 321
United Nations 8, 38, 44, 52, 60, 66, 95, 97, 101, 124, 153, 157, 180, 236, 313, 314, 341, 342, 347, 354-357, 360, 362, 364
United Arab Republic 360, 361, 363, 364
Arab League 2

Codenames

Operation Boathook 176
Operation Kadesh Chapter 7
Operation Matate 54
Operation Musketeer Chapters 8-17
Operation Sunray 3
Operation Telescope 292
Operation Velveta 2 33
Exercise Contentment 17
Exercise Gestic 8